Understanding Security South Asia

This book explores the ways in which non-state actors (NSAs) in South Asia are involved in securitizing non-traditional security challenges in the region at the sub-state level.

South Asia is the epicentre of some of the most significant international security challenges today. Yet, the complexities of the region's security dynamics remain under-researched. While traditional security issues such as inter-state war, border disputes and the threat of nuclear devastation in South Asia remain high on the agendas of policy-makers and academics both within and beyond the region, insufficient attention has been paid to non-traditional or 'new' security challenges.

Drawing on various case studies, this work offers an innovative analysis of how NSAs in South Asia are shaping security discourses in the region and tackling such security challenges at the sub-state level. Through its critique of Securitization Theory, the book calls for a new approach to studying security practices in South Asia – one which considers NSAs as legitimate security actors.

This book will be of much interest to students of security studies, Asian security, critical security studies, securitization studies and IR in general.

Monika Barthwal-Datta is a research fellow at the Centre for International Security Studies, University of Sydney.

Asian Security Studies

Series Editors: Sumit Ganguly, *Indiana University, Bloomington*, Andrew Scobell, *US Army War College* and Joseph Chinyong Liow, *Nanyang Technological University, Singapore*.

Few regions of the world are fraught with as many security questions as Asia. Within this region it is possible to study great power rivalries, irredentist conflicts, nuclear and ballistic missile proliferation, secessionist movements, ethnoreligious conflicts and inter-state wars. This book series publishes the best possible scholarship on the security issues affecting the region, and includes detailed empirical studies, theoretically oriented case studies and policy-relevant analyses as well as more general works.

Understanding Security Practices in South Asia

Securitization Theory and the role of non-state actors

Monika Barthwal-Datta

Routledge
Taylor & Francis Group

LONDON AND NEW YORK

First published 2012
by Routledge
2 Park Square, Milton Park, Abingdon, Oxon OX14 4RN

Simultaneously published in the USA and Canada
by Routledge
711 Third Avenue, New York, NY 10017

Routledge is an imprint of the Taylor & Francis Group, an informa business

First issued in paperback 2013

British Library Cataloguing in Publication Data
A catalogue record for this book is available from the British Library

Library of Congress Cataloging-in-Publication Data
Barthwal-Datta, Monika, 1980-
Understanding security practices in South Asia : securitization theory and the
role of non-state actors / Monika Barthwal-Datta.
p. cm. -- (Asian security studies ; 34)
Includes bibliographical references and index.
1. Security, International--South Asia. 2. Non-state actors (International
relations)--South Asia. I. Title.
JZ6009.S64B37 2012
355'.033054--dc23
2011044047

ISBN13: 978-0-415-61631-7 (hbk)
ISBN13: 978-0-415-74107-1 (pbk)
ISBN13: 978-0-203-12068-2 (ebk)

Typeset in Baskerville
by Taylor & Francis Books

To Dhyan Chand Barthwal and Krishna Barthwal

Contents

Illustrations

Figures

Preface

South Asia provides rich pickings for international relations (IR) and security studies scholars. Its empirical puzzles are packed with complexities and contradictions, and offer fertile grounds for testing theories and conceptual frameworks. Yet, this vast potential for theoretical and empirical investigations remains unexploited to an extent by scholars within and beyond the region. At least two factors may be responsible for this state of affairs. One, the historic dominance of realist thinking within the discipline of IR in general, and in South Asia in particular (both within policy-making and academic circles). Two, the enduring historic rivalry between India and Pakistan, which serves to reinforce the perceived relevance of realism in understanding security dynamics in the region.

This book is an effort to contribute to the small but growing volume of security studies literature on South Asia that breaks with this tradition. It is an attempt to create a wider understanding of security concerns and practices in South Asia – one which accommodates the insecurities of those who are most marginalized, discriminated or excluded in the politics of the region. The book is also premised on the belief that the practice of security in South Asia, as elsewhere, is no longer the exclusive domain of the state. With the increasing relevance of a number of 'new' or non-traditional threats to the security of different groups, the role of non-state actors (NSAs) in identifying these threats, and devising and implementing measures to respond to them adequately at the sub-state level, requires closer scrutiny. This book aims to provide such an analysis of security practices in South Asia, and for the first time investigates the analytical utility of Securitization Theory in studying these dynamics.

Acknowledgements

This book emerged out of a process to which many people contributed in various ways. I am deeply grateful to Alister Miskimmon, who supervised the doctoral thesis on which the book is based. A tremendous supervisor, Alister has remained a solid source of guidance and support in my professional life afterwards. In the process of converting the thesis into this book, he provided much-needed clarity of thought in times of intellectual despair, and also gave invaluable comments on draft chapters. I am thankful to Evelyn Goh and Edward Newman who examined the thesis and through their constructive criticisms helped me to refine it further. I am also grateful to Michael Foley, who mentored me during my postgraduate studies at Aberystwyth University. His guidance, support and generosity of spirit were instrumental in setting me on the path to a PhD.

I would like to thank the Department of Politics and International Relations (IR) at Royal Holloway College (University of London) for the Thomas Holloway scholarship, which enabled me to pursue my doctoral research within the department. The Gilchrist Trust (UK) funded my fieldwork in South Asia, where I was lucky to have the help and advice of a number of people, some of whom also commented on draft chapters in the thesis. I am particularly thankful to Vishal Chandra, Mallika Joseph and Avilash Roul for their guidance and help in New Delhi; Madhuri Singh Rana in Kathmandu; Shaheen Anam and Hossain Zillur Rahman in Dhaka, and Peter Bashford in the UK. For their insightful and helpful comments on draft book chapters, I am also thankful to Christian Kaunert and Prachi Bhuchar.

My postdoctoral research fellowship at the Centre for International Security Studies (CISS), University of Sydney, funded by the MacArthur Foundation, allowed me to have the time and resources required to convert the thesis into this book. My colleagues at CISS have been a great source of encouragement and support during this process. They include Alan Dupont, Gemma Connolly, Vivian Puccini-Scuderi, Sarah Phillips, Thomas Wilkins and Peter Curson – who constantly supplied good humour and good advice while generously accommodating me in his office. I am thankful to Benjamin Shepherd and Christopher Baker for their cheerful support and intellectually stimulating discussions over weekly coffees. Michael Safi gave me invaluable research assistance in the final weeks of updating and preparing the book manuscript, and I am grateful to the Faculty of Arts and Social Sciences at Sydney for funding Michael's efforts.

While doing my doctoral research, I had the opportunity to work with a number of amazing people who supported my efforts in different ways. I learnt a great deal from Gabrielle Rifkind as I worked with her at the Oxford Research Group (ORG) – an experience which enriched my life in so many ways. At ORG, I was also fortunate enough to work with Paul Rogers, Oliver Ramsbotham and John Sloboda – all of whom inspired me by their humility and kindness, and also by their efforts to bridge the divide between academic scholarship and the policy world in meaningful and effective ways. I am grateful to Lawrence Saez for his careful guidance in helping to shape the proposal for this book. Colleagues at the BBC World Service Radio in London were fantastic sources of expertise on South Asia and different issues discussed in the book.

In all my efforts, I was spurred on by my family – Himanshu Barthwal, Minakshi Barthwal, Tanisha Barthwal, Tarika Barthwal, Pulkit Datta, Preeti Datta-Nemdharry, Bhaskar Nemdharry, Ishaan Nemdharry, Narbada Datta and Sushil Kumar Datta. I am thankful to them all.

The affairs of South Asia are close to my heart, and for this my father is largely responsible. His job as an Indian diplomat gave me a taste for the region's international politics early on in life, and the experiences of growing up as an Indian in different parts of the world shaped my world-view in many ways. I am grateful to him and my mother for always believing in me, and for giving me a head start towards learning the skills necessary to understand the world in all its complexities.

The one person without whom this book would not have been possible is my husband, Puneet. He valiantly put up with the trials and tribulations of my PhD years, and gave me unflinching support as I immersed myself into producing this book. His faith in my abilities is remarkable, and inspires me to aim higher every time.

Abbreviations

AATWIN – Alliance Against Trafficking of Women and Children in Nepal
ABC Nepal – Agro Forestry and Basic Cooperatives Nepal
ACB – Anti-Corruption Bureau
ACC – Anti-Corruption Commission
ADB – Asian Development Bank
ATSEC – Action against Trafficking and Sexual Exploitation of Children
BHRC – Bangladesh Human Rights Commission
BNP – Bangladesh Nationalist Party
CA – Constituent Assembly
CAN – Climate Action Network
CANSA – Climate Action Network South Asia
CBMs – confidence-building measures
CHT – Chittagong Hill Tracts
CO_2 – Carbon Dioxide
COP – Conference of the Parties
CPI-M – Communist Party of India-Marxist
CPN – Communist Party of Nepal
CSE – Centre for Science and Environment
CSS – Critical Security Studies
CTG – caretaker government
CWIN – Child Workers in Nepal Concerned Centre
DFID – UK Department for International Development
DSDS – Delhi Sustainable Development Summit
DTF – District Task Forces
ECDPM – European Centre for Development and Policy Management
EDF – Environmental Defence Fund
EPA – Environmental Protection Agency
EU – European Union
FPTP – first past the post
FTS – Free the Slaves
FWLD – Forum for Women, Law and Development
G8 – Group of Eight
GAATW – Global Alliance Against Trafficking in Women

GDP – gross domestic product
GFW – Global Fund for Women
GHGs – greenhouse gases
GLOFs – glacial lake outburst floods
GNP – gross national product
HimRights – Himalayan Human Rights Monitors
HIV – Human Immunodeficiency Virus
IAC – InterAcademy Council
ICC – International Criminal Court
IDPs – Internally Displaced Persons
IGO – Intergovernmental Organizations
IGP – Indo-Gangetic Plains
ILO – International Labour Organization
INGO – international non-government organization
IOM – International Organization for Migration
IPCC – Intergovernmental Panel on Climate Change
IPKF – Indian Peacekeeping Force
IR – International Relations
ISI – Inter-Services Intelligence
JAMA – Journal of American Medical Association
LACC – Legal Aid and Counseling Centre
LoC – Line of Control
LTTE – Liberation Tigers of Tamil Eelam
MDGs – Millennium Development Goals
MEA – Ministry of External Affairs (India)
MEF – Ministry of Environment and Forests (India)
MNC – multinational corporation
MSWCSW – Minister of State for Women, Children and Social Welfare
MWCSW – Ministry of Women, Children, and Social Welfare
NAPCC – National Action Plan on Climate Change
NATO – North Atlantic Treaty Organization
NCTSN – National Conference of Trafficking Survivors of Nepal
NGO – Non-Governmental Organization
NHRC – National Human Rights Commission
NNAGT – National Network against Girls Trafficking
NPA – National Plan of Action
NPT – Non-Proliferation Treaty
NSA – non-state actor
NTF – National Taskforce on Trafficking
NWDTA – Narmada Water Dispute Tribunal Award
OHCHR – Office of the High Commissioner for Human Rights
ONRT – Office of the National Rapporteur on Trafficking in Women and Children
PDS – public distribution system
PMCCC – Prime Minister's Council on Climate Change
PRC – Peace Rehabilitation Centre

SAARC – South Asian Association for Regional Cooperation
SACCS – South Asian Coalition on Child Servitude
SPA – Seven Party Alliance
SPC – scientific policy community
SRP – Special Rehabilitation Package
SSD – Sardar Sarovar Dam
STOP – Stop Trafficking and Oppression
SWCYP – Street Working Children and Young People
TDH – Terre des Hommes
TERI – The Energy and Resources Institute
TIB – Transparency International Bangladesh
TIP – United States Department of State Trafficking in Persons Report
TNC – Transnational Corporation
UK – United Kingdom
ULFA – United Liberation Front of Assam
UN – United Nations
UN.GIFT – United Nations Global Initiative to Fight Human Trafficking
UNCED – United Nations Conference on Environment and Development
UNDP – United Nations Development Programme
UNEP – United Nations Environment Programme
UNFCCC – United Nations Framework Convention on Climate Change
UNHCR – United Nations High Commissioner for Refugees
UNICEF – United Nations Children's Fund
UNIFEM – United Nations Development Fund for Women
UNSC – United Nations Security Council
UPA – United Progressive Alliance
US – United States
USAID – United States Agency for International Development
WBGU – The German Advisory Council on Global Change
WG – Working Group
WMO – World Meteorological Organization
WOREC – Women's Rehabilitation Centre
WRI – World Resources Institute
WSDF – World Sustainable Development Forum
WWF – World Wildlife Fund

1 Introduction

South Asia, non-state actors and Securitization Theory

This book highlights the significance of non-state actors (NSAs) in security practices in South Asia.[1] It makes a contribution to the understanding of security challenges affecting sub-state groups in the region, and the role played by NSAs in identifying and politicizing these issues; shaping public policy responses to them, and in some instances also providing vulnerable and affected communities with the necessary measures to tackle these challenges. It argues that in doing so, these NSAs effectively operate as security actors, fulfilling a role traditionally ascribed to the state. The book also explores the utility of Securitization Theory when investigating security practices in developing socio-political contexts such as in South Asia, and sheds light on how its analysis in such scenarios may be improved.

In South Asia, states have generally been poor at dealing with the insecurities of their people. The processes of nation and state-building in the region have proved long and arduous, and preoccupied state agendas for decades. Historically, the focus has been on efforts to protect the territorial integrity of the state, and the safety and stability of ruling regimes – usually at the cost of adequate socio-economic development and political freedoms for those living inside and across borders. This focus continues to dominate security policy-making in the region even today, and is also to an extent reflected in the bulk of the international relations (IR) and security studies literature on South Asia, which deals overwhelmingly with inter-state hostilities, wars and disputes over territories and international borders; intra-state conflicts including armed insurgencies and ethno-nationalistic movements, and the seemingly ever-present threat of nuclear conflict between India and Pakistan.[2] Consequently, there exists relatively little scholarship from IR and security studies perspectives which attempts to grapple with those *issues* which are perceived as sources of deep insecurities by *sub-state* groups in South Asia,[3] and the range of *actors* operating in these realms particularly in the absence of effective state-led efforts.

As Booth has pointed out, 'insecurity involves living in fear, with dangers arising from one or more types of threat'.[4] Sub-state groups in South Asia – such as caste or religion-based communities, gendered groups, ethnic minorities or socio-economic groups – battle with a range of insecurities in relation to their physical, social, political and economic survival and well-being. Multidimensional poverty – encapsulating

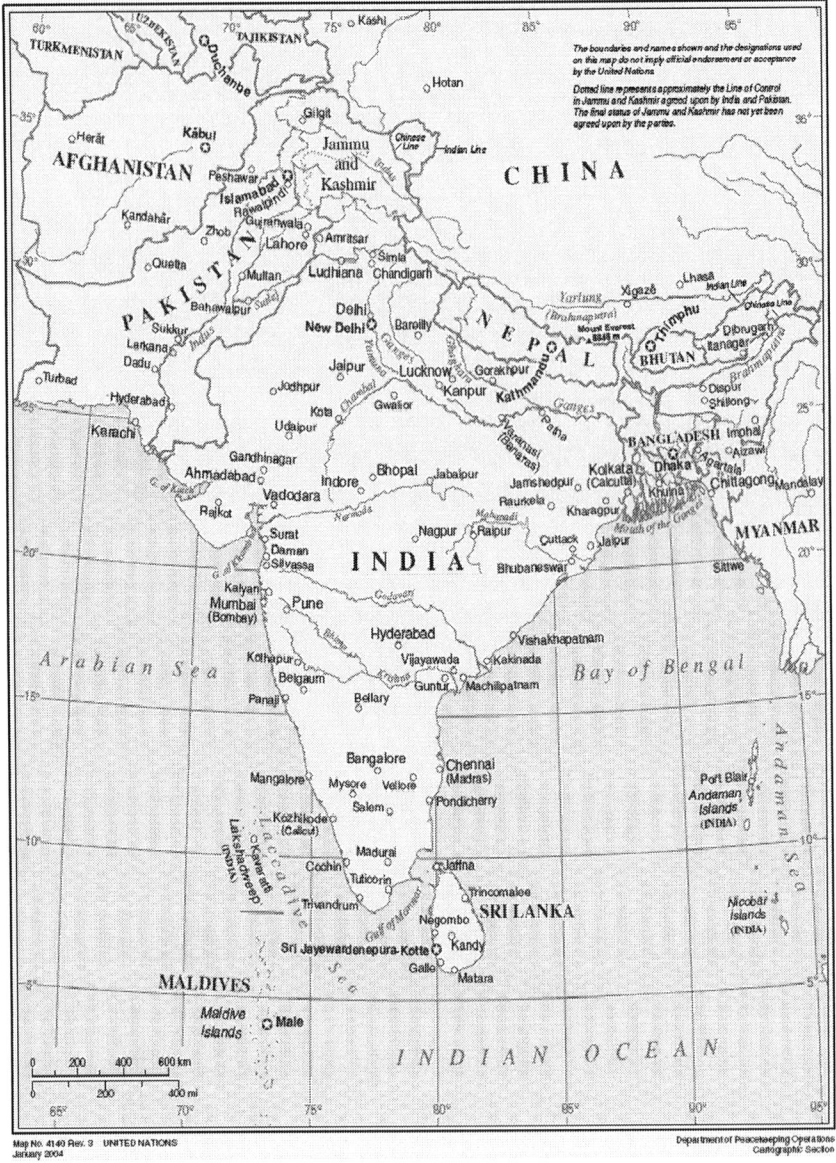

Map 1.1 South Asia and neighbouring countries
Source: United Nations

inadequate income as well as 'poor health and nutrition, low education and skills, inadequate livelihoods, bad housing conditions, social exclusion and lack of participation' – affects around 40 per cent of South Asians.[5] The region is home to around 400 million of the world's chronically hungry, and more than half its underweight children.[6] Ethnic minorities in South Asia have historically faced oppression by states and traditionally privileged communities. State institutions in the region are prone to varying levels of corruption, rule of law is fragile in most countries and state agencies are often subjected to little accountability. Political instability is therefore a key characteristic of South Asia, with political processes within states often being criminalized and violent. India, the largest and most populous country in the region, is relatively more stable than its neighbours, yet sub-state groups in different parts of India continue to suffer from the same set of problems which trouble their counterparts across borders, be it corruption, political exclusion and violence, ethnic discrimination, multidimensional poverty and hunger, and internal displacement due to factors such as political violence and conflict, or ill-conceived developmental projects. Not surprisingly, it is those who are the least empowered – socially, politically and economically – who suffer the most devastating consequences of these challenges.

States in South Asia have largely been unsuccessful in adequately dealing with, or at times even acknowledging, the different insecurities faced by their people. Under these circumstances, a range of NSAs in the region have been taking it upon themselves to identify and deal with those issues perceived as being key sources of insecurity for vulnerable and affected sub-state groups. Through activities ranging from research, advocacy and lobbying, to implementing measures on the ground which directly address such issues and their impacts, NSAs such as non-governmental organizations (NGOs), civil society groups, media actors and epistemic communities are increasingly becoming involved in issue areas which security studies and IR scholars usually know as 'non-traditional' – i.e. non-military sources of threats to the survival and well-being of groups other than (but not excluding) the state.

It is useful here to cite an example related to one of the case studies in the book, focusing on human trafficking in Nepal as a source of insecurity for women and children in particular. In February 1996, police in the Indian state of Maharashtra raided several brothels in the state capital of Mumbai, resulting in the rescue of around 500 women and girls. The group included around 200 Nepalese nationals.[7] The Nepalese government at the time refused to repatriate these individuals, demanding proof of their Nepali citizenship which few, if any, of those rescued were in a position to provide. For five months, the trafficking survivors waited in government-run rehabilitation centres in India – some continuing to face physical and mental abuse at the hands of their keepers – as their own state took no action to help them.[8] During this time, a small group of NGOs in Kathmandu joined forces and devised a detailed plan to repatriate and rehabilitate these individuals. They petitioned the Maharashtra High Court for the release of the girls, and subsequently 124 Nepalese women and girls were returned to Kathmandu in July 1996, where these NGOs helped to move them into seven different rehabilitation centres.[9] In this way, these NSAs achieved what the state failed to do – they acknowledged and gave expression to the state of insecurity in which the rescued group of Nepalese women and girls were suffering, made an extraordinary and successful effort to lift them out of the conditions which were the source of their insecurities, and subsequently worked to provide them with essential rehabilitative measures in order to help facilitate their reintegration into society. Thus, it may be argued that these NGOs effectively performed the role of security actors in the absence of political will and action by the Nepalese state.

Expanding the security studies agenda: actors, issues and approaches

The traditional, realist approach to security has dominated the sub-field of security studies for much of its history. In recent decades however, awareness of and arguments around threats to the safety of individuals, communities and states arising from sources other than inter-state war or the military sector have grown significantly.[10] The study and analysis of issues such as poverty, misgovernance, gender-based violence, infectious diseases, trafficking in humans and drugs, piracy, climate change and resource scarcity in the context of the security of states and other groups has become a distinct area of engagement for a growing number of security studies scholars, aided to an extent by the emergence of fresh ways of conceptualizing and theorizing security, such as Human Security,[11] the Welsh School of Critical Security Studies (CSS)[12] and the Copenhagen School's Secur-itization Theory.[13] While the security studies landscape has evolved in recent times to accommodate concerns for such non-military threats on the one hand, and understandings of security which prioritise the safety and well-being of indivi-duals and communities on the other, it continues to be dominated by a focus on states as the primary security *actors*. This focus has restricted the attention given to the role of NSAs in security practices, particularly those operating at the sub-state level. This is not to say that the role of NSAs in IR has been entirely neglected in the literature. Indeed, IR scholars have historically accounted for and investigated the role of religious organizations, armed insurgent groups, private security organizations, civil society groups and NGOs amongst others in domestic and international politics.[14] In 2005, an edited volume on *New Threats and New Actors in International Security* pointed out the 'growing role of [NSAs]—both as the cause of new security threats ... and as security providers, including nongovernmental organizations (NGOs), private security companies, and international regimes.'[15] Nonetheless, the literature examining NSAs as security providers remains sparse, and very little exists by way of scholarly analysis of the role they may play in the absence of, or in parallel to, state-led action in dealing with non-military chal-lenges to security at the sub-state level.[16] NSAs such as NGOs, civil society groups, epistemic communities, media organizations and others are often highly active in identifying, raising and/or dealing with non-military challenges which have in recent times been widely acknowledged as having security consequences for groups other than (but not excluding) the state. This phenomenon demands the attention of security studies scholars in order to generate a systematic and nuanced understanding of NSAs and how they may operate in the realm of security, in whose interest and with what implications for wider security dynamics within and outside states.

Focusing on NSAs in South Asia, this study is an effort to address this gap in the security studies literature. The book undertakes an in-depth study of how NSAs in South Asia – NGOs, media organizations, epistemic communities and civil society groups in particular – are involved in different security practices around those issues which challenge the survival and well-being of sub-state groups. In particular, the study analyses two dynamics within the context of these security practices. First, how NSAs attempt to 'securitize' issues which they perceive as threatening to distinct groups. Often, such issues are considered as threats to Human Security by a range of actors, yet there is little or no attempt on the part of state authorities to deal with them as such. Second, it explores how NSAs, in the absence of sufficient and adequate state-led policies, step in to address these challenges directly. In doing so, they become securitizing agents or security practitioners themselves, a role which is traditionally ascribed to the state. The case studies in the book also reveal the complexities which characterize security practices in developing socio-political contexts such as in South Asia where, as described earlier, state institutions are plagued by corruption, political processes are criminal and violent, law enforcement is weak, and respect for human rights takes a backseat. In such settings, security-related responses may be located outside the public policy realm, especially when it comes to non-traditional issue areas.

In conducting this analysis, the book draws on Securitization Theory as proposed by the Copenhagen School, and more recent theoretical developments within the securitization studies literature.[17] It demonstrates that despite substantial progress made by scholars over the last decade or so in developing Securitization Theory beyond the work of the Copenhagen School, certain weaknesses continue to affect the theoretical framework's analytical prowess when studying security dynamics in relation to the role played by NSAs, particularly in developing socio-political contexts. Securitization Theory provides the most sophisticated and systematic approach yet to the study of security practices. In the realm of issues which fall outside the traditional security concerns of the state, and particularly at the sub-state level, it is often NSAs which are at the frontline of identifying, raising and dealing with threats to referent groups emerging from non-military issue areas. Securitization Theory however arguably overlooks many of these dynamics because of its ambiguous stance on how an issue is securitized, and also by focusing on public policy responses by state-led agencies as the only legitimate 'security' responses. In doing so, it misses out significantly on the work of NSAs such as those mentioned earlier as security practitioners, i.e. legitimate security actors providing groups perceived as threatened with adequate protective and preventative measures to deal with the threat in question. The case studies use insights from the Human Security and CSS perspectives to develop the argument that in South Asia, in instances where sub-state groups suffer from insecurities arising particularly from non-military issue areas, NSAs often not only speak on their behalf in terms of identifying the dangers faced by the groups, but in the absence of adequate state action often provide the protective and preventative measures considered essential to deal with the insecurities in question. This dynamic is not something Securitization Theory seems to be able to capture adequately, given its emphasis on state-led public policy responses at the institutional level. The following section briefly maps the evolution of Securitization Theory since it was first proposed by the Copenhagen School, and subsequent work done by securitization studies scholars to further develop its theoretical framework.

Securitization Theory and developing socio-political contexts

According to the Copenhagen School, 'securitization studies aims to gain an increasingly precise understanding of who securitizes, on what issues (threats), for whom (referent objects), why, with what results, and, not least, under what conditions …'[18] Thus, Securitization Theory offers a unique approach to analysing security dynamics in a range of issue areas in IR. The Copenhagen School argues that securitization involves the construction of a discourse which presents a particular issue as a 'security' threat, i.e. it poses an immediate and existential danger to the referent group(s) in question, and which must be dealt with as a matter of urgency and priority using 'emergency measures'. As the authors point out,

> The way to study securitization is to study discourse and political constellations: When does an argument with this particular rhetorical and semiotic structure achieve sufficient effect to make an audience tolerate violations of rules that would otherwise have to be obeyed? If by means of an argument about the priority and urgency of an existential threat the securitizing actor has managed to break free of procedures and rules he and she would otherwise be bound by, we are witnessing a case of securitization.[19]

Thus, the Copenhagen School highlights three elements in its theorising: a securitizing move, a securitizing actor and the audience. A securitizing move is defined as a speech act, i.e. the discursive act of presenting something as an existential threat to a referent object using the language of security. A securitizing actor is the one who actually carries out the speech act. Although this may be an individual, he or she usually represents a larger collective which ultimately decides on the action which needs to be taken. 'Common players in this role are political leaders, bureaucracies, governments, lobbyists, and pressure groups … their arguments will normally be that it is necessary to defend the security of the state, nation, civilization, or some other larger community, principle, or system.'[20] The authors advocate that 'if [the individuals] are locked into strong roles it is usually more relevant to see as the 'speaker' the collectivities for which individuals are designated authoritative representatives (e.g. parties, states, or pressure groups)'.[21] Lastly, according to the Copenhagen School, a successful securitization requires the acceptance of the relevant securitizing move, and thereby the status of a threat as existentially endangering a referent object, by a 'sufficient audience'.

It has already been pointed out that Securitization Theory as developed by the Copenhagen School is 'theoretically vague and … does not provide clear guidance for empirical studies'.[22] Over the last decade or so a number of security studies scholars have engaged with the framework in depth, detailing some of its theoretical ambiguities and structural underdevelopment while offering specific remedial measures or modifications to the framework.[23] Key critiques have revolved around issues such as the Copenhagen School's reliance on the speech act as the only 'act' of securitization[24] and the lack of consideration of other forms of expressions such as visual images.[25] The ambiguity surrounding the relationship between the securitizing actor and the audience of the securitizing move has also been cited as a major weakness in the theoretical framework, with little clarity on who or what the role of the audience is, and the prospect of multiple audiences in the process of securitization.[26] Much of this critique has emerged in favour of a 'sociological approach' to securitization.[27] This approach proposes a central role for audiences in different stages of the securitizing process, a deeper consideration of the wider socio-political contexts within which the securitizing moves take place and the nature and types of policy tools and practices which are involved. Such an approach promises a richness to the theoretical framework which has otherwise been lacking. It provides potential grounds for a more comprehensive theory of securitization to emerge and be used for empirical analyses. At the same time, there are some important aspects of the original Copenhagen School approach to Securitization Theory which have not necessarily been sufficiently addressed in these recent developments within securitization studies.

It may be safe to say that if 'theory is always *for* someone and *for* some purpose',[28] then Securitization Theory – the original Copenhagen School variant as well as the variant suggested by a more contextualized or sociological approach – is best-suited to the pursuits of those who wish to understand how state-led security policy is negotiated by state elites. While this is a perfectly useful project, the problem arises when it is suggested that Securitization Theory opens up the security analysis to include a consideration of non-traditional security issues and the role of NSAs, something which traditional security studies, based on realist assumptions, fails to do. This claim is only partly qualified by the analysis the theory produces. The theoretical framework follows the process by which an issue may be accepted as a 'security' issue *by the state*. As far as the process leading up to this acceptance or rejection by state institutions is concerned, the theoretical framework allows (to an extent) a consideration of NSAs in terms of their efforts to propel the issue onto the state security agenda. What it does not consider, however, is that the acceptance of an issue as a matter of 'security' may also be reflected outside the public policy realm – e.g. by NSAs and the communities and groups who perceive the particular issue as a source of insecurity. This may be reflected in expressions made and measures taken by NSAs on the ground in response to the threat perception in question. It may be argued here that the lack of focus on NSAs and their role in security practices results more from how the theory has been applied so far – i.e. to understand the security practices of states and state-led institutions such as the EU – and not necessarily from an inherent fault in the theory which prevents a similar analysis around NSAs. While the former may be true, the latter is not self-evident given the level of ambiguity which continues to plague Securitization Theory. The following two points elaborate on the specific aspects of Securitization Theory which are critical in this respect.

Conditions for a successful securitization

The Copenhagen School is ambiguous when it comes to defining a successful securitization. It argues that 'the security act is negotiated between the securitizer and the audience', and if the audience accepts the argument being made, 'the securitizing agent can obtain permission to override rules that would otherwise bind it'. Such a linear construction of how an issue may come to be seen as a 'security' threat, and the ambiguity around who constitutes the 'audience', have been extensively critiqued and addressed by authors who argue for a contextualized or sociological approach to Securitization Theory.[29] The qualifying condition for a successful securitization, however, remains a subject of disagreement amongst securitization studies scholars. Salter, for example, places emphasis on (1) the rejection, or (2) the acceptance but lack of implementation, of the suggested 'emergency measures' to deal with the threat constructed by the securitizing actor, by those with the power to implement it.[30] In this view, the mobilizations of 'emergency measures' in the form of specific state-led public policy action is key. Trombetta, however, argues that invoking security does not always result in an 'emergency' policy response, and using the case of the securitization of global environmental problems, locates the success of securitizations in public policy responses (national or international) which relate to 'prevention, risk management and resilience'.[31] She makes an important argument, one that urges analysts to move away from a rigid understanding of how 'security' issues may be dealt with at the policy level. However, both arguments remain committed to the idea of *some* kind of public policy response as the qualifying condition for a successful securitization. Thus, the practice of 'security' is ultimately confined to the state-led public policy realm.

Securitizing actor–securitizing agent relationship

According to the Copenhagen School, a successful securitization consists of a securitizing actor making an argument regarding the priority and urgency of a threat and thereby '[breaking] free of procedures and rules he or she would otherwise be bound by'.[32] There is, however, little clarity around the relationship between the securitizing actor (i.e. the one who 'speaks' security to construct the narrative of a threat in relation to a referent group) and the securitizing agent or security practitioner (i.e. the one who *does* security and may have the relative authority and power to legitimize the breaking of 'normal procedures and rules', according to the Copenhagen School).[33] The Copenhagen School is unclear in its theorizing whether there is a distinction between the two in the securitization process.[34] The idea of both being one and the same is problematic, particularly if public policy is to be pivotal for a successful securitization, as implied by the Copenhagen School and argued more forcefully by those mentioned earlier. It may be argued that the power and legitimacy to break or override 'normal procedures and rules' or to take 'extraordinary' or 'emergency' measures (generally interpreted as referring to public policy) lies with state authorities. In this context, it becomes logical to conclude that if indeed the securitizing actor is envisioned to be the same as the securitizing agent, state actors can be described as having exclusive powers to make a successful case of securitization, as ultimately it is they who decide whether the securitizing move has been accepted or not, and whether they are in a position to override 'normal procedures and rules'.[35]

Thus, by continuing to focus on the actions of states and state-led institutions domestically and internationally through an emphasis on public policy outcomes, and on breaking 'normal procedures and rules' in order to securitize, together with a lack of distinction between who may securitize and who may *act* to deal with the threat in question, Securitization Theory struggles to look beyond the realm of state-led practices and the security agendas of states.

> What matters for the [Copenhagen] School is 'top leaders', 'states', 'threatened elites' and 'audiences' with agenda-making power. Those without discourse-making power are disenfranchised, unable to join the securitization game.[36]

The sociological approach, while expanding the scope of Securitization Theory beyond that of the Copenhagen School approach, is not excluded from this critique. For these scholars too, 'the *existence* and salience of a security issue' still depends on 'the political success of an actor reaching a political audience'.[37] In all practical terms, for Securitization Theory, the case finally rests with the state. The above-discussed limitations are particularly problematic when analysing security dynamics in developing socio-political contexts which may not conform, in varying degrees, to the western liberal democratic practices shaping the European context within which Securitization Theory originally developed and from where the majority of the scholarship on Securitization Theory continues to emerge.[38] When security practices are firmly rooted in institutionalized, democratic processes and there is the scope for extensive negotiations over what may or may not be a security threat, identifying threats to security purely by their construction by political actors, and security perceptions in relation to public policy responses, might be a convincing approach. Such an approach is also particularly relevant in contexts where state institutions are deeply entrenched and robust, political processes are inclusive (i.e. 'fair and free'), largely uncorrupt and not determined or heavily influenced by vested political interests. However, this is not always the case in most developing countries where people do not always have the freedom (without making themselves more insecure) to negotiate with others in relative positions of power and authority, about what is or is not a threat to their 'security'. In fact, the argument for the need to negotiate such action with relevant audiences in the first place highlights Securitization Theory's reliance on the western liberal democratic example. In countries where democracy is weak or does not exist, and political power and practices are highly centralized, where corruption and vested political interests have for decades corroded government institutions, state actors often coerce or even bribe audiences into accepting public policy responses which the former deem appropriate. In such scenarios, Securitization Theory is in danger of producing an analysis which is predominantly constructed by, and in, the interests of the state, and one which does not necessarily resonate with 'real situations of urgency' for sub-state groups. This study emphasizes the notion that responses to expressions of insecurity may arise from outside the realm of public policy and by actors other than state-led institutions. In non-military issue areas in particular, when the state fails to respond adequately, NSAs often provide what are arguably necessary measures required on the ground to alleviate the insecurities of those vulnerable and affected. In this way, they often bypass the public policy realm and become security practitioners themselves.

Analysing non-traditional security issues in South Asia: Securitization Theory, Human Security and Critical Security Studies (CSS)

In South Asia, NSAs have been actively involved in identifying and highlighting the insecurities of different sub-state groups. At times, they have substantially shaped public policy outcomes to tackle the sources of these insecurities by lobbying the state and working with state agencies to implement resulting policies. At other times, they have been involved in providing protective and preventative measures to vulnerable and affected groups in the absence of adequate state-led action. In order to provide a security analysis which genuinely extends beyond the traditional focus on the state, these dynamics at the sub-state level need to be accounted for. While Securitization Theory is useful to an extent in tracing how NSAs may help raise certain issues onto the security agendas of states and work with state agencies to shape and implement desired policies, it is less capable of acknowledging the role of NSAs as securitizing agents or practitioners on their own accord. Here, two key non-traditional security approaches are helpful – CSS as proposed by the Welsh School and Human Security. Like Securitization Theory, both CSS and Human Security aim to broaden the security analysis and generally open it up to the consideration of non-military threats, non-state referent groups and NSAs. While Securitization Theory maintains its focus at the state level and is most interested in the actions of state-led institutions, CSS and Human Security pro-vide the conceptual tools for analysts to delve into the sub-state level and examine the work of NSAs as those speaking on behalf of less powerful groups who may be battling with insecurities arising from a range of issue areas, and also as those acting to prevent and mitigate these insecurities.

Placing the individual at the heart of the security analysis, both Human Security and CSS reject the state-centricism of realist traditional security studies, and wish to broaden the study of security to include non-military threats to indi-viduals and communities. They both challenge the neorealist orthodoxy within security studies, but do so in different ways. As Newman points out, Human Security is predominantly policy-oriented, and does not 'generally engage in epistemological, ontological or methodological debates'.[39] Human Security remains primarily 'problem-solving', i.e. it focuses on how to improve the 'real-world' conditions of individuals and communities by tackling the insecurities they face within their socio-economic and political settings. Human Security scholars generally concede the importance of the state as part of the solution to dealing with these challenges.[40] CSS on the other hand fundamentally questions 'existing structures and institutions of power, gender and distribution in relation to economic and political organisation'.[41] While an exhaustive review of Human Security and CSS and their critiques is not possible here, the following is a brief overview of the two approaches with respect to how they relate to one another and their utility for the purpose of this study.

The concept of Human Security – which has many formulations, and scholars and analysts have yet to find consensus over a universal definition – derives from an 'embedded stock of ideas' comprising human rights, conflict prevention, and the principles and practices of humanitarianism which took root in the second half of the twentieth century.[42] The germination of these ideas took place within the UN well before the much-cited 1994 UNDP *Human Development Report* articulated the concept in a more detailed and forceful manner.[43] Nonetheless, the political discourse on Human Security in the late 1990s and early 2000s was shaped significantly by the discussion of Human Security embedded in the report, which argued against the narrow interpretation of security in realist terms, 'as security of territory from external aggression, or as protection of national interests in foreign policy or as global security from the threat of nuclear holocaust … [Forgetting] the legitimate concerns of ordinary people who sought security in their daily lives.'[44] It called for an equal emphasis on the two main aspects of security as envisioned by the UN – freedom from fear and freedom from want – to be provided through sustained human development.[45] The UNDP's formulation of Human Security is broad, referring to various categories of 'security', e.g. economic security, food security, health security, environmental security, personal security, community security, and political security.[46] Japan has notably been the most solid proponent of this approach to Human Security, while others such as Canada and the EU have favoured a narrower, relatively more focused conceptualization of Human Security that prioritizes the physical well-being and human rights of people in armed conflict situations as its key aim.[47]

Human Security has been critiqued extensively for lacking conceptual clarity and for expanding the security agenda to the point of analytical incoherence.[48] Far more damning, however, have been critiques emerging from critical security scholars who have accused Human Security of 'associations ranging from the imposition of neoliberal practices and values on non-western spaces to the legitimization for attacks on Iraq and Afghanistan'.[49] In this view, Human Security is seen as a 'biopolitical security technology' used by the liberal West to control people living in developing countries, or 'surplus life'.[50] It has been argued that:

> What was intended in an expansive sense as a means of securing a greater number of civilians from a broader range of threats has been manipulated to legitimate violent Liberal interventionism, including 'humanitarian bombing' and 'cosmopolitan police-keeping.'[51]

Consequently, calls have been made for a revitalization of Human Security by appealing to its 'emancipatory' aspect. This, it is proposed, is best done by engaging in 'local-local understandings of security, and to recognize difference, enable agency and to respect autonomy as far as possible'.[52] Others like Mandy Turner, Neil Cooper and Michael Pugh are far more pessimistic, dismissing any possibility of Human Security to be 'rescued', for they see it as having been 'institutionalized and co-opted to work in the interests of global capitalism, militarism and neoliberal governance'.[53]

'Emancipation' also lies at the centre of the concerns of those identified with the Welsh School of security. Associated with the works of Ken Booth and Richard Wyn Jones, among others, CSS is devoted to the development of a 'critical theory approach to the study of security'.[54] CSS scholars argue that security is a derivative concept, and the task of CSS is to challenge the underlying theoretical structures of traditional security studies. They believe that security can be achieved only through emancipation, defined by Booth as,

> The freeing of people (as individuals and groups) from the physical and human constraints which stop them carrying out what they would freely choose to do … [such as] war and the threat of war, … poverty, poor education, political oppression and so on.[55]

To put it succinctly, CSS scholars argue that our understandings of security are premised upon certain 'underlying and contested theories about the nature of world politics' and they wish broaden the security agenda beyond its current statist realm.[56] They urge analysts not to accept prevailing social and political organizational structures as given frameworks for action, but to look beyond them to investigate how they came to be in the first instance, and where their interests lie.[57] In this thinking, it becomes imperative to ask why certain issues raise security concerns, while others do not.[58] What motivates the actors who raise these concerns? The absence of such questions focuses the analyst's attention on following a pattern of behaviour of state actors and on explaining how their actions unfold within the given context. Significantly, unless these questions are addressed, there is little scope for finding out if or how this behaviour may change over time.

Much like Human Security, CSS has been critiqued for reducing the level of analysis to the individual and for stretching the security agenda to potentially unmanageable limits. The emancipatory aim of CSS has also met with much disapproval by those who point out that 'emancipation' as a concept is deeply associated with western liberal values rooted in Enlightenment, and with western hegemonic practices.[59] Given that there is no universal definition of emancipation, it is argued that this risks the potential hijacking of the concept to legitimate the actions of those with power and vested interests. At the same time, others have pointed out that emancipation does not necessarily, as CSS scholars insist, guarantee security, and that such a perspective is indeed misguided. Ayoob, for example, has argued that in the context of the Third World, to equate emancipation with security is actually a dangerous move.[60] Alker suggests that rather than surrendering this commitment to 'human improvement and emancipatory development' at the heart of CSS, work needs to be done 'to achieve the fuller inclusion of multiple Western *and* non-Western perspectives on the meanings of freedom' in order to render it insightful in both contexts.[61]

As far as the value that a CSS approach brings to the study of security, Wæver admits,

> The big contrast to Critical Security Studies [read: Welsh School] is that the analyst cannot step in on behalf of actors who do not speak security and tell that *really* their main security problem is this or that, only they suffer from false consciousness. Speaking from some general emancipatory ideal, Critical Security Studies can deal with exactly the blind spot of the Copenhagen School and thus the two might be complimentary.[62]

Thus, the 'blind spot' in Securitization Theory may be something an approach based on insights from Human Security and CSS could help overcome. Rather than simply focusing on expressions of security as part of a certain kind of process, CSS and Human Security may help identify the *insecurities* of communities and groups at the sub-state level which may not necessarily have found expression in such a manner, or have not been addressed by policy action by the state for whatever reason. This would ensure that the study of 'security' does not focus exclusively on the threat perceptions and powers of persuasion of certain kinds of actors, but also includes 'real situations of urgency' where a referent object is threatened in indisputable circumstances.[63] Both CSS and Human Security are in favour of expanding the security agenda to include those issues which threaten the 'survival plus'[64] of individuals, and it is this notion of security – one which refers to freedom from threats to the physical survival of *communities*, but also to their livelihoods and way of life – which characterizes the analytical frame adopted in this study.

In this way, this study does not presuppose as inherently positive the notion of 'desecuritization' as does the Copenhagen School. This is because first, as Acharya points out, to distinguish neatly between 'politicization' and 'securitization' is rather problematic, especially when considering security practices in developing socio-political contexts.[65] Also, to call for 'desecuritization' implies a limited understanding of responses to the identification of an issue as a 'security' threat as it associates it only with the 'threat–defence' logic which the Copenhagen School warns against. It emphasizes a certain *kind* of policy response which is distinctly associated with this logic, and fails to recognize that responses to 'security' vary, and can be located within as well as outsidethe public policy realm.[66] Finally, it considers more carefully instances which may appear as 'failed' securitizations by most securitization studies scholars – where the issue perceived as a matter of security by NSAs has not resulted in a direct public policy response, but may have gained cognizance amongst the actors, communities or groups which perceive it as a 'real and urgent' threat. Also, this may have resulted in non-state responses in terms of the implementation of measures to assist relevant referent groups in dealing with the immediate danger presented by the threat and in mitigating its impact on those who have suffered by it. In such instances, arguing for a 'failed' case of securitization may be short-sighted, and there needs to be a wider consideration of whether the above-mentioned dynamics are at play in the absence of a state-led response, and implications for the security analysis.

Analytical framework

Thus, in studying security dynamics in South Asia with respect to the role of NSAs in identifying and dealing with insecurities to sub-state groups within the region, the analytical framework in this book takes into account the recent theoretical developments in the field of securitization studies and, drawing on the above-discussed insights from CSS and Human Security, first proposes *a wider consideration of 'threats' and responses to expressions of insecurity*. It is argued here that for any security analysis to be comprehensive, 'Threats have to be dealt with *both in terms of perceptions and in terms of the phenomena which are perceived to be threatening.*'[67] When it comes to analysing security in developing socio-political contexts, this becomes even more imperative as communities living in these countries continue to suffer from insecurities arising from threats which have been or are being dealt with successfully in developed countries, such as political violence, ethnic discrimination (institutionalized and informal), widespread corruption, developmental projects which uproot communities without providing adequate rehabilitation, among others. This may be because developing states suffer from situations which reduce their capacity to deal with such threats, such as 'financial limitation, bureaucratic deadlock, weak governance, and ongoing political instability'.[68] In the context of this investigation, a threat refers to a 'passive sense of an impending danger, rather than in its active sense of an undertaking by one actor to impose a sanction on another.'[69] Other than threats which may be existential in nature, those which endanger a group or community's way of life or livelihood, or lead to political violence (as more often than not, political violence itself results in great disruption in the socio-political realm, causing severe damage to or loss of life and livelihood) are also considered. The success of a securitization in this context is no longer solely reliant on certain kinds of public policy responses (i.e. those associated with 'emergency measures' breaking 'normal procedures and rules'), but also takes note of other responses located outside the public policy realm, as well as the actual and perceived threatening quality of the issue in question.

Second, it takes *a broader view of who may securitize, and how*. The Copenhagen School argues that a securitizing actor must be someone with 'social capital and authority'.[70] The 'authority' alluded to by the Copenhagen School, given its emphasis on 'emergency measures' which break 'normal procedures and rules' and focus on public policy measures, can be safely interpreted as state authority. It is argued here that while the element of having social capital is still important, the question of having direct political authority is less so. A sociological approach to Securitization Theory points to multiple audiences and different 'streams' but it appears also to focus primarily on policy outcomes when determining whether an issue has been accepted as a matter of 'security' or not. This study proposes an analytical approach which does not emphasize the breaking of 'normal procedures and rules' as demanded by the Copenhagen School (and not necessarily questioned by those who have proposed a sociological approach) in calling for an issue to be recognized as a security threat. In this way, a wider range of actors may be opened to consideration as those who can securitize and those who may act as security agents on the ground. Simultaneously, actions outside the public policy realm may also be included in the security analysis.

Finally, given the focus on NSAs in the study, it becomes essential to identify the different types of NSAs involved and briefly consider the possible motivations in their behaviour. As generally understood, state actors are considered those which act in the name of the state, i.e. representatives of state institutions. According to realists, the state is a unitary and rational actor motivated by national interests (defined by power in terms of military capabilities and influence) to compete with other states in the presence of an anarchic international system.[71] Since governments have ordered preferences, they act in a rational manner by calculating costs and benefits of policies and opt for those which maximize interests and minimize costs.[72] Therefore, in the realist analysis, states are the only actors whose actions are worth considering. The rise of international organizations such as the United Nations, multi-national corporations (MNCs), and transnational groups in the 1970s challenged these assumptions and provided ground for other IR traditions to question the realist emphasis on states as sole actors in IR.[73] While realists maintain that such NSAs actors are 'extensions of states with little influence on nation-state interactions', liberal pluralists argue that these actors may play a direct role in world politics. In their 1977 book, *Power and Independence*, Keohane and Nye developed a model of 'complex interdependence' which proposed that states are not sole unitary actors (as they may have competing bureaucracies) in IR. The model suggested that the world exists of 'multiple channels that connect societies including inter-state, trans-governmental and transnational relations' with an agenda 'consisting of multiple issues that are not arranged in a clear and consistent hierarchy' and with 'economic interests on the same footing as military ones'.[74]

When it comes to the definition and classification of NSAs, there is considerable disagreement within the literature.[75] According to Clemens, for example, NSAs in IR are simply 'players that are not states', including intergovernmental organizations (IGOs), NGOs, MNCs and transnational corporations (TNCs).[76] Others such as Higget and colleagues outline NSAs in two realms – private sector corporate actors (further divided into TNCs and MNCs), and NGOs (further divided into societally sponsored NGOs, state-sponsored NGOs and so on).[77] Yet others classify NSAs as those which are transnational, i.e. 'consisting of individuals or groups residing in two or more states', and 'formally organized'.[78] In 'A User's Guide for Non-State Actors' to the Cotonou Agreement, the European Centre for Development and Policy Management (ECDPM) defines NSAs as 'the private sector, economic and social partners, including trade union organisations, and civil society in all its diversity'.[79] Included in this definition are actors such as 'community-based organisations, women's groups, human rights associations, NGOs, religious

organisations, farmers' cooperatives, trade unions, universities and research institutes, the media, etc ... [as well as] informal groups such as grassroots organisations,
informal private sector associations, etc.'.[80] It is this group of NSAs (not representative of or substantially funded by one or more governments or states), which
this study focuses on.[81] Such actors play a variety of roles in the socio-political
realm, and have varying and at times even conflicting motivations for their
actions. What unites these different actors is 'their distinct "unofficial" nature as
compared to state actors, their greater flexibility and often unaccountability under
national and international laws.'[82] Finally, the study focuses on NSAs primarily
operating at the sub-state level, but also as part of wider transborder and international networks.

In relative terms, it may be easier to trace the motivations of state actors than
to discern the motivations of NSAs.[83] In most cases, NSAs declare their interests
in taking particular actions. For example, an armed group such as the Liberation
Tigers of Tamil Eelam (LTTE) may declare its interest in achieving greater
autonomy for the Tamil-majority regions in Sri Lanka. An NGO in the education
sector in Cambodia may cite improving primary education among girls in the
country as the key motivation behind its drive to increase the enrolment of young
girls in secondary school. An MNC is most likely to be driven in its strategies by
the pursuit of profit and creating favourable market conditions for itself. In
instances where NSAs are funded at least in part by states, however, it may be
argued that the latter may influence the former's agenda for action. Moreover,
the issues of accountability and transparency are also important considerations
when trying to establish the motivations of NSAs.[84] While a government may be
held accountable to its people or elite populations, depending on the socio-political
nature of the governing system, there are no formal institutions making NSAs
accountable to stakeholders. In any analysis of motivations for NSA behaviour,
these issues need to be taken into account, along with the situational context of
their actions.

The structure of the book

Chapter 2 contextualizes the study by presenting an overview of a range of issues
identified as key sources of insecurity for different groups in South Asia, by state
actors and NSAs in the region and beyond. The aim of the chapter is to highlight
contesting security understandings and priorities in South Asia. A number of
traditional as well as non-traditional issue areas are identified, and in each case
the dynamics are explored in terms of the threats perceived and by whom, and
any relevant responses by actors involved. Chapters 3, 4 and 5 then investigate
the roles played by NSAs in South Asia at the sub-state level in three different
non-traditional security issue areas respectively. Each case study focuses on a
particular issue which has been identified as a threat or source of insecurity in
South Asia by various actors and within the relevant literature, and uses Securitization Theory to examine the role of NSAs involved. In each context, the analysis
also tests the ability of Securitization Theory to accommodate the wider spectrum

of security practices in which NSAs may be involved, both when operating outside the immediate public policy realm in relation to the issue in question, and when directly involved in the process of policy-making on the same issue.

Chapter 3 presents an investigation into perceived threats to societal security in Bangladesh and the issue of 'misgovernance'. It examines why aspects related to misgovernance have been cited as major sources of insecurity in the country and the wider region, and analyses the role of English-language national daily newspapers in raising these issues as threats to the safety and well-being of the people of Bangladesh. Problems such as corruption, a violent and criminal political process, a politicized judiciary and weak law enforcement have gained widespread cognizance in Bangladeshi society as sources of deep insecurity for its people. This cognizance is arguably both reflected in and, to some extent, perpetuated by the focus placed on these issues by the country's highly active media organizations. In examining the role of three main English-language national daily newspapers in the country – *The Daily Star*, *New Age* and *The Bangladesh Today* – the case study investigates them as securitizing actors, and in doing so illuminates continuing ambiguities within Securitization Theory around the role of the securitizing actor and the securitizing agent or security practitioner respectively, as well as lack of clarity around what constitutes a successful securitization.

Chapter 3 further deepens the investigation at the heart of the book by focusing on an instance where NSAs have gone beyond articulating a threat in relation to vulnerable and affected referent groups, to providing them with necessary measures to prevent and deal with the threatening phenomenon and the insecurities it creates. In doing so, these NSAs may at times work with the state, but often also fill the gap left by state agencies and effectively become securitizing agents or security practitioners in the given context. The case study focuses on the phenomenon of human trafficking in Nepal and analyses the role of NGOs such as those run by trafficking survivors, in raising the issue as a threat to, and cause of insecurity for, women and children in Nepal, and their role in (1) influencing policy in this issue area at the state level, (2) providing communities considered most vulnerable to the risk of being trafficked with preventative knowledge, and (3) providing rescued trafficked victims with rehabilitative measures to equip them with livelihood skills and facilitate their reintegration into the families and communities from which they were trafficked. It demonstrates how NSAs often work outside the state-led public policy realm and provide security measures to those who need it, and argues that Securitization Theory misses out on these dynamics owing to its predominant focus on state-led action, and its preference for state actors as the main security actors.

Chapter 5 presents the final case study which examines the role of scientific policy communities (SPCs) in shaping India's National Action Plan on Climate Change (NAPCC) launched in 2008. It focuses on the work of two SPCs, The Energy and Resources Institute (TERI) and the Centre for Science and Environment (CSE), which have been at the forefront of efforts to securitize the issue as an existential threat to the people to India, particularly the poor; those living in areas most vulnerable to the adverse impacts of climate change, and those who rely on the agricultural sector for their way of life and livelihoods. The case study analyses how these SPCs have, through their research, analysis and outreach activities, significantly influenced the Indian state's perceptions of climate change as a security threat, and have been an integral part of the formulation of the NAPCC in this context. The analysis demonstrates that, given the proximity of these SPCs to state agencies working in the area of climate change (and the formers' role in helping to produce the NAPCC), Securitization Theory largely accommodates these NSAs in its analysis, in terms of their role as both securitizing actors and security actors. In conclusion, the book brings together insights gained from the case studies in a systematic manner to emphasize the need to acknowledge and better understand the different ways in which NSAs operate in the realm of security practices in South Asia, with implications for developing cooperative approaches to tackling common security challenges in the region and for the continuing development of securitization studies and Securitization Theory.

Notes

1 In this study, South Asia is defined by the seven founding member states of the South Asian Association for Regional Cooperation (SAARC): Bhutan, Bangladesh, India, Maldives, Nepal, Pakistan and Sri Lanka.

2 For example, see S. Ganguly, *Conflict Unending: India Pakistan Tensions Since 1947*, New York: Columbia University Press, 2001; R.G.C. Thomas (ed.), *Perspectives on Kashmir: the Roots of Conflict in South Asia*, Boulder, CO: Westview Press, 1992; S. K. Khatri (ed.), *Regional Security in South Asia*, Kathmandu: Centre for Nepal and Asian Studies, Tribhuvan University, 1987; C. K. Tiwari, *Security in South Asia: Internal and External Dimensions*, London: University Press of America, 1989; R. G. C. Thomas, 'South Asian Security in the 1990s', Adelphi Paper 278, International Institute for Strategic Studies, July 1993; V. T. Patil and N. K. Jha, *Peace and Cooperative Security in South Asia*, Delhi: P R Books, 1999; P. Sahadevan, (ed.), *Conflict and Cooperation in South Asia*, New Delhi: Lancer's Books, 2001 and R. M. Basrur, *South Asia's Cold War*, London: Routledge, 2008, among others.

3 In the last decade or so, a small but growing number of scholars have started to focus on non-military threats to states and communities in South Asia. For example, see P. R. Chari, M. Joseph and S. Chandran (eds.), *Missing Boundaries: Refugees, Migrants, Stateless and Internally Displaced People in South Asia*, New Delhi: Manohar, 2003; Chari (ed.), *Security and Governance in South Asia*, Colombo: Manohar, 2001; V. T. Patil, P. R. Trivedi, *Migration, Refugees and Security in the 21st Century*, New Delhi: Authorspress, 2000; P. S. Ghosh, *Migrants and Refugees in South Asia: Political and Security Dimensions*, Shillong: ICSSR-NERC, 2001; P. Bhattacharya and S. Hazra (eds.), *Environment and Human Security*, New Delhi: Lancer's Books, 2003; J. Richter and C. Wagner (eds.), *Regional Security, Ethnicity and Governance: The Challenges for South Asia*, New Delhi: Manohar, 1998.

4 K. Booth, *Theory of World Security*, Cambridge: Cambridge University Press, 2007, p. 101.

5 United Nation Development Programme (UNDP), 'The Real Wealth of Nations: Pathways to Human Development', *Human Development Report 2010*, p. 98. Online. HTTP: <http://hdr.undp.org/en/media/HDR_2010_EN_Complete_reprint.pdf> (accessed 12 June 2011).

6 'A Matter of Magnitude: The Impact of the Economic Crisis on Women and Children in South Asia', *UNICEF*, June 2009. Online. HTTP: <http://www.unicef.org/rosa/Latest_Matter_of_magnitude.pdf> (accessed 12 Mar. 2011).

7 Y. Fujikura, 'Repatriation of Nepali Girls 1996: Social Workers' Experience', *Himalayan Research Bulletin*, vol. 21, no. 1, 2001, p. 1. Online. HTTP: <http://digitalcommons. macalester.edu/cgi/viewcontent.cgi?article=1674&context=himalaya> (accessed 10 July 2011). As Fujikura points out, different reports often provide conflicting figures in terms of the number of girls. The total number of those rescued varies from 477 to 538, while the number of Nepali girls among them ranges from 218 to 238.

8 Ibid. Also see 'The Story of a Nepali Girl Sold into Sexual Slavery', *Kanchenjunga Social Network*, 17 Apr. 2009. Online. HTTP: < http://www.ksnonline.org/profiles/blogs/ survivor-the-story-of-a-nepali> (accessed 12 July 2011).

9 Fujikura, 'Repatriation of Nepali Girls', p. 1.

10 For example, see K. Krause and M. Williams, 'Broadening the Agenda of Security Studies: Politics and Methods', *Mershon International Studies Review*, vol. 40, no. 2, Oct. 1996, pp. 229–54; 'Emerging Non-Traditional Security Challenges in Asia', *Centre for Strategic and International Studies*, Washington DC, 6 Mar. 2007; R. Thakur and E. Newman, *Broadening Asia's Security Discourse and Agenda*, Tokyo: United Nations University Press, 2004; 'Policy Bulletin: Nontraditional Security Threats in South East Asia', *The Stanley Foundation*, Warrenton, Virginia, 16–18 Oct. 2003; and 'Non-Traditional and Human Security in South Asia', *Institute of Regional Studies: National Commission for Human Development*, Islamabad, 2006.

11 For example, see E. Newman and O. P. Richmond (eds), *The United Nations and Human Security*, Basingstoke: Palgrave Macmillan, 2001; J. P. Burgess and T. Owen (eds), 'Special Section: What Is Human Security?', *Security Dialogue*, vol. 35, no. 3, Sept. 2004, pp. 345–87; K. Keith, 'The Key to a Powerful Agenda, If Properly Defined', in Burgess and Owen (eds), 'Special Section: What Is Human Security?', pp. 367–68; P. R. Chari and S. Gupta (eds), *Human Security in South Asia: Energy, Gender, Migration and Globalisation*, New Delhi: Social Science Press, 2003; S. Tadjbakhsh and A. M. Chenoy, *Human Security: Concepts and Implications*, London: Routledge, 2007; M. Kaldor, *Human Security: Reflections on Globalization and Interventions*, Cambridge: Polity Press, 2007; M. Den Boer and J. de Wilde (eds), *The Viability of Human Security*, Amsterdam: Amsterdam University Press, 2008; and D. Chandler and N. Hynek (eds), *Critical Perspectives on Human Security: Rethinking Emancipation*, Abingdon: Routledge, 2011.

12 This refers specifically to the work emerging from the Aberystwyth or Welsh school of critical security studies, led by Ken Booth and Richard Wyn Jones. For example, see Booth, *Theory of World Security*; R. Wyn Jones, *Security, Strategy, and Critical Theory*, CO: Lynne Rienner, 1999; K. Booth, 'Security and Emancipation', *Review of International Studies*, vol.17, no. 4, Oct. 1991, pp. 313–26; K. Booth, 'Human Wrongs and International Relations', *International Affairs*, vol. 71, no. 1, Jan. 1995, p. 103–26; K. Booth and T. Dunne (eds), *Worlds in Collision: Terror and the Future of Global Order*, Houndmills and New York: Palgrave Macmillan, 2002; K. Booth (ed.), *Critical Security Studies and World Politics*, CO: Lynne Rienner, 2004; R. Wyn Jones, 'Message in a Bottle? Theory and Praxis in Critical Security Studies', *Contemporary Security Policy*, vol. 16, no.3, Sept. 1995, pp. 299–319. Also see K. Fierke, *Critical Approaches to International Security*, London: Polity Press, 2007, and T. McCormack, *Critical Security Theory and Contemporary Power Relations: Emancipation, Critique and the International Order*, London: Routledge, 2009.

13 For example, see B. Buzan, O. Wæver and J. de Wilde, *Security: A New Framework for Analysis*, CO: Lynne Rienner, 1998; O. Wæver, 'Securitization and Descuritization', in R. Lipschutz (ed.), *On Security*, New York: Columbia University Press, 19950; O. Wæver, B. Buzan, M. Kelstrup et al., *Identity, Migration and the New Security Agenda in Europe*, London: Pinter, 1993, and B. Buzan and O. Wæver, *Regions and Powers: The Structure of International Security*, Cambridge: Cambridge University Press, 2003.

14 For example, see S. Strange, *The Retreat of the State: The Diffusion of Power in the World Economy*, Cambridge: Cambridge University Press, 1996; P. Willetts (ed.), *The Conscience of the World: The Influence of Non-governmental Organisations in the UN System*, London:

Hurst & Co., 1996; W. Korey, *NGOs and the Universal Declaration of Human Rights*, New York: Palgrave, 1998; S. J. Kaufman, 'Approaches to Global Politics in the Twenty-First Century: A Review Essay', *International Studies Review*, vol. 1, no. 2, Summer 1999, pp. 201, 218; V. D. Cha, 'Globalization and the Study of International Security', *Journal of Peace Research*, vol. 37, no. 3, May 2000, pp. 391–403; R. A. Higgott, G. Underhill and A. Bieler (eds), *Non-State Actors and Authority in the Global System*, London: Routledge, 2000; J. True and M. Mintrom, 'Transnational Networks and Policy Diffusion: The Case of Gender Mainstreaming', *International Studies Quarterly*, vol. 45, no. 1, Mar. 2001, pp. 27–57; J. Haynes, 'Transnational Religious Actors and International Politics', *Third World Quarterly*, vol. 22, no. 2, Apr. 2001, pp. 143–58; B. Arts, M. Noortmann and B. Reinialda (eds), *Non-State Actors in International Relations*, Aldershot: Ashgate, 2001; D. Held and A. McGrew (eds), *Governing Globalization: Power, Authority and Global Governance*, Cambridge: Polity Press, 2002; C. Knill and C. Lehmkuhl, 'Private Actors and the State: Internationalization and Changing Patterns of Governance', *Governance*, vol. 15, no. 1, Jan. 2002, pp. 41–63; T. M. Shaw, 'The Commonwealth(s): Inter- and Non-State: At the Start of the Twenty-First Century: Contributions to Global Development and Governance', Third World Quarterly, vol. 24, no.4 (Aug. 2003), pp. 729–44; I. Parmar, *Think Tanks and Power in Foreign Policy: A Comparative Study of the Role and Influence of the Council on Foreign Relations and the Royal Institute of International Affairs, 1939–1945*, New York: Palgrave Macmillan, 2004; and M. Barnett and R. Duvall (eds), *Power in Global Governance*, Cambridge: Cambridge University Press, 2005.

15 E. Krahmann, 'From State to Non-State Actors: The Emergence of Security Governance' in E. Krahmann (ed.), *New Threats and New Actors in International Security*, New York: Palgrave Macmillan, 2005, p. 3.

16 This sub-set of the security studies literature is small but growing. For example, see Krahmann (ed.), *New Threats and New Actors*; C. Bruderlein, *Role of Non-State Actors in Building Human Security: The Case of Armed Groups in Intra-State Wars*, Geneva: Centre for Humanitarian Dialogue, 2000; B. Hadiwinata, 'Poverty and the Role of NGOs in Protecting Human Security in Indonesia', in M. Caballro-Anthony, R. Emmers and A. Acharya (eds), *Non-Traditional Security in Asia: Dilemmas in Securitization*, Aldershot: Ashgate, 2006, pp. 198–224, and R. Datta, '"Hum honge kamiyab … [We shall overcome …]": Non-governmental Organizations, The State and Human Security in India', in R. Thakur and O. Wiggen (eds), *South Asia in the World: Problem Solcing Perspectives on Security, Sustainable Development, and Good Governance*, Tokyo: United Nations University Press, 2004, pp. 335–54; E. Krahmann (ed.), *New Threats and New Actors in International Security*.

17 For example, see H. Stritzel, 'Towards a Theory of Securitization: Copenhagen and Beyond', *European Journal of International Relations*, vol. 13, no. 3, Sept. 2007, pp. 357–83; J. Vaughn, 'The Unlikely Securitizer: Humanitarian Organizations and the Securitization of Indistinctiveness', *Security Dialogue*, vol. 40, no. 3, June 2009, pp. 263–85; T. Balzacq (ed.), *Securitization Theory: How Security Problems Emerge and Dissolve*, London: Routledge, 2011; T. Balzacq, 'The Three Faces of Securitization: Political Agency, Audience and Context', *European Journal of International Relations*, vol. 11, no. 2, June 2005, pp. 171–201 and more.

18 B. Buzan, et al., *Security: A New Framework for Analysis*, p. 32. Conversely, the authors also wish to study how desecuritization – the removal of an issue or threat from the security agenda – occurs, by whom and to what consequences.

19 Ibid., p. 25.

20 Ibid., p. 37.

21 Ibid., p. 41.

22 Stritzel, 'Towards a Theory of Securitization', p. 368.

23 See J. Erikkson, 'Observers or Advocates? On The Political Role of Analysts', *Cooperation and Conflict*, vol. 34, no. 3, Sept. 1999, pp. 311–30; J. Huysmans, 'Revisiting Copenhagen: Or, On the Creative Development of a Security Studies Agenda in

Europe', *European Journal of International Relations*, vol. 4, No. 4, Dec. 1998, pp. 479–505; B. McSweeney, 'Identity and Security: Buzan and the Copenhagen school', *Review of International Studies*, vol. 22, no. 1, 1996, pp. 81–89; L. Hansen, 'The Little Mermaid's Silent Security Dilemma and the Absence of Gender in the Copenhagen school', *Millennium*, vol. 29, no. 2, 2000, pp. 285–306; A. Kent, 'Reconfiguring Security: Buddhism and Moral Legitimacy in Cambodia', *Security Dialogue*, vol. 37, no. 3, Sept. 2006, pp. 343–61; Stritzel, 'Towards a Theory of Securitization', pp. 357–83.

24 See Hansen, 'The Little Mermaid's Silent Security Dilemma', pp. 285–306; D. Bigo, 'Security and Immigration: Toward a Critique of the Governmentality of Unease', *Alternatives: Global, Local, Political*, vol. 27, no. 1, Jan. 2002, pp. 64–92; Balzacq, 'The Three Faces of Securitization', pp. 171–201.

25 See M. Williams, 'Words, Images, Enemies: Securitization and International Politics', *International Studies Quarterly*, vol. 47, no. 4, Dec. 2003, pp. 511–31; L. Hansen and H. Nissenbaum, 'Digital Disaster, Cyber Security and the Copenhagen School', *International Studies Quarterly*, vol. 53, no. 4, 2009, pp. 1155–75.

26 See Stritzel, 'Towards a Theory of Securitization', pp. 357–83; M. Salter, 'Securitization and Desecuritization: Dramaturgical Analysis and the Canadian Aviation Transport Security Authority', *Journal of International Relations and Development*, vol. 11, no. 4, 2008, pp. 321–49; Vaughn, 'The Unlikely Securitizer', pp. 263 – 85; S. Leonard and C. Kaunert, 'Reconceptualising the Relationship Between the Audience and the Securitizing Actor', in Balzacq (ed.), *Securitization Theory*, pp. 57 – 76.

27 See Balzacq (ed.), *Securitization Theory*. This approach is identified with the 'Paris school' of critical security studies, consisting primarily of scholars based at the Paris Institute of Political Studies (Sciences Po).

28 R. Cox, 'Social Forces, States and World Orders: Beyond International Relations Theory', *Millennium: Journal of International Studies*, vol. 10, no. 2, 1981, p. 128.

29 For example, see C. Wilkinson, 'The Copenhagen School on Tour in Kyrgyzstan: Is Securitization Theory Usable Outside Europe?', *Security Dialogue*, vol. 38, no. 1, Mar. 2007, p. 13.

30 M. Salter, 'When Securitization Fails', in Balzacq (ed.), *Securitization Theory*, p. 126.

31 M.J. Trombetta, 'Rethinking the Securitization of the Environment', in Balzacq (ed.), *Securitization Theory*, p. 143.

32 B. Buzan, et al. *Security: A New Framework for Analysis*, p. 25.

33 Ibid., p. 26.

34 See B. Buzan, et al. *Security: A New Framework for Analysis*.

35 The state-centric outlook inherent within the Copenhagen school's approach is obvious in other places too. For example, in *Security: A New Framework for Analysis*, Buzan et al. argue that when an issue is securitized it becomes 'so important that it should not be exposed to the normal haggling of politics but should be dealt with decisively by top leaders prior to other issues.' As quoted in K. Booth, *Theory of World Security*, Cambridge: Cambridge University Press, 2007, p. 166.

36 K. Booth, *Theory of World Security*, p. 166.

37 Ibid., p. 167.

38 Huysmans, 'Revisiting Copenhagen', pp. 479–505; E. Krahmann, 'The Emergence of Security Governance in Post-Cold War Europe', Working Paper 36/01, *E S R C "One Europe or Several?" Programme*, Sussex European Institute, Sussex: University of Sussex, 2001. Online. HTTP: <http://www.one-europe.ac.uk/pdf/w36krahmann.pdf> (accessed 3 Mar. 2010); M. Williams, 'The Continuing Evaluation of Securitization Theory', in Balzacq (ed.), *Securitization Theory*, p. 221.

39 E. Newman, 'Critical Human Security Studies', *Review of International Studies*, vol. 36, no.1, Jan. 2010, p. 77.

40 Ibid. As discussed later in the section, a small group of these scholars has attempted to take a more theoretical approach to human security and how it has been applied by

global governance institutions. It remains however that the bulk of Human Security scholarship is policy-oriented and not of a critical orientation.

41 Ibid., p. 89.

42 A. Suhrke, 'Human Security and the Interests of States', *Security Dialogue*, vol. 30, no. 3, Sept. 1999, pp. 268–69.

43 As pointed out in an illuminating piece by D. Bosold, 'Development of the Human Security Field: A Critical Examination', in D. Chandler and N. Hynek (eds), *Critical Perspectives on Human Security*, Abingdon: Routledge, 2011, pp. 28–42.

44 'New Dimensions of Human Security', *UNDP Human Development Report 1994*, Oxford University Press, 1994, p. 22. Online. HTTP: <http://hdr.undp.org/en/reports/global/hdr1994/chapters/> (accessed 30 Jan. 2011).

45 Ibid., pp. 22–23.

46 Ibid., p. 24.

47 See G. Shani, 'Securitizing "Bare Life": Critical Perspectives on Human Security Discourse', in D. Chandler and N. Hynek (eds), *Critical Perspectives on Human Security*, Abingdon: Routledge, 2011, p. 56–68.

48 For example, see T. Owen, 'Human Security – Conflict, Critique and Consensus: Colloquium Remarks and a Proposal for a Threshold-Based Definition', *Security Dialogue*, vol. 35, no. 3, 2004, pp. 373 – 87; R. Paris, 'Human Security: Paradigm Shift or Hot Air?', *International Security*, vol. 26, no. 2, 2001, pp. 87–102; Y. Foong Khong and S. N. MacFarlane, *Human Security and the UN: A Critical History*, Indiana: Indiana University Press, 2006; D. Roberts, 'Human Security or Human Insecurity? Moving the Debate Forward', *Security Dialogue*, vol. 37, no. 249, 2006, pp. 249–61.

49 D. Chandler and N. Hynek, 'Emancipation and Power in Human Security' in D. Chandler and N. Hynek (eds), *Critical Perspectives*, p. 1.

50 For example, see D. Roberts, *Global Governance and Biopolitics: Regulating Human Security*, Zed: London, 2009.

51 D. Roberts, 'Human Security, Biopoverty and the Possibility for Emancipation' in D. Chandler and N. Hynek (eds), *Critical Perspectives*, p. 69.

52 O. Richmond, 'Post-Colonial Hybridity and the Return of Human Security', in D. Chandler and N. Hynek (eds), *Critical Perspectives*, pp. 43–44.

53 M. Turner, N. Cooper and M. Pugh, 'Institutionalised and Co-opted: Why Human Security Has Lost Its Way', in D. Chandler and N. Hynek (eds), *Critical Perspectives*, p. 7.

54 R. Wyn Jones, *Security, Strategy, and Critical Theory*, CO: Lynne Rienner, 1999, p. 2. Critical theory in IR literature can be traced to writings of Kant, Hegel and Marx, among others. For example, see I. Kant in H. Reiss (ed.), *Kant's Political Writings*, Cambridge: Cambridge University Press, 1989; G.W.F. Hegel, *The Philosophy of Right*, Oxford: Oxford University Press, 1967, and *Phenomenology of Spirit*, Oxford: Oxford University Press, 1977; K. Marx, *Capital Vol. 1*, London: Penguin Books, 1990; A. Gramsci, *Prison Notebooks*, New York: International Publishers, 1971; and F. Nietzsche, *The Birth of Tragedy and the Geneology of Morals*, trans.F. Golffing, London: Doubleday, Random House Inc., 1956. More recently, it has been associated with the work of scholars linked to the Frankfurt Institute of Social Research (also known as the Frankfurt school) such as Max Horkheimer and Jürgen Habermas. For example, see T. Adorno and M. Horkheimer, *Dialectic of Enlightenment*, trans. J.Cumming, London: Vereso, 1979; M. Horkheimer, 'Traditional and Critical Theory', trans. M.J. O'Connell et. al., in *Critical Theory: Selected Essays*, New York: Seabury Press, 1972, pp. 188–243; J. Habermas, *Between Facts and Norms: Contributions to a Discourse Theory of Law and Democracy*, trans. W. Rehg, Cambridge: Polity Press: 1996; J. Habermas, *The Theory of Communicative Action, Volume 1: Reason and the Rationalization of Society*, trans. S. Verlg, Boston: Beacon Press, 1981, and more. For a useful overview of the first generation of theorists of Frankfurt school, see M. Jay, *The Dialectical Imagination: The History of the Frankfurt School and the Institute of Social Research: 1923–1950*, Berkeley: University of California Press, 1973.

55 K. Booth, 'Security and Emancipation', *Review of International Studies*, vol. 17, no. 4, Oct. 1991, p. 319.
56 K. Booth, 'Security. Introduction', in K. Booth (ed.), *Critical Security Studies and World Politics*, CO: Lynne Rienner, 2004, p. 14.
57 R. Cox in K. Krause and M. Williams (eds), *Critical Security Studies: Concepts and Cases*, Minneapolis: University of Minneapolis Press, p. xi.
58 D. Skidmore, 'Review: Security: A New Framework for Analysis by Barry Buzan et al.', *The American Political Science Review*, vol. 93, no. 4, Dec. 1999, p. 1010–11.
59 H. Alker, 'Emancipation in the Critical Security Studies Project', in Booth (ed.), *Critical Security Studies and World Politics*, London: Lynne Rienner, 2005, pp. 189–214.
60 M. Ayoob, 'Defining Security: A Subaltern Realist Perspective' in K. Krause and M. Williams (eds), *Critical Security Studies: Concepts and Cases*, London: UCL Press, 1997, p. 125.
61 Alker, 'Emancipation in the Critical Security Studies Project', p. 200.
62 O. Wæver in R. Taureck, 'Positive and Negative Securitization – Bringing Together Securitization Theory and Normative Critical Security Studies', paper prepared for the *COST Doctoral Training School, 'Critical Approaches to Security in Europe, ACTION A24: The Evolving Social Construction of Threats'*, Centre Européen, Institut d'Etudes Politiques de Paris, France, June 2005, p. 7.
63 O. Knudsen, 'Post-Copenhagen Security Studies', *Security Dialogue*, vol. 32, no. 3, p. 360. Human security proponents argue that certain threats such as those arising from human trafficking, gendered violence, ethnic discrimination, and armed conflict carry with them a sense of real urgency, i.e. if they are not dealt with immediately, the referent group's physical existence, way of life or livelihood is endangered. Such threats, therefore, are arguably real and imminent in nature.
64 Booth, *Theory of World Security*, p. 106.
65 A. Acharya, 'Securitization in Asia', in M. Caballero-Anthony, R. Emmers and A. Acharya (eds), *Non-Traditional Security in Asia*, Aldershot: Ashgate, 2006, p. 250.
66 On this, see M.J. Trombetta, 'Rethinking the Securitization of the Environment', in Balzacq (ed.), *Securitization Theory*, pp. 135–49.
67 Knudsen, 'Post-Copenhagen Security Studies', p. 359.
68 B. S. Hadiwinata, 'Securitizing Poverty: The Role of NGOs in the Protection of Human Security in Indonesia', paper presented at *IDSS, Nanyang University-Ford Foundation workshop on 'The Dynamics of Securitization in Asia'*, Singapore, 3–5 Sept. 2004, p. 4. Online. HTTP: <http://www.rsis-ntsasia.org/resources/publications/research-papers/poverty/Bob%20Hadiwinata.pdf> (accessed 16 Feb. 2011).
69 R. Cohen, 'Threat Perception in International Crisis', in *Political Science Quarterly*, vol. 93, no. 1, Spring 1978, p. 95.
70 Buzan et al., *Security*, p. 33.
71 B. Russett and H. Starr, *Choices in World Politics: Sovereignty and Interdependence*, New York: Freeman, 1989, p. 28.
72 R. O. Keohane (ed.), *Neorealism and Its Critics*, New York: Columbia University Press, 1986, p. 11.
73 M. P. Sullivan, 'Transnationalism, Power Politics, and the Realities of the Present System', in M. Williams (ed.), *International Relations in the Twentieth Century*, London: MacMillan, 1989, pp. 255–74.
74 R. O. Keohane and J. Nye, *Power and Interdependence*, 2nd ed., Glenview: Scott Foresman, 1977, 1989, pp. 24–25.
75 P. Taylor, *Non-State Actors in International Politics: From Transregional to Sub-State Organizations*, Boulder, CO: Westview Press, 1984, p. 20.
76 W.C. Clemens, Jr., *Dynamics of International Relations*, 2nd ed., Boulder: Rowman and Littlefield Publishers Inc., 2004, p. 517.
77 R. Higgott, R. Underhill and A. Bieler (eds), *Non-State Actors and Authority in the Global System*, London: Routledge, 2000, pp. 1–2.

78 P. Taylor, *Non-State Actors in International Politics*, p. 20.
79 ECDPM, 'The Cotonou Agreement: A User's Guide for Non-State Actors', *African, Caribbean and Pacific (ACP) Secretariat*, Brussels, Belgium, Nov. 2003, p. 4. Online. HTTP: <?twb=0.25w> http://www.acpsec.org/en/nsa/nsa_users_guide_en_rev1.pdf> (accessed 22 June 2011).
80 Ibid.
81 In doing so, the definition acknowledges that it is not necessarily unproblematic to distinguish NSAs completely from states and their operations. Indeed, often NSAs are closely linked to states and their decision-making processes. For example, former government officials often sit on boards of NGOs and MNCs, and employees of such organizations are often contracted to work for government agencies on a project-basis. Given this reality, the definition attempts to make an abstraction which can then be applied to individual cases in the context of the thesis which would allow the analysis to engage with the complexities of each case.
82 Bruderlein, 'The Role of Non-State Actors in Building Human Security', 2000.
83 This is not to say that state actors always have identifiable interests, or interests which align with those of the government of the day. Indeed, competing bureaucracies within states often have conflicting interests and do not act in harmony with each other.
84 S. Burall and C. Neligan, 'The Accountability of International Organizations', *GPPi Research Paper Series No. 2*, Global Public Policy Institute, 2005. Online. HTTP: <http://www.gppi.net/fileadmin/gppi/IO_Acct_Burall_05012005.pdf> (accessed 12 Jan. 2011).

2 Understanding security in South Asia

An overview

This chapter provides a brief overview of the main issues which have been identified as 'security' threats by a variety of actors (state or non-state) in South Asia, and their perceived impacts on different groups.[1] Many of these challenges have been met by public policy responses at the national and regional levels, primarily addressing the security concerns of states, while the insecurities of sub-state groups have often been sidelined. In other cases, the absence of adequate policy measures has seen the emergence of non-state actors (NSAs) such as Non-governmental organizations (NGOs), civil society groups and epistemic communities as key actors involved in tackling these challenges at the sub-state level. In providing an overview of these issues, this chapter also aims to develop a broad understanding of the interconnected and complex nature of challenges in South Asia, and how they may relate to the insecurities of different groups in the region.[2]

The nature of security dynamics in South Asia

The majority of states in South Asia emerged at the end of British colonial rule in the region.[3] In many ways, the history of the creation of these states holds the key to understanding some of the current hostilities within and among them.[4] Even after almost sixty-five years since they gained independence from British colonial rule, relations between the two largest South Asian states – India and Pakistan – remain tenuous.[5] For much of this period, countries in the region have been immersed in efforts to preserve their state borders and territorial unity, and their security perceptions have been dominated by these tasks. It is, therefore, hardly surprising that the main body of literature on regional security in South Asia is primarily concerned with balance-of-power politics, inter-state disputes, nuclear rivalry and intra-state conflicts.[6] In the traditional security analysis, which prioritizes the safety of the state against military aggression, South Asia remains a hotbed of hostilities, with a nuclear rivalry between historic arch rivals India and Pakistan, and several ethno-nationalistic movements and armed insurgencies. This focus on military-political threats to states in South Asia in the name of 'national' security has not only meant that the insecurities of sub-state groups caught up in these dynamics are largely ignored, but also that calls to address other issues causing insecurity amongst sub-state groups also remain inadequately unaddressed. In recent years, a growing body of literature has emerged urging the policy-makers, analysts, academics and political elites of South Asian countries to re-focus their 'security' perspectives to include issues which fit under the rubric of human security and are seen as threatening sub-state communities on a daily basis.[7]

According to Gopinath, security dynamics in South Asia are 'a complex amalgam of domestic and external factors, linked with the crisis of governance'.[8] They represent interrelated phenomena where often one aspect cannot be studied in isolation from the other. For instance, when talking about the nuclear threat to security in South Asia, analysts cannot ignore the Kashmir dispute between India and Pakistan. The roots of this problem lie in history, yet the problem itself is aggravated by misgovernance, lack of adequate development, cross-border terrorism and a political armed insurgency which first emerged in 1989 and continues to rear its head from time to time.[9] The grievances of Kashmiris in India with respect to widespread unemployment and lack of opportunities, inadequate infrastructure such as educational and health facilities, underdevelopment and lack of adequate political representation are further compounded by the insecurity created by the insurgency and the heavy presence of the armed forces.[10] Living under such circumstances, members of affected communities have in the past resorted to violent confrontations with the state security apparatus to express their frustrations, and often become easy recruits for violent factions. In June 2010, the killing of innocent Kashmiris by Indian security forces led to mass protests on the streets and by November over a hundred Kashmiris had died, the majority being teenagers.[11]

The flow of refugees across borders in South Asia has been a significant cause of inter-state tensions and insecurity within recipient countries. The ongoing insurgency in India's north-eastern state of Assam is a useful example.[12] Even after the secession of East Pakistan and the creation of Bangladesh in 1971, the flow of refugees across the Indian border into Assam carried on in large numbers, changing the demographic make-up of the region. This, together with the phenomenon of names of immigrants who were not Indian citizens appearing on electoral rolls, created high levels of resentment amidst local communities.[13] In 1979, a movement to identify illegal immigrants with the purpose of removing their names from voting lists and deporting them back to Bangladesh gained momentum. This was shortly followed by the establishment of the United Liberation Front of Assam (ULFA) with the aim of creating an Assam which was independent, socialist and free from 'foreigners'.[14] The ULFA continues to accuse the Indian state of ignoring the development-related needs of the Assamese people, and holds it responsible (together with foreigners) for exploiting the resources of the region.[15] The mix of problems in Assam – numerous other tribal, linguistic, religious or cultural sub-groups demanding separation from the others, ethnic sub-nationalism, radical demographic shifts and a long history of misgovernance – is extremely volatile and affects not only local and national security perceptions, but also has regional implications.

Wars and conflicts between states

South Asia has experienced a wide range of armed conflicts over the last six decades.[16] While intra-state conflicts in the region have largely revolved around ethno-nationalistic movements within national boundaries,[17] inter-state conflicts and their causes have both internal and external dimensions. In some instances, for example, intra-state conflicts have spilled over borders and stimulated inter-state conflict (e.g. the Indo-Pakistan war of 1971). Thus, in the case of South Asia, there has historically been a strong link between intra- and inter-state conflicts.[18] Inter-state war has been a frequent phenomenon, although so far only India and Pakistan, the two regional giants, have gone to war with each other.[19] Since independence, they have engaged in four wars: in 1947–48, 1965, 1971 and 1999. 'The first two were fought over the possession and control of [the territory of] Kashmir.'[20] The Kashmir dispute is widely described as 'the core issue' between the two rival neighbours. The origins of the dispute lie in the division of the subcontinent.[21] At present, Kashmir is divided by the Line of Control (or LoC) into 'Indian-administered Kashmir' to the east and south (with a population of around nine million), which falls within the Indian state of Jammu and Kashmir, and 'Pakistan-administered Kashmir' to the north and west (with a population of around 3 million), which is labelled by Pakistan as *Azad* or 'free' Kashmir. China also controls a small portion of Kashmir.[22] The LoC also serves as a *de facto* border between India and Pakistan. Both countries claim ownership of the territory, and the issue remains unresolved despite several attempts at negotiations in the past.

The third war between India and Pakistan was fought over East Pakistan and led to the independence of Bangladesh. In 1971, the Pakistani military dictator General Yahya Khan violently suppressed a movement by the East Pakistani people for regional autonomy. Consequently, around 9.8 million refugees fled from East Pakistan to the different parts of East and North-East India, particularly West Bengal and Assam. The Indian government at the time decided to intervene in Pakistan's civil war by assisting the insurgents and eventually facilitated the breaking up of Pakistan and the independence of Bangladesh.[23] The fourth war between India and Pakistan was also over the territory of Kashmir. Although it was not officially declared a war, it met the criteria for a full-scale war and is now referred to as such.[24] It occurred between May and July 1999 in the Kargil district of Indian-administered Kashmir. The Indian army accused Pakistani soldiers and militants of having infiltrated the Indian side of the LoC. At the time, Pakistani authorities denied any involvement and blamed independent Kashmiri insurgents for the infiltration and ensuing conflict. However, during the Kargil war and since, evidence of the involvement of the Pakistani army emerged in the form of documents recovered from casualties and in statements made by Pakistani officials. The Indian Army retaliated with land and air attacks on the positions taken up by the infiltrators. In late July 1999, the Indian army, with great international diplomatic backing, forced the Pakistan-backed infiltrators to withdraw back to the Pakistani side of the LoC.[25]

Given its history of violent conflict, the India–Pakistan rivalry continues to cast a long shadow over the prospects of stability in the region and remains a potential, and perhaps the only, source of inter-state war in South Asia. This was powerfully illustrated in the aftermath of the terror attacks in Mumbai in November 2008. Immediately after the attacks, there was a huge wave of anti-Pakistan sentiments in India, as evidence linked the attacks to Pakistani nationals.[26] The Indian government took a tough stand, suspending the composite dialogue between the two countries and raising its assessment of security in the country to 'war level'.[27] Pakistan, in turn, diverted 20,000 troops from its border with Afghanistan towards its border with India, further escalating tensions between the two sides.[28] Ultimately, an inter-state war in the region did not take place, although the episode caused a distinct souring in bilateral relations between India and Pakistan following what had been a period of relative optimism. More recently, there has been an easing of tensions between New Delhi and Islamabad following a round of 'cricket diplomacy',[29] although it remains to be seen if it will actually lead to an overall improvement in relations between the two sides.

While there have been no other incidences of inter-state war in the region, a number of bilateral disputes exist, some as deeply entrenched in history as the India–Pakistan rivalry. For example, since the partition of the subcontinent, Kabul and Islamabad have never had normal neighbourly relations. Until the rise of the Taliban regime in 1996, successive Afghan governments resented Pakistan and viewed it as an illegitimate state, believing that the Pashtun and Baluch tribes living in Afghan territory were forced to become part of the newly independent Pakistan at the end of British colonial rule.[30] Pakistan, on the other hand, regarded the latter with suspicion in relation to its involvement in Pashtun and Baluch affairs within its national borders, and also because Afghanistan and India historically shared friendly relations, particularly during the Cold War because of their mutual friendship with the Soviet Union.[31] Post-Taliban, Afghanistan–Pakistan relations remained cordial until the attack on the Pakistani Embassy in Kabul in July 2003, which returned the state of affairs to allegations and counter-allegations. In recent years, the Karzai government has accused Pakistani authorities of failing to clamp down on pro-Taliban activities within its borders, and sought to 'break up the support network created by that Pakistan's Inter-Services Intelligence (ISI) working through religious establishments along the Afghan border'.[32] Pakistani authorities, on the other hand, have denied any role in the internal affairs of Afghanistan, suggesting that Afghanistan look inwards to find the roots of its problems in the tribal areas along their common border. In May 2011, the killing of Osama Bin Laden in Abbottabad shattered the credibility of Pakistani authorities and severely strained relations between Pakistan and the US.[33] Afghan officials, on the other hand, felt 'vindicated after years of insistence that Pakistan was responsible for harbouring Bin Laden as well as Taliban leaders'.[34] Despite their quarrels, there is no evident threat of an inter-state war between Pakistan and Afghanistan. This is particularly because both continue to be heavily embroiled in assisting the US in its fight against the Taliban and are fighting other extremist forces within their own borders.[35]

Another long-standing inter-state dispute in the region has been over the question of Bhutanese refugees in Nepal. Since the early 1990s, more than 100,000 Bhutanese refugees have been living in UN-sponsored refugee camps in Nepal.[36] All belong to Nepalese ethnic groups, and most were stripped of their citizenship by Bhutan or expelled after campaigning for democracy.[37] Historically, Nepal has insisted that Bhutan should take back all the refugees, as they have valid documents to prove their Bhutanese nationality. Bhutan disagrees, however, claiming that only a few thousand are genuine Bhutanese citizens and the rest are economic migrants or those who have forfeited Bhutanese citizenship by voluntarily leaving the country.[38] Despite numerous talks between the two sides, no solution to the dispute is in sight.[39] While the dispute is certainly an irritant in bilateral relations between Nepal and Bhutan, it is highly unlikely that either side will resort to violence in the context of an inter-state war to bring about an end to the problem.

The above is a brief overview of the key inter-state hostilities in South Asia.[40] The region's only multilateral organization for facilitating inter-state cooperation is the South Asian Association for Regional Cooperation (SAARC).[41] With its Secretariat in Kathmandu, SAARC was established in 1985 with the aim to

> promote the well-being of the populations of South Asia and improve their standards of living; to speed up economic growth, social progress and cultural development; to reinforce links between the countries of this area; and lastly, to promote mutual collaboration and assistance in the economic, social, cultural, technical and scientific fields.[42]

Over the years, however, regional progress through SAARC has been throttled by factors such as inter-state rivalry and intra-state socio-economic and political turmoil. While SAARC has provided a much-needed platform for the countries of South Asia – particularly the smaller states – to come together to discuss regional issues in a multilateral fashion, it bars any discussion of bilateral disputes. Officially, this effectively renders it useless in terms of having any direct impact on the region's inter-state conflicts.[43] Nevertheless, SAARC annual summit meetings, which are attended by the heads of states, have often provided the opportunity to diffuse tensions via sideline talks, particularly in the case of India and Pakistan.[44]

Needless to say, when two or more states go to war, the repercussions are felt both locally and regionally. While the direct effects of war may at times be confined to the areas which bear the brunt of the military operations, the effects at the national level – economic fall-out, rationing, black-outs, interruption of normal politics, low national morale, etc. – are felt by most. When it comes to the prospect of inter-state war in South Asia, the relationship between India and Pakistan is critical. Over the last sixty-five years or so, wars between the two countries have succeeded in creating a high level of instability and fear within the region. It is important to note here that historically, South Asia has been an extremely violent region. The tragic events of the partition of the subcontinent, which led to widespread bloodshed, loss of property and broken familial ties, sowed the seeds for the most dangerous inter-state rivalry in the region.[45] In this context, many believe that the prospect of inter-state war in South Asia remains a distinct possibility, whether in the context of the Kashmir issue, international terrorism or border disputes.

The threat of nuclear conflict

The threat of nuclear conflict in South Asia has caused much concern within the region and beyond. In May 1998, India announced its nuclear capabilities to the world by conducting a series of nuclear test explosions. These were quickly followed by Pakistan conducting its own set of nuclear tests and declaring itself a nuclear weapon state.[46] Further events served to worsen relations and escalate tensions between the two countries – the Kargil war, the military coup in Pakistan (which ousted Prime Minister Nawaz Sharif and brought to power General Pervez Musharraf), and the attack on the Indian Parliament in December 2001, which Indian authorities claimed involved members of two Pakistan-based Islamic militant outfits, Lashkar-e-Toiba and Jaish-e-Mohammad.[47] The last was followed by a significant mobilization of Indian troops along the LoC in Kashmir in a massive show of military muscle by India. India also launched a diplomatic offensive against its neighbour, arguing to the international community that Pakistan was a sponsor of terror and had to be forced to stop supporting Jihadist elements in Kashmir. Following pressure from the US, in July 2002 General Musharraf promised to halt extremist elements operating from within Pakistan, leading to a slight ease in tensions. A cease-fire offer was extended in November 2003, and India responded positively.[48] In the following five years, joint attempts by both sides led to a further easing of tensions, including the establishment of a composite dialogue and confidence-building measures (CBMs) such as starting a cross-border bus service across the LoC between Srinagar in Indian-administered Kashmir and Muzzaffarabad in Pakistan-administered Kashmir.[49] Following the Mumbai terror attacks in November 2008, however, bilateral relations once again nose-dived and although talks between the two sides have now once again resumed, the relationship remains volatile and mired in mistrust.

Regardless of the level of tensions between the two countries, the nuclear policies of both India and Pakistan are not particularly reassuring. Following the 1971 defeat at the hands of India, the perception in Islamabad became increasingly that having a nuclear capability would be the best deterrent to a military attack from India. Since then, Pakistani leaders and officials have continuously proclaimed that Pakistan would use its nuclear weapons to deter conventional war.[50] Although India's nuclear stance appears more restrained than Pakistan's, and while India's draft nuclear doctrine expresses a no-first-use policy, 'a good part of the draft nuclear doctrine concerns itself with nuclear war fighting … [and] despite the goal of nuclear disarmament being lauded, the need to establish a triad has also been emphasized'.[51] There is little doubt that distinct uncertainty marks the future of the use of nuclear weapons by India and Pakistan.[52] This depends on various factors, including the quality of command and control in peacetime and crisis, as well as the role of the US in influencing the relationship between the two sides to bring about key policy changes which would herald a measure of security against a nuclear war in South Asia.[53] History shows that despite engaging in talks and confidence-building measures from time to time, India–Pakistan relations remain volatile. For the international community, as much as for other South Asian states, the region is constantly under the shadow of nuclear rivalry between the two countries.

Inter-state hostilities, when on the rise, are generally expressed quickly and often directly in the rhetoric and subsequent policy action adopted by the representatives of states involved. For example, in the aftermath of the Mumbai terror attacks in November 2008, the language adopted by the Indian administration clearly indicated it held 'Pakistani elements' responsible for the attacks.[54] Pranab Mukherjee, India's Foreign Minister at the time, stated that, 'Terrorism emanating from Pakistan is of course a direct threat to India' and 'the primary onus of responsibility lies on Pakistan to fully unveil the conspiracy, identify those guilty and act in a transparent and verifiable manner'.[55] The bilateral composite dialogue was promptly suspended as a response at the policy level. Significantly, Mukherjee refused to rule out the option of a military strike against Pakistan in response to the attacks, and insisted that 'every sovereign country has a right to protect its territorial integrity and take appropriate action as and when it feels necessary'.[56] Accompanied by a raising of the security level in the country to 'war level', these statements arguably amounted to a plausible securitizing move on behalf of the Indian state, and one which could be viewed as successful if looking for policy responses as the qualifying condition. Given that the tide of public opinion in India had already turned vehemently against Pakistan in the aftermath of the attacks, and the fact that there was real evidence to prove Pakistani involvement, it was also not difficult to convince the public at large that Pakistan remained the enemy, and the ultimate threat to national security.[57]

Intra-state conflict

According to Bard O'Neill, an insurgency may be defined as:

> A struggle between a non-ruling group and the ruling authorities in which the non-ruling group consciously uses political resources (e.g., organisational expertise, propaganda, and demonstrations) and violence to destroy, reformulate, or sustain the basis of legitimacy of one or more aspects of politics.[58]

In South Asia, insurgencies are a familiar phenomenon and have been carried out usually along the lines of ethnic identities and in demand for either greater political autonomy within, or to secede from, the supranational state.[59] In pre-colonial South Asia, ethnic and communal divisions were largely managed through the caste-system, which restricted social cohesion and therefore mobility, and through the plurality of religious belief systems.[60] Since the end of British colonial rule and the advent of the state-system in the region, South Asia has been struggling with an upsurge in ethnonationalistic movements. Here, 'ethnonationalism' refers specifically to the sentiment of nationalism driven by ethnic compulsions. Connor argues that there is no real difference between 'nationalism' and 'ethnonationalism' if the former is used in its true meaning.[61] Others like Anthony Smith, however, feel the need to differentiate 'ethnic' nationalism from 'civic' and 'territorial' nationalism:

> Ethnic nationalism [or ethnonationalism] conceives of a nation as a genealogical and vernacular cultural community. Whereas civic and territorial concepts of the nation regard it as a community of shared culture, common laws and territorial citizenship, ethnic concepts of the nation focus on the genealogy of its members, however fictive; on popular mobilisation of 'the folk'; on native history and customs and on the vernacular culture. As a vernacular community of genealogical descent, the ethnic nation seeks to create itself in the image of an ancestral ethnie. In so doing, it often helps to recreate that ethnie.[62]

States in South Asia are still deeply embroiled in their respective nation-building projects. They are particularly diverse in their ethnic, cultural and linguistic make-up, and this has complicated the task of nation-building on the part of the states significantly. State borders in South Asia are overlapped by distinct ethnic communities, creating a situation where the welfare of an ethnic community in one state becomes the cause for concern for its counterpart in the neighbouring state. In India, the largest and most diverse of states in the region, the challenge of nation-building has been the greatest. The Indian state shares its borders with most other South Asian states. These borders virtually divide large ethnic communities which have existed in the region for centuries and continue to share familial and other bonds regardless of their state nationalities. It is of little surprise, then, that India has been the most affected in terms of being home to numerous insurgencies throughout its independent history. Within the Indian state's boundaries, there have been several ethnonationalistic struggles which have found support in parallel communities in neighbouring countries. The latter is a unique aspect of the international politics of South Asia, where one state has supported insurgencies in another. Chari puts his finger on the pulse when he argues that 'the security problematique in South Asia [is] exacerbated by the malevolence of inimical neighbours'.[63] For example, in the 1970s and 1980s, the Kashmiri and Sikh ethno-nationalistic movements in India were covertly supported by Pakistan;[64] India supported the Bangladeshi nationalistic force 'Mukti Bahini' in its fight against the East Pakistan government which facilitated the independence of Bangladesh,[65] and the ethnonationalistic movements in north-east India have found support from China in the past.[66]

In the last few years, some of the longest-running armed insurgencies in South Asia have come to an end. In Nepal, the decade-long Maoist insurgency ceased with a Comprehensive Peace Agreement signed between the ruling government and Maoists rebels in November 2006.[67] In Sri Lanka, in early 2009 the country's armed forces concluded a massive military offensive against the 26-year-old Tamil insurgency led by the Liberation Tigers of Tamil Eelam (LTTE), decisively crushing the rebels.[68] The main cause of the insurgency was a separate nation-state for the Tamils on the island, in the North and Eastern provinces. The conflict stemmed from a deep sense of humiliation, disempowerment and feeling of inequality in Sri Lanka's Tamil minority.[69] The country's Muslim minority was also inevitably dragged into the conflict, creating 'deep cleavages among these groups'.[70] Despite attempts to mediate the conflict by India in the 1980s[71] and more recently by Norway, it continued to prove intractable and the government finally 'abandoned the pursuit of a negotiated solution'.[72] The military campaign concluded in May 2009 was the final phase of a sustained military offensive against the LTTE, which resulted in around 280,000 people being displaced.[73] Sri Lanka's civil war has cost about 100,000 lives over the past twenty-six years,[74] and the prospects for long-term peace and stability in the country are yet to be determined.

Insurgencies in India have proved to be tough challenges for the state. The Sikh insurgency of the 1980s was crushed with the exercise of overwhelming state power during the late 1980s and early 1990s.[75] The insurgency in Kashmir peaked during the early 1990s, but still rears its head from time to time and eats away at the socio-economic fabric of Kashmiri society.[76] The Indian state continues to face ethnonationalistic insurgencies in the north-eastern states of Assam, Meghalaya, Mizoram, Manipur, Nagaland and Tripura. In eastern and central parts of India, the state is battling with what has been called its most significant national security challenge in present times – a Maoist insurgency which began in the 1960s and, according to official estimates, has claimed the lives of more than 10,000 civilians and security-force personnel since 2005.[77]

Insurgencies, particularly those which are organized along ethnic, communal and sectarian lines, pull away at the very fabric of society. At the local level, they create terror, suspicion, mistrust and chaos among people who are going about their ordinary lives. At the national level, insurgencies violently interrupt and attempt to reverse the nation-building processes over which South Asian states have been labouring since the late 1940s. For a region such as South Asia, an insurgency in the form of an ethnonationalistic movement within a particular country can quite often easily mobilize the mirroring community across the border and therefore create a regional movement which affects more than the country of its origin. This was seen clearly in the case of the Tamil insurgency in Sri Lanka (with repercussions for India), and also observed in the case of the Maoist insurgencies in parts of India and neighbouring Nepal where each found sympathy and support in the other.

The inherent nature of insurgencies is such that they attempt to challenge the ruling authorities to submit to specific political demands which have been neglected or denied, or even to bring about regime change. In this context, the ruling authorities are quick to label any insurgency as a national 'security' threat, as it is perceived in no unclear terms as an existential threat to the survival of the state or ruling regime. Therefore, it is swiftly articulated as such by those in power, who then seek to deploy whatever means deemed necessary – whether consented to by the wider public or not – in order to tackle this challenge. Securitization Theory is illuminating when applied to such a context, although it could be argued that it privileges the threat perceptions and constructions of state representatives, as opposed to, for example, those of the communities which are caught in the middle. One such example is the case of tribal communities living in parts of India affected by the Maoist insurgency.[78] What began as a small but violent peasant protest against land seizures in Naxalbari, a village in the state of West Bengal, is today a raging conflict affecting twenty of the country's twenty-eight states.[79] The so-called 'Red Corridor' stretches for around 40,000 square kilometres across the central and eastern parts of India, and primarily affects the states of Jharkhand, Chhattisgarh, West Bengal, Orissa and Bihar.[80] The region is rich in minerals, with significant deposits of coal and bauxite, but its tribal communities are amongst India's poorest.[81] The Maoists claim to be fighting for these communities and their land rights, while the state, which has severely neglected the socio-economic development needs of these communities for decades, is keen to open up the region for significant private investment. In April 2006, Prime Minister Manmohan Singh called the insurgency the 'greatest internal security challenge' faced by India.[82] Affected communities have not only lost thousands of lives in the cross-fire between the insurgents and state security forces, but have been displaced in the tens and thousands from their homes, recruited forcefully by both Maoists and government-backed vigilante groups, and threatened with deadly violence by both sides for various reasons.[83] An analysis using Securitization Theory may capture state-led securitizations well here; however, its emphasis on institutional responses in identifying the success of a securitization means it may not be as analytically useful when considering the insecurities of the communities that are suffering on a daily basis and in the most fundamental ways as a consequence of the dynamics of this conflict. It is unlikely that the challenges faced by such communities would amount to 'security' threats given that policy responses in this situation have revolved primarily around safeguarding the state and its interests in the affected areas.

Misgovernance

The phenomenon of poor governance or 'misgovernance' is a familiar one to the countries and people of South Asia. Good governance is arguably one of the most significant tools by which the state can provide security to its people. According to the United Nations Development Project (UNDP), governance is the

> exercise of economic, political and administrative authority to manage a country's affairs at all levels. It comprises mechanisms, processes, and institutions through which citizens and groups articulate their interests, exercise their legal rights, meet their obligations, and mediate their differences.[84]

While in the conventional view of governance, the state comprises the parliament, government and judiciary, in the 'revised' view with respect to good governance, it includes the private sector, local government and civil society.[85] It is argued that, in essence, the minimum requirement for good governance should be: promotion of efficiency and transparency in public administration; respect for human rights and the rule of the law, and a greater role for civilian bodies in monitoring and managing the security sector.[86]

Misgovernance is often cited as a key source of insecurity for sub-state communities in South Asia.[87] This is yet to be recognized fully by the states in the region, and there is some way to go before a consensus emerges on the need to balance the needs of the security of the state and the security of sub-state communities.[88] Misgovernance in South Asia at the state and sub-state levels plays a major part in provoking violence and reducing the ability of governments to 'use democratic means to bring about social justice and change in a peaceful manner'.[89] Various manifestations of misgovernance are reportedly prevalent in South Asia. These include poor representation; lack of accountability; lack of ethos of public service; nationalism; the role of local 'big men'; poor standards of policing; rigged elections; discrimination; distortions in government spending; resettlement schemes; the power of corporate actors, and regional imperialism.[90]

In Bangladesh, for example, the polarization of society happened early on, and the constitution reflects this in its bias for the 'Bangali nation'. Bangladesh's religious and ethnic minority communities have no space in the constitution, and an increasing 'Islamization' of the constitution and the politics of the country has resulted in a civil and political society that is 'violently polarized'.[91] The electoral process remains widely corrupt, with plenty of room for money and muscle power to play a big role. For example, there is no residency requirement for an electoral candidate in the constituency he or she is contesting or is elected from, meaning any one with enough money and muscle power can contest an election, contributing to the problem of poor representation.[92] Within this scenario, women and poorer segments of society have little scope to make their voices heard. This also means that almost half the population of Bangladesh (women constitute 48.6 per cent of the country's population) are effectively prevented from taking part in national politics.[93] Parliamentary proceedings are highly autocratic with little consideration for opposition voices. All these elements have combined to create an atmosphere of heightened insecurity for the people of Bangladesh.[94] The state, through its own institutions and activities, has marginalized ethnic and religious minorities and created a system that is corrupt, biased and inadequate in providing security to its people.[95]

As the largest democracy in the world, India is the only country in the region which has maintained a secular democratic system of governance since independence. Nonetheless, the roots of some of the key challenges perceived as undermining its security – such as the various insurgencies which plague it – may be located in issues of misgovernance. It is a country divided economically and socially along the lines of religion, caste, gender and community. Thus, the challenges to good governance are relatively more complex than in, for example, a country devoid of such divisions. Unfortunately, these challenges are compounded by widespread corruption within state institutions, and the growing phenomenon of communal emphasis in politics at different levels. Corruption has particularly emerged as a significant issue of concern in India in recent years, following a series of high-level scams involving huge sums, senior government officials and ministers.[96] In 2011, an anti-corruption movement generated by members of civil society, called 'India against Corruption', gained momentum in various parts of the country. In August, the Indian government's refusal to introduce in Parliament a strong anti-corruption draft bill as proposed by those behind the movement saw a huge swell of non-violent protests across the country.[97] The scale of the protests, spearheaded by Anna Hazare – a septuagenarian social activist and war veteran who undertook a 'fast unto death' to put moral pressure on the government to submit to civil society's demands – shook the government. It was only when Parliament passed a resolution which agreed in principle to key demands being made on the nature of the bill that Hazare ended his fast and protests de-escalated.[98]

The issue of misgovernance strikes a chord with people across South Asia. At the local level, misgovernance means communities lack adequate structures required for basic socio-political and economic existence. South Asians are the most deprived in the world, with over 260 million not having access to basic health facilities, more than 337 million without safe drinking water and 830 million without basic sanitation.[99] Because of inadequate representation at the sub-state level they have little say in how their lives in the socio-political and economic realms should be managed. To have access to the most basic amenities, they often have to bribe corrupt officials and struggle with corrupt and distant bureaucracies. The judicial systems in most South Asian countries are slow and the process fraught with challenges, as the volume of cases far outweighs the capacity and efficiency of these systems. This has a direct impact on the law-and-order situation, as a slow and creaking legal system creates a certain disregard for the law. There is widespread corruption in the law enforcement system, which further compounds the problem. At the state level, misgovernance distorts the process of state-building, with which each South Asian state continues to struggle. Instead of strengthening the structures of the state, the current structures are further weakened. Misgovernance within states is reflected at the regional level in many ways, such as a distinct lack of trust when it comes to bilateral or multilateral relations and a lack of capacity to fulfil commitments. The treatment of minorities, such as ethnic and religious groups with state borders, may also become a contentious issue at the regional level, given that borders in South Asia often divide such communities which share familial and cultural ties.

Aspects of misgovernance, such as a politicized judiciary, partisan politics, weak and ineffective institutions and violent and corrupt electoral processes, are often identified as threats to the security of sub-state communities in South Asia by sections of civil society, the media and other NSAs rather than state officials in the first instance. To what extent such moves are followed by policy decisions that take into account the measures recommended by these actors as necessary in order to deal with the issues in question, is the subject of a different analysis. What is worth noting, however, is that threats associated with misgovernance usually emanate from those in positions of political influence and authority themselves, usually embedded within wider networks of influence which in themselves may be perceived as threatening by referent groups.

Terrorism

In the decade following 9/11, South Asia has felt the repercussions of the terrorist attacks on the World Trade Center perhaps more than anywhere else in the world. It emerged as the epicentre of the US 'war on terror' immediately after, and continues to be the primary theatre where the US-led coalition battles with al Qaeda forces and the Taliban. Prior to this, South Asian countries like Sri Lanka, India, Pakistan, Nepal and Bangladesh had all been struggling with terrorist activities within their borders. Since then, the situation has only deteriorated, particularly with al Qaeda and Taliban forces fleeing across the border from Afghanistan into Pakistan. Both Afghanistan and Pakistan have seen a significant rise in the number of terror attacks and resulting casualties in recent years.[100]

Observed independently from the post-9/11 developments, the links between terrorism, political agitation and insurgencies within South Asia are strong and cannot be ignored. Various religious, ethnic and sectarian groups have in the past resorted to, and continue to adopt, violent and terrorist methods to further their political and social goals by destabilizing civil society.[101] In fact, South Asia is unique in its tradition of violence in public life, even for states which have formerly been subjects of colonialism. As De Silva points out, one of the ways this is reflected is in the number of heads of government or state, senior leaders, politicians and other public figures who have been assassinated in South Asia in the last fifty years.[102] This phenomenon has been particularly prevalent in India, Pakistan and Sri Lanka.

Some of the key cases of terrorism in South Asia include: the Kashmir conflict and separatist groups in India and Pakistan using terror to further their political objectives; Tamil militant groups (particularly the LTTE) in Sri Lanka using terror against the government and local populations in aid of their own political goals and the Sri Lankan government in turn carrying out terror tactics among its Tamil population as a measure to fight LTTE and its supporters; political insurgents in north-east India and Maoists in eastern and central parts of India resorting to terror tactics against the central Indian state and local communities; the Taliban in Afghanistan using terror tactics to fight the national government in place and the foreign armed forces present on Afghan soil, and more recently the Taliban in Pakistan carrying out terrorist attacks to weaken the government's control over the country.

The ethnic conflict in Sri Lanka serves as a good example of how terrorism, linked with political insurgency, has played out at various levels in the region, and how it impacts communities and states in South Asia. The conflict found its roots in a historic rivalry between the two communities on the island: the majority Sinhala community and the Tamil minority. The politicization of the ethnic divide took the form of successive governments passing policies against the welfare of the Tamils.[103] As the Tamil community became increasingly marginalized, a movement for greater autonomy for Tamils soon grew into a separatist movement which further developed rapidly into a violent and militarized force. The LTTE took up the cause of a separate Tamil state in the north and east of Sri Lanka, and soon became notorious for using terror tactics to fight the Sri Lankan army as well as terrorizing the local Sinhala and Tamil populations. The Sri Lankan state, on the other hand, did not abstain from using similar methods to retaliate and to pressurize the Tamil community. At the local and national levels, this created a perpetual cycle of fear, mistrust and violence. In May 2009, following a major military offensive against the LTTE, the Sri Lankan authorities declared an end to the civil war. According to UN estimates, around 7,000 ethnic Tamil civilians were killed in the last three and a half months of the military onslaught.[104]

In South Asia, as in any other part of the world affected by the phenomenon, terrorism has had a profound effect on local communities. Apart from the loss of life and property, it has created and stimulated an atmosphere of perpetual fear and mistrust within which it is no longer possible to live a 'normal' life. This has been the experience of people, for example, in Kashmir, Punjab, Tamil Nadu and Assam in India, and those living in Sri Lanka, Pakistan, Bangladesh and Afghanistan. At the national level, terrorism in South Asia has further hardened the attitude of states, which have always favoured a tough approach to dealing with political insurgencies and not giving an inch to their demands. Regionally, terrorism has been a key cause of souring inter-state relations in the past, and continues to be a bone of contention between states which accuse each other of sponsoring terrorism in their respective countries, e.g. India and Pakistan, India and Bangladesh, and Pakistan and Afghanistan. An issue which has such a substantial presence in various parts of South Asia is an essential consideration when mapping security dynamics in the region. Terrorist attacks shake the confidence of the public at large in a state's ability to protect them, and are often carried out for this very purpose, i.e. to destabilize the regime in power. Therefore, states are usually quick to condemn terrorists and terrorist attacks verbally and decisively, citing them as threats to the security of both citizens and the state. In doing so, states also often take policy actions which may be seen as breaking 'normal rules and procedures' in order to respond in the aftermath of terrorist attacks or to prevent them. In the immediate aftermath, the wider public reaction may be to agree with the measures being taken, thereby arguably indicating an acceptance of the securitizing move by the government. Thus, the dynamics involved fit well within the conditional framework outlined by the Copenhagen School's approach to Securitization Theory.

Forced migration: refugees and Internally Displaced Persons (IDPs)

In the last sixty-five years, more than 35 million South Asians have moved across borders,

> in search of security, running from threats to life, honour and property, or in
> search of protection from religious and other kinds of persecution, or to

avoid strife and wars, or for work and food, or just by drives towards ethnic, racial, ideological or religious homogenisation.[105]

These population movements have included people migrating voluntarily or involuntarily across international borders within the region as well as across villages, towns and cities within borders. When such migration is involuntary or 'forced' and international in nature, migrants are classified as refugees; those who involuntarily migrate within the boundaries of a state are referred to as internally displaced persons, or IDPs.[106] According to the UN High Commissioner for Refugees (UNHCR), refugees are generally 'people who flee their country because of a well-founded fear of persecution for reasons of race, religion, nationality, political opinion or membership of a particular social group. A refugee either cannot return home or is afraid to do so.'[107]

South Asia is home to over a quarter of the world's refugee population.[108] Immediately before and after the partition of the Indian subcontinent in 1947, around 15 million people scrambled to get on the right side of the India–Pakistan border, their decisions based on religious and nationalistic considerations which had a direct impact on their physical safety. During the struggle for Bangladesh's independence in 1970–71, around 10 million Bangladeshi refugees fled into the bordering Indian states of West Bengal and Assam. Pakistan today is host to over a million Afghan refugees, who left their homes earlier to escape the brutality of the Taliban regime, or more recently the instability and insecurity caused by the complex dynamics stemming from the NATO intervention. Nepal is home to hundreds of Tibetan and Bhutanese refugees since as early as 1959 and 1990 respectively.[109] Sri Lankan Tamils have been crossing the Palk Straits into the South Indian state of Tamil Nadu (literally, the 'Tamil Nation') since the 1950s and continue to do so even today. According to the Rehabilitation Commission in Tamil Nadu, there are over 70,000 Sri Lankan Tamil refugees living in around 112 camps in the state, and over 32,000 living outside these camps.[110]

At the same time, the internal displacement of people within state boundaries is also a widespread phenomenon in the region.[111] This movement of people is heavily linked with the problems of misgovernance, and the processes of state and nation-building. In Sri Lanka for example, the ethnic conflict between the Sinhala majority and the Tamil minority has forced hundreds of thousands of men, women and children to flee their homes in fear of their lives. Often, those who died or were maimed in conflict were the income-earners and left entire families without the means to cope, with no shelter or food, vulnerable to malnutrition and starvation. At the end of the armed conflict, there were approximately 280,000 IDPs in Sri Lanka. At present, about 35,000 IDPs remain in camps and face persistent obstacles to a 'sustainable return' to their place of origin.[112]

Without the financial means to leave the country, IDPs are dependent on the local or national authorities for assistance, and even for basic survival. Often, IDPs are at the mercy of those who are enforcing their displacement in the first place. One such case is the plight of those being displaced by the building of the Sardar Sarovar Dam (SSD) in Gujarat. SSD is the largest dam in a project to build a series of dams on the River Narmada,[113] and has been fiercely opposed by a huge number of people across India since the late 1980s. The Narmada Bachao Andolan, or 'Save the Narmada' movement, has been at the forefront of these protests, and consists of civil society groups concerned with the socio-economic, environmental and human rights implications of the project. The environmental and ecological effects of the dam are widely debated. Currently at a height of 121.92 metres, the final and yet to be completed phase of installing radial gates will raise the dam's height to its final peak of 138.68 metres.[114] At full reservoir level, the dam will measure 142 metres high at completion. According to a recent independent report by the Tata Institute for Social Sciences, the cumulative number of families that have already been displaced by the dam and are yet to be rehabilitated, and those who will be affected if the height is increased to the final peak height, is around 40,000. Rehabilitation so far has been limited, exclusionary and arbitrary, with differential enumeration policies between the three affected federal states. In many instances, state governments have failed to comply with the binding rehabilitation norms as laid out by the Supreme Court and the Narmada Water Dispute Tribunal Award (NWDTA) to provide those displaced with 'cultivable and irrigable land, and alternative house plots with civic amenities in rehabilitation villages.'[115] The Madhya Pradesh government has reportedly made it clear that it cannot find land for the evictees, and has been giving out cash to affected families under its 2001 Special Rehabilitation Package (SRP), in contradiction of the rehabilitation norms laid down by the Indian Supreme Court.[116]

Refugees and IDPs arguably face immense challenges to their physical survival and wider well-being.[117] These include lack of shelter and medical care, unemployment, starvation, human rights abuses, and more. Also, at the local level, refugees and IDPs are often perceived as disruptive to the well-being of communities and societies they enter, as they may be alien to the prevailing socio-cultural norms, and have no jobs or homes.[118] The plight of refugees and IDPs, who are usually destitute, is worsened by the hostile attitudes with which they are often received – or rejected – by the communities in which they find themselves. For states, the issue of refugees can quickly become a 'national' security matter, as it did in South Asia for East Pakistan in 1971, and Sri Lanka in the early 1980s. In the case of the former, 'Bengali refugees from Pakistan in 1971 formed the "Mukti Bahini", fought against the Pakistani armed forces and facilitated the break-up of Pakistan which created the new and independent state of Bangladesh.'[119] Similarly, the Tamil diasporas passionately sympathized with the plight of Sri Lankan refugees in the subcontinent and elsewhere, and worked hard to generate international pressure on Sri Lanka 'not only on the question of human rights violations in the UN and other fora, but also made it vulnerable to its international donors, demanding an early and peaceful resolution of its ethnic conflict'.[120] In a region such as South Asia, where ethnic conflict and communal tensions often underpin the movement of people, and ethnic communities are divided by national borders, the issue of refugees can create tensions which cut across many countries and thus threaten to create instability and insecurity across the region.

Human trafficking

According to Article Three of the UN Protocol to Prevent, Suppress and Punish Trafficking in Persons, Especially Women and Children, Supplementing the United Nations Convention against Transnational Organized Crime,

> trafficking in persons shall mean the recruitment, transportation, transfer, harbouring or receipt of persons, by means of the threat or use of force or other forms of coercion, of abduction, of fraud, of deception, of the abuse of power or of a position of vulnerability or of the giving or receiving payments or benefits to achieve the consent of a person having control over another person, for the purpose of exploitation. Exploitation shall include, at a minimum, the exploitation of the prostitution of others or other forms of sexual exploitation, forced labour or services, slavery or practices similar to slavery, servitude or the removal of organs.[121]

Trafficking in persons in South Asia is not a recent phenomenon. However, the recognition of this phenomenon as a 'security' issue in the region and elsewhere has come about only recently. In South Asia, the alarming rate at which the trafficking of persons, particularly women and children but also including boys and men, has been growing and has caught the attention of many within and outside South Asia. The 1990s saw 'the proliferation of frontline organisations, NGOs, government programmes and activist research focusing on the issue of trafficking.'[122] In 1993, for example, the World Conference on Human Rights adopted the Vienna Declaration and the Programme of Action which addressed the problem of trafficking of persons as a human rights violation. Article 27 of the Declaration of the SAARC Ninth Annual Summit in Male in 1997 notes that:

> Expressing grave concern at the trafficking of women and children within and between countries, the Heads of State of Government pledged to coordinate their efforts and take effective measures to address this problem. They decided that this should include simplification of repatriation procedures for victims of trafficking. They also decided that the feasibility of establishing a Regional Convention on Combating the Crime of Trafficking in Women and Children for Prostitution be examined by the relevant Technical Committee.[123]

In January 2002, SAARC member countries adopted the SAARC Convention on Preventing and Combating Trafficking in Women and Children for Prostitution (the SAARC Trafficking Convention), which was further ratified in 2005.[124] At the national level, many South Asian states have adopted policies to combat trafficking in persons, particularly women and children. According to the Asian Development Bank (ADB), trafficking in the region is a highly complex process and affects many different actors: – trafficked persons; their families; communities; and other third parties who recruit, transport, harbour and use trafficked labour.[125] It attacks the very fabric of society, exploiting the weakest and most vulnerable of its sections. Human trafficking involves gross violations of human rights and great human suffering, and is a very difficult and complex problem to combat. Although today there is growing concern and investments from governments, donors, NGOs and civil-society organizations, 'evidence seems to suggest an increasing incidence of human trafficking as the demand for this form of exploitable labour persists'.[126] Traffickers also change their modus operandi frequently in response to changing immigration regulations and economic considerations, and go to great lengths to obscure their activities and seek to involve a wide range of actors in order to make the likelihood of their own implication in the crime more remote.[127] This complex nature of trafficking means the phenomenon varies from country to country and between regions.

In South Asia, 'dynamics of trafficking reach across ... the region, where, despite specific and different historical and cultural circumstances, similarities are clear'.[128] According to the data available, the worst forms of trafficking relate to the illegal movement of women and children for the purposes of exploitation in sectors such as commercial sex work, and child labour of all forms. Unfortunately, the elusive nature of the problem means statistics regarding its magnitude widely vary and are unreliable. Studies point out that India and Pakistan are the major destination countries for trafficked women and girls in South Asia.[129] Moreover, India and Pakistan also serve as transit points for the trafficking of persons from Bangladesh to Middle Eastern countries. The latter receive trafficked boys for exploitation as, for example, cheap labour and camel jockeys, and girls and women for sexual exploitation. For Bangladeshi women and girls, India is also a transit point en route to Pakistan.[130]

A range of domestic and external factors are cited as fuelling the problem of human trafficking. The predicament of dim employment prospects and lack of opportunities is worsened by other socio-political factors, making people easy targets for traffickers.[131] 'The importance of economic factors in deciding to migrate is, in all probability, due to a lack or low level of education among women and men resulting in poor job prospects in their native countries.'[132] Also, 'discrimination against women ... also plays an important role in pushing women to look for independent lives inside or outside the country'.[133] The forces of globalization have also worked in ways that have been detrimental to local economies, weakening rural sources of employment and forcing people out of villages to cities and townships in search for jobs. Many are then exploited by those looking for cheap labour, and by traffickers. Often, conflicts and natural disasters drive people from their homes in search for the means to survive. 'When such individuals have no marketable skills or education, and are exposed to health risks, their capacity to secure sustainable livelihoods is limited and their risk of being trafficking is heightened.'[134] Thus, although the threat of trafficking in human beings is most profound at the individual and sub-state level (as it directly affects those who are being trafficked and their families and communities), it is a problem common to all SAARC countries. At the state level, it poses a unique problem for countries as they try to impose standards for labour and human rights. As trafficking in South Asia is both an internal problem as well as a transnational one, it requires a collective response at the regional level in order to be dealt with effectively.

Human trafficking has been referred to as a 'security' threat by many countries including the US and UK, and international organizations such as NATO.[135] These articulations have generally been framed around the phenomenon posing a threat to 'national' security, or in the case of NATO, to its missions in countries where human trafficking is 'a significant source of revenue for criminal organisations whose activities may destabilize legitimate governments and undermine the NATO mission'.[136] As is the case with the approach to the issue of refugees and IDPs, human trafficking has been understood primarily as a threat to the state in South Asia, as opposed to being dealt with in terms of how it impacts those who are directly affected by it. In the absence of adequate state-level recognition of and responses to the challenge of human trafficking to vulnerable groups in South Asia, NSAs have often stepped in to provide those affected or threatened with the measures required to help prevent and deal with the impacts of trafficking on individuals, families and wider communities effectively.

Climate change

The impacts of climate change have been identified as threats to the security and stability of states and communities by actors around the world. Scientists and environmental analysts have been joined by a host of others, including states and civil society groups, in warning of the threats posed by the phenomenon. Climate refers to the average weather experienced over a long period, including temperature, wind and rainfall patterns. The earth's climate changes over time as it responds to a range of natural causes. The key concern today is that humans are influencing the planet's climate through the emission of greenhouse gases (such as methane and carbon dioxide (CO_2)), leading to global warming. Currently, approximately 6.5 billion tonnes of CO_2 are emitted globally each year, mostly through burning coal, oil and gas for energy. According to analysts, climate change has already begun, with the ten hottest years on record globally all experienced since the beginning of the 1990s. The UN Inter-governmental Panel on Climate Change (IPCC) has reported that the average surface temperature of the Earth is likely to increase by 1.1–6.4°C by the end of the twenty-first century.[137]

For a region which already suffers from high levels of food insecurity (being home to the largest number of the world's poor) and water scarcity, the impacts of climate change are particularly worrisome. In June 2006, Sabihuddin Ahmed, the High Commissioner of Bangladesh to the UK, while speaking at a public gathering, announced that the threat of climate change and global warming to his country was greater than that of global terrorism.[138] Bangladesh's economy is largely agricultural, with the cultivation of rice being the single most important activity. Most Bangladeshis earn their living from the rice crop, which is dependent on the increasingly erratic monsoon cycle. Analysts warn that Bangladesh is highly vulnerable to the threat of climate change, because it is low-lying, located on the Bay of Bengal in the delta of the Rivers Ganges, Brahmaputra and Meghna, and densely populated. Consequences of global warming, such as increases in sea levels and temperatures, increased evaporation, changes in precipitation and in cross-boundary river flows, are identified as the agents of change, which cause the most threatening impacts in the natural, social and economic systems of a country.[139] In Bangladesh, these agents are predicted to create havoc, given the country's geographical characteristics, and are expected to lead to problems of drainage congestion, reduced fresh water availability, disturbance of morphologic processes[140] and increased intensity of flooding and disasters.

The situation Bangladeshis find themselves in is shared by those living in the many low-lying areas along India's coastline, which stretches for over 7,500 kilometres. It is argued that climate change is being observed in the increasing temperatures and heat spells all over northern India, with 2009 being the warmest year since records began in 1901.[141] By the end of the twenty-first century, annual mean surface temperature is expected to increase by 2°C to 4°C, and it is proposed that the monsoons have also been affected, spelling disaster for India's agricultural and water needs. Scientists at the Indian Institute for Technology in New Delhi have noted subtle changes in the monsoon rain patterns, and warn that by the 2050s there will be a decline in the summer rainfall in India. Increased temperatures will also affect crop cycles, resulting in low yields and food shortage. According to analysts, sea level rise due to thermal expansion of sea water in the Indian Ocean is expected to be about 25–40 centimetres by 2050. This would overwhelm low-lying areas, 'drown coastal marshes and wetlands, erode beaches, exacerbate flooding and increase the salinity of rivers, bays and aquifers'. Deltas are also threatened by flooding, erosion and salt intrusion, while the fishing industry is expected to suffer hugely from the loss of coastal mangroves.[142]

Most South Asian countries like Nepal, Bhutan, Pakistan, Sri Lanka and India are mainly agrarian economies, and depend heavily on the climate cycles for good harvests of the various crops they grow, such as rice, wheat, jute, sugarcane, and other cereals and pulses. Thus, climate change is perceived as threatening food and water security in the region, as well as livelihoods and the way of life of the majority of people who inhabit it. Moreover, for small island states like Sri Lanka and the Maldives, the threat of climate change appears even more sinister. Eighty per cent of the Maldives' 1,200 islands, for example, are no more than one metre above sea level. Analysts predict that within 100 years, the Maldives could become uninhabitable and its population of over 300,000 would have to evacuate.[143] In the wake of the Stern Report on global warming published by the British government in October 2006, analysts believe that the mass migration resulting from climate change will be far more destabilizing than any other fallout of the phenomenon. China, India and Brazil are among those countries which are projected as the ones to be most affected by this.[144]

Climate change is one non-traditional issue which appears on the national security agendas of most South Asia states. In 2007, India's Prime Minister Manmohan Singh identified climate change as a 'security' threat to the people of India.[145] As previously stated, Bangladesh and Maldives also identify the issue as a security threat. Apart from states in South Asia, a number of NSAs have raised the issue as a threat to livelihoods and the physical safety of people within and across state borders in the region.

Conclusion

As the above discussion demonstrates, the range of issues which have been raised as security challenges to the communities and states in South Asia is wide and diverse, with the challenges themselves complex and interconnected in many ways. For example, without acknowledging the insecurities faced by South Asians in their daily socio-economic and political experiences, the nature of forced migration in South Asia cannot be fully understood. Similarly, the role of conflict, developmental projects authorized by the state and climate change-related phenomena is significant in explaining why such a vast number of people in the region are living as refugees or IDPs. Some of these issues have been identified by states in the region as 'security' threats – such as nuclear conflict, inter-state war, climate change, various border disputes and political insurgencies within countries. Others, such as misgovernance and human trafficking, have been dealt with as law and order issues by these states, despite a number of NSAs identifying them as sources of insecurity for various groups and communities at the sub-state level in South Asia. In studying security dynamics in the region, it is important to identify these activities at the sub-state level for several reasons. The first may seem obvious: they are often critical in shifting and shaping state-led positions on a given issue, with direct or indirect impact on relevant policy-making. A contextualized, sociological variant of Securitization Theory takes into account the wider context within which security practices take place, which includes such dynamics. Beyond this, there are at least two further reasons. First, NSAs are often not only involved in identifying issues which are perceived as posing a security threat to communities and groups within and across borders, but in providing these referent groups with the measures considered as necessary in order to protect them from and mitigate the impacts of the threat in question. Second, NSAs also fill an analytical gap when identifying issues which are perceived as threatening by certain communities and groups, when these issues and referent groups are not sufficiently acknowledged by state actors. Despite not always leading to responses at the public policy level, such expressions by NSAs define a realm of insecurity in South Asian states which has a huge impact on the daily lives of its people.

Notes

1 Afghanistan has been included in some discussions, for instance in the context of its relationship with Pakistan and wider security implications for the region. Also, it is important to state that to provide an overview of all issues which may be perceived as sources of insecurity by different groups in the region is not possible here. Concerns around water and food security, for example, have not been discussed although they are touched upon briefly in the discussion on climate change.

2 The complex and interconnected nature of these issues hinders to an extent the ability to present them systematically, given the dynamics related to each issue often overlap

or are linked and therefore reappear many times in discussions as relevant. The chapter has attempted to deal with this challenge by only getting into detailed discussions of such overlapping dynamics where they appear most relevant.

3 The exceptions are Nepal and Bhutan, and while Bangladesh was previously East Pakistan (created in 1947 following the partition of British India), it gained independence in 1971.

4 For an excellent account of the history of the partition of the subcontinent, see Y. Khan, *The Great Partition: The Making of India and Pakistan*, New Haven: Yale University Press, 2008.

5 See S. Ganguly, *Conflict Unending: India Pakistan Tensions Since 1947*, New York: Columbia University Press, 2001 and R.G.C. Thomas (ed.), *Perspectives on Kashmir: the Roots of Conflict in South Asia*, Boulder, CO: Westview Press, 1992.

6 For example, see S. K. Khatri (ed.), *Regional Security in South Asia*, Kathmandu: Centre for Nepal and Asian Studies, Tribhuvan University, 1987; C. K. Tiwari, *Security in South Asia: Internal and External Dimensions*, London: University Press of America, 1989; R.G.C. Thomas, 'South Asian Security in the 1990s', Adelphi Paper 278, International Institute for Strategic Studies, July 1993; V. T. Patil and N. K. Jha, *Peace and Cooperative Security in South Asia*, Delhi: P R Books, 1999; P. Sahadevan (ed.), *Conflict and Cooperation in South Asia*, New Delhi: Lancer's Books, 2001 and R. M. Basrur, *South Asia's Cold War*, London: Routledge, 2008, among others.

7 For example, see P. R. Chari, M. Joseph and S. Chandran (eds), *Missing Boundaries: Refugees, Migrants, Stateless and Internally Displaced People in South Asia*, New Delhi: Manohar, 2003; P. R. Chari (ed.), *Security and Governance in South Asia*, Colombo: Manohar, 2001; V. T. Patil and P. R. Trivedi, *Migration, Refugees and Security in the 21st Century*, New Delhi: Authorspress, 2000; P. S. Ghosh, *Migrants and Refugees in South Asia: Political and Security Dimensions*, Shillong: ICSSR-NERC, 2001; P. Bhattacharya and S. Hazra (eds), *Environment and Human Security*, New Delhi: Lancer's Books, 2003; J. Richter and C. Wagner (eds), *Regional Security, Ethnicity and Governance: The Challenges for South Asia*, New Delhi: Manohar, 1998.

8 In M. Gopinath, 'Trenches, Boundaries, Spaces: The Dialectics of Governance and Security in India', in Chari (ed.), *Security and Governance*, p. 52.

9 For more on the armed insurgency in Kashmir, see S. Ganguly, 'Explaining the Kashmir Conundrum: Prospects and Limitations', *Asia Policy*, no. 3, Jan. 2007, pp. 196–98; S. Ganguly and S. Paul Kapur, 'The Sorcerer's Apprentice: Islamist Militancy in South Asia', *The Washington Quarterly*, vol. 33, no. 1, Jan. 2010, pp. 47–59; R. Tavares, 'Resolving the Kashmir Conflict: Pakistan, India, Kashmiris and Religious Militants', *Asian Journal of Political Science*, vol. 16, no. 3, pp. 276–302 and R. Ganguly, 'India, Pakistan and the Kashmir Insurgency: Causes, Dynamics and Prospects for Resolution', *Asian Studies Review*, vol. 25, no. 3, pp. 309–34.

10 For a recent and insightful account of the situation in Kashmir, see A. Mattoo, 'Summer of Discontent', *Harvard International Review*, vol. 32, no. 4, Winter 2011, pp. 54–58.

11 Ibid. To a large extent, the anger of Kashmiris is directed at the inefficiency of the government and the existence of the Armed Forces Special Powers Act (Jammu and Kashmir) 1990, which 'permits Indian security forces to use extensive coercive powers (including deadly force) when acting in good faith in the conduct of counterinsurgency operations. Under the aegis of this sweeping legislation, security forces sometimes resorted to deliberate, extrajudicial killings.' In S. Ganguly, 'Six Decades of Independence', *Journal of Democracy*, vol. 18, no. 2, 2007, pp. 33–34.

12 For more, see J. B. Bhattacharjee (ed.), *Roots of Insurgency in Northeast India*, New Delhi: Eastern Book Corporation, 2007; J. Madhab, 'North East: Crisis of Identity, Security and Underdevelopment', *Economic and Political Weekly*, vol. 34, no. 6, Feb. 6–12, 1999, pp. 320–22; H. Gohain, 'Ethnic Unrest in the North-East', *Economic and Political Weekly*, vol. 32, no. 8, Feb. 22–28, 1997, pp. 389–91; M. Hussain, 'Governance and Electoral Processes in India's North-East', *Economic and Political Weekly*, vol. 38, no. 10,

Mar. 8–14, 2003, pp. 981–90; K. S. Aggarwal, *Dynamics of Identity and Intergroup Relation in North East India*, Shimla: Indian Institute of Advanced Studies,` 1999 and S. Bhattacharjee and R. R. Dhamala, *Human Rights and Insurgency: The North-East India*, New Delhi: Shipra Publications, 2002.

13 P. N. Chopra, *India at The Crossroads*, New Delhi: Sterling Publishers Pvt. Ltd., 2004, p. 81–80.

14 Ibid., p. 81.

15 'Assam Playing Host to Anti-Insurgency Plays', *The Indian News*, 15 Mar. 2009. Online. HTTP: <http://www.thaindian.com/newsportal/india-news/assam-playing-host-to-anti-insurgency-plays_100166637.html> (accessed 26 May 2010).

16 For a comprehensive list of recent conflicts in South Asia, see M. Ahmar, *Chronology of Conflict and Cooperation in South Asia 1947–2001*, Karachi: Karachi University Press, 2001.

17 For more, see I. Ahmed, *State, Nation and Ethnicity in Contemporary South Asia*, London: Pinter, 1996; U. Phadnis, *Ethnicity and Nation Building in South Asia*, New Delhi: Sage Publications, 1990 and R. Ganguly, *Kin State Intervention in Ethnic Conflicts: Lessons from South Asia*, New Delhi: Sage Publications, 1998.

18 R. Harshe, 'Understanding Conflicts in South Asia', in S. George (ed.), *Intra and Inter-State Conflicts in South Asia*, New Delhi: South Asian Publishers Pvt. Ltd., 2001, p. 19.

19 The war between West Pakistan and East Pakistan which resulted in the independence of the latter as Bangladesh is classified as a civil war. Also, while China and India fought a border war in 1961–62, China is not a South Asian country, although it is widely acknowledged as an extra-regional power.

20 S. Ganguly, 'India's Territorial Disputes with Pakistan and China: Understanding Security Relations', in P. Sahadevan (ed.), *Conflict and Cooperation in South Asia*, New Delhi: Lancer's Books, 2001, p. 198.

21 For a detailed account, read V. Schofield, *Kashmir in the Crossfire*, London: I. B. Tauris, 1996; S. Ganguly, *The Crisis in Kashmir*, Washington, D.C: Woodrow Wilson Center Press, 1997 and A. Lamb, *Kashmir: A Disputed Legacy 1846–1990*, Hertingfordbury: Roxford Books, 1991.

22 'Q and A: Kashmir Dispute', *BBC News*, 6 Nov. 2008. Online. HTTP: <http://news.bbc.co.uk/1/hi/world/south_asia/2739993.stm> (accessed 31 Oct., 2010).

23 Ganguly in Sahadevan (ed.), *Conflict and Cooperation*, pp. 198–99.

24 See S. Bose, 'Kashmir: Sources of Conflict, Dimensions of Peace', *Survival*, vol. 41, no. 3, Autumn 1999, pp. 149–71.

25 Ibid.

26 R. Ramesh and V. Dodd, 'Mumbai Terror Attacks: India Fury at Pakistan as Bloody Siege is Crushed', *Guardian*, 30 Nov. 2008. Online. HTTP: <http://www.guardian.co.uk/world/2008/nov/30/mumbai-terror-attacks-india3> (accessed 12 Feb. 2011).

27 See J. Perlez and S. Masood, 'Pakistanis Deny Any Role in Attacks', *The New York Times*, 29 Nov. 2008. Online. HTTP: <http://www.nytimes.com/2008/11/30/world/asia/30pstan.html> (*accessed* 12 Feb. 2010); 'India–Pakistan Composite Dialogue On Hold', *The Hindu*, 5 Dec. 2008. Online. HTTP: <http://www.hindu.com/thehindu/holnus/000200812051421.htm>, 12 Feb. 2009; 'India Talks Tough with Pakistan over Mumbai Terror Attack', *Rediff India Abroad*, 28 Nov. 2008. Online. HTTP: <http://www.rediff.com/news/2008/nov/28mumterror-india-talks-tough-with-pakistan.htm> (*accessed 12* Feb. 2009) and R. Ramesh and J. Burke, 'At War Level: India Raises Security Status Amid Grief', *Guardian*, 1 Dec. 2008. Online. HTTP: <http://www.guardian.co.uk/world/2008/dec/01/mumbai-terror-attacks-india-pakistan3> (accessed 12 Feb. 2009).

28 Z. Hussain, 'Pakistan Sends 20,000 Troops to Indian Frontier', *The Times*, 17 Dec. 2008. Online. HTTP: <http://www.timesonline.co.uk/tol/news/world/asia/article5400650.ece> (accessed 12 Feb. 2010).

29 'Cricket World Cup: India PM Invites Pakistan Leaders', *BBC News*, 25 Mar. 2011. Online. HTTP: <http://www.bbc.co.uk/news/world-south-asia-12864679> (accessed 4 April 2011).

30 A. Tarzi, 'South Asia: Pakistan–Afghanistan Conflicts Continue', *Radio Free Europe/ Radio Liberty*, 29 Sept. 2006. Online. HTTP: <http://www.rferl.org/featuresarticle/ 2006/09/260c90a0–1f41–44ab6-a580–21bcc8a914f5.html> (*accessed 12* Nov. 2010).

31 Ibid.

32 Ibid.

33 For example, see L. Millar, 'Bin Laden operation strains US-Pakistan ties', ABC News, 27 May 2011. Online. HTTP: <http://www.abc.net.au/news/2011-05-10/ bin-laden-operation-strains-us-pakistan-ties/2713696> (accessed 16 Jun. 2011).

34 'World Reaction to Osama Bin Laden's Death', NPR, 2 May 2011. Online. HTTP: <http://www.npr.org/2011/05/02/135919728/world-reaction-to-osama-bin-ladens-death> (accessed 16 Jun. 2011).

35 Ibid. For more, see K. A. Kronstadt, 'International Terrorism in South Asia', *CRS Report for Congress No. RS21658*, Washington, DC, 3 Nov. 2003. Online. HTTP: <http://www.fas.org/irp/crs/RS21658.pdf > (accessed 10 Mar. 2009); P. Gossman, 'Afghanistan in the Balance', *Middle East Report*, no. 221, Winter 2001, pp. 8–15; P. Rogers, *A War on Terror: Afghanistan and After*, London: Pluto Press, 2004; Z. Hussain, *Frontline Pakistan: The Path to Catastrophe and the Killing of Benazir Bhutto*, London: I. B. Tauris, 2008; L. T. Hadar, 'Pakistan in America's War against Terrorism Strategic Ally or Unreliable Client?', *Policy Analysis*, no. 436, CATO Institute, 8 May 2002. Online. HTTP: <http://www.cato.org/pubs/pas/pa436.pdf> (accessed 27 Feb. 2009); A. J. Tellis, 'Pakistan and the War on Terror: Conflicted Goals, Compromised Performance', Carnegie Endowment Report, Jan. 2008. Online. HTTP: <http:// www.carnegieendowment.org/files/tellis_pakistan_final.pdf> (accessed 27 Feb. 2009); S. G. Jones, 'Pakistan's Dangerous Game', *Survival*, vol. 49, no. 1, Spring 2007, pp. 15–32 and B. R. Rubin, 'Saving Afghanistan', *Foreign Affairs*, vol. 86, no. 1, Jan./Feb. 2007, pp. 57–78.

36 'IOM Resettles Over 10,000 Bhutanese Refugees from Nepal', *United Nations Radio*, 17 Feb. 2009. Online. HTTP: <http://www.unmultimedia.org/radio/english/detail/ 69588.html> (accessed 19 Mar. 2010).

37 For more on the background of this issue, see H. A. Ruiz and M. Berg, 'Unending Limbo: Warehousing Bhutanese Refugees in Nepal', *U.S. Committee for Refugees and Immigrants*, Report 98 – 105, Washington DC, 2004. Online. HTTP: <www.cnsp.ca/ pdf%20files/bhutanese_refugees_in_nepal.pdf> (accessed 23 Nov. 2010).

38 C. Haviland, 'Despair of Nepal's Unwanted Exiles', *BBC News*, 30 Aug. 2005. Online. HTTP: <http://news.bbc.co.uk/1/hi/world/south_asia/4194616.stm> (accessed 10 Mar. 2010).

39 'Bhutanese Refugees in Nepal: Point of No Return', *The Economist*, 15 Jan. 2009. Online. HTTP: <http://www.economist.com/world/asia/displaystory.cfm?story_id= 12941086> (accessed 10 Mar. 2009). Similar disputes over refugees exist between Pakistan and Afghanistan, and India and Bangladesh.

40 This overview is by no means exhaustive as there are numerous other political disputes which characterize inter-state relations in South Asia. However, it is not possible to give an account which encapsulates them all in this space.

41 For a recent evaluation of SAARC, see L. Saez, *The South Asian Association for Regional Cooperation (Saarc): An Emerging Collaboration Architecture*, London: Routledge, 2011.

42 'SAARC Charter', *South Asian Association for Regional Cooperation (SAARC)*. Online. HTTP: <http://www.saarc-sec.org/SAARC-Charter/5/> (accessed 10 Mar. 2009).

43 For more, see S. Pattanaik, 'Making Sense of Regional Cooperation: SAARC at 20', *Strategic Analysis*, vol. 30, no. 1, Jan.–Mar. 2006, pp. 139–60; S. Kashani, 'SAARC: 25 Years of Existence but Little to Show', *The Hindustan Times*, 28 April 2010. Online.

HTTP: <http://www.hindustantimes.com/SAARC-25-years-of-existence-but-little-to-show/Article1–536770.aspx > (accessed 23 Feb. 2011); S. Pattanaik, 'SAARC at 25: Time to Reflect', IDSA Comment, 7 May 2010. Online. HTTP: <http://www.idsa.in/idsacomments/SAARCat25TimetoReflect_sspattanaik_070510> (accessed 23 Feb. 2011).

44 For example, in January 2004 the leaders of both countries held talks on the sidelines of the SAARC annual summit in Islamabad. The talks marked the first such official-level contact between the two sides since July 2001, and eventually led to the establishment of a composite dialogue between the two countries. For more, see 'India Pakistan Leaders Meet at South Asia Summit', *USA Today*, 4 Jan. 2004. Online. HTTP: <http://www.usatoday.com/news/world/2004-01-04-summit_x.htm> (accessed 10 Mar. 2010) and A. Quraishi, 'Chance of India, Pakistan Thaw', *CNN News*, 22 July 2004. Online. HTTP: <http://edition.cnn.com/2004/WORLD/asiapcf/07/21/saarc.meeting/index.html> (accessed 10 Mar. 2009).

45 For more see Khan, *The Great Partition*.

46 This is not to say that the nuclearization of South Asia occurred overnight. India's first nuclear test was in fact conducted as far back as 1974, following the India–Pakistan war of 1971. The defeat spurred Pakistan to develop its own nuclear strength, and it acquired the capability to assemble a nuclear device at short notice in 1987. For more, see K. Matinuddin, *The Nuclearization of South Asia*, Oxford: Oxford University Press, 2002, p. 94; R. B. Rais, 'Post-Cold War Security Studies in Pakistan: Continuity and Change', in D. Banerjee (ed.), *Security Studies in South Asia: Change and Challenges*, New Delhi: Vedam Books, 2000, pp. 127–28.

47 S. Ganguly and K. L. Biringer in L. Dittmer (ed.), *South Asia's Nuclear Dilemma: India, Pakistan and China*, New York: M. E. Sharpe Inc., 2005, pp. 30–31.

48 For more, see M. J. Akbar, 'India–Pakistan: Take the Good News Cautiously', *International Herald Tribune*, 30 Oct. 2002. Online. HTTP: <http://www.nytimes.com/2002/10/30/opinion/30iht-edakbar_ed3_.html> (accessed 12 July 2011).

49 For example, see 'New India–Pakistan Bus on Trial', *BBC News*, 11 Dec. 2005. Online. HTTP: <http://news.bbc.co.uk/2/hi/south_asia/4518096.stm> (accessed 4 July 2011); M. Rama Rao, 'India–Pakistan Begin a New Round of Talks on Nuke CBMs', *Asian Tribune*, 5 Aug. 2005. Online. HTTP: <http://www.asiantribune.com/news/2005/08/05/india-pakistan-begin-new-round-talks-nuke-cbms> (accessed 4 July 2011).

50 Emirates Center for Strategic Studies (ECSS), *The Balance of Power in South Asia*, Abu Dhabi: I. B. Tauris, 2003, pp. 98–99.

51 P. R. Chari, 'India's Nuclear Doctrine: Confused Ambitions', *The Non-Proliferation Review*, Fall–Winter 2000, p. 126.

52 S. Cohen, 'Nuclear Weapons and Nuclear War in South Asia', in R. Thakur and O. Wiggen, *South Asia in the World: Problem Solving Perspectives on Security, Sustainable Development and Good Governance*, Hong Kong: United Nations University Press, 2004, pp. 39–57.

53 Ibid.

54 Indian External Affairs Minister Pranab Mukherjee's statement in Parliament on the Mumbai terror attacks, 13 Feb. 2009. Online. HTTP: <http://www.satp.org/satporgtp/countries/india/document/papers/09fab13.htm> (accessed Mar. 11 2009).

55 Ibid.

56 R. Bedi, 'India Reserves Right to Attack Pakistan in Response to Mumbai Attack', *Jane's Defence News*, 5 Dec. 2008. Online. HTTP: <http://www.janes.com/news/defence/triservice/jdw/jdw081205_1_n.shtml> (accessed 11 Mar. 2009).

57 For example, see M. Sappenfield and H. Yusuf, 'Public Anger Strains Indian–Pakistani Cooperation', *The Christian Science Monitor*, 5 Dec. 2008. Online. HTTP: <http://www.csmonitor.com/2008/1205/p06s02-wosc.html> (accessed 11 Mar. 2009) and 'Blame and Retribution', *The Economist*, 4 Dec. 2009. Online. HTTP: <http://www.economist.com/world/asia/displaystory.cfm?story_id=12724858> (accessed 11 Mar. 2010).

58 B. E. O'Neill, *Insurgency & Terrorism: Inside Modern Revolutionary Warfare*, Washington, DC: Brassey's, 1990, p. 13.
59 For more see V. Balachandran, 'Insurgency, Terrorism and Transnational Crime in South Asia', *Transnational Trends: Middle Eastern and Asian Views*, June 2008, pp. 117–19. Online. HTTP: <http://kms1.isn.ethz.ch/serviceengine/Files/ISN/95193/ichaptersection_single document/c8178933-7827-4b08-ad45-27e6b6284a83/en/6.pdf> (accessed 11 Mar. 2009).
60 I. Ahmed, *State, Nation and Ethnicity in Contemporary South Asia*, London: Pinter, 1996, p. 2.
61 For Connor, 'Nationalism connotes identification with and loyalty to one's nation' as per his definition given above. In W. Conner, *Ethnonationalism: The Quest for Understanding*, Princeton: Princeton University Press, 1994, p. xi.
62 A. D. Smith, *The Ethnic Origin of Nations*, Oxford: Blackwell, 1986, pp. 29–49.
63 Chari in Chari (ed.), *Security and Governance*, p. 10.
64 As pointed out in the 'Asia Overview' chapter in 'Patterns of Global Terrorism 2000', Report by the *Office of the Coordinator for Counterterrorism*, US Department of State. Online. HTTP: <http://www.state.gov/s/ct/rls/crt/2000/2432.htm> (accessed 11 Mar. 2010).
65 O. Marwah, 'India's Military Intervention in East Pakistan, 1971–72', *Modern Asian Studies*, vol. 13, no. 4, 1979, p. 564.
66 For more, see M. Mehta, 'India's Turbulent Northeast', *The South Asia Monitor*, no. 35, 5 July 2001. Online. HTTP: <http://www.ciaonet.org/pbei/csis/sam/sam35/index.html> (accessed 11 Mar. 2009).
67 For more, see 'Nepal's Peace Agreement: Making it Work', International Crisis Group Asia Report No.126, 15 December 2006. Online. HTTP: <http://www.crisisgroup.org/~/media/Files/asia/south-asia/nepal/126_nepals_peace_agreement-making_it_work.ashx> (accessed 20 Jul. 2010).
68 For more, see B. Ghosh, 'How to Defeat Insurgencies: Sri Lanka's Bad Example', *Time*, 10 May 2009. Online. HTTP: <http://www.time.com/time/world/article/0,8599, 1899762,00.html> (accessed 26 May 2009).
69 For more on the Tamil insurgency in Sri Lanka, see S. U. Kodikara, 'The Separatist Eelam Movement in Sri Lanka: An Overview', *India Quarterly*, vol. 37, April–June 1981, pp. 194–212; O. N. Mehrotra, 'Ethnic Strife in Sri Lanka', *Strategic Analysis*, vol. 21, Jan. 1988, pp. 346–61; N. De Silva, *An Introduction to Tamil Racism in Sri Lanka*, Colombo: Chintana Prashadaya, 1997; D. Hellman-Rajanayagam, *The Tamil Tigers' Armed Struggle for Identity*, Stuttgart: Franz Steiner Verlag, 1994; D. Jayatilleke, *Sri Lanka: The Travails of a Democracy, Unfinished War, Protracted Crisis*, Colombo: ICES, 1995; S. Nadarajah and D. Sriskandarajah, 'Liberation Struggle or Terrorism? The Politics of Naming the LTTE', Third World Quarterly, vol. 26, no. 1, 2005, pp. 87–100.
70 Ahmed, *State, Nation and Ethnicity*, p. 2.
71 In the early 1980s, support for Sri Lankan Tamils and the LTTE was great amidst the Tamils living in the South Indian state of Tamil Nadu, just across the Palk Straits. India's key concerns with respect to the conflict involved fears of separatist tendencies in Tamil Nadu getting a new lease of life, and the prospect of extra-regional powers (such as the US and China) intervening in the conflict at the behest of the Sri Lankan state. India's own role in the ethnic conflict progressed from an initial mediatory role in 1983 to the deployment of the Indian Peacekeeping Force (IPKF) on the island-state in 1987 following the signing of an Indo-Sri Lankan 'peace accord'. The military intervention proved disastrous. The IPKF ended up fighting the LTTE for many reasons; it lost over 1,100 troops by the time its withdrawal was complete in March 1990, and IPKF troops came to be seen as 'aliens and enemies trying to dominate the lives of the Tamils.' S. K. Hennayake, 'The Peace Accord and the Tamils in Sri Lanka', *Asian Survey*, vol. 29, no. 4, Apr. 1989, p. 413. Also see D. T. Hagerty, 'India's Regional Security Doctrine', *Asian Survey*, vol. 31, no. 4, Apr. 1991, pp. 351–63.
72 B. Ghosh, 'How to Defeat Insurgencies: Sri Lanka's Bad Example'.

73 P. Wonacott, 'Sri Lanka Declares Rebel Chief Dead, Ending War', *The Wall Street Journal*, 18 May 2010. Online. HTTP: <http://online.wsj.com/article/SB1242634793620298 41.html> (accessed 26 May 2009).
74 Ibid.
75 For more, see G. Singh, 'Punjab Since 1984: Disorder, Order and Legitimacy', Asian Survey, vol. 36, no. 4, Apr. 1996, pp. 410–21.
76 For more, see S. Bose, 'Kashmir: Sources of Conflict, Dimensions of Peace', Economic and Political Weekly, vol. 34, no. 13, 27 Mar. 27–2 Apr. 1999, pp. 762–68; S. Ganguly, 'Explaining the Kashmir Insurgency: Political Mobilization and Institutional Decay', International Security, vol. 21, no. 2, Autumn 1996, pp. 76–107; P. Ghate, 'Kashmir: The Dirty War', Economic and Political Weekly, vol. 37, no. 4, 26 Jan. 1 Feb. 2002, pp. 313–22 and B. Puri, *Kashmir: Insurgency and After*, New Delhi: Orient Longman Private Limited, 2008.
77 'India's Maoist Challenge', *IISS Strategic Comments*, vol. 16, no. 24, Sep. 2010.
78 See 'Profile: India's Maoist Rebels', BBC News, 4 March 2011. Online. HTTP: <http://www.bbc.co.uk/news/world-south-asia-12640645> (accessed 14 June 2011).
79 M. Bahree, 'India's Dirty War', *Forbes Magazine*, 10 May 2010. Online. HTTP: <http://www.forbes.com/forbes/2010/0510/global-2000-2010-maoists-naxalites-tata-steel-india-dirty-war.html> (accessed 14 Jun. 2011). Also see S. A. Weiss, 'India's Maoist Insurgency', *The Washington Times*, 9 July 2010. Online. HTTP: < http://www.washingtontimes.com/news/2010/jul/9/on-thursday-heavily-armed-maoist-rebels-attacked-a/> (accessed 14 Jun. 2011).
80 'India's Maoist Challenge'.
81 K. Banerjee and P. Saha, 'The NREGA, the Maoists and the Developmental Woes of the Indian State', *Economic and Political Weekly*, vol. 45, no. 28, 10 July 2010, pp. 42–47.
82 'Profile: India's Maoist Rebels', BBC News.
83 The complexity of the situation with regard to the plight of these communities is too great to be discussed here. For a recent and very informative account, see M. Bahree, 'The Forever War: Inside India's Maoist Conflict', *World Policy Journal*, vol. 27, no. 2, Summer 2010, pp. 83–89.
84 'Human Development Report 1997', *United Nations Development Report*. Online. HTTP: <http://hdr.undp.org/reports/global/1997/en/> (accessed 11 Mar. 2009).
85 M. Mamun, 'The Challenge of Governance in South Asia: Good Governance in Bangladesh', *Occasional Paper 2000*, Peace Studies Group, University of Calcutta.
86 *The Conflict, Security & Development Group Bulletin*, The Conflict, Security & Development Group, Oct. 1999, p. 3.
87 Chari in Chari (ed.), *Security and Governance*, p. 15.
88 Ibid.
89 J. Boyden, J. Hart, J. de Berry and T. Feeney, 'Children Affected by Armed Conflict in South Asia: A Review of Trends and Issues Identified Through Secondary Research', *RSC Working Paper Series 7*, International Development Centre, 2002, Oxford University, p. 13.
90 Ibid., pp. 13–20.
91 Interviews with Bangladesh experts and journalists in London and Dhaka. Also see A. Riaz, 'The Politics of Islamization in Bangladesh', in Riaz (ed.), *Religion and Politics in South Asia*, Abingdon: Routledge, 2010, pp. 45–70.
92 A. Mohsin, 'Governance and Security: The Experience of Bangladesh', in Chari (ed.), *Security and Governance*, pp. 22–47.
93 Ibid. Also see A. Riaz, 'Bangladesh in 2004: The Politics of Vengeance and the Erosion of Democracy', *Asian Survey*, vol. 45, no. 1, Jan.–Feb. 2005, pp. 112–18, and S. R. Sen, 'Bangladesh: Retrospect and Prospect', *Economic and Political Weekly*, vol. 26, no. 13, 30 Mar., 1991, p. 826.
94 Interview with senior South Asia expert at the BBC World Service Radio, London.

95 Mohsin in Chari (ed.), *Security and Governance*, pp. 22–47. Also see F. A. Osman, 'Bangladesh Politics: Confrontation, Monopoly and Crisis in Governance', *Asian Journal of Political Science*, vol. 18, no. 3, 2010, pp. 310–33.
96 For more, see 'India's Corruption Scandals', BBC News, 19 August 2011. Online. HTTP: <http://www.bbc.co.uk/news/world-south-asia-12769214> (accessed 24 Aug. 2011).
97 See R. Deshpande, 'Centre Won't Bypass House rules for Lokpal', *The Times of India*, 22 Aug. 2011. Online. HTTP: <http://articles.timesofindia.indiatimes.com/2011-08-22/india/29914533_1_anna-hazare-agitation-lokpal-anti-corruption-ombudsman> (accessed 26 Aug. 2011).
98 D. Halder, 'Anna domini', Mid-Day, 28 Aug. 2011. Online. HTTP: <http://www.mid-day.com/news/2011/aug/280811-News-Mumbai-Indian-Parliament-Anna-Hazare.htm> (accessed 29 Aug. 2011).
99 A. Najam, 'The Environmental Challenge to Human Security in South Asia', in Thakur and Wiggen (eds), *South Asia in the World*, p. 234.
100 L. C. Baldor, 'Terror Attacks Spike in Pakistan, Afghanistan', *MSNBC*, 28 Apr. 2010. Online. HTTP: <http://www.msnbc.msn.com/id/36820196/ns/world_news-south_and_central_asia/> (accessed 12 Mar. 2011).
101 J. L. N. Rao, 'Jihad and Cross-Border Terrorism in South Asia', in A. S. Raju (ed.), *Terrorism in South Asia: Views from India*, New Delhi: India Research Press, 2004, p. 182.
102 K. de Silva, 'Terrorism and Political Agitation in Post-Colonial South Asia: Jammu-Kashmir and Sri Lanka', in Thakur and Wiggen (eds), *South Asia in the World*, p. 86.
103 S. D. Muni, *Pangs of Proximity: India and Sri Lanka's Ethnic Crisis*, New Delhi: Sage Publications, 1993, p. 42.
104 'Sri Lanka Probe Urged as Video Airs in US', *Agence France-Presse*, 15 July 2011. Online. HTTP: http://news.yahoo.com/sri-lanka-probe-urged-video-airs-us-2131525 66.html (accessed 29 July 2011).
105 P. S. Ghosh, *Migrants and Refugees in South Asia: Political and Security Dimensions*, Shillong: ICSSR-NERC, 2001, p. iv.
106 P. R. Chari, 'Refugees, Migrants and Internally Displaced Persons in South Asia: an Overview', in P. R. Chari, M. Joseph and S. Chandran (eds), *Missing Boundaries: Refugees, Migrants, Stateless and Internally Displaced People in South Asia*, New Delhi: Manohar, 2003, p. 17.
107 UNHCR. Online. HTTP: <www.unhcr.org> (*accessed 12* Mar. 2010).
108 P. Saxena, 'Creating Legal Space for Refugees in India: The Milestones Crossed and the Roadmap for the Future', *International Journal of Refugee Law*, vol. 19, 2007, pp. 246–72.
109 S. Kanitkar, *Refugee Problems in South Asia*, New Delhi: Rajat Publications, 2000, pp. 30–45.
110 R. Radhakrishnan, 'More Tamil Refugees Expected to Return: UNHCR', The Hindu, 10 Jan. 2011. Online. HTTP: <http://www.thehindu.com/news/international/article1076016.ece> (accessed 4 Apr. 2011).
111 For a detailed account, see P. Banerji, S. B. R. Chaudhury and S. K. Das (eds), *Internal Displacement in South Asia*, London: Sage Publications, 2005.
112 See '2011 Regional Operations Profile – South Asia', *UNHCR*. Online. HTTP: <http://www.unhcr.org/pages/49e45b156.html> (accessed 15 Apr. 15 2011).
113 The Narmada, the fifth-longest river in India, originates in the central Indian state of Madhya Pradesh and empties into the Arabian Sea after flowing through the western Indian states of Maharashtra and Gujarat.
114 'TISS Report on the Narmada Dam: Sardar Sarovar Project', Tata Institute of Social Sciences, 20 Aug. 20 2008. Online. HTTP: <http://aidindia.org/main/content/view/764/376/> (accessed 4 Apr. 2011).
115 Ibid.

116 Ibid. The SRP (Cash for Land) was suspended by the Review Committee of the Narmada Control Authority on 21 March 2005, only to be revived again by the Madhya Pradesh government on 16 June 2005.

117 For example, see J. W. Heffernen, 'Being Recognised as Citizens: A Human Security Dilemma in South and Southeast Asia', Nov. 2002. Online. HTTP: <http://www.humansecuritychs.org/activities/research/citizenship_asia.pdf> (accessed 12 Mar. 2011) and 'Protecting Refugees and the Role of UNHCR', *UNHCR*, Report 2007–8. Online. HTTP: <http://www.unhcr.org/basics/BASICS/4034b6a34.pdf> (accessed 12 Mar. 2009).

118 It is important to point out here that more than 80 per cent of refugees worldwide are women and children, which highlights the gendered nature of the phenomenon. In South Asia, this has been linked with 'the marginalisation of women by the South Asian states. These states at best patronise women and at worse infantilise, disenfranchise and de-politicise them.' In conflicts between states and communities, women are often deliberately targeted and displaced, disempowering them at many levels. Refugee women 'emerge as the symbol of difference between us/citizens and its other/refugees/non-citizens.' From 'Refugee Watch Special Issue', *Maharniban Calcutta Research Group*, nos. 24–26, Oct. 2005. Online. HTTP: <www.mcrg.ac.in/rw%20files/RW24.doc> (accessed 12 April 2011).

119 'Protecting Refugees', *UNHCR*.

120 S. Kanitkar, *Refugee Problems in South Asia*, New Delhi: Rajat Publications, 2000, p. 113.

121 'UN Protocol to Prevent, Suppress and Punish Trafficking in Persons Especially Women and Children, supplementing the United Nations Convention against Transnational Organised Crime', *United Nations*, 2000. Online. HTTP: <http://www.uncjin.org/Documents/Conventions/dcatoc/final_documents_2/convention_%20traff_eng.pdf> (*accessed 12* Mar. 2009).

122 J. Sanghera in H. Johnston and S. Khan (eds), *Trafficking in Persons in South Asia*, Alberta: Shastri Indo-Canadian Institute, 1998, p. 120.

123 Article 27 of the Declaration of the Ninth SAARC Summit, *SAARC*, Male, Maldives, 12–14 May 1997. Online. HTTP: http://www.saarc-sec.org/userfiles/Summit%20Declarations/09%20-%20Maldives%20-%209th%20Summit%201997.pdf (accessed 14 May 2010).

124 R. Bhowmick, 'Preventing Trafficking of Women', *The New Nation*, 28 July 2006. Online. HTTP: <http://www.wunrn.com/news/2006/07_31_06/080106_trafficking_south.htm> (accessed 19 May 2009).

125 'Combating Trafficking of Women and Children in South Asia', *Asian Development Bank*, Manila, 2003, p. 4.

126 Ibid.

127 Ibid., p. 3.

128 Ibid.

129 For example, see A. K. M. Masud Ali, 'Treading along a Treacherous Trail: Research on Trafficking in Persons in South Asia', *International Migration*, vol. 42, nos. 1–2, Jan. 2005, pp. 141–64.

130 Ibid., p. 141.

131 Interview with senior staff at the Office of Health and Planning, USAID, Kathmandu.

132 Masud Ali, 'Treading along a Treacherous Trail', pp. 141–42.

133 Ibid.

134 Ibid., p. 142.

135 For example, former US Secretary of State Colin Powell has described human trafficking as a global security threat. See K. Broendel and G. Goodwin, 'State Dept. Releases Human Trafficking Report', *All Africa*, 17 June 2004. Online. HTTP: <http://allafrica.com/stories/200406170721.html> (accessed 10 Mar. 2009). Also see S. L. Keefer, 'Human Trafficking and the Impact on National Security for the United States', *USAWC Strategy Research Project*, 15 Mar. 2006. Online. HTTP: <http://stinet.

dtic.mil/cgi-bin/GetTRDoc?AD=ADA448573&Location=U2&doc=GetTRDoc.pdf>
(accessed 10 Mar. 2009) and K. J. Allred, 'Analysis: Combating Human Trafficking',
NATO Review, Summer 2006. Online. HTTP: <http://www.nato.int/docu/review/
2006/issue2/english/Analysis.html> (accessed 10 Mar. 2009).

136 Allred, 'Combating Human Trafficking'.

137 'Climate Change 2007: The Physical Science Basis', *Contribution of Working Group I to
the Fourth Assessment Report of the Intergovernmental Panel on Climate Change*, IPCC, 2007.
Online. HTTP: <http://www.ipcc.ch/publications_and_data/publications_ipcc_fourth_
assessment_report_wg1_report_the_physical_science_basis.htm> (accessed 20 July
2011).

138 For more, see 'Address to the IISS by HE Mr Sabiluddin Ahmed, High Commissioner
for Bangladesh to the UK', *International Institute for Strategic Studies*, 30 June 2006. Online.
HTTP: <http://www.iiss.org/recent-key-addresses/sabiluddin-ahmed-address/>
(accessed 15 Mar. 2011).

139 'Potential Impact of Sea-Level Rise on Bangladesh', *UNEP*. Online. HTTP: <http://
www.grida.no/publications/vg/climate/page/3086.aspx> (accessed 12 Mar. 2010)
and A. U. Ahmed et al., 'Considering Adaptation to Climate Change: Towards a
Sustainable Development of Bangladesh', *Report Prepared for South Asia Region, World Bank,
Washington DC*, Oct. 1999. Online. HTTP: <http://www.mungo.nl/CC_Bangla.htm>
(accessed 12 Mar. 2008).

140 Bangladesh riverine and coastal morphological processes are extremely dynamic, to a
large extent because of the tidal and seasonal variations in river flows and run-off.
Climate change is expected to increase these variations, giving rise to further disruptive events. For more, see Ahmed, 'Considering Adaptation to Climate Change'.

141 'Climate Change Debate Hots Up', *The Times of India*, 13 April 2010. Online. HTTP:
<http://articles.timesofindia.indiatimes.com/2010-04-13/delhi/28137197_1_highest-
temperature-degree-climate-change> (accessed 12 Jan. 2011).

142 Ibid.

143 N. Bryant, 'Maldives: Paradise Soon to be Lost', *BBC News*, 28 July 2004. Online.
HTTP: <http://news.bbc.co.uk/1/hi/world/south_asia/3930765.stm> (accessed 27
Apr. 2008).

144 P. Rogers, 'Climate Change: Threat and Promise', *Open Democracy*, 2 Nov. 2006.
Online. HTTP: <http://www.opendemocracy.net/conflict/climatechange_4055.jsp>
(accessed 27 Apr. 2008).

145 'Climate Change Threat Real, Change Lifestyle: PM', *Hindustan Times*, 5 June
2007. Online. HTTP: <http://www.hindustantimes.com/storypage/storypage.aspx?
id=7aba6298-7bcc-4c6a-8b6d-2f78fad93ce2&ParentID=90fc013b-af57-40d2-b066-
a5ac1995828d&MatchID1=4468&TeamID1=2&TeamID2=4&MatchType1=1&Series
ID1=11> (accessed 15 Aug. 2010).

3   Securitizing misgovernance in Bangladesh

The Daily Star, New Age and *The Bangladesh Today**

In the experiences of the people of South Asia, misgovernance and insecurity appear to be intimately linked. In most states in the region, corruption is rampant, state institutions are often weak and inefficient, electoral processes are riddled with violence and crime, and judiciaries are often politicized. Structural violence is a brutal reality for most South Asians, and on many occasions paired with the threat of physical violence. Ethnic and religious minorities in South Asian states have generally faced oppression, persecution or discrimination, be it the tribal communities in Northeast India, people of Nepalese ethnicity in Bhutan, the Tamil minority in Sri Lanka or the hill people of the Chittagong Hill Tract in Bangladesh. Socio-economic divides are still vast in South Asian countries. In most cases, for those situated outside and without any links to the traditional realms of power within socio-economic and political structures, or those who lack the resources to bribe their way to access the most basic services and exercise the most fundamental rights, it is a traumatic and harsh way of life, riddled with deep insecurities.

In recent times, several non-state actors (NSAs) operating in Bangladesh have persistently cited aspects of misgovernance – such as partisan politics, weak governance institutions, a corrupt and politicized judiciary, and a similarly corrupt and violent electoral process – as key causes of insecurity for people in the country. This chapter explores the main arguments which link these issues to the safety and well-being of Bangladeshi people, and analyses the attempts of three main national English-language dailies – *The Daily Star, New Age* and *The Bangladesh Today* – to highlight these links. The case study begins with a brief conceptual discussion of 'misgovernance' and contextualizes the phenomenon in South Asia through a historical overview of socio-political instability in the region. It goes on to outline the political landscape in Bangladesh since independence, followed by a detailed examination of the key dynamics of misgovernance in the country. The case study then analyses editorials published in the three newspapers mentioned above in the years leading up to and immediately following the imposition of a state of emergency in Bangladesh

* Barthwal-Datta, M., 'Securitising Threats without the State? A case study of misgovernance as a security threat in Bangladesh', *Review of International Studies*, vol. 35, no. 2, Apr. 2009, pp. 277–300. Copyright © British International Studies Association doi: 10.1017/S0260210509008523. Reproduced with permission.

in January 2007. These editorials specifically link aspects of misgovernance and insecurity amongst the people of Bangladesh, and call for urgent action at the state level towards mitigating them. Using Securitization Theory, the case study carefully explores these efforts as attempts to securitize misgovernance in Bangladesh. In doing so, it highlights the weaknesses in the theory when applied to such a case, particularly its lack of adequate distinction between who 'speaks' security and who 'does' security, its requirement of a securitizing actor breaking free of 'normal procedures and rules' in making a securitizing move, and (to a lesser extent) its focus on policy outcomes in determining the success or failure of a securitizing move.

Defining misgovernance

Before exploring what is meant by the term 'misgovernance', it is helpful to locate the dynamics of this phenomenon in the societal sector. The Copenhagen School insists that security must be viewed in its dual form, i.e. state security and societal security.[1] While the former is concerned with sovereignty, the latter is 'about identity, the self-conception of communities and of individuals identifying themselves as members of a community'.[2] Thus, while 'social' security is about individuals and mainly economic issues, societal security refers to the level of collective identities and action taken to defend such 'we identities'.[3] It follows that threats to societal security are those which threaten society as a collective, rather than 'threats primarily to individuals (threats *in* society); only if they threaten the breakdown of society do they become societal security issues.'[4] Embedded within these conceptualizations is the idea that security is 'not only about survival, it is, as a general rule, about *collective* survival'.[5] Insecurities arising from misgovernance manifest themselves not only at the individual level (where they may be experienced in different ways and to varying extents by individuals), but also at the collective, societal level – whether experienced by members of ethnic minority groups in the form of partisan politics and a lack of political representation, or by members of Bangladeshi society in general through corruption, weak rule of law and a criminalized and violent electoral process. It is, however, important to note that such insecurities do not relate only to the fear of being unable to survive physically, but extend to wider fears around, for example, being able preserve one's way of life and livelihood. The distinction made by Booth between 'survival' and 'security' is illuminating here, and allows for a more nuanced security analysis of the phenomenon of misgovernance and its impact on people in Bangladesh.[6]

Misgovernance as a term has been used in South Asia to signify a lack of or extremely poor standards of governance. The social science literature deals with the issue of governance from two angles: 'rational choice theory and public policy studies on the one hand, and historical sociology of institutions, on the other', the difference being that while 'the former approaches governance as the best political framework for policy-making and provides its theoretical foundations, the latter is more critical and comparative'.[7] According to Rhodes, governance signifies 'a change in the meaning of government, referring to a new process of governing or a changed condition of ordered rule; or the new method by which society is governed'.[8] While there is no consensus over a universal definition of governance in the academic literature, it is widely understood as a process of interaction between people and government institutions. It has been used in many contexts, such as 'the growing interaction between the private and public sectors' in Europe in particular, 'in criticism of the welfare state, or, in the sphere of IR, to express the increasing distrust of certain intergovernmental organizations and … the state authoritarianism persisting in many new nations'.[9]

In the realm of public policy-making and advocacy-based research, the vast and growing body of literature on governance may be roughly be divided in four subsets.[10] The first relates to definitions and efforts to clarify conceptually the idea of governance.[11] The second deals with providing indicators and measurements for governance, or more specifically, 'good governance'.[12] The third subset of this literature investigates the links between governance and development.[13] The fourth and final subset which can be identified within the governance literature is relatively younger and concerns itself with the nexus between governance, security and development. In this context, the governance agenda is tied closely to that of development on the one hand, and of security to the other. This conceptualization of governance reinforces the idea that security and development are intrinsically linked, and that this nexus is particularly relevant for countries still on the path to development.[14] The literature on human security derives heavily from the work done on the links between governance and development to support its argument that human development is essential in order for individuals to be safe from threats to their physical safety and general well-being. Without meeting the governance and development needs of its citizens, it is argued that the state cannot provide security to its people.[15]

Given the lack of a single conceptual definition of governance, and the specific problems of misgovernance that are widely present in South Asian states, this case study adopts an 'ideal type'[16] model of governance. According to Weber,

> an ideal type is formed by the one-sided accentuation of one or more points of view and by the synthesis of a great many diffuse, discrete, more or less present and occasionally absent concrete individual phenomena, which are arranged according to those one-sidedly emphasized viewpoints into a unified analytical construct.[17]

In the South Asian scenario, the ideal type model of governance considers the following issues:[18]

- Public institutions through which a government exercises its powers and functions (accountability, legitimacy and transparency);
- the authority and functioning of the judiciary;
- the administrative system and culture;
- the role of civil society and its relationship with the government;
- underlying socio-political dynamics which influence the functioning of the above.

Security and misgovernance in South Asia

In 1999, Mahbub-ul-Haq pointed out that:

> South Asia has emerged now as one of the most poorly governed regions in
> the world, with exclusion of the voiceless majority, unstable political regimes
> and poor economic management. The systems of governance have been
> unresponsive and irrelevant to the needs and concerns of people ... The most
> vulnerable in South Asia remain the most abused.[19]

Several South Asia analysts point to misgovernance as a key threat to the
security of people in the region.[20] Some insist that the region is in fact a prime
example of misgovernance, where

> Scarce resources are inefficiently deployed or frittered away, the administration
> is getting increasingly divided on ethnic and sectarian lines, law enforcement
> is arbitrary and political leadership is obviously inadequate. This situation
> largely derives from a lack of participatory government accompanied by a
> rapid erosion of political government ... a 'We–They' syndrome has devel-
> oped between the governing elites and the governed masses, with the
> bureaucracy becoming the masters rather than the servants of the people.[21]

In this context, regional analysts argue that for countries in South Asia, the
problems arising from misgovernance are far from an 'esoteric past time for the
intellectual elite of [the region]. They bear heavily on the day-to-day life of over
1.3 billion people making their life and living miserable, almost unliveable.'[22]
These problems are wide-ranging and have real-world consequences for individuals
and communities. The course of development in South Asia has been particularly
erratic and paradoxical.[23] Where it has taken place in the form of economic
progress, such as in India, it may have brought political empowerment to back-
ward sections of society, but these communities have not experienced relief from
their poverty-ridden, deprived socio-economic context. On the other hand, even
economic progress and political empowerment to an extent have not been able to
eliminate the effects of long-established and deeply entrenched ethnic and caste-
based discrimination, leaving huge sections of the population outside the political
and social (and therefore economic) mainstream.[24]

According to Marwah, the rise in political violence in South Asian countries is
due to economic, political and social factors, 'most of [which] are interrelated and
directly linked to the decline in the quality of governance'.[25] He argues that
given the huge and increasing disparities in socio-economic wealth in South Asian
countries, political empowerment has come to symbolize 'the key to social and
economic justice'.[26] Deprived and undermined groups seek increasingly to get
their voice heard within state institutions, which are widely undemocratic and
polarized on the lines of religion, community, ethnicity and caste. Consequently,
such groups turn to violence as 'the dominant mode of political action'.[27] Thus,

there appears to be a strong link between aspects of misgovernance and the rise of the threat of political violence in South Asia.

The effects of misgovernance manifest themselves most emphatically at the sub-state level in South Asia, with spillover effects at the national and regional levels.[28] As political power in South Asia remains tied to the supranational state, or the 'centre',[29] it is governance at the local level which is neglected. Most governments in South Asia, including India, Pakistan, Bangladesh, Sri Lanka and Nepal, have historically adopted an authoritarian approach to governance within their boundaries.[30] In this approach, most of the constitutional, administrative and fiscal power remains with the centre. Such a model of governance in South Asia has meant that there is little local representation at the relevant levels of power. The diversity of South Asian states in terms of socio-political and cultural disparities is huge, and therefore communities feel a great need to find representation for themselves at the relevant levels of power – something which has historically been met with great resistance by the central authorities in these states.[31]

As a result of the iron-fisted approach by South Asian states to separatist movements and demands for greater autonomy by sub-state groups, there is a high degree of insecurity amongst the minorities within these countries.[32] These groups feel existentially threatened by those in power, and lack adequate representation at the various levels of authority. Too often, minority groups are treated as pawns by political parties which woo them during the run-up to elections for votes, only to disregard the promises made to these groups for votes afterwards.[33] In many instances, these sub-state groups turn to political violence and armed insurgencies as the means to express their discontent with the state and to fight for the survival of their communities on their own terms.[34]

The nature of the demographics within the region makes misgovernance particularly problematic at the regional level. Because state boundaries here dissect ethnic communities, which share familial ties going back to pre-colonial times, cross-border communities often feel sympathetic to the plight of their counterparts in neighbouring countries.[35] For example, the suppression of Tamils in Sri Lanka generated a huge wave of sympathy among the Tamils in India in the 1980s. The Indian Tamil community assisted their counterparts in Sri Lanka by giving financial support to the Liberation Tigers of Tamil Eelam (LTTE), setting up training camps for the rebels in the Indian state of Tamil Nadu, and putting intense pressure on the central government to intervene in the Sri Lankan civil war.[36] Similarly, the insurgency in Indian-administered Kashmir in the 1990s was implicitly supported by Pakistan.[37] Sympathy and support for a mirroring community across the border suffering at the hands of its state is usually expressed through financial aid, covert arms supply and demands on the home state to pressure relevant governments to act to protect the sister community.[38]

Misgovernance is also held accountable for human suffering in South Asia on a day-to-day basis. Corruption, a symptom as well as cause of misgovernance, permeates the key institutions of most South Asian states.[39] Money, political influence and power are key motivators for politicians and bureaucrats, and the marginalized and poorer sections of society are the ones who suffer the most.[40] As the gap between the rich and the poor continues to increase rapidly in South Asian countries, bribery has taken deep root as a means to supplement modest salaries in administrations, and has provided an easy mode of bypassing the law of the land. The situation is so bad in some South Asian countries (especially in India and Bangladesh, where corruption infects almost every public institution) that it has led to a complete lack of faith in the system amongst their civil societies. With a majority of the population living below the poverty line, most people are unable to find work and access basic services such as healthcare, electricity and water without bribing government officials or using the support of someone influential whom they may know and by whom they could get recommended to the relevant official. In India, for example, 'ration shops' licensed to sell government-subsidized food such as grains and cereals under the public distribution system (PDS) are notorious for selling only a fraction of these goods at subsidized prices. Many shopkeepers sell the rest on the black market at exorbitant prices, denying the public access to these goods at affordable prices and pushing up market prices further.[41] Often it is the case that government officials in charge of issuing these licences get a cut of the profit these shopkeepers make. Therefore, while those in power manipulate their positions to expropriate funds and resources which are meant for the public, the poor live in deep insecurity about matters such as their ability to afford the next meal, to have a fair environment in which to compete for jobs and to be able to access and afford adequate healthcare. Such daily hardship as a consequence of misgovernance has been a significant cause of political violence in many parts of South Asia. For example, the key causes of the Maoist insurgency in Nepal have been identified as:

> the significant economic disparity in Nepal, particularly when comparing the financial means of rural Nepalis to the wealth of the urban middle and upper classes in Kathmandu ... endemic gender, ethnic, and caste-based discrimination embodied by the longstanding hegemonic rule of the caste and class elite ... and the disenchantment that occurred after dysfunctional and corrupt politicians dashed the people's hopes for change after 1990.[42]

For non-traditional security analysts, the case for misgovernance as a 'security' threat to states as well as sub-state groups in South Asia is a strong one. In this perspective, the nature of the phenomenon is such that it threatens not only the physical safety of the referent groups, but also fundamentally challenges their ability to live without the fear of being persecuted and being unable to provide themselves and their families with the most basic requirements for daily survival. The following analysis explores the nature of misgovernance and its impacts in Bangladesh in particular, and the role which national English-language daily newspapers in the country have been playing to raise the issue as a matter of 'security'.

Contextualizing misgovernance in Bangladesh: a brief political history

Misgovernance as a cause of political violence has deep roots in Bangladesh, a country with a volatile socio-political past. In order to establish a link between misgovernance and security in Bangladesh, it is necessary to briefly analyse the trajectory of politics and governance in the country since its inception. According to Rehman Sobhan, 'the character of the Bangladesh state is a society which is not so much over or misgoverned but is barely governed at all'.[43] Political instability has been endemic in Bangladesh, which gained independence from West Pakistan in 1972 to form a parliamentary democracy under a constitution.[44] Elections in 1973 resulted in a landslide victory for Sheikh Mujibur Rahman of the Awami League, who quickly began to rule the country in an authoritarian style, paid little attention to institution-building and tried to establish one-party rule.[45] In 1975, Mujibur Rahman was assassinated and the government overthrown in a military coup by General Ziaur Rahman. Thus began a period of fifteen years of military rule in Bangladesh's political history. In 1981, General Ziaur Rahman was assassinated in a failed military coup attempt, and within the next year was replaced by a new military leader in General Ershad. Under military rule, political parties were far from developing into democratic institutions, and served as little more than 'political vehicles for powerful individual leaders'.[46] Nonetheless, demands for a restoration of democracy in Bangladesh snowballed in the late 1980s, spearheaded by the Awami league (led by Sheikh Hasina) and the other main political party, the Bangladesh Nationalist Party (BNP, led by Begum Khaleda Zia). The protests gained wide public support, becoming a mass movement to overthrow the Ershad regime and to hold free and fair elections to bring a democratically elected government to power. In early December 1990, under immense pressure, General Ershad was forced to resign.

The first 'free and fair' elections in Bangladesh were held in March 1991, marking the advent of a fresh, if not altogether new, period of democracy in the country. The BNP swept to power under Begum Khaleda Zia as Prime Minister, but inherited – and further entrenched – polarized politics infested with corrupt and partisan values.[47] In 1994, the opposition in Parliament walked out and boycotted the government on charges of rigging elections earlier in the year, and shunned elections in February 1996, leading to a BNP victory. Riots and protests erupted on the streets. Under increasing pressure from all quarters, the government gave in to demands to amend the constitution, allowing the incumbent government to vacate office at the end of its five-year term and hand over power to a non-party caretaker government (CTG) which would be headed by the outgoing Chief Justice as Chief Adviser for ninety days, and would oversee the election of the new government.[48] In June 1996, under the first such CTG, fresh elections monitored by international observers took place, and brought the Awami League under Sheikh Hasina's leadership to power.

The CTG system also worked smoothly in the run-up to the next elections in 2001, which brought to power a four-party alliance of BNP and right-wing Islamist parties. It failed, however, to succeed a third time, as Bangladesh succumbed to political upheaval at the heels of violent demonstrations and protests by opposition parties accusing the incumbent government of corruption and demanding reforms for the elections due in January 2007.[49] The opposition argued that the CTG appointed in October 2006 was partisan, as the incumbent government had managed to fill all key positions from which the caretaker administration was drawn with their own allies in the preceding months. Even as the Zia government handed over power to the caretaker administration, opposition parties led by the Awami League claimed the Chief Election Commissioner and his deputies were hand-in-glove with the government, and that elections would not be free and fair.[50] Unless their reform demands were met and they were given a say in who would be the Chief Adviser of the CTG, the opposition threatened to boycott elections. The army was deployed onto the streets to prevent political protests and safeguard elections,[51] but as demands for the Chief Adviser's resignation and for the postponement of elections grew, so did pressure from the international community. The UN and EU suspended their election observer missions in the country and withdrew all technical support, claiming that conditions for credible elections did not exist.[52] On 11 January, the head of the CTG President Iajuddin Ahmed resigned, hours after declaring a state of emergency in the country.[53] Dr Fakhruddin Ahmed, a noted economist and former civil servant approved of by both sides, took charge of the interim government shortly after, and vowed to crack down on corruption and violence, which he claimed were undermining democracy in Bangladesh.[54] Almost two years later, in December 2008, the CTG finally lifted the emergency to allow elections to take place at the end of the month.[55] The verdict was a landslide victory for an alliance led by Hasina, making her Prime Minister for a second time.[56] The losing BNP-led alliance accused the other side initially of widespread ballot-rigging and forgery,[57] yet by early January 2009 it agreed to give the administration a chance to govern and pledged its support to the same.[58] In the past two years since then, the opposition has boycotted Parliament several times and politics in the country remains largely mired in hate and attrition, shaped by the personal vendettas of its political leaders.[59]

Bangladesh's political volatility has been accompanied by hardships from a hostile physical environment. Although relatively small in area, Bangladesh has a population of over 164 million, making it the world's eighth most populous country.[60] Over 80 per cent of the population lives in rural areas, and around two-thirds still depend on agriculture for their livelihoods.[61] Bangladesh is located in the delta plains formed by three great rivers – Ganges, Brahmaputra and Meghna – and their tributaries. Only 8 per cent of the catchment area (approximately 1.75 million square miles) lies inside Bangladesh, giving it little control over the flood discharges that flow into its boundaries. Hundreds of tonnes of sediment brought in by these rivers block river and drainage channels in Bangladesh, and the problem is worsened by heavy monsoon rains and Bangladesh's location in the Bay of Bengal, which makes it susceptible to storm surges. Consequently, flooding (both natural – flash, river and rainwater floods – and man-made) is a recurrent phenomenon in the country.[62] The risk of flooding is compounded by Bangladesh's propensity for cyclones due to its location by the warm waters of the Bay of Bengal. The high-speed winds create havoc by regularly destroying dams and river banks. Every year, millions are made homeless and thousands die as a direct or indirect consequence of floods. The country's health services are severely tested year after year, as the receding of flood waters gives way to a number of water-borne diseases and post-flood diseases such as pneumonia, typhoid, hepatitis, conjunctivitis, as well as a number of skin infections.[63]

Key problems of misgovernance in Bangladesh

According to Odhikar, a local human rights watchdog, life in Bangladesh continues to be crippled by 'the overwhelming lack of political tolerance, absence of necessary and effective institutions to ensure a democratic polity and blatant violations of human rights'.[64] This analysis chimes with the view that:

> The failure of the state to deliver basic service to the people, widespread corruption and appropriation of State resources by the regimes in power and the opposition, weak political institutions, lack of democratic spirit in the party in power and in the Opposition has turned Bangladesh into one of the most violent and polarized societies in [South Asia].[65]

A growing number of voices in the country and the wider region are now focusing on misgovernance as a major cause of insecurity in Bangladesh. They focus on partisan politics, weak government institutions, corruption, a politicized judiciary, and a criminalized and violent political process.[66]

Partisan politics

Politics in Bangladesh has been increasingly polarized along ethnic and religious lines since the country adopted its constitution following independence in 1972.[67] This was 'a highly nationalist and undemocratic document, ensuring the hegemony of the dominant Bangali nation in all sphere of life'.[68] It embraced 'Bangali nationalism', which was premised on the priority of the Bangali language and culture over all others within the borders of the newly created state. This was done at the cost of leaving no space for other ethnic nations – numbering around forty groups – which existed within these boundaries. By 1977, the constitution had become further polarized along religious lines, with an emphasis on Islam as the dominant religion.[69] This appealed to Bangali Muslims, the majority in the country, as it distinguished Bangladesh from its Hindu counterpart across the border in the Indian state of West Bengal; but Bangali Hindus, the Chakmas and other ethnic groups in the country were further marginalized.[70] Historically, these ethnic minorities have been widely discriminated against through practices such as discriminatory land laws, lack of representation in Parliament, not being allowed to vote or having their names being taken off electoral lists.[71] The insurgency in the Chittagong

Hill Tracts (CHT) in south-west Bangladesh lasted twenty years, and provides an example where such 'ethnocultural factors [and] … faulty nation-building' combined with 'strategies undertaken by past and present governments, and inappropriate development projects' to create a violent crisis.[72] Although the insurgency ended when a peace treaty was signed between the government and the insurgents in 1997, the local hill people of CHT continue to be largely administered by the army, which is accused of widespread human rights violations. Refugees returning to CHT have been unable to reclaim land which was theirs, and the indigenous people continue to suffer discrimination and physical attacks from the Bangali community, which has been systematically settled into the area over decades.[73]

Despite having around 100 political parties, politics in Bangladesh has been dominated since independence by its two main parties, the BNP and the Awami League. Over the years, it became increasingly polarized around the leaders of these parties rather than ideologies, fuelled by the intense contempt and dislike each had for the other.[74] Forming governments soon became a 'winner takes all' situation, and as one party would come to power, the other would take its place in opposition with the sole purpose of bringing the government down.[75] Money and muscle power increasingly became the tools with which to win elections, yielding a corrupt and power-obsessed political and governance climate. Consequently, political violence has become a common tool for those in power to maintain control, for the opposition to create trouble for the government, and for the public to express grievances and demand attention from those who rule. The Awami League government promised to ensure good governance, transparency and accountability in its election manifesto, but since coming to power it has failed to deliver. It has been unable to stop extra-judicial killings and torture, and to rein in its youth and student wings, who have been involved in intra-party clashes. It has also failed to curb tender manipulation, extortion and violence in educational institutions, reflecting broadly 'the political culture of major political parties'.[76]

Criminal and violent political processes

The electoral process in Bangladesh has historically been violent, corrupt and tipped towards those with power. The system which has prevailed over the years has been one influenced 'not by the free will of the people, but by the manipulation of elections through money and muscle'.[77] Since independence, Bangladesh adopted a system of representation for its Parliament which followed the majoritarian first-past-the post (FPTP) system adopted by most Commonwealth countries.[78] Over the years, however, this system has 'failed to reflect [the] true opinion of the electorate in the distribution of seats in the Parliament elections' in relation to 'the percentage of votes received by the contesting parties in the elections held since the changeover in the 1990s'.[79] The influence of money and muscle over the system means a large number of the seats in Parliament are occupied by people from the business community. In a country where half the population lives below the poverty line, this is a glaring lack of representation. The situation is not helped by the fact that a candidate running for parliamentary elections is not required to be a resident of the constituency he or she is campaigning to represent. This effectively means that the chances of women candidates and those from poorer segments of society winning remain highly unlikely.

Consequently, these sections of Bangladeshi society have had little representation at the political level.[80] At present, 45 of the 345 seats in Parliament are reserved for women, and are allocated to parties in proportion to their overall share of the vote.[81] These parties then elect the candidates for the reserved seats. Such a system means that for women to have access to these seats they are dependent on those in the higher echelons of power within the political parties. While ethnic and religious minorities have faced added challenges to the right to cast their votes, critics and opponents of the ruling parties have also historically faced harassment and impediments to exercising their franchise.[82]

Weak institutions, corruption and a politicized judiciary

According to Subhash Kashyap, a key problem of governance in Bangladesh has been 'the inability to develop sustainable representative institutions that can provide a democratic and yet reasonably stable government'.[83] With every government has come the breaking down of institutions to rebuild new institutions which suit the political needs of the incoming regime.[84] Additionally, successive governments have done little to change the corrupt nature of these institutions as it has provided them with a means to further their own interests and agendas. The judiciary in Bangladesh has historically been exceptionally weak and unable to function as a non-partisan institution. This is because nepotism pervades politics in Bangladesh, and successive governments, particularly during Bangladesh's extended period of military rule, have rendered it a mere tool in the hands of those with money, power and influence. During the rule of General Ershad, Bangladesh was declared an Islamic state despite the constitution guaranteeing freedom of religion. Corruption was rampant and even encouraged. As Rehman reveals, 'The entire cabinet and most members of [Ershad's] Jatiya Party were motivated to join politics with the single-minded goal of holding public office and using state power to accumulate wealth ... Political power was nasty, brutish and short.'[85] Years of corrupt governance have led to a widespread politicization of the judiciary, arguably one of the most significant institutions for governance within a state. This created a scenario where a politician belonging to the party in power, or a government official, could make a call to a particular judge, demand a certain judgement and the judge would deliver. In 2005, the German watchdog Transparency International ranked Bangladesh as the world's most corrupt country for the fifth consecutive year.[86] Though it has since risen in the rankings, it remains the twelfth most corrupt country in the world.[87] It is widely acknowledged that corruption in the country is rife and that 'its roots lie deep in bureaucratic, business and political institutions'.[88] Previous surveys by Transparency International's Bangladesh arm (TIB) found that the police, revenue and land departments were the most corrupt among the country's public institutions.[89] Until 2004, Bangladesh's Anti-Corruption Bureau (ACB) was the key institutional mechanism for battling corruption. Ironically, the ACB itself became a symbol of corrupt institutions in Bangladesh, as it became:

> a totally dysfunctional agency ... said to have been used by successive governments, politicians and administrators or their allies either to victimize people belonging to opposing political camps or to frighten off competitors in the corruption game. The general public perception would seem to be that the ACB is not only a further source of corruption, but has actually increased the quantum of bribery and spread corruption to previously untainted areas.[90]

In 2004, the ACB was replaced with the Anti-Corruption Commission Act or ACC, which has since been amended once in 2007, and the Awami League government has proposed another set of twenty-three amendments to the Act recently. Concerns around political interference in the ACC's work also remain high, with organizations such as Transparency International Bangladesh (TIB) and the Bangladesh Human Rights Commission (BHRC) saying the recently proposed amendments – including the requirement of permission from the government to file cases against public officials, making the ACC accountable to the president, and for the ACC to no longer be a self-governed body – would deprive the body of its independence and neutrality.[91]

Administrative interference in the judiciary remains a feature of misgovernance in Bangladesh. This is despite the last CTG's work to separate the judiciary from the executive.[92] The courts in the country remain 'prone to corruption and severely backlogged; pretrial detention is lengthy, and many defendants lack counsel. The indigent have little access to justice through the courts.'[93] According to the Asian Centre for Human Rights,

> hundreds of juveniles are illegally held in prisons in contravention of the 1974 Children's Act. Suspects are routinely subjected to warrantless arrest and detention, demands for bribes, and physical abuse (including torture) at the hands of law enforcement officials. Torture is routinely used to extract confessions and intimidate political detainees.[94]

Bangladesh is a receiver of a huge amount of international aid towards development and eradicating poverty. A major proportion of these funds flow directly to the government institutions in charge of allocating them to appropriate institutions and organizations. However, much of this aid money goes straight into the pockets of those in government. According to one report, 'the country's politicians, bureaucrats, commission agents, consultants and construction contractors take away about 30 per cent ... of the total foreign aid' entering Bangladesh, while the high-income and middle-class groups in urban and rural areas receive about 20 per cent. The poor, who are the main target group of the aid, get only 25 per cent of the funds.[95]

Corruption in Bangladesh is facilitated by a number of factors, such as lack of transparency in government processes, undemocratic principles guiding political parties whose actions are guided by the desire to grab power by any means, the use of political power and positions of influence in government institutions for personal and political gain, and so on. It strips away vital opportunities from those individuals, communities and socio-economic groups which do not have positions of influence in the government and politics and belong to the lower strata of society, defined in terms of caste and socio-economic indicators. Corrupt practices deny basic services to citizens such as access to housing, health and education facilities, and often render them in worse-off situations unless they are able to bribe officials, or influence those in positions of power.[96] These problems are further intensified when combined with lack of adequate representation and partisan politics.

Bangladesh does, however, have a vibrant media, and an alert and active civil society and non-government organization (NGO) community. These actors have been increasingly expressing their concern about the high levels of insecurity in Bangladeshi society in relation to the problems discussed above. The following section analyses attempts made by three different NSAs in Bangladesh to raise aspects of misgovernance as security threats to the people of the country, and whether the securitization framework is able to identify these attempts as valid securitizing moves. The analysis concludes with key observations around how the framework can become more receptive to such attempts to securitize non-traditional security threats by NSAs.

Securitizing misgovernance in Bangladesh

As discussed earlier, the phenomenon of misgovernance is common to the countries of South Asia. Since the end of colonial rule in the region, states have battled with their respective state-building and nation-building processes. This has often inevitably involved resorting to authoritarian rule to suppress local identities and ethno-nationalistic movements which have been a key characteristic of the region. The plight of ethnic minorities and other socio-economic groups in the region has been exacerbated systematically through violent, partisan and corrupt political practices and institutions, adopted and maintained by political elites with vested interests. In Bangladesh, it is argued that people suffer the consequences of misgovernance in their daily lives to the extent that their security – in the widest sense referring to human security and in the strictest terms referring to physical survival from political violence – is threatened on a regular basis. The preceding analysis has identified the key aspects of misgovernance which are cited as the sources of these threats. Mainly, they include partisan politics, weak governance institutions, a corrupt and politicized judiciary, and an equally corrupt and violent electoral process.

Amongst those actors raising different aspects of misgovernance as threatening the security of people in Bangladesh are the country's media organizations. The following analysis examines the role of three key English-language national daily newspapers in raising misgovernance-related issues as threats to the security of the people of Bangladesh. As the analysis reveals, Securitization Theory is useful in identifying these actions as attempts to securitize misgovernance. Where it is less conclusive, however, is whether the issue of misgoverance may be considered successfully securitized, considering the nature of these securitizing actors and following the response from the public at large.

The Daily Star, New Age *and* The Bangladesh Today

Despite having suffered from the phenomenon of misgovernance for decades, Bangladesh has had an active print media which has flourished in recent years. It has been significant in offering an outlet for civil society to express its grievances and challenge the state in its actions. The print media played an important role in the mass movement of the people and the opposition in 1990 which brought down Bangladesh's last military ruler, General Ershad. Today, the print media continues to be bold and vigorous in its attempts to create public awareness and act as a forum for important debates around the country's future.[97] Before examining the role of *The Daily Star, New Age* and *The Bangladesh Today* in raising misgovernance-related issues as a matter of security, it is important to establish what kind of power an NSA such as a newspaper may hold in Bangladeshi society. This is because Securitization Theory stipulates that a key facilitating condition for a successful securitization is the 'social capital of the enunciator ... who must be in a position of authority, although this should not be defined as official authority'.[98] In general, this is a contentious issue, especially as social capital and authority are relative to the social contexts within which they may be located. For example, representatives of groups who are marginalized or discriminated against and abused in society may have social capital and authority within the groups they represent, but not necessarily among those groups whose abusive and discriminatory practices they may be challenging. Here, a sociological approach to analysing security practices is more insightful as it takes into account the socio-political contexts within which these actors are embedded, and the relative significance of their words and actions to their different audiences.

In order to understand the kind of power or authority actors such as the newspapers under observation may wield in society, it is helpful to identify the two forms of power – direct and indirect.[99] In this formulation, direct power refers to power as 'conduct-shaping', which is 'immediate, visible and behavioural, and is manifest in such practices as physical and psychological coercion, persuasion or blackmail'. Alternatively, indirect power refers to power which is 'context-shaping', and where power is 'mediated by, and instantiated in, structures ... Indirect power is evidenced in the capacity of a government, say, to pass legislation.'[100] Political communication analysts insist it is this form of power with which the media can be most identified.[101] For newspapers, a key means to influence public opinion is through 'editorials' which are projections of their own political identity and perspectives on current affairs. Editorials also '[seek] to articulate what the newspaper's editors believe to be the collective voice of its readers'. Thus, 'newspapers use their power as information disseminators to influence the policy-making environment; to move their readers in certain directions if they can, and to put pressure on decision-makers in government'.[102]

This context is useful in ascertaining the power a national newspaper may have in Bangladesh's socio-political setting. The *Daily Star*, *New Age*, and *The Bangladesh Today* are three of the most popular and influential English-language daily newspapers in Bangladesh. According to a number of Bangladesh specialists both at home and abroad, they are also among the best-informed.[103] *The Daily Star*'s sister publication in Bangla, called *Prothom Alo* (meaning 'first light'), is also the number one vernacular daily in the country. The editorials in *The Daily Star* are therefore considered a useful source of information and analyses with insights into the current socio-political mood in the country.[104] Over the last few years, the newspaper has consistently reported on activities in the academic and civil society spheres around the notion of good governance and human security.[105] Similarly, *New Age* and *The Bangladesh Today* are known as newspapers with their fingers firmly on the pulse of Bangladeshi politics and society, and are reputed as well-informed and influential press organs.

The ideas embedded within the concepts of misgovernance, state, societal and human security, and the links between them, have been underlying themes in articles published in all these three newspapers in recent years. Many analysts believe that through such articles, these newspapers along with other parts of the vernacular press have played a key role in highlighting political violence, lack of representation, and corruption within state institutions and the electoral process as real challenges to the security of Bangladeshi society. These efforts, together with the work of other actors such as national and international organizations, NGOs, research bodies and academic institutions, have helped make misgovernance a hotly debated issue in Bangladeshi politics and society, with an increasing number of state agencies and NSAs becoming involved in the issue-area in different ways.[106]

Between 2005 and 2007, *The Daily Star*'s assistant editor Zafar Sobhan wrote a series of editorials which carried a consistent underlying message of misgovernance (with all its aspects of corruption, weak judiciary and government institutions, and criminal and violent politics) being a key cause of insecurity in Bangladeshi society. On 25 February 2005, for example, Sobhan's column 'Straight Talk' focused on the socio-political situation in the light of the events of preceding months.[107] In the editorial, he argues

> we no longer enjoy the most fundamental of freedoms – the freedom from fear. If you cannot even go to campaign in your constituency without fear for your security – if you cannot hold a political rally for fear of death – then where can you go and what kind of politics can you engage in?[108]

Sobhan makes a direct link between recent terrorist attacks in Bangladesh and an unravelling of the democratic process in the country. He suggests that the collapse of 'meaningful participatory democracy' in Bangladesh has become a key threat to the security of Bangladeshi state and society:

To my mind there is no greater threat to both our short and long-term stability and security than that the democratic process seems to be breaking down and that the respect for democracy that has sustained and enriched us for the past decade and a half seems to be in retreat. To my mind this is the prism through which our choices should be viewed.[109]

Thus, Sobhan clearly frames the deteriorating state of governance and democracy in the country as a threat to society as well as the state, as exemplified by the bomb blasts which rocked the country in August 2004.[110] He cites a lack of freedom from fear as both a cause and a consequence of this development in Bangladesh.

Similarly, in 2007 Sobhan wrote an editorial titled 'Freedom from Fear' in the same column in *The Daily Star*.[111] At the time the article was published, a state of emergency had been in place in the country for four months since 11 January 2007, and a CTG was in place with parliamentary elections due at the end of the year. The editorial focused specifically on the state of governance in Bangladesh in previous decades and what kind of security Bangladeshis should expect and demand from their government in the coming times. In his own answer to the question, he relates

The security that we will not be killed in cross-fire. The security that we will not be subjected to any extra-judicial punishment. The security that we will not be subject to arbitrary arrest. The security that we will not have to worry about being disappeared ... [112]

Here, Sobhan once again implies a direct link between governance institutions and the way they operate, and the physical (and psychological) security of the people. He continues further to argue that 'freedom from fear' is the most crucial freedom a society can have. Again, he frames his argument around the importance of freedom from fear not just in terms of fear of physical harm or death from violence, but also in terms of fear from the threat of being persecuted unjustly, from the threat of a corrupt policing institution and from the threat of criminal politics. Sobhan's editorials evoked strong responses from readers, received in communications to Sobhan directly and indirectly.[113]

Misgovernance issues as security challenges facing the Bangladeshi state and society also cropped up frequently in editorials in *New Age* during the same period.[114] In a January 2005 editorial, for example, titled 'People's freedoms and development in Bangladesh', Qazi Kholiquzzaman Ahmad highlights that 'Governance in Bangladesh remains extremely poor, characterized by pervasive corruption, wastefulness, bureaucratic procrastination, lack of coordination, favouritism, and politically motivated decisions.'[115] He suggests that this has led to little or no transparency and accountability, and 'the country ... being run by a system which may be best described as "democratic autocracy" or "autocratic democracy" ... excluding the people at large'. Ahmad concludes by asking 'how to ensure that freedoms are actually enjoyed by the people of Bangladesh, whose unfreedoms and adversities are overwhelming ... '.[116] While Ahmed does not make an explicit link between security and misgovernance, he indicates that his editorial is inspired by Amartya Sen, co-Chair of the Commission on Human Security, and Sen's linking of human security with freedoms such as freedom from want and freedom from fear.[117]

Another example is 'Democracy and State Security', an unaccredited editorial in *New Age* on 28 January 2007, commenting on a report on human development in South Asia.[118] The writer argues that in the context of Bangladesh (as in other developing countries), 'injustice and disempowerment are the cause of conflict as much as its effect'.[119] The author insists that Bangladeshi society and state needed to take the cited report, which pointed to aspects of misgovernance as key causes of conflict, and economic and political instability in South Asian states, as a warning. The editorial urges that in the context of Bangladesh, 'democracy with its electivity must be restored within the shortest possible time preparatory to making democracy more mature, inclusive and sensitized'. This key task is described as a 'human need, security need as well'.[120] Thus, writing only days after the most recent state of emergency was imposed in Bangladesh, the columnist urgently calls for dealing with misgovernance issues such as lack of representation, corruption and criminal politics through a democratic system which is inclusive, representative and corruption-free for the security of Bangladeshi state as well as society.

On the first anniversary of this period of emergency, *The Bangladesh Today* published an editorial titled 'Where is the Emergency Leading Us?'.[121] In the article, the writer accuses the interim CTG (in power since January 2007) of plunging the country further into socio-political chaos since its inception. He argues that key elements within Bangladesh society, including the majority of the 'media, educationists, economists and the common citizenry' were of the opinion that the CTG had not only failed to deliver a safe and conducive environment for holding free and fair elections, 'it [had] in fact aggravated and accelerated the breakdown of our already fragile economic and social systems'. In dramatic language, he creates a link between the CTG's failings and the danger of socio-political tensions in the country exploding into political violence:

> We have a deteriorating economy imposing unending hardships on the people, pushing people, particularly the poorest section, to the limits of their physical and psychological endurance. As people reach those limits, they will invariably burst out, in frustration and blind anger, in waves of protests suffused with violence and like a bursting dam, they will destroy a state which has not been able to provide them with the minimum requisites for survival as human beings.

Thus, the author warns that unless the CTG improves its performance to provide the Bangladeshi people with the level and quality of governance they so desperately require, the country and society at large face the stark threat of political violence erupting on its streets, with the potential to produce widespread destruction of lives and property.

Impact of securitizing moves

To proponents of Human Security and Critical Security Studies (CSS), misgovernance is a phenomenon which creates deep insecurities for individuals and communities in Bangladesh on a daily basis. From a Human Security perspective, aspects of misgovernance threaten the ability of individuals to live without freedom from fear (e.g. of death, injury and disruption or destruction of livelihood from political violence, social or ethnic discrimination in political and electoral processes, etc.) and freedom from want (e.g. of basic necessities such as shelter, food, employment, healthcare, etc.). For CSS scholars, misgovernance represents severe constraints on the people of Bangladesh, which stop them from making the choices they would freely choose to make in their socio-political and economic capacities.

Using Securitization Theory, the question of whether or not misgovernance is a security threat to people in Bangladesh in objective terms becomes less significant. Instead, the focus is on whether the articulations of actors such as the newspapers under scrutiny may qualify as securitizing moves around the issue of misgovernance, and whether their attempts to securitize succeed or not. As securitizing actors, it may be argued that the newspapers within which the analysed articles were published have a degree of political and social influence in Bangladesh, by virtue of the indirect power of the media to influence public opinion and set agendas. In the context of Bangladesh, it is important to note that adult literacy stands at 56.5 per cent,[122] and among the literate, the vast majority are educated in the vernacular. The readers of these dailies, therefore, are those who belong to the middle class, upper middle class and elite groups in the country. However, despite the limited reach of the newspapers as English-language dailies, the fact remains that these are some of the most important newspapers in the country and their readers include government officials, bureaucrats, the research and analysis community, and the NGO sector. Moreover, the fact that *Prothom Alo*, *The Daily Star*'s sister publication, is the number one Bangla daily in the country supports *The Daily Star*'s status as an influential and significant newspaper, read not least by those who are in power, those who wish to be in power and those in civil society who see it as their voice. *Prothom Alo* is known to carry reports and editorials which are of the same political and editorial tone as those which are published in *The Daily Star*. In fact, the former is considered by some to push the governance agenda even more vigorously than its sister publication.[123]

The direct audience of each editorial appears to be implicit within the article. For example, throughout his editorials cited in *The Daily Star*, Sobhan makes direct appeals to the people of Bangladesh, identifying himself as one of them. He uses terms such as '*our* choices',[124] '*our* security and freeing *us* from fear', and '*we* ... as a nation'.[125] Similarly, in 'Where is the Emergency Leading Us?' in *The Bangladesh Today*, the author argues, 'Now that the entire *nation* has watched ... *we* can all get down to the business of surviving as individuals and as a collectivity ... '[126] In the *New Age* editorial titled 'Democracy and State Security', the author urges in the context of the Human Development Report, 'this is a warning bell for *us*'.[127]

Thus, it can be concluded that as a member of civil society, the author is referring to the citizens of Bangladesh. During the period within which the articles analysed were published, a state of emergency was imposed and the head of the CTG resigned shortly after announcing the move. It could be argued that the latter is the equivalent of a breaking of normal 'procedures and rules' in the process by which successive governments come into power in Bangladesh, although an argument which cites this development as an indication of misgovernance being successfully securitized is problematic on several counts.

While the status of the discussed newspapers as securitizing actors and the direct audiences of their securitizing moves may not be difficult to establish, the problem arises when trying to determine whether the phenomenon of misgovernance has been successfully securitized in Bangladesh. The Copenhagen School argues that a successful securitization consists of a *securitizing actor* making an argument regarding the priority and urgency of a threat and thereby '[breaking] free of procedures and rules he or she would otherwise be bound by'.[128] Exactly how a securitizing actor may do so remains unclear, however, mainly because of a lack of explanation of what 'breaking' normal 'procedures and rules' means. If this refers to breaking or overriding the law, then it may be argued that in articulating misgovernance as a security threat in Bangladesh, the relevant newspapers have done no such thing. Here, the Copenhagen School appears to be asking for the securitizing actor to also be the security *agent* (i.e. the actor who 'does' security).[129] This is problematic because if the above interpretation of breaking normal 'procedures and rules' is appropriate, then securitizing actors, such as media actors and others who do not have the legitimacy to go against the rule of law, by logic are incapable of doing so without actually violating the law and risking punishment from the ruling authorities. By this logic, only in instances where such actors break the law or go against official ordinance of some sort would a successful securitization be identified.

The Copenhagen School also contends that a successful securitization takes place only when a 'sufficient' audience has accepted the securitizing move(s) made in a particular context. By eliciting such an acceptance, the securitizing actor-agent can 'obtain permission to override rules that otherwise bind it'. This makes audience acceptance the critical enabling factor to the success of a securitization, yet the Copenhagen School is again ambiguous about how audience acceptance may be recognized or measured.[130] Several scholars have now focused on this weakness in the theoretical framework offered by the Copenhagen School, and subsequently suggested ways to reconceptualize the audience in the securitization process.[131] Most recently, Leonard and Kaunert have proposed a reconceptualization of the audience within the securitization process using Kingdon's 'three streams' framework of public policy.[132] They argue that the three streams – problem stream, policy stream and politics stream – should be included in the securitization framework 'in order to allow researchers to allow their conceptualisation of "the audience" as comprising different audiences … in the securitization framework'.[133] To them, these different streams and the audiences within are 'inter-linked as they are involved in a single policy-making process'.[134]

In the case of Bangladesh, it could be argued that the notion of misgovernance itself as a threat may have evolved out of securitizing moves around specific aspects of the phenomenon (such as corruption, lack of political representation, violent electoral politics) made by actors and accepted by – or rather, as Leonard and Kaunert point out, negotiated with – different relevant audiences.[135] In Bangladesh, it is safe to propose that the idea of misgovernance as a source of deep insecurity amongst Bangladeshi people has gained cognizance. To what extent this development can be attributed to the above-analysed editorials is, however, difficult to ascertain in any hard terms. Aspects of misgovernance such as corruption, weak government institutions, and violent electoral politics, etc. have been rife in Bangladesh since the country gained independence. Thus, the debate on governance-related issues in the country has been ongoing for almost four decades.[136] This provides credible grounds to contemplate whether securitizing moves by elements in the national press – vernacular and English-language – around misgovernance have been inspired by these debates or vice versa. The debate has also found contributors in the form of a host of foreign aid donors, international developmental agencies and governments, which are among the drivers of the 'good governance agenda' in Bangladeshi politics and society.[137] According to some analysts, it is a combination of these voices which has served to create a strong awareness in Bangladeshi society of the dangers of misgovernance, and to try to unravel which expressions have led to the sedimentation of this thinking, and inspired the other expressions in a greater or lesser way, is a convoluted task.[138]

As Wilkinson has argued, visualizing securitization as a linear process – i.e. a securitizing actor making a speech act around a particular threat which is then to be accepted or rejected by an audience (as suggested by the Copenhagen School) – is misleading, as it may 'in practice start at any point, with the component parts developing simultaneously and contributing to each other's construction'.[139] This argument could be extended further by the prospect that an audience acceptance – in terms of a cognizance around the phenomenon of misgovernance being an existential threat to the people of Bangladesh in their daily lives – may already exist prior to the securitizing moves in focus. In such a scenario, when a strong narrative on misgovernance as a threat to the people of Bangladesh, rooted in the direct and indirect experiences of the same in daily life, has already been established, the question arises: should analysts continue to look for the breaking of 'procedures and rules' (interpreted widely in the literature as 'emergency' public policy action by state agencies) in the wake of relevant speech acts as a qualifying condition for a successful securitization? In the case of Bangladesh, it may be argued that the imposition of a state of emergency further enabled securitizing actors to strengthen their arguments around the problems of misgovernance in the country and their impact on the security of average Bangladeshis. It is, however, difficult to consider this argument before resolving the question of the securitizing actor-agent ambiguity in Securitization Theory. The question remains – *who* needs to be breaking normal 'procedures and rules' in order to securitize the issue in question, and what exactly does this mean?

Conclusion

The phenomenon of misgovernance presents significant challenges to the people of Bangladesh in their daily lives. This has been widely recognized by different elements in Bangladeshi society, and the country's national media have been at the forefront of raising aspects of misgovernance as a challenge to the physical safety of the people of Bangladesh, as well as their social, political, economic, and even psychological well-being. A number of NGOs, civil society groups, educational institutions and think-tanks have also been identifying misgovernance issues in such a way and demanding greater action at the state level to deal with these challenges. Applying Securitization Theory to study the dynamics around securitizing misgovernance in Bangladesh gives insight into how actors such as national English-language daily newspapers in the country have been articulating issues of misgovernance as threats to the security of Bangladeshis. At the same time, it amplifies the continuing ambiguities within securitization studies around key aspects of Securitization Theory. The question of what signifies a successful securitization, for example, remains unresolved, as does the notion of breaking 'normal procedures and rules', and the role of the securitizing actor and the securitizing agent in this context. A lack of clarity around these issues risks attention being focused exclusively at the policy-making level, which offers an ideal fit for Securitization Theory with respect to its conditionalities. State authorities, for example, are relatively easily identified as securitizing actors and securitizing agents. Audiences at this level may also be more apparent, such as ruling authorities and specific policy-making bodies with whom negotiations may be undertaken, and policy change may be identified as the breaking of 'normal procedures and rules'. Such a focus inevitably results in the security analysis remaining tied to the security agenda of the state, rather than being inclusive of the security concerns of NSAs. In a socio-political context like that of Bangladesh, such an approach impoverishes the empirical analysis considerably and delivers a security assessment that resonates with the views and policies of predominantly state actors.

This analysis applies widely beyond Bangladesh, to the region of South Asia, as well as other similar developing socio-political contexts. As discussed, misgovernance is a problem of great proportion in South Asian countries, where democratic institutions and practices are in various stages of being established and implemented, to differing effects. Successive governments in the region have been consistently preoccupied with traditional security threats to regime security, sovereignty and territorial integrity. A preference for the realist view of security and the presence of weak governance institutions, widespread corruption, politicized judicial processes, lack of adequate political representation and violent electoral politics are common features of the type of governance South Asians have found themselves under for decades. The acute crisis of governance in Pakistan continues without any signs of ebbing in the near future, and persists as the cause of enormous insecurities in the daily lives of ordinary people in the country.[140] In Afghanistan, reconstruction efforts which have been ongoing since large amounts of aid began flowing into the country in 2002 to rebuild it from the ruins of its civil war have amounted to little, given 'the misgovernance, misrule and corruption' in the country.[141] The problem has been exacerbated by Afghanistan's own rising Taliban insurgency, which is surging to fill the vacuum in the absence of functioning and effective political and legal government institutions, as in the case of Pakistan.[142] In Sri Lanka, the government has succeeded in crushing the insurgency led by the LTTE using a sustained, ruthless military campaign since 2007, which brought chaos and bloodshed to the lives of hundreds of thousands. Yet it remains to be seen how the Sri Lankan state now approaches the genuine grievances of the country's Tamil minority, which led to the insurgency in the first place. In Nepal, a shaky truce ended the Maoist insurgency in 2006, and two years later a new Parliament, or Constituent Assembly (CA), was elected and given a two-year mandate to draft a new constitution. Unfortunately, the CA has failed to deliver even after it was granted a year's extension for the task, thanks to the ongoing power struggle between Nepal's major political parties. As a constitutional crisis looms, the people of Nepal once again find themselves on the brink of a political conflict, and living under the threat of political violence.[143] Even in India, considered a beacon of democracy in South Asia, misgovernance is a widespread phenomenon and has contributed, for example, to fuelling the violent Maoist insurgency affecting twenty of the country's twenty-eight states.[144] Ordinary people trapped between the Maoists and state forces live deeply insecure lives, in fear of being caught in the crossfire and with little or no access to the most basic infrastructure and facilities.[145]

While symptoms of misgovernance such as insurgencies and worsening law and order situations have been cited as security threats by state actors in South Asia, underlying causes of the problem, i.e. different aspects of misgovernance, are often neglected by these actors. NSAs in the region, such as media actors and NGOs, have often been at the forefront of identifying misgovernance issues as sources of insecurity for sub-state communities and groups. In the next chapter, the role of NGOs in Nepal is analysed with respect to their efforts not only to highlight the phenomenon of human trafficking as a source of insecurity to vulnerable and affected groups in Nepal, but also to provide these groups with the means to protect themselves from being trafficked, and to deal with the insecurities of being a trafficking survivor, among other things.

Notes

1 Wæver et al. (1993), in K. Krause and M. Williams, 'Broadening the Agenda of Security Studies: Politics and Methods', *Mershon International Studies Review*, vol. 40, no. 2, Oct. 1996, p. 243.
2 B. Buzan, O. Wæver and J. de Wilde, *Security: A New Framework for Analysis*, Boulder, CO: Lynne Rienner, 1998, p. 119.
3 The authors clarify that 'societal' in their use of the term does not refer to the entire population of a country, e.g. Bangladeshi society (which in itself may contains many societal units). For them, societal refers to 'communities with which one identifies'. For more, see ibid., p. 120.
4 Ibid., p. 121.
5 L. Hansen, 'The Little Mermaid's Silent Security Dilemma and the Absence of Gender in the Copenhagen School', *Millennium*, vol. 29, no. 2, 2000, p. 290.

6 K. Booth, *Theory of World Security*, Cambridge: Cambridge University Press, 2007, pp. 106–7.

7 P. Le Gales and J. Leca in A. Kazancigil, 'Governance and Science: Market-Like Modes of Managing Society and Producing Knowledge', *International Social Science Journal*, vol. 50, no. 155, Mar. 1998, p. 69.

8 Rhodes (1996), in G. Stoker, 'Governance as Theory: Five Propositions', *International Social Science Journal*, vol. 50, no. 155, Mar. 1998, p. 17.

9 J. P. Gaudin, 'Modern Governance, Yesterday and Today: Some Clarifications to be Gained from French Policies', *International Social Science Journal*, vol. 50, no. 155, Mar. 1998, pp. 47–56. For more, see M.C. Smouts, 'The Proper Use of Governance in International Relations', *International Social Science Journal*, vol. 50, no. 155, Mar. 1998, pp. 81–89.

10 The first three subsets identified here are as mentioned in H. Z. Rehman (ed.), 'Unbundling Governance: Bangladesh Governance Report 2007', *Power and Participation Research Centre (PPRC)*, Dhaka: PPRC, 2007.

11 Ibid. For example, see P. Landell-Mills and I. Seregeldin, 'Governance and the External Factors', *Proceedings of the 1991 World Bank Annual Conference on Economic Development*, Washington DC: World Bank, 1991; M. Haq, *Human Development in South Asia 1999: The Crisis of Governance*, Karachi: Oxford University Press, 1999 and 'Our Global Neighbourhood', *Report of The Commission on Global Governance*, Oxford University Press: Oxford, 1995.

12 For example, see 'Governance Matters 2007: Worldwide Governance Indicators 1996–2006', *The Worldwide Governance Indicators (WBI) Project*. Online. HTTP: <http://info.worldbank.org/governance/wgi2007/> (accessed 1 Oct. 2009). Other existing indicators include Transparency International's *Corruption Perception Index*, Freedom House's *Index of Political Freedom and Civil Liberties*, the *International Country Risk Guide* (ICRG) indicators produced for sale by the PRS Group of Syracuse, New York, and the *Business Environmental Risk Intelligence* indicators of BERI, Washington D.C., USA.

13 For example, see R. Bates, *States and Markets in Tropical Africa*, Berkeley: University of California Press, 1981; N. Douglas, *Institutions, Institutional Change and Economic Performance*, Cambridge: Cambridge University Press, 1990 and H. de Sotto, *The Other Path: The Invisible Revolution in the Third World*, New York: Harper and Row, 1989. For empirical analyses, see P. Keefer and S. Knack, 'Why Don't Poor Countries Catch Up? A Cross-Country Test for an Institutional Explanation', *Economic Enquiry*, vol. 35, no. 3, 1997, pp. 590–602, and P. Mauro, 'Corruption and Growth', *Quarterly Journal of Economics*, vol. 110, 1995, pp. 681–712.

14 For example, see R. Sobhan, 'Problems of Governance in South Asia: An Overview', in V. A. P. Panandikar (ed.), *Problems of Governance in South Asia*, Dhaka: University Press Limited, 2000, pp. 3–5.

15 For example, see C. Thomas, *Global Governance, Development and Human Security*, London: Pluto, 2000; D. Lamberton, *Managing the Global: Globalization, Employment and Quality of Life*, London: I. B. Tauris in association with the Toda Institute for Global Peace and Policy Research, 2002; S. J. MaClean, D. R. Black and T. M. Shaw (eds), *A Decade of Human Security: Global Governance and New Multilateralisms*, Ashgate: Aldershot, 2006, and P. R. Chari (ed.), *Alternative Approaches to Security: National Integration, Governance, Non-Military Challenges*, Dhaka: The University Press Limited, 2000.

16 For more discussion of the concept of 'ideal type', see G. B. Pepper, 'A Re-Examination of the Ideal Type Concept', *The American Catholic Sociological Review*, vol. 24, no. 3, Autumn, 1963, pp. 185–201; W. J. Cahnman, 'Ideal Type Theory: Max Weber's Concept and Some of Its Derivations', *Sociological Quarterly*, vol. 6, no. 3, Summer, 1965, pp. 268–80; B. Nefzger, 'The Ideal-Type: Some Conceptions and Misconceptions', *Sociological Quarterly*, vol. 6, no. 2, Spring, 1965, pp. 166–74; S. J. Hekman, 'Weber's Ideal Type: A Contemporary Reassessment', *Polity*, vol. 16, no. 1, Autumn, 1983, pp. 119–37; and D. McIntosh, 'The Objective Bases of Max Weber's Ideal Types', *History and Theory*, vol. 16, no. 3, Oct. 1977, pp. 26–79.

17 M. Weber, *The Methodology of the Social Sciences*, New York: Free Press, 1949, p. 90.

18 As listed by Sobhan in Panandikar (ed.), *Problems of Governance*, p. 2.

19 M. Haq, 'Human Development Report in South Asia 1999 – The Crisis of Governance', Mahbub ul Haq Human Development Centre, 1999, p. 3, 7. Online. HTTP: <http://www.mhhdc.org/reports/HDRSA%201999.pdf> (accessed 12 Oct. 2009).

20 As reflected in interviews with social commentators, analysts and security experts in New Delhi, Dhaka, Nepal and London, Jul.–Aug. 2007.

21 P. R. Chari, 'Security and Governance in South Asia: Their Linkages', in P.R. Chari (ed.), *Security and Governance in South Asia*, Manohar: New Delhi, 2001, pp. 14–15.

22 V.A.P. Panandiker, 'Introduction', in Panandiker (ed.), *Problems of Governance* , p. xi.

23 V. Marwah, 'Rise in Violence and Governance in South Asia', in Panandiker (ed.), *Problems of Governance*, p. 231.

24 Ibid. Also see M. Shehzad, 'The South Asian Paradox', *Frontline*, vol. 20, no. 3, Feb. 2003. Online. HTTP: <http://www.hinduonnet.com/fline/fl2003/stories/20030214010508000.htm> (accessed 6 Dec. 2007).

25 V. Marwah, 'Rise of Violence and Governance in South Asia', in Panandiker (ed.), *Problems of Governance*, p. 229.

26 Ibid.

27 Ibid., p. 230. Also see S. M. Gurung, 'Good Governance, Participation, Gender and Disadvantaged Groups', *Dialogue on National Strategies for Sustainable Development in Nepal*, 23 Dec. 2000. In the report, the author argues that the Maoist insurgency in Nepal was

> clearly associated with poor governance and the dissatisfaction of rank and file people who have been affected by it on a daily basis. Associated with it is the lack of law and order and security in the country, which [forced] people to join the Maoist movement and retaliate against the government.

28 See 'National Security Internal & External Dimensions for India', *India International Centre ARSIPSO Seminar Summary*; P. R. Chari and S. Gupta (eds), *Human Security in South Asia: Gender, Migration and Globalisation*, New Delhi: Social Science Press, 2003; M. Joseph, 'Security Threat Assessment of Naxalites in India', *IPCS*, 15 Aug. 2001. Online. HTTP: <http://www.ipcs.org/article/naxalite-violence/security-threat-assessment-of-naxalites-in-india-541.html> (accessed 23 Oct. 2009) and R. Sobhan, 'South Asia's Weak Development: The Role Of Governance', *Centre for Policy Dialogue Dhaka*, November 1999. Online. HTTP: <http://www.cias.org/publications/briefing/1999/weakdev.pdf.pdf> (accessed 23 Oct. 2009).

29 That is, the overarching national government, as opposed to federal states or districts within the country, such as India and its states of Punjab, Gujarat and Tamil Nadu, etc.

30 Interviews in New Delhi, Kathmandu and Dhaka. Also see R. Chanda, 'Internal Politics in Bangladesh: An Insight', *IPCS*, 4 Oct. 1999. Online. HTTP: <http://www.ipcs.org/article/bangladesh/internal-politics-in-bangladesh-an-insight-269.html> (accessed 23 Oct. 2009) and 'Authoritarianism and Political Party Reform in Pakistan', *International Crisis Group*, no. 102, 28 Sept. 2005. Online. HTTP: <http://www.crisisgroup.org/en/regions/asia/south-asia/pakistan/102-authoritarianism-and-political-party-reform-in-pakistan.aspx> (accessed 27 Oct. 2009). For an understanding of the development of democracy in South Asia in a comparative perspective, see A. Jalal, *Democracy and Authoritarianism in South Asia: A Comparative and Historical Perspective*, Cambridge: Cambridge University Press, 1995.

31 Interviews with South Asia experts in New Delhi, Kathmandu, Dhaka and London. See 'Insecurity of the Marginalised', in 'Democracy: Object of Desire', *Special Report in Himal South Asian*, vol. 20, no. 1, Jan. 2007. The article discusses the key findings of 'State of Democracy in South Asia: A Report', *Prepared by the Centre for the Study of*

Developing Societies (CSDS) New Delhi in collaboration with International IDEA and the Department of Sociology, Oxford University, 4 Dec. 2006.

32 As identified in 'State of Democracy in South Asia: A Report', *CSDS.*

33 Interviews with security experts in New Delhi.

34 For more, See 'Bad Governance Breeds Militancy, Says Expert', *The Tribune*, 22 Oct. 2007.

35 For more on the inter-linkages between ethnic communities involved in conflict in South Asia, see P. Sahadevan, 'Ethnic Conflict and Militarism in South Asia', *Kroc Institute Occasional Paper*, vol. 16, Joan B. Kroc Institute for International Peace Studies, University of Notre Dame, June 1999. Online. HTTP: <http://www.ciaonet.org/wps/sap01/> (accessed 5 Dec. 2009).

36 R. Gunaratna, *Indian Intervention in Sri Lanka: The Role of India's Intelligence Agencies*, Colombo: South Asian Network on Conflict Research, 1994, pp. 92–93. For a detailed discussion of India's role in Sri Lanka's ethnic conflict, see S.D. Muni, *Pangs of Proximity: India and Sri Lanka's Ethnic Crisis*, New Delhi: Sage Publications, 1993; D. Jayatilleka, *The Indian Intervention in Sri Lanka, 1987–1990: The North-East Provincial Council and Devolution of Power*, Kandy: International Centre for Ethnic Studies, 1991; R.K. Dubey, *Indo-Sri Lankan Relations with Special Reference to the Tamil Problem*, New Delhi: Deep & Deep Publications, 1989; S. Bose, *States, Nations and Sovereignty: Sri Lanka, India and the Tamil Eelam Movement*, New Delhi: Sage Publications, 1994; and R. Manivannan, *Shadows of a Long War: Indian Intervention in Sri Lanka*, New Delhi: Kumar & Manivannan, 1988.

37 For more on Pakistan's role in the insurgency in Indian-administered Kashmir in the 1990s, see P. Chalk, 'Pakistan's Role in the Kashmir Insurgency', *Jane's Intelligence Review*, 1 Sept. 2001. Online. HTTP: <http://www.rand.org/commentary/090101JIR.html> *(accessed 12 Oct. 2010).*

38 Interviews with South Asia experts in New Delhi.

39 Interviews in New Delhi, Kathmandu and Dhaka. For more on corruption in South Asia, see R.J. May and B. Ray (eds), *Corruption, Governance and Democracy in South Asia: Bangladesh, India and Pakistan*, Kolkata: Towards Freedom, 2006; T. Lindsey and H. Dick, *Corruption in Asia: Rethinking the Governance Paradigm*, Annadale: Freedom Press, 2002 and Haq, 'Human Development in South Asia 1999'. For more on corruption in government institutions in the region, see S.C. Kashyap, *Institutions of Governance in South Asia*, New Delhi: Konark Publishers, 2000.

40 Interviews in Dhaka.

41 See S. Bhaumik, 'Mob Attacks India Grain Warehouse', *BBC News*, 18 Sept. 2007. Online. HTTP: <http://news.bbc.co.uk/2/hi/south_asia/7000535.stm> (accessed 6 Dec. 2007) and 'Minister Vows to Root Out Corruption in PDS', *The Hindu Online*, 28 May 2006. Online. HTTP: <http://www.hinduonnet.com/thehindu/2006/05/28/stories/2006052812270100.htm> (accessed 6 Dec. 2009).

42 C.P. Anderson, 'Causes and Consequences of the Maoist Rebellion in Nepal: 1996–2006', *International Affairs Journal at UC Davis*, vol. 3, no. 2, Winter 2007.

43 In A. Mohsin, 'Governance and Security: The Experience of Bangladesh', in Chari (ed.), *Security and Governance*, p. 21.

44 See M. Rashiduzzaman, 'Political Unrest and Democracy in Bangladesh', *Asian Survey*, vol. 37, no. 3, Mar. 1997, pp. 254–68; M. Ahmed, *Democracy and the Challenge of Development: A Study of Politics and Military Interventions in Bangladesh*, Dhaka: University Press Ltd., 1995 and T. Maniruzzaman, *Politics and Security of Bangladesh*, Dhaka: University Press Ltd., 1994.

45 'Bangladesh Today', *International Crisis Group Report*, 23 Oct. 2006, p. 3. Online. HTTP: <http://www.crisisgroup.org/home/index.cfm?id=4462> (accessed 27 May 2009).

46 Ibid. For more on Bangladesh under military rule, see E. Ahmed, 'The Military and Democracy in Bangladesh', in R.J. May and V. Selochan, *The Military and Democracy in Asia and the Pacific*, Canberra: ANU E-Press, 2004.

47 See I. Ahmed, 'Bangladesh: Amid Hope and Despair', *South Asia Journal*, vol. 13, July–Sept. 2006. Online. HTTP: <http://www.southasianmedia.net/magazine/journal/13_amid-hope.htm> (accessed 15 Mar. 2008).

48 For a discussion of the CTG system in Bangladesh and what brought it about, see 'Reform of the Caretaker Government', *Keynote paper given by Shah A.M.S. Kibria at a seminar organized by Bangladesh Foundation for Development Research (BFDR)*, 31 Jan. 2005. Online. HTTP: <http://www.kibria.org/publications/caretaker_govt.pdf> (accessed 12 Mar. 2008).

49 See J. Huggler, 'Bangladesh Gripped By Rioting As Political Rivalry Threatens Election', *The Independent*, 8 January 2007. Online. HTTP: <http://news.independent.co.uk/world/asia/article2134843.ece> (*accessed 4 Oct.* 2007) and W. Rahman, 'Is Bangladesh Heading Towards Disaster?', *BBC News*, 8 Jan. 2007. Online. HTTP: <http://news.bbc.co.uk/2/hi/south_asia/6241263.stm> (accessed 4 Oct. 2009).

50 See S. Samad, 'Awami League and Its Allies Said They Will Boycott Forthcoming Parliamentary Elections', *Durdesh Weekly*, 3 Jan. 2007; 'Grand Alliance Boycotts Jan 22 Election', *The Daily Star*, 4 Jan. 2007. Online. HTTP: <http://www.thedailystar.net/2007/01/04/d7010401011.htm> (accessed 4 Oct. 2009) and 'Hasina Urges People to Resist Jan 22 Elections', *New Age*, 5 Jan. 2007. Online. HTTP: <http://www.bangladesh-web.com/view.php?hidRecord=144963> (accessed 10 Oct. 2009).

51 'Army to Stop Election Violence', *BBC News*, 4 Jan. 2007. Online. HTTP: <http://news.bbc.co.uk/2/hi/south_asia/6230965.stm> (accessed 4 Oct. 2009).

52 See 'Bangladesh: EU Commission Suspends Election Observation Mission', *European Commission*, 11 Jan. 2007. Online. HTTP: <http://www.europa-eu-un.org/articles/en/article_6669_en.htm> (accessed 10 Oct. 2009) and N. Islam, 'Military Role May Bear on Dhaka's Peacekeeping UN, EU Suspend Election Observation missions', *New Age*, 12 Jan. 2007.

53 'Emergency Declared; Iajuddin Quits As Chief Adviser', *The Daily Star*, 12 Jan. 2007. Online. HTTP: <http://thedailystar.net/2007/01/12/d7011201011.htm> (accessed 10 Oct. 2009) and P. Foster and R. Zaman, 'Riots Halt Bangladesh Elections', *The Telegraph*, 12 Jan. 2007. Online. HTTP: <http://www.telegraph.co.uk/news/main.jhtml?xml=/news/2007/01/12/wbangla12.xml> (accessed 4 Oct. 2009).

54 'Bangladesh Leader Vows Crackdown', *BBC News*, 22 Jan. 2007. Online. HTTP: <http://news.bbc.co.uk/2/hi/south_asia/6285685.stm> (accessed 10 Oct. 2009).

55 'Bangladesh "Will Lift Emergency"', *BBC News*, 10 Dec. 2008. Online. HTTP: <http://news.bbc.co.uk/2/hi/south_asia/7776085.stm> (accessed 12 Jan. 2009); 'Bangladesh State of Emergency Lifted', *The Age*, 18 Dec. 2008. Online. HTTP: <http://www.theage.com.au/world/bangladeshs-state-of-emergency-lifted-20081217-70q9.html> (accessed 12 Jan. 2009) and 'Bangladesh Emergency Laws Lifted', *Al Jazeera*, 17 Dec. 2008. Online. HTTP: <http://english.aljazeera.net/news/asia/2008/12/2008121620156401684.html> (accessed 12 Jan. 2009).

56 Hasina's first stint as PM was between 1996 and 2001.

57 This was despite international monitors declaring the results largely free and fair, and 'accurately [reflecting] the will of Bangladeshi voters'. See 'Bangladesh Results Seen As Fair, Though Loser Disputes Results', *International Herald Tribune*, 30 Dec. 2008. Online. HTTP: <http://www.iht.com/articles/2008/12/30/asia/bangla.php> (accessed 12 Jan. 2009) and 'Bangladesh Election Winner Urges Loser to Concede', *International Herald Tribune*, 31 Dec. 2008. Online. HTTP: <http://www.iht.com/articles/ap/2008/12/31/asia/AS-Bangladesh-Election.php> (*accessed 12 Jan.* 2009).

58 S. Liton and R. Hasan, 'BNP Pledges to Work with Govt for Nation's Progress', *The Daily Star*, 2 Jan. 2009. Online. HTTP: <http://www.thedailystar.net/newDesign/news-details.php?nid=71529> (accessed 19 Jan. 2009).

59 See 'Politics of Hate: An Ancient Vendetta Continues To Eat Away At Public Life', *The Economist*, 10 Nov. 2010. Online. HTTP: <http://www.economist.com/node/

17525830> (accessed 20 Apr. 2011). Also see 'Present "EC" Must Go: Khaleda', *The Daily Star*, 1 May 2011. Online. HTTP: <http://www.thedailystar.net/newDesign/latest_news.php?nid=29590> (accessed 2 May 2011).
60 'Bangladesh Today', *International Crisis Group*, p. 3. Also see 'Bangladesh Has a Population of 164.4 Million: UN', *Sify News*, 21 Oct. 2010. Online. HTTP: <http://www.sify.com/news/bangladesh-has-a-population-of-164-4-million-un-news-international-kkvpawhdead.html> (accessed 20 Apr. 2011).
61 H. Wiebe, 'Flood Action Plan in Bangladesh', *Contributing Paper, Northwest Hydraulic Consultants, Canada*. Online. HTTP: <http://www.slideshare.net/willwilliams7/bangladesh-flood-action-plan> (accessed 23 Oct. 2007).
62 C. Duenas, 'Water Champion: Hamidur Khan on Flood Management – Coping with the Worst of Floods', *Asia Development Bank*, August 2004. Online. HTTP: <http://www.adb.org/Water/Champions/khan.asp#footnote> (accessed 6 Oct. 2009).
63 'Bangladesh: Flood Waters Recede, But Challenges Remain', *IRIN Humanitarian News and Analysis*, 27 Aug. 2007. Online. HTTP: <http://www.irinnews.org/report.aspx?ReportId=73966> (accessed 23 Oct. 2007) and M. Khan and M. Rahman, 'Partnership Approach to Disaster Management in Bangladesh: A Critical Policy Assessment', *Natural Hazards*, vol. 41, no. 2, May 2007, p. 359.
64 'Human Rights Report 2010', *Odhikar Report on Bangladesh*, 1 Jan 2011, p. 4. Online. HTTP: <http://www.odhikar.org/documents/2010/English_Reports/Annual_Human_Rights_Report_2010_Odhikar.pdf> (accessed 12 Apr. 2011).
65 Mohsin in Chari (ed.), *Security and Governance*, p. 22.
66 See 'Weak Governance, Judiciary Root Cause of Human Insecurity', *The Daily Star*, 26 Jan. 2007. Online. HTTP: <http://www.thedailystar.net/2007/01/26/d70126060171.htm> (accessed 12 Nov. 2009). Also, as pointed out in interviews with analysts at PPRC, Bangladesh Centre for Advanced Studies (BCAS) in Dhaka, Research Initiative Bangladesh and the Manusher Jonno Foundation, Dhaka, 21 Aug. 2007.
67 Interviews in Dhaka. Also see S. Datta, 'Bangladesh's Political Evolution: Growing Uncertainties', *Strategic Analysis*, vol. 27, no. 2, Apr.–Jun. 2003. Online. HTTP: <http://www.idsa.in/publications/strategic-analysis/2003/april/Sreeradha%20Datta.pdf> (accessed 12 Mar. 2010) and 'Political Unrest and Democracy in Bangladesh', *Asian Survey*, vol. 37, no. 3, Mar. 1997, pp. 254–68.
68 Mohsin in Chari (ed), *Security and Governance*, p. 23.
69 Ibid. Also see T. Maniruzzaman, 'Bangladesh Politics: Secular and Islamic Trends', in R. Ahmed (ed.), *Religion, Nationalism and Politics in Bangladesh*, New Delhi: South Asian Publishers, 1990.
70 For a detailed discussion of the treatment of ethnic minorities in Bangladesh, see S. Samad, 'State of Minorities in Bangladesh: From Secular to Islamic Hegemony', *Country Paper presented at 'Regional Consultation on Minority Rights in South Asia' organised by South Asian Forum for Human Rights (SAFHR)*, Kathmandu, Nepal, 20–22 Aug. 1998. Online. HTTP: <http://www.sacw.net/DC/CommunalismCollection/ArticlesArchive/ssamad_Bangaldesh.html> (accessed 23 Sept. 2009).
71 For example, see R. Thakur, 'Minorities, Women and Elections in Bangladesh – Part-II', *Asian Tribune*, 17 Oct. 2007. Online. HTTP: <http://www.asiantribune.com/index.php?q=node/7845> (accessed 6 Dec. 2009).
72 S. Aziz-al Hasan and B. Chakma, 'Problems of National Integration in Bangladesh', *Asian Survey*, vol. 29, no. 10 Oct. 1989, pp. 960–61.
73 'Freedom in the World – Bangladesh', *Freedom House*, 16 Apr. 2007. Online. HTTP: <http://www.unhcr.org/cgi-bin/texis/vtx/refworld/rwmain?docid=473c55ad48> (accessed 10 Dec. 2009).
74 See J. Alamgir, 'We Need Local Leaders Not National Personalities', *The Daily Star*, 15 Feb. 2007. Online. HTTP: <http://www.thedailystar.net/2007/02/15/d70215020324.htm> (accessed 24 Oct. 2009); N. Rahman, 'A Civil War of the Soul', *Forum*, vol. 2, no. 1, Jan. 2007. Online. HTTP: <http://www.thedailystar.net/forum/2007/january/

civil.htm> (accessed 23 Oct. 2007); 'Analysis: A Tale of Two Women', *BBC News*, 2 Oct. 2001. Online. HTTP: <http://news.bbc.co.uk/2/hi/south_asia/1575704.stm> (accessed 12 Oct. 2007).

75 T. Hashmi, 'Power Politics in Bangladesh', *Countercurrents.org*, 16 Nov. 2006. Online. HTTP: <http://www.countercurrents.org/bangla-hashmi160107.htm> (accessed 12 Mar. 2008).

76 'Human Rights Report 2010', Odhikar, p. 4.

77 M. R. Chowdhury, 'Bangladesh State Emergency an Opportunity', *Washington Post*, 7 May 2007. Online. HTTP: <http://newsweek.washingtonpost.com/postglobal/needtoknow/2007/05/bangladeshs_political_emergenc.html> (accessed 6 Dec. 2009).

78 R. K. Menon, 'A Case for Proportional Representation', *The Daily Star*, 31 Jan. 2004. Online. HTTP: <http://www.thedailystar.net/suppliments/anni2004/demo_04.html> (accessed 6 Dec. 2009).

79 Ibid.

80 Mohsin in Chari (ed.), *Security and Governance*, pp. 22–39.

81 'Bangladesh Parliament', *National Web Portal of Bangladesh*. Online. HTTP: < http://www.bangladesh.gov.bd/index.php?option=com_content&task=view&id=116&Itemid=190> (accessed 10 Mar. 2010)

82 Interviews with South Asia experts in New Delhi and London. Also see K. Hossain, 'Struggling for Democracy 1986–2006', *Forum*, 21 Jan. 2007. Online. HTTP: <http://www.thedailystar.net/forum/2006/november/struggling.htm> (accessed 12 Mar. 2010).

83 Kashyap, *Institutions of Governance in South Asia*, p. 18.

84 Ibid.

85 Ibid., p.10.

86 'Transparency International Corruption Perceptions Index 2005', *Transparency International*, 2005. Online. HTTP: <http://www.transparency.org/news_room/in_focus/2005/cpi_2005#cpi> (accessed 30 Nov. 2010). Also see M. Rahman, S. Hossain and F. Ahmed, *Endemic Corruption in Bangladesh: A Handful of Corrupt Hurt Millions*, Dhaka: News Network, p. 7.

87 'Transparency International Corruption Perceptions Index 2010', *Transparency International*, 2010. Online. HTTP: <http://www.transparency.org/policy_research/surveys_indices/cpi/2010/results> (accessed 30 Nov. 2010). Also see 'Graft level Stays Same', *The Daily* Star, 27 Oct. 2010. Online. HTTP: <http://www.thedailystar.net/newDesign/news-details.php?nid=160096> (accessed 12 Jan. 2011).

88 'Corruption in the Public Sector: Its Manifestations, Causes and Suggested Remedies', *Report by Transparency International Bangladesh*. Online. HTTP: <http://www.ti-bangladesh.org/index.php?page_id=338> (accessed 11 Nov. 2009).

89 'Bangladesh Tops Most Corrupt List', *BBC News*, 18 Oct. 2005. Online. HTTP: <http://news.bbc.co.uk/2/hi/south_asia/4353334.stm> (accessed 11 Nov. 2009).

90 'Corruption in the Public Sector', *Transparency International Bangladesh*.

91 For example, see 'Amendment to Strip ACC of Freedom: TIB', *BDnews24.com*, 29 Jan. 2011. Online. HTTP: <http://www.bdnews24.com/details.php?id=185894&cid=2> *(accessed 19 Feb.* 2011) and 'Graft Level Stays Same', *The Daily Star*.

92 'Freedom in the World – Bangladesh', *Freedom House*, 2010. Online. HTTP: <http://www.freedomhouse.org/template.cfm?page=22&year=2010& country=7778> (accessed 12 Jan. 2011).

93 Ibid.

94 Ibid.

95 Ahmed, *Endemic Corruption in Bangladesh*, p. 13.

96 See 'Human Security in Bangladesh: Recent Trends and Responses', *Centre for Policy Dialogue*, no. 77, November 2003. Online. HTTP: <http://www.cpd.org.bd/pub_attach/DR-77.pdf> (accessed 14 Jan. 2011).

97 It is important to note that during the last emergency period between January 2007 and December 2008, there were incidences where newspapers critical of the establishment

faced intimidation from the authorities. Consequently, the press in general exercised a certain amount of caution when criticizing the CTG's actions and politics.

98 Buzan et al., *Security: A New Framework for Analysis*, p. 33.
99 C. Hay, *Political Analysis*, New York: Palgrave, 2002, pp. 184–87. For more on power as a concept and relevant critiques, see P. Bachrach and M. S. Baratz, 'Two Faces of Power', *The American Political Science Review*, vol. 56, no. 4, Dec. 1962, pp. 947–52; R. A. Dahl, 'The Concept of Power', *Behavioural Science*, vol. 2, no. 3, 1957, pp. 201–15; N. W. Polsby, *Community Power and Political Theory* (2nd edn), New Haven: Yale University Press, 1980; R. A. Dahl, 'A Critique of the Ruling-Elite Model', *American Political Science Review*, vol. 52, no. 2, June 1958, pp. 463–69; L. J. R. Herson, 'In the Footsteps of Community Power', *American Political Science Review*, vol. 51, Dec. 1961, pp. 817–31; R. Merelman, 'On the Neo-Elitist Critique of Community Power', *American Political Science Review*, vol. 62, no. 2, 1968, pp. 451–60 and S. Lukes, *Power: A Radical View* (2nd edn), New York: Palgrave Macmillan, 2005.
100 Hay, *Political Analysis*, p. 186.
101 For example, see B. McNair, *An Introduction to Political Communication*, Abingdon: Routledge, 2003, and M. McCombs, *The Agenda-Setting Role of the Mass Media in the Shaping of Public Opinion*, Oxford: Polity Press, 2004, pp. 4–5.
102 McCombs, *The Agenda-Setting Role of the Mass Media*, pp. 4–5.
103 As pointed out by academics, journalists, civil society representatives and other analysts in the course of research.
104 Ibid.
105 For example, see A. M. M. Shawkat Ali, 'What are the signposts of a Failed State?', *The Daily Star*, 11 May 2004. Online. HTTP: <http://www.thedailystar.net/2004/05/11/d40511020330.htm> (accessed 10 Dec. 2009); E. Kabir, 'Why Small Arms Jeopardise Human Security', *The Daily Star*, 23 Sept. 2004. Online. HTTP: <http://www.thedailystar.net/2004/09/23/d40923020527.htm> (accessed 10 Dec. 2009); A. Bayes, 'Beyond the Border Basics', *The Daily Star*, September 28, 2004; 'Strong Democratic Institutions a Must to Face External Threats', *The Daily Star*, 30 Mar. 30 2005. Online. HTTP: <http://www.thedailystar.net/2005/03/30/d50330060269.htm> (accessed 10 Dec. 2009) and Z. Sobhan, 'Freedom from Fear', *The Daily Star*, 4 May 2007. Online. HTTP: <http://www.thedailystar.net/2007/05/04/d70504020330.htm> (accessed 5 Dec. 2009).
106 For example, there are a range of international actors such as the Asian Development Bank (ADB), UK Department for International Development (DFID), United States Agency for International Development (USAID) amongst others, assisting local partners in Bangladesh in various areas of governance including financial management reform, transparency, accountability and anti-corruption, local governance, decentralization and rural development, etc. For more, see 'Governance Programmes and Activities for Development Partners in Bangladesh', *Local Consultative Groups in Bangladesh (LCG Bangladesh)*, 2007. Online. HTTP: <http://www.lcgbangladesh.org/inventory/13_inventory.pdf> (accessed 12 June 2011).
107 These included 'a massive unsolved arms haul in Chittagong … the British High Commissioner narrowly [escaping] assassination … virtually the entire opposition leadership [escaping] death by seconds on August 21, and … senior opposition leaders … killed by assassins'. See Sobhan, 'Tribal Loyalties', *The Daily Star*, 25 Feb. 2005. Online: <http://www.thedailystar.net/2005/02/25/d50225020328.htm>.
108 Ibid.
109 Ibid.
110 For more, see 'Grenades Kill 18 at Rally in Bangladesh', *CNN*, 21 Aug. 2004. Online. HTTP: <http://edition.cnn.com/2004/WORLD/asiapcf/08/21/bangladesh.blasts/index.html> (accessed 20 May 2010) and 'Blasts Hit Bangladesh Party Rally', *BBC News*, 22 Aug. 2004. Online. HTTP: <http://news.bbc.co.uk/2/hi/south_asia/3586384.stm> (accessed 20 May 2010).

111 Sobhan, 'Tribal Loyalties', *The Daily Star*.
112 Ibid.
113 As indicated by Sobhan. For more such writings by him and others in *The Daily Star*, see M. Asadullah Khan, 'Poor Governance Fuels Corruption', 17 May 2008. Online. HTTP: <http://www.thedailystar.net/story.php?nid=36841> (accessed 23 May 2010); G. M. Quader, 'The Ultimate Target', 22 Oct. 2007. Online. HTTP: <http://www.thedailystar.net/story.php?nid=8282> (accessed 23 May 2010); Z. Sobhan, 'Human Security in Bangladesh', 17 Oct. 2004. Online. HTTP: <http://www.thedailystar.net/2004/10/17/d41017020320.htm> (accessed 23 May 2010) and 'More Democracy, Not Less', 29 Sept. 2006. Online. HTTP: <http://www.thedailystar.net/2006/09/29/d60929020319.htm> (accessed 19 May 2010).
114 For example, see 'Democracy and State Security', *New Age*, 28 Jan. 2007; Q. K. Ahmad, 'People's Freedoms and Development in Bangladesh', *New Age*, 8 Jan. 2008; C. I. A. Siddiky, 'Coercive Stability Needs to be Transformed into Consensual Stability', *New Age*, 9 July 2007; T. Hashmi, 'An Open Letter', *New Age*, 18 Sept. 2007.
115 Ahmad, 'People's Freedoms and Development in Bangladesh', *New Age*.
116 Ibid.
117 For more, see 'Human Security Now', *Report of the Commission on Human Security*, 2003. Online. HTTP: <http://reliefweb.int/sites/reliefweb.int/files/resources/91BAEED BA50C6907C1256D19006A9353-chs-security-may03.pdf> (accessed 18 May 2009).
118 'Democracy and State Security', *New Age*.
119 Ibid.
120 Ibid.
121 'Where is the Emergency Leading Us?', *The Bangladesh Today*, 12 Jan. 2008.
122 'International Human Development Indicators: Bangladesh', *UNDP Human Development Report*. Online. HTTP: <http://hdrstats.undp.org/en/countries/profiles/BGD.html> (accessed 21 Jan. 2010).
123 As pointed out by a senior Bangladesh expert at the School of Oriental and African Studies (SOAS), University of London.
124 Sobhan, 'Tribal Loyalties', *Daily Star*, emphasis added.
125 Sobhan, 'Freedom From Fear', *Daily Star*, emphasis added.
126 'Where is the Emergency Leading Us?', *The Bangladesh Today*, emphasis added.
127 'Democracy and State Security', *New Age*, emphasis added.
128 Buzan et al., *Security: A New Framework for Analysis*, p. 25.
129 See Ibid., p. 26.
130 For more, see S. Leonard and K. Kaunert, 'Reconceptualising the Audience', in T. Balzacq (ed.), *Securitization Theory: How Security Problems Emerge and Dissolve*, Abingdon: Routledge, 2011, pp. 58–61.
131 For example, see T. Balzacq, 'The Three Faces of Securitization: Political Agency, Audience and Context', *European Journal of International Relations*, vol. 11, no. 2, 2005, pp. 171–201; J. Vuori, 'Illocutionary Logic and Strands of Securitization: Applying the Theory of Securitization to the Study of Non-Democratic Political Orders', *European Journal of International Relations*, vol. 14, no. 1, 2008, pp. 65–99; M. Salter, 'Securitization and Desecuritization: Dramaturgical Analysis and the Canadian Aviation Transport Security Authority', *Journal of International Relations and Development*, vol. 11, no. 4, 2008, pp. 321–49; P. Roe, 'Actor, Audience(s) and Emergency Measures: Securitization and the UK's Decision to Invade Iraq', *Security Dialogue*, vol. 39, no. 6, 2008, pp. 615–35.
132 Leonard and Kaunert in Balzacq, *Securitization Theory*, p. 69.
133 Ibid.
134 Ibid.
135 Such actors include NGOs such as Manusher Jonno and think tanks such as the Power and Participation Research Centre (PPRC).

136 R. Sobhan, 'Aid, Governance and Policy Ownership in Bangladesh', *Centre for Policy Dialogue*, Dhaka, January 2003. Online. HTTP: <http://www.cpd-bangladesh.org/publications/rs/rs1.PDF> (accessed 7 Apr. 2009).

137 For a list of the various international actors involved in the governance and development programmes in Bangladesh, including USAID, UNDP and DFID, see 'Governance Programmes and Activities', *LCG Bangladesh*, 2007. Online.

138 As pointed out in interviews with journalists, academics and practitioners in Dhaka and Delhi.

139 Ibid.

140 For example, see M. A Qadeer, 'Will the Falling Dominoes Reach Pakistan?', *Open Democracy*, 30 Mar. 2011. Online. HTTP: <http://www.opendemocracy.net/mohammad-aqadeer/will-falling-dominoes-reach-pakistan> (accessed 4 Apr. 2011). Also see I. H. Malik, 'Pakistan: Misgovernance to Meltdown', *Open Democracy*, 19 Nov. 2007. Online. HTTP: <http://www.opendemocracy.net/article/conflicts/india_pakistan/pakistan_meltdown> (accessed 12 Apr. 2011).

141 S. Denyer, 'Ghani Says Afghanistan Must Take Its "Second Chance"', *Reuters India*, 3 Mar. 2009. Online. HTTP: <http://in.reuters.com/article/southAsiaNews/idINIndia-38310720090303> (accessed 7 Apr. 2009).

142 For more, see 'The Insurgency in Afghanistan's Heartland', *International Crisis Group*, Asia Report no. 207, 27 June 2011. Online. HTTP: <http://www.crisisgroup.org/en/regions/asia/south-asia/afghanistan/207-the-insurgency-in-afghanistans-heartland.aspx> (accessed 2 July 2011). Also see 'Pakistan Government Does Deal with Taliban on Sharia law', *CNN*, 18 Feb. 2009. Online. HTTP: <http://www.cnn.com/2009/WORLD/asiapcf/02/16/pakistan.taliban.sharia.law/index.html> (accessed 7 Apr. 2009) and A. Gopal, 'Afghanistan: Taliban Fill Power Void in Kabul?', *IPS News*, 20 Aug. 2008. Online. HTTP: <http://ipsnews.net/news.asp?idnews=43614> (accessed 7 Apr. 2009).

143 D. Adhikari, 'Nepal Risks Political Chaos over Constitutional Task', *Agence France-Presse*, 20 June 2011. Online. HTTP: <http://au.news.yahoo.com/world/a/-/world/9679744/nepal-risks-political-chaos-over-constitution-task/> (accessed 26 June 2011).

144 M. Bahree, 'India's Dirty War', *Forbes Magazine*, 10 May 2010. Online. HTTP: <http://www.forbes.com/forbes/2010/0510/global-2000-10-maoists-naxalites-tata-steel-india-dirty-war.html> (accessed 14 Jun. 2011). Also see S. A. Weiss, 'India's Maoist Insurgency', *The Washington Times*, 9 July 2010. Online. HTTP: <http://www.washingtontimes.com/news/2010/jul/9/on-thursday-heavily-armed-maoist-rebels-attacked-a/> (accessed 14 Jun. 2011); 'Red Storm Rising: India's Intractable Maoist Insurgency', Jane's Information Group, 20 May 2008. Online. HTTP: <http://www.janes.com/news/security/countryrisk/jir/jir080520_1_n.shtml> (accessed 7 Apr. 2009).

145 For example, see 'India: Desperately Seeking Doctors in Orissa's Red Zone', *Radio Netherlands Worldwide*, 23 June 2011. Online. HTTP: <http://www.rnw.nl/english/article/india-desperately-seeking-doctors-orissas-red-zone> (accessed 28 June 2011).

4 Tackling human trafficking in Nepal

Shakti Samuha and Maiti Nepal

This chapter analyses the role of non-governmental organizations (NGOs) in Nepal in dealing with the challenge of human trafficking. It explores the key characteristics of the phenomenon in South Asia and Nepal respectively, and undertakes a detailed examination of the activities of Shakti Samuha and Maiti Nepal, two prominent anti-trafficking NGOS in the country. It analyses the activities of these NGOs in two main areas: (1) the public policy realm, focusing on lobbying activities ahead of the introduction of a new anti-trafficking law in Nepal in July 2007, and (2) initiatives taken by these NGOs to help prevent trafficking, provide care and support to survivors and at-risk groups, and engage in advocacy and law enforcement-related activities. The analysis reveals that through their efforts to highlight the insecurities of those who have experienced trafficking and those who are vulnerable to the dangers of being trafficked, these NGOs have played a significant role in influencing Nepal's anti-trafficking legislation. Moreover, by undertaking activities to help prevent trafficking in vulnerable communities and rehabilitate trafficking survivors, they have filled a gap where the state has been relatively less effective. In this way, Shakti Samuha and Maiti Nepal have been significant security actors in the realm of human trafficking in Nepal.[1] The investigation also demonstrates that by privileging public policy responses in the context of security practices, or how security is 'done', Securitization Theory misses out on those dynamics which occur outside the state-dominated realm of public policy, where often it is actors such as the NGOs under analysis who are most actively engaged in dealing with the insecurities of sub-state groups.[2]

Contextualizing human trafficking in South Asia

Human trafficking is a global phenomenon affecting millions within and across state borders. According to the UN's International Labour Organization (ILO), at any given point, around 2.5 million people are in forced labour globally, including sexual exploitation, as a result of trafficking.[3] It is a complex, multi-faceted problem which, in recent years, has become the focus of policy measures by states as well as international organizations.[4] It has generated increasing attention in the media, and there has been a surge in the number of NGOs dedicated to advocacy around the issue.[5] In South Asia, trafficking presents an immense challenge and has increased drastically over the past few decades.[6] The surge in NGO-driven activity around the issue has also been witnessed in South Asian countries, and in many cases such organizations are going beyond lobbying and advocacy to deal with the threat and consequences of trafficking directly in at least two ways – by raising awareness amongst those at risk, and providing rehabilitative measures to rescued victims of trafficking. As an area of policy and advocacy focus, and considerable academic interest, human trafficking has generated a growing amount of literature on different aspects of the phenomenon. Within this body of literature, key areas of concern include defining human trafficking and identifying its causes, discussions on human trafficking within a human rights framework,[7] human trafficking in relation to migration and sex work,[8] laws and conventions around the phenomenon in relation to the role of governments and public policy,[9] literature which focuses on traffickers (in terms of profiling) and on victims (in terms of rescue and rehabilitation), and more.

Although there is no single definition of human trafficking, the ideas common to most definitions include the movement of the victim away from their original community through deception or coercion, and the exploitation of the victim sexually, in slavery or in servitude without pay. Variations amongst these definitions are usually along lines of gender (with some focusing exclusively on women as victims, others on women and children, with yet others making no such distinctions) and external and internal trafficking.[10] In 2000, the UN adopted the Protocol to Prevent, Suppress and Punish Trafficking in Persons, Especially Women and Children, Supplementing the United National Convention Against Transnational Organized Crime, which defined trafficking as:

> the recruitment, transportation, transfer, harbouring, or receipt of persons by means of threat or use of force, or other forms of coercion or abduction, of fraud, of deception, of the abuse of power or of a position of vulnerability or of the giving control over another person, for the purpose of exploitation. Exploitation shall include, at a minimum, the exploitation of the prostitution of others or other forms of sexual exploitation, forced labour or services, slavery or practices similar to slavery, servitude or the removal of organs.[11]

This is a broad understanding of human trafficking which does not limit victimization to females, and considers a wide range of forms of exploitation in relation to trafficking.[12] The definition emphasizes 'the *activities* that constitute human trafficking … the *means* being used [and] … the *purpose*, which is exploitation'.[13] The UN 2000 Protocol further identifies that the consent of a victim of trafficking for purposes of exploitation as outlined above becomes irrelevant 'where any of the means [outlined] have been used'.[14] This distinguishes trafficking from the phenomenon of smuggling of migrants, although there is much debate around this issue, as a person may believe they are paying to migrate illegally to another location for work, but are actually being deceived into believing so, and in fact are being trafficked for exploitation.[15] In July 2011, 146 states were party to the Protocol and 117 countries had signed it.[16] This study adopts the definition of human trafficking as outlined in the UN 2000 Protocol, which embraces the notion that a trafficked person may be a man, woman or child, trafficked for the purposes of exploitation for sexual and other purposes, and regards consent as irrelevant in situations where the person trafficked is being exploited.

In South Asia, human trafficking is often cited as one of the fastest-growing forms of transnational organized crimes.[17] According to sources such as the UN Development Programme (UNDP), the Asian Development Bank (ADB) and the International Organization for Migration (IOM), Bangladesh and Nepal are key source countries in South Asia, with India and Pakistan being the prime destinations as well as transit countries to other regions, especially the Middle East.[18] Such sources cite South Asia as having the second-largest number of trafficked persons in the world, with an overall estimate of 150,000–200,000 South Asians trafficked annually for various reasons – sex work, labour, forced marriages and organ trade.

It is, however, highlighted that the bulk of trafficking in South Asia takes place for commercial sexual exploitation.[19] Around 9,000 girls are trafficked from Nepal to India and from Bangladesh to Pakistan every year, with more than half of all female sex workers in India coming from Nepal or Bangladesh.[20] In Sri Lanka, the sex tourist industry has been a burgeoning phenomenon 'especially along its coastal belt, where the demand from European tourists for young male sex workers or "beach boys" is high'.[21] Child trafficking is also rife in other parts of South Asia, and is considered 'an extension of a serious child labour problem' in the region.[22] Increasing demands for cheap labour in the form of domestic help in South Asia's rapidly growing urban areas have been met by rural families, often willingly giving their children over to intermediaries who guarantee a better life for them in the cities.[23] According to the ILO, bonded labour systems continue to persist in South Asia – despite the establishment of laws against bonded labour, together with the existence of mechanisms to identify, release and rehabilitate those working as bonded labourers.[24] Unfortunately, although there are clear indications from existing reports that human trafficking in South Asian countries is on the rise at alarming rates, the clandestine and criminal aspects of the phenomenon make it difficult to ascertain exact figures and the extent of the problem.[25]

According to UN agencies, a number of factors make individuals and communities vulnerable to trafficking in South Asia. Poverty is the most commonly cited factor underpinning trafficking in the region: 'The necessity to meet basic needs, *in combination with other factors*, is the most commonly identified motivation to migrate or to encourage a family member to leave.'[26] Other factors include gender-based and other forms of discrimination, violence and abuse at home, within the community and wider institutions, lack of employment opportunities, limited access to education, political instability, war and conflict, and social, economic and cultural exclusion and marginalization.[27] Weak governance and legal frameworks, trade and migration policies, unsafe migration, environmental disasters (to which the region is very prone) and internal displacement also create circumstances where individuals become increasingly vulnerable to traffickers.[28] The impacts of globalization and rapid urbanization have led to a sharp decline in traditional income sources and rural employment, in turn driving poor or unskilled people to migrate in search of means to survive. Simultaneously, South Asia's rising demand for low-cost labour has resulted in a booming informal work sector and employers' illegal practices like bonded labour in order to lower production costs.[29]

Human trafficking as a security issue

Human trafficking has been argued to be a threat to state security as well as a source of insecurity to vulnerable and affected individuals and communities. For states, human trafficking presents a fundamental challenge to their authority, legitimacy and control over sovereign territory and state borders. It thrives on corruption as traffickers use links with politicians, business persons, state officials, police, customs officials and border police to facilitate trafficking.[30] The IOM estimates that human trafficking generates more than US$8 billion every year in revenues.[31] Criminal organizations may use these funds to create political instability for governments by funnelling money into activities against the state. In developing countries where corruption is rife and rule of law is already weak, trafficking is seen as a particularly destabilizing phenomenon.[32] The links between drug trafficking on the one hand and insurgent guerrilla groups, terrorists and paramilitary forces on the other have been well established. Human trafficking is another activity with which such groups have been involved across the world.[33] As Shelley points out, terrorists in Pakistan have been known to buy children to use as suicide bombers, and Maoist insurgents in Nepal trafficked girls to India to fund their political cause during the civil war. In countries like Uganda and Sudan, rebel groups have relied on trade in children to fund their conflicts and recruit child soldiers.[34] In 2002, a report by the Task Force on Organized Crime in the Baltic Sea Region revealed links between terrorism and organized crime, especially illegal migration, corruption, money laundering, and other types of financial crime providing illegal funding of terrorist activities. About half the countries represented on the Task Force reported that they had found indications of links between organized crime and terrorism within their own borders.[35] In Columbia, the nexus between drugs trafficking and paramilitary forces, insurgent guerrilla groups and terrorist has also been confirmed.[36]

Adopting a Human Security or Critical Security Studies (CSS) approach to understanding human trafficking reveals the phenomenon as a multi-faceted and complex source of insecurity to vulnerable and affected groups. Victims of trafficking face gross violations of their human rights. 'Every stage of the trafficking process can involve physical, sexual and psychological abuse and violence, deprivation and torture, the forced use of substances, manipulation, economic exploitation and abusive working and living conditions.'[37] Men, women and children trafficked for forced labour usually end up working in appalling health and safety conditions, with little or no access to medical assistance or health care, and inadequate food leading to malnourishment or starvation. They are often confined to single locations (such as factories or sweatshop premises), and are stripped of any official documents of identification such as a passport or other documents, and prohibited from making social contact outside their area of confinement. Working hours in such cases tend to be long and illegal, with insufficient or no payment for their labour. Often, victims are sexually abused and forced to pay for their subsistence or return the alleged cost of being trafficked out of their meagre wages, or face further physical and sexual abuse. Those trapped within bonded labour systems – a particular problem in South Asian countries – spend years, indeed often lifetimes, paying off debts their employers claim they owe.[38] As the UN Office of the High Commissioner for Human Rights (OHCHR) points out, 'although in theory a debt is repayable over a period of time, a situation of bondage arises when in spite of all his efforts, the borrower cannot wipe it out'.[39] In such scenarios, the debt is normally inherited by the bonded labourer's children, continuing the cycle of extreme poverty, suffering and deprivation.[40]

Children trafficked for commercial sexual exploitation and other forms of forced labour suffer significant impediments to their physical and mental development. Trafficked children, particularly those in debt bondage, have little or no access to education. Their experiences leave them traumatized for life, profoundly shaping their psyche and severely diminishing their prospects of leading a socially functional life as they grow older. Families of trafficked persons, whether children or adults, are also left deeply traumatized and, where the trafficked family member was the sole income earner, without financial means to survive.[41] In cases where families pay for their loved ones being smuggled across borders lured by the promise of jobs, and discover that he or she has been trafficked, they are devastated at the breach of trust and struggle to deal with immense levels of guilt and trauma.[42]

In 2008, the Nepalese anti-trafficking NGO Shakti Samuha published a study which revealed that of the 463 trafficking survivors interviewed, a staggering 91 per cent 'did not file a complaint against their traffickers because of lack of awareness about filing complaints, fear of social stigma, threats from criminals and fear of family hatred and lack of proof'.[43] Caste discrimination may also play a part, in the way the police and judiciary may view the victim, and the manner in which the case may be dealt with. In social terms, returnees often go back to their communities and face harsh discrimination, at times rejected by their own families. They may even be treated as outcasts, and these experiences profoundly shape the lives of survivors post-rescue. Most face great difficulties in reintegrating within their communities, finding jobs and partners.[44] The links between human trafficking and the rise of HIV/AIDS in South Asia have also been highlighted in recent years. According to the UNDP, HIV and human trafficking have in common several causal and consequential factors, including 'gender inequalities, poverty, lack of economic opportunities for women, stigma and discrimination, rights violations and a life without dignity'.[45] In 2007, a study carried out by the *Journal of the American Medical Association* (JAMA) concluded that 'trafficking of women across South Asia to work as prostitutes is likely a key factor in the spread of HIV/AIDS across the region'.[46] It analysed Nepalese girls and women who had been trafficked to brothels across the border in India and then repatriated to their home communities. The study revealed that 'nearly 40 per cent of them were HIV-positive with the figure rising beyond 60 per cent among those trafficked before age 15'.[47]

In 1997, the South Asian Association for Regional Cooperation (SAARC) at its Ninth Annual Summit in Male issued a declaration on trafficking in women and children, whereby the heads of states pledged to 'coordinate their efforts and take effective measures to address [human trafficking]'.[48] It was, however, only in 2002 that SAARC member countries adopted the SAARC Convention on Preventing and Combating Trafficking in Women and Children for Prostitution (the SAARC Trafficking Convention).[49] Ratified in 2005, the Convention represented a significant step towards combating human trafficking at a regional level, 'the first regional treaty of its kind and the first treaty in Asia to address human trafficking'.[50]

The SAARC Trafficking Convention fell short of the expectations of human rights campaigners and anti-trafficking lobbyists in the region, who critiqued it on several counts. Article 1.3 of the Convention defines trafficking in a very narrow manner, referring only to the 'moving, selling or buying of women and children *for prostitution* within and outside a country for monetary or other considerations with or without the consent of the person subjected to trafficking'.[51] Similarly, 'persons subjected to trafficking' refers only to 'women and children victimized or forced into *prostitution* by traffickers by means of deception, threat, coercion, kidnapping, sale, fraudulent marriage, child marriage, or any other unlawful means'.[52] Thus, the Convention does not differentiate trafficking from prostitution, nor does it acknowledge the differences in the needs and capacities of adult women and children.[53] Critics have also pointed out that although the Convention identifies trafficking as a violation of basic human rights, it does not actually adopt a rights-based perspective (including human, gender and child rights) in dealing with the problem, and 'was primarily drawn up to protect the state party's interest in clamping down on criminal activity instead of upholding the rights of the individual'.[54] Moreover, while the obligations conferred by the SAARC Trafficking Convention upon member states are legally binding, the obligations themselves – particularly on provisions for regional and legal cooperation and state prevention measures – are worded in a weak and insufficiently binding manner.[55] The Convention does not provide a mechanism for overseeing the implementation of its obligations by member states,[56] and lacks clarity over issues such as the extent to which the recipient country is responsible for the rescue, rehabilitation, repatriation and reintegration of victims, and their well-being post-rescue in terms of providing healthcare, psychological support, legal advice and financial compensation.[57]

Governments in South Asia have generally approached trafficking as a law and order issue, and therefore focused predominantly on punishing the perpetrators.[58] This remains the dominant regional trend, despite an increasing volume of voices including international actors such as UNIFEM and USAID, regional actors like the South Asian Coalition on Child Servitude (SACCS), Action against

Trafficking and Sexual Exploitation of Children (ATSEC), ADB and the Asia Foundation, as well as other, grassroots organizations demanding that human trafficking should be viewed through a rights-based framework, one which places the victim of trafficking at the centre of its focus and emphasizes the protection, rehabilitation and welfare of the victim, as opposed to just the punishment of traffickers.[59]

South Asian countries traditionally turn to their own domestic legislation in order to fight trafficking, which include provisions in general criminal codes as well as specific trafficking legislation.[60] Most trafficking cases in South Asian countries are dealt with at the local level, and in their concern for determination of guilt and the sentencing of the convicted person, local judges tend to give little regard to international standards.[61] Domestic or cross-border trafficking cases which end up in higher courts tend to be those involving discussions on constitutional standards of protection for citizens and non-citizens, which are not uniform across the region. For example, in India and Nepal the respective constitutions deem all forms of trafficking and forced labour illegal. In Nepal, members of both the police and judiciary at times have either little knowledge of or ignore legislation with regard to the manner in which the victim should be treated and the gathering of admissible evidence. In Bangladesh, the constitution does not mention trafficking but prohibits forced labour and calls for the state to take effective measures to prevent prostitution. The Sri Lankan constitution does not include any such references 'beyond invoking a general obligation on the State to protect children'.[62] Finally, there is little by way of consensus on the definition of trafficking amidst countries in the region, and the SAARC definition, although useful for cooperative purposes and in moving towards regional policies to deal with trafficking, 'has little practical significance where the punitive law continues to follow a different definition'.[63]

Human trafficking in Nepal: key dynamics

Human trafficking has become a severe problem in Nepal, with persons being trafficked both within and across its national borders. Nepal is primarily a source country for men, women, and children trafficked for commercial sexual exploitation and other forced labour such as domestic servitude, begging, work in factories and mines, and in the entertainment industry such as circuses and pornography.[64] International destinations for trafficked Nepalese women and children for sexual exploitation include India, countries in the Middle East, as well as in Southeast Asia such as Malaysia, Hong Kong and South Korea. Nepalese boys and men are also trafficked for forced labour within Nepal, where bonded labour is found particularly in brick kilns, the stone-breaking industry, agriculture and the embroidered textiles industry.[65]

A lack of sufficient research on the issue means it is difficult to verify figures for trafficked persons in Nepal. According to one estimate, around 5,000–7,000 Nepalese women and girls are annually trafficked for sex work in India alone.[66] The main destination cities for trafficked Nepalese women and girls in India are

Delhi, Mumbai, Kolkata and Bangalore, for the purpose of 'bondage based commercial sex'.[67] Underpinning the phenomenon of trafficking are the key 'push' and 'pull' factors in the context of human trafficking in South Asia, such as poverty and increasing income disparities, human rights violations within communities and families, armed conflict, corruption in the police and armed forces, and the forces of globalization. Nepal is one of the poorest and least developed countries in the world. With a population of more than 28.5 million, it is a mainly agricultural economy, where about 78 per cent of the population depends on farming for its income and survival. Almost one-third of Nepal's citizens live below the national poverty line.[68] The country has a diverse ethnic, linguistic and cultural fabric, and Nepalese society continues to revolve around the ancient Hindu caste system, which also prevails in neighbouring India.[69]

Modern-day Nepal was established as a kingdom in 1768, and has since endured the rule of several monarchs.[70] The country was never subjected to colonial rule, and consequently it has 'neither the colonial experience of institution-building nor the infrastructure for economic development that accompanied colonisation' in much of the rest of South Asia.[71] Nepal's successive monarchs maintained tight control over the country's people and its resources, with ordinary people given no access to education in order to complete their isolation from external influences.[72] In 1959, the country voted in a government for the first time, but the experiment did not last long. In 1960, King Mahendra dissolved the government, banned all political parties and assumed direct rule through a party-less *panchayat* system.[73] It was not until 1990, in the context of a rapidly deteriorating economic situation and huge pressure from political parties and sections of the public in the form of political protests, that the succeeding monarch King Birendra restored multi-party parliamentary democracy in Nepal.[74] For the first time, the constitution guaranteed basic civil liberties, including freedom of speech, freedom of assembly and freedom to join political parties.[75] The king's powers were reduced to that of a constitutional monarch, thus transferring sovereignty into the hands of the people of Nepal for the first time. Unfortunately, Nepal continued to be run by

> a small elite, composed mainly of Brahmins and Chetris, ethnic groups who made up less than 30 per cent of the population. The 57 other ethnic groups in Nepal were excluded from power and thus felt alienated from the state.[76]

Divisions along several lines – caste, religion, ethnicity as well as the rural–urban divide – continue to shape Nepalese politics to this day, and the country's transition from monarchy to democracy remains a difficult and volatile process. Between 1994 and 1999, Nepal saw six minority and coalition governments, even as the country fell further into the abyss of socio-economic chaos.[77] The situation was made drastically worse between 1996 and 2006, when the country was ravaged by a civil war, or the 'people's war' launched by Maoist rebels belonging to the Communist Party of Nepal (CPN) to overthrow the constitutional monarchy and establish a republic.[78] During this period, Nepal witnessed 'an explosion of serious human rights violations, including increased extra-judicial killings, enforced disappearances, arbitrary detention and a breakdown in the rule of law'.[79] The raging insurgency and the government's inability to quell it presented King Gyanendra with the grounds to sack the government and take charge in February 2005. Declaring a period of emergency, he suspended civil liberties and gave the army sweeping powers in the fight against the Maoists.[80] Under intense pressure from the international community, King Gyanendra ended emergency rule on 29 April, but political and press freedoms in Nepal continued to be curtailed.[81] A year later, the Seven Party Alliance (SPA), representing seven of Nepal's largest political parties, and the CPN came together over their common desire to see the end of the monarchy and signed a ceasefire.[82] Within a month, the Nepalese parliament voted to curtail the king's powers, and six months later the Maoists and the SPA signed a comprehensive peace agreement.[83]

Nepal's civil war lasted a decade, cost more than 13,000 lives (many of them civilians caught in the cross-fire), saw over 100,000 displaced internally and was hugely detrimental to the country's economy. 'Economic growth slowed to an average of 1.9 per cent over the [financial year] 2002–4 period compared to 4.9 per cent in the decade preceding that.'[84] The country's physical infrastructure was shattered and while 'economic disruptions … increased … , development expenditures … [declined] sharply', with significant poverty implications for the country and its people.[85] In April 2008, Nepal held its first democratic Constituent Assembly elections in almost a decade, making it a parliamentary republic. The country is still in the nascent stages of becoming a functioning parliamentary democracy: three years on, the constituent Assembly has been unable to produce a draft constitution, and political instability and the prospect of political violence remain high.[86]

It is against this backdrop that human trafficking in Nepal, both domestically and across the porous border it shares with India, has flourished. Historically, the internal trafficking of girls and women dates at least as far back as 1846, which marked the reign of the Ranas who bought girls from villages for sexual slavery. While these girls were molested, raped and 'even murdered after the terror of being hunted', 'those set free were rejected by family … and … [turned] to prostitution in a dowry-fuelled society where family is everything'.[87] Trafficking of Nepalese girls and women to India also became widespread during this time, supplying the country's growing brothel systems.[88]

Sociological factors such as the caste system have also played a key role in the fuelling of the trafficking trade in Nepal, with certain communities becoming more vulnerable to trafficking than others. The Badi community, for example, has seen a rapid decline in demand for their traditional role as ceremonial religious dancers in temples.[89] The caste system meant the Badis who belong to the lowest caste – 'Dalit' or untouchable – could not break out of their caste restrictions to take up another trade, and trapped in conditions of extreme poverty, unemployment and lack of education, they 'turned to selling their women into prostitution. Their children were groomed into prostitution and on reaching puberty accepted their role just as a tailor's son would take to his father's trade.'[90] Selling daughters to traffickers for trade across the border became the next logical step in the process.[91] This sociological dimension is further explained within the context of gender and caste discrimination, which usually go hand in hand in Nepal. The Dalits sit at the bottom of the caste-based social hierarchy, and are condemned to carry out 'tasks and occupations that are deemed too "filthy" or "polluting" for "upper-caste communities" such as those of laborers, cobblers, and manual scavengers'.[92] Nepal is a patriarchal society, and when a woman marries into another family, her caste changes to that of her husband and his family. In this perspective, the woman is seen as the property first of her parents, and then of her husband and in-laws, and is engaged in family labour from early on in life.[93] According to one survey conducted in twenty-six of Nepal's seventy-five districts, 'the higher rate of female child labour resulted mainly due to discriminatory treatment to the girl child in the family'.[94] The Badis are a prime example of the caste system shackling communities to traditional roles, and when these roles become obsolete, forcing them to turn to prostitution in order to survive without exposing themselves to social and communal violence. This is further made possible because of the lower status women (or daughters) are given within these communities in comparison to men (or sons).[95]

Other factors which have served to entrench further gender and caste discrimination within the country and exacerbate the phenomenon of trafficking include poor standards of education, high levels of unemployment and the recently ended civil war. In Nepal, only 35 per cent of women are literate, compared to 63 per cent of men.[96] The level of unemployment among women in cities is twice as high as that among Nepalese men.[97] The decade-long conflict created widespread political repression, violence and fear in the country. It heightened the conditions where traffickers could operate successfully and without fear of punishment. In September 2007, Nepal's Senior Superintendent of Police Lok Bahadur Karki admitted that human trafficking in Nepal had increased in recent times due to lax security at some of the checkpoints along its borders as a consequence of the country's internal conflict.[98] Traffickers particularly targeted women and young girls raped in the course of the armed conflict, as well as those desperate to escape the violence, and find work and a new, safer life elsewhere.[99]

Anti-trafficking NGOs in Nepal

As mentioned earlier, in South Asia states have reacted to the phenomenon of human trafficking by treating it primarily as a crime, as opposed to a human rights or Human Security issue. Within SAARC itself, human trafficking is seen as a sociological phenomenon without any security implications per se, and one which is individual to each country, with limited regional externality.[100] In Nepal, the state-led approach has been similar. In 1986, the Human Trafficking (Control) Act was established as the primary law dealing with trafficking and remained so until 2007. The act made human trafficking a criminal offence, punishable by a maximum imprisonment term of twenty years, or a fine equivalent to the amount of money involved in the trafficking transaction. In essence, the law was based on the notion that trafficking can be controlled through harsher punishment for the perpetrator, and 'seriously failed to address the interests and concerns of the victims'.[101] For example, while the law dealt with the buying and selling of human beings, it did not deal with the 'recruitment by deception or for the purposes of bonded labour within and outside the country'.[102] It also failed to tackle the incidence of 'separating a person from their legal guardian for the intention of selling without taking that person out of the country', with no 'provision for punishment of the person buying the victim'.[103] Moreover, the law did not deal with the rehabilitation of trafficking victims and no provisions were made for this or for the compensation of victims in any way.[104] Although the law presumed guilt on part of the accused, relieving prosecutors and investigators from the need to secure evidence beyond any reasonable doubt, in reality the rate of prosecution has been very low, with a success rate of only 40 per cent.[105] Often, women and young girls in Nepal are trafficked by family members, and are usually reluctant to file a case against them. Most are unaware of existing laws around trafficking, and when informed, are fearful of a backlash from trafficking networks that may have links with the local police force.[106]

It is important to note here that the Nepalese state has generally demonstrated an aversion to accepting universal human rights standards embedded in international treaties and conventions.[107] It has, for example, failed to ratify a number of important international rights conventions, such as the International Convention on the Status of Refugees 1954, the International Convention on Migrant Workers 1990, the Convention on Consent to Marriage, Minimum Age for Marriage and Registration of Marriages 1962, the Statute of the International Criminal Court (ICC) 1998 as well as the UN Trafficking Protocol 2000.[108]

These concerns – particularly around the inadequacy of the Human Trafficking Act 1986 in terms of its focus on the criminal nature of the phenomenon with little regard for the victim's security, needs and welfare; the lack of awareness amongst vulnerable communities about the dangers of trafficking and existing laws, and the lack of adequate mechanisms for support to rescued victims and their rehabilitation and reintegration into their communities and within society at large – became the focus of a growing number of NGOs and international non-government organizations (INGOs) in Nepal from the early 1990s. The last two decades have seen unprecedented growth in the number of NGOs, civil society and youth groups, and the development of policy networks including such actors in Nepal particularly, and the wider region in general. The role of local NGOs has been identified in the key areas of 'prevention', 'care and support', and 'advocacy and networking'.[109] In their efforts to prevent trafficking, NGOs in Nepal are involved in activities such as awareness raising, advice-giving, social mobilization, providing opportunities to improve livelihood activities (e.g. different ways to generate income, micro-credit, vocational training, etc. such as animal husbandry, credit for buying livestock, developing vegetable gardens, setting up tea shops, sewing/tailoring, and so on).[110] They are also involved in intercepting girls and women potentially being trafficked through community-based surveillance and rescue programmes at border checkpoints. Some NGOs are also involved in brothel-based rescue programmes in India and Nepal.

Care and support activities include measures to rescue and repatriate victims of trafficking, and then facilitate their rehabilitation and reintegration into communities. These include individual and family counselling, medical check-ups, residential care, and skills training in order to provide them with livelihood opportunities. Those women and girls who are unable to return home upon being rescued, owing to the stigma of being trafficked and having been forced into prostitution, are provided with long-term housing, medical care, job placements and even the opportunity to marry. In some cases, NGOs also offer medical care and counselling to those rescued victims who have been infected with HIV, and provide legal assistance to prosecute traffickers and assist trafficking victims to present their cases in court.[111]

Leading anti-trafficking NGOs in Nepal who are at the forefront of such activities include Maiti Nepal, the Agro Forestry and Basic Cooperatives Nepal (ABC Nepal), Peace Rehabilitation Centre (PRC), Child Workers in Nepal Concerned Centre (CWIN), Shakti Samuha, the Himalayan Human Rights Monitors (HimRights), the Women's Rehabilitation Centre (WOREC) and the Legal Aid and Consultancy Centre (LACC), among others. The two major national networks of NGOs working against trafficking in Nepal are the Alliance Against Trafficking of Women and Children in Nepal (AATWIN) and the National Network against Girls Trafficking (NNAGT). Both focus on campaigning, advocacy, lobbying and awareness raising, and have played a key role in the development and adoption of Nepal's anti-trafficking 'National Plan of Action' (NPA), and the adoption of Human Trafficking (Control) Act 2064 and Foreign Employment Act 2064 in 2007.[112] These national networks are affiliated with different INGOs and members are often supported in their work by organizations such as World Education, Save the Children US, UK, Sweden and Norway, The Asia Foundation, Terre des Hommes (TDH) and others.

NGOs as securitizing actors and security practitioners: Shakti Samuha and Maiti Nepal

NGOs in Nepal have now been raising human trafficking as a significant threat to vulnerable groups in the country for over two decades, also pointing out the deep insecurities victims continue to face even after being rescued. UN agencies such as UNIFEM South Asia and UNICEF who have a visible presence in the country have clearly defined human trafficking as a Human Security issue, and this language has been adopted by local NGOs working in partnership with them.[113] Interestingly, while some of the most active anti-trafficking NGOs may not specifically employ the term 'Human Security' in their discourse, they do emphasize human trafficking particularly as a threat to young girls, women and children, and use issues such as violence, loss of livelihood and human rights abuses, such as the loss of freedom of movement and the ability to take decisions on one's own behalf, to emphasize the nature of the threat and its consequences for those involved.[114]

Over the last couple of decades, anti-trafficking NGOs in Nepal have found significant motivation in the lack of initiative shown by the state in tackling the problem of trafficking in a holistic manner, and in acknowledging and addressing the interests and concerns of the victims of trafficking in particular. Nepalese state representatives as well as non-governmental practitioners, analysts and academics focusing on human trafficking in the country agree that the collective work done by many NGOs working in the anti-trafficking sector created a strong social force lobbying the government over the years to change its perspective on trafficking and trafficking victims.[115] As the following analysis demonstrates, these NGOs have not only played an important role in shaping and influencing the new anti-trafficking law in the country through their lobbying and advocacy work, but they have also successfully filled the gap where state efforts have been missing in terms of leading the work on rehabilitating rescued victims and assisting their reintegration back into communities. At the forefront of such efforts have been Shakti Samuha, Maiti Nepal, HimRights, the Forum for Women Law and Development (FWLD), Women Rehabilitation Centre (WOREC), and ABC Nepal.[116]

Before examining the role of such actors, and the wider networks within which they are embedded, in influencing the onset of the new anti-trafficking law, it is crucial to acknowledge more definitively the relationship between local NGOs in Nepal and INGOs and funding agencies which contribute to the financial sustainability of the former. As Bashford has pointed out, despite the hard work and achievements of NGOs and INGOs, they are often guilty of things such as 'duplication of work, misuse of funds, research projects with few or no tangible outcomes, projects not funded to completion, fragmentation and lack of cooperation'.[117] In a local context, this is often a direct consequence of NGOs being forced to act in this way to meet the demands of INGOs and funding agencies 'who tend to demand either their own project applications or will only fund new projects rather than the continuation of grassroots activity or existing projects'.[118] In the competition for funds, NGOs often undertake projects, research and working methods as determined by INGOs and those which may not necessarily align completely with their own agenda.

While anti-trafficking work has been a prime focus for many NGOs and INGOs in Nepal since the early 1990s, the Nepalese state has been slower to take initiatives which deal with the issue in practical terms. In August 2002, the Office of the National Rapporteur on Trafficking in Women and Children (ONRT) was established by the National Human Rights Commission (NHRC). The mandate of the ONRT includes monitoring human trafficking, coordinating 'national, regional and international efforts to combat the crime of trafficking', and generating 'a high level of commitment aimed at improving the human rights situation of women and children'.[119] Responsibilities include advocacy and training, awareness-raising, capacity-building, collaboration with local, national, regional and international actors, as well as producing an annual report critically analysing efforts to combat trafficking in the country.[120]

In its 2005 report, the ONRT highlighted that in the preparation of the anti-trafficking bill which became the 2007 Trafficking Act, it held a series of consultations with a range of actors including NGOs, INGOs and donor communities.[121] These included representatives from AATWIN and NNAGT, including member organizations such as Maiti Nepal, Shakti Samuha, HimRights, ABC Nepal and WOREC.[122] During the consultations, these actors presented their own views on the proposed bill and made specific recommendations regarding its contents. The proposals were then forwarded by the ONRT to the Nepalese Parliament. The report specifically mentions that these actors have 'contributed to the development ... and adoption of Human Trafficking (Control) Act 2064 (2007) and Foreign Employment Act 2064 (2007)'.[123] There is also general agreement amongst the different stakeholders involved that the first 'National Conference of Trafficking Survivors of Nepal' or NCTSN, held in Kathmandu in March 2007, put a great deal of pressure on the interim government in Nepal to accept the final draft of the new anti-trafficking bill and adopt it as law.[124] The conference was organized by Shakti Samuha,[125] meaning 'Group of Power', an NGO which came into being in 1996 when a group of Nepali trafficking victims rescued from Indian brothels decided to take matters into their own hands and formed the organization with 'the realisation that the victims of trafficking themselves should come forward and raise their voice in an organized manner'.[126] A key goal of the national conference was to pressure the Nepalese state into amending its anti-trafficking legislation by putting the trafficking victim at the centre of the legal framework.[127] The conference was highlighted in the Trafficking in Persons (TIP) report 2007, which stated that:

> Shakti Samuha, the first NGO in the world formed by trafficking survivors, organized a conference attended by more than 120 survivors ... assembled to focus on preventing human trafficking of vulnerable populations, particularly adolescent girls, and providing rehabilitative services for trafficking survivors. The organization upholds human rights at the core of its human trafficking strategy and compels policy makers to work from the perspective of victims of trafficking and their vulnerability.[128]

Shakti Samuha is engaged in anti-trafficking work in the areas of prevention, care and support as well as advocacy. It runs a safe shelter home in Kathmandu for trafficking survivors and an emergency shelter for street/working and young children (SWCYP) in Pokhara. It is engaged in several outreach programmes for at-risk communities such as young girls and women working in the entertainment and commercial sex industry, dance bars and massage parlours as well as in domestic servitude in the country. It provides these groups with information and advice on prevention, protection and risk reduction in relation to the threat of being trafficked, as well as counselling and medical support. Shakti Samuha also carries out organized rescue operations and provides legal support to trafficking survivors, should they wish to or are able to prosecute their traffickers. It facilitates vocational training for survivors in order to provide them with livelihood opportunities, and also allows them access to seed money in the form of small loans to help launch small businesses such as confectionary and newspaper shops, cattle rearing, etc.[129] It also engages in advocacy with the media, government agencies such as the Ministry of Women, Children and Social Welfare (MWCSW), and the police.

Shakti Samuha's activities are financed by a number of INGOs and other funding bodies. Its partner organizations include Save the children International, Asha Nepal UK, Free the Slaves (FTS), TDH, IOM, UN.Gift and the Japanese Embassy in Nepal. Oxfam GB was the first organization to support the work of Shakti Samuha financially, and also shared information and helped develop its strategies and programmes, as well as facilitating the communication of its work and messages to national and international forums.[130] The organization's rehabilitation centre in Kathmandu is funded by a UK-registered charity, Asha Nepal,[131] which also runs a sponsorship programme where it funds placements through Shakti Samuha for rescued victims and those at risk of trafficking and sexual violence, enabling them to learn a trade and giving them a seed loan to facilitate the setting-up of an independent lifestyle, or helping them to find a relevant job placement.[132] Shakti Samuha is also connected to the wider region of South Asia through partnerships with similar organizations in neighbouring countries such as Stop Trafficking and Opression of Children and Women (STOP) in India and Vision in Pakistan, and it is also a member of GAATW. In the 2011 Trafficking in Persons (TIP) Report published by the US Department of State, one of Shakti Samuha's board members, Charimaya Tamang, was honoured as a 'TIP Hero', recognized for her work as part of the organization and in her current role as a member of the government-led National Committee to Combat Human Trafficking, formed in 2009.[133]

Given the experiences of the individuals who founded the organization, it is not surprising that Shakti Samuha has been actively raising concerns around the Nepalese state's failure to protect vulnerable groups from being trafficked, and for treating survivors like criminals themselves rather than providing them with adequate care and support. Over the years, it has organized several rallies and workshops to educate other NGOs and government agencies about the plight of victims after rescue, and the lack of adequate support structures to facilitate the reintegration and rehabilitation of rescued victims back into the community. Until 2007, the Nepalese law on human trafficking focused on the phenomenon as affecting only women for the purpose of prostitution. Shakti Samuha was on the forefront of lobbying efforts to change this perception of trafficking, which it viewed as inaccurate, to include men as potential victims and reasons for trafficking other than for the sole purpose of prostitution (e.g. bonded labour, including working in circuses, organ-selling rackets and more). It actively highlighted the social challenges faced by victims post-trafficking, which often lead to victims committing suicide. In recent years, it has formulated detailed recommendations on these fronts and proposed them to relevant governments on various occasions.[134]

Maiti Nepal is another leading anti-trafficking NGO in Nepal. It was established in 1993 by 'a group of socially committed professionals like teachers, journalists and social workers' with a special focus on 'preventing trafficking for forced prostitution, rescuing flesh trade victims and rehabilitating them'. Its donors include organizations such as ECPAT International, Friends of Maiti Nepal and the CarMax Foundation. The organization does extensive work in the area of prevention through its 'prevention homes', which provide short-time shelter to girls perceived to be at 'high risk' of being trafficked. Here, they receive information on safe migration, how to protect themselves against trafficking and sexually transmitted infections including HIV, and training in life skills and income generation, primary health care support, counselling and non-formal education.[135] Maiti Nepal also has ten 'transit homes' located in towns along the India–Nepal border for trafficking survivors rescued from India and also for those intercepted in the process of being trafficked. At these homes, rescued individuals receive medical attention, counselling, and help in locating their families. Surveillance teams at these transit homes work closely with the border police, responding quickly to requests for assistance by actual or even potential victims.[136] Its rehabilitation centre in Kathmandu accommodates survivors of domestic violence and rape, street children, and trafficked children and women. It provides meals, arranges for non-formal as well as formal education, vocational skills training, facilitates medical check-ups, runs counselling sessions and helps residents to identify family members. It also encourages them to become self-sufficient financially.[137] In March 2008, Maiti Nepal's founder and Executive Director Anuradha Koirala was awarded the United Nations Women's Organization Prize for 'her outstanding contribution in promoting the cause of women's and children's development in the field of social development in Nepal'.[138]

Both Shakti Samuha and Maiti Nepal are members of AATWIN, which carries out lobbying activities to influence the state's anti-trafficking policies towards adopting a more human rights-oriented approach. Apart from its member organizations, it works with the National Task Force on Trafficking (NTF) and District Task Forces (DTFs) set up by the state to combat trafficking, as well as with other state institutions such as MWCSW, and other anti-trafficking networks such as GAATW.[139] Shakti Samuha and Maiti Nepal are also members of NNGAT, which focuses on the problem of girl trafficking for sexual exploitation, and comprises of local and national NGOs and capacity-building organizations. NNGAT in turn collaborates in various projects with INGOS such as the South Asia Forum against Human Trafficking, Coalition against Trafficking in Women – Asia Pacific, The Asia Foundation and regional organizations such as UNIFEM South Asia.[140]

A victim-focused lens: the Human Trafficking (Control) Act, 2007

In March 2007, Shakti Samuha organized the first NCTSN. The timing of the conference was significant: in January 2007, a new anti-trafficking bill was tabled in Parliament by the Minister of State for Women, Children and Social Welfare (MSWCSW). The bill had been drafted following extensive consultations by the MSWCSW, ONRT and NHRC with other actors perceived by the agencies as leading the anti-trafficking work in Nepal. These included Shakti Samuha, Maiti Nepal and other members of AATWIN and NNAGT.[141] The draft bill contained a strong victim-centred focus and included many of the recommendations made by these actors. However, the bill was not adopted as law until July 2007 and the delay was seen as resulting primarily from a lack of political will to pass the legislation.[142]

The first NCTSN brought together a large number of NGOs, INGOs and others involved in anti-trafficking efforts in Nepal, many of whom had already been offering their expertise and assistance to state-led anti-trafficking programmes. The conference was also attended by trafficking survivors who related their experiences of being trafficked as part of efforts to raise awareness and sensitize the media. They also contributed to discussions on difficulties faced by trafficked individuals upon rescue. According to Shakti Samuha, following the conference 'many trafficking survivors who were in hiding in the community ... contacted [the organization] with the knowledge that they will be supported to regain their lost rights', and the fact that the conference is going to be an annual event 'has created a hope amongst them that they will once again be granted the opportunity to come together to raise a united voice to the government of Nepal to secure their fundamental rights'.[143]

The conference culminated in the formulation of a declaration consisting of twenty-five demands signed by all participants at the conference, which was then presented to representatives from MWCSW on 8 March 2007. The declaration made key references to the security and safety of trafficking survivors, and called on the government to undertake specific measures to ensure this. Demands included the right of confidentiality to the survivor prosecuting his or her trafficker, rehabilitation centres and healthcare facilities for survivors and more (see Figure 4.1).

The conference received substantial media attention in Nepal and was also mentioned in the TIP Report 2007. Most importantly, it generated significant momentum behind the draft anti-trafficking bill and helped mount the pressure on the government in this regard.[144] In July 2007, the 'Human Trafficking and Transportation (Control) Act, 2064' was brought into effect and the new legislation tackled many of the shortcomings which were embedded within the 1986

- The state must provide education, skills and employment to trafficking survivors.
- The state must run the rehabilitation centre to re-establish the trafficking survivors.
- The state should provide free medicine and medical treatment to trafficking survivors.
- The children of trafficking survivors must be provided free education, health check-ups and security.
- The state should guarantee the life of security and without violence to trafficking survivors.
- There must be provisions of compensation for trafficking survivors.
- Life imprisonment must be given to both traffickers (for both seller and buyer).

Figure 4.1 Key demands contained in the declaration by trafficking survivors at the First NCTSN, March 4–7 2007.
Source: Report of the First NCTSN 2007, Shakti Samuha.

human trafficking law, and had been highlighted repeatedly by NGOs in their lobbying efforts in previous years. Most significantly, the legislation dealt specifically with the some of the key points raised in the declaration which emerged out of the NCTSN earlier that year. (see Figure 4.2). For example, it further criminalized the act of trafficking and provided for structural support to victims who petitioned against their perpetrators. It also allowed for compensation, rehabilitation and healthcare for victims (including centres with facilities to provide physical and psychological support), and detailed more stringent punishment to officers found complicit in assisting traffickers in their crime. It even called for a code of conduct for the media to protect victim confidentiality, as demanded in the NCTSN declaration.

Prosecution

- Age of 'child' in relation to trafficking increased from 16 to 18 years.
- Accused should be under custody while undergoing investigation except in cases of seeking sexual service (prostitution).
- Burden of proof on the accused.
- Provision to hire a lawyer to represent the victim/survivor.
- Provision for a translator for the victim/ survivor.
- Confidentiality of the petitioner ensured encouraging victim/witness protection policy.

Rescue, Rehabilitation and Reintegration

- Government of Nepal should take responsibility of rescue;, rehabilitation and reintegration facilities for those trafficked outside Nepal.
- Government should make provisions to establish rehabilitation centres that provide physical and mental treatment to survivors and ensure social rehabilitation and family reintegration of the survivors.

Punishment

- Stringent punishment to perpetrator and compensation provision to victims/survivors is ensured by the Act. Harsher punishment is stated for trafficking children.
- If the victim/survivor injures or harms the perpetrator (resulting in fatal consequences) in an act of self- defensedefence, the victim shall not be punished.

Compensation

- Victims will receive 50 per cent% or more compensation as stated by the court from the fine paid by the perpetrator.

Publicity

- Media is are expected to comply by a certain code of conduct to protect the rights of survivors and to maintain confidentiality while publicising publicizing the case of trafficking.

Figure 4.2 Salient features of the Human Trafficking and Transportation (Control) Act, 2064 (2007).
Source: USAID Nepal, Kathmandu.

'Speaking' and 'doing' security: Securitization Theory and NGOs in Nepal

The discourse around human trafficking as a source of insecurity particularly to young girls, women and children in Nepal has at least in part evolved out of the experiences and articulations of survivors, their families, larger communities and those who work with them in terms of rescue and rehabilitation. As Fujikura points out, the rescue, repatriation and rehabilitation of a group of Nepalese girls and women in July 1996,

> marked one of the major shifts in public debates along with the urgent demands of recovery, rehabilitation, and family reunion of the rescued girls. During the process, activists placed a strong emphasis on the stories of 'innocent victims', based on their direct interactions with the girls as well as their concern about the girls' difficult re-integration into society.[145]

The sharing of experiences by the survivors over time helped to build further on the perception around trafficking as a threat to the physical, psychological and economic security of the victims and their families. The civil war in Nepal raged between 1996 and 2006, and during this period it is thought to have significantly increased the incidence of human trafficking in women and young girls.[146] As concerns around the issue intensified, together with NGO-led activities in the areas of prevention, care and support, advocacy and law enforcement, state agencies were eventually forced to take note of the shortcomings of existing mechanisms to combat trafficking and adopt a more victim-centred approach in devising a new national anti-trafficking law.

Using a contextualized approach to the securitization process allows insight into these wider dynamics within which the state-led policy responses to the challenge of human trafficking in Nepal have been embedded. It highlights a number of different audiences and securitizing actors involved: trafficking survivors and their families, NGOs, INGOs, state agencies and the media. It also helps to identify the different levels – and their inter-linkages and even overlaps – where these different actors and audiences may be located; where their activities have been concentrated and where they may have had an impact. Securitization Theory as outlined by the Copenhagen School describes a securitizing actor as a figure with social capital and authority, representing a larger collective or referent group around which the representative constructs an existential threat using the language of security.[147] It has already been argued that to understand threats or insecurities only in relation to physical survival is inadequate. A broader understanding which encapsulates threats to, or insecurities around fear of losing one's way of life and livelihood, is more useful, particularly when analysing security concerns in developing socio-political contexts. The NGOs examined here are lobbying for the rights and protection of trafficking survivors, and campaigning for adequate measures to be adopted by the state in order to protect vulnerable communities from the threat of being trafficked. As leading anti-trafficking NGOs in the country, both Shakti Samuha and Maiti Nepal are held in high regard by the Nepalese state, those who have experienced the dangers of trafficking as well as other actors engaged in the realm of anti-trafficking work and policy-making.[148] Given the pioneering and significant nature of their anti-trafficking work, it may also be argued that these NGOs maintain a certain degree of indirect power with respect to their ability to influence the context within which socio-political decisions in relation to anti-trafficking measures are made in the country. This power is further derived from and reinforced by the wider national and international networks within which they are embedded, and is evident in the admission stated in the ONRT 2006–7 report that they, among other NGOS and INGOs in Nepal, contributed to the development and adoption of the new anti-trafficking law in 2007.[149] These affiliations also serve to bolster the credibility of these actors at home and abroad. Maiti Nepal, for example, is affiliated to ECPAT International, which is a global network of individuals and NGOs engaged in anti-trafficking initiatives. It has worked in collaboration with organizations such as UNHCR[150] and has received funding from USAID.[151] It is also supported in its work and fundraising efforts by Friends of Maiti Nepal, a US-based NGO.[152] Such relationships give Maiti Nepal the ability to make its voice heard by a variety of actors and audiences, and to have impact on the work of other NGOs in Nepal and to be able to influence state-led policy.

It is also necessary to consider the requirement within the securitization framework that these actors must be using the language of security when articulating human trafficking as a threat to vulnerable groups. Securitization Theory is at its heart a theory about the *practice* of security, i.e. it identifies how an issue is raised into the realm of 'security politics', thus sanctioning the use of 'extraordinary' and 'emergency' measures to deal with the threat in question. It does not concern itself with the question of whether the threat is 'real' or perceived, but only whether the threat has been constructed successfully using the language of security and existential threats. In their campaigning and lobbying work and when discussing rescue and rehabilitation measures for trafficking survivors, Shakti Samuha and Maiti Nepal describe human trafficking as a powerful threat to women and children which violates the most basic freedoms and rights of the victims, and is a continuing source of insecurity to trafficking survivors. There is a strong link between such articulations and the principles of Human Security, revolving around the security of the individual, groups and communities in terms of freedom from want and freedom from fear. The demands raised in the declaration, for example, which emerged out of the March 2007 NCTSN, included that the state must guarantee 'social security'[153] and safety of trafficking survivors, their families and those helping them prosecute their traffickers in court. This demand is implicit in its contention that trafficking survivors face the fear and threat of physical and structural violence when seeking redress, and that the state needs to take greater responsibility in protecting these groups and individuals from this threat. Similarly, other demands – e.g. trafficking survivors should be assured their rights to food, shelter, clothing and security, and the state must guarantee education and skill-based employment for women trafficking survivors – indicate that Shakti Samuha, Maiti Nepal and other participating organizations and individuals at the first NCTSN were calling for the Nepalese state to treat trafficking survivors in an exceptional manner as they face a distinct threat to their physical, economic and psychological safety and well-being, and asking for the mobilization of what may be deemed as 'extraordinary' or 'emergency' measures to do so.

Thus, applying Securitization Theory to the dynamics of human trafficking in Nepal points to Shakti Samuha and Maiti Nepal, individually as well as part of wider national and international networks, as legitimate securitizing actors. Also, if the success of a securitization is determined by a public policy response, either in the form of a change in policy or in the introduction of a new one, it may be concluded that human trafficking has been successfully securitized in Nepal. In taking such an approach, however, an extremely significant aspect of the security dynamics in relation to the issue in question is overlooked. While such an analysis acknowledges the role of NGOs such as Shakti Samuha and Maiti Nepal in attempts to securitize human trafficking in the country, it does not acknowledge their efforts to prevent human trafficking and provide care and support to those vulnerable to and affected by trafficking. Here, these actors are fulfilling the role of securitizing agents or security practitioners – a role which the Copenhagen School reserves for the state. This is evident in much of its theorizing, such as the emphasis on institutionalized, state-led responses to securitizing moves, the breaking of 'normal procedures and rules', and the importance of public policy as a signifier of the incidence of a successful securitization. In the case of human trafficking in Nepal, it is NGOs and INGOs rather than state agencies which have been at the frontline of caring for and supporting trafficking survivors.[154] Where the state has failed to respond adequately, these actors have stepped in and met the urgent needs of trafficking survivors and provided them with the care and support required for their short-term and even long-term safety and welfare.

It remains unclear whether such action by NGOs in Nepal would classify as the breaking of 'normal procedures and rules' – a condition imposed on securitizing actors in making a securitizing move – or as 'emergency' and 'extraordinary' measures to deal with the threat of trafficking. Given Securitization Theory's preference for the state as the main security actor, both could be interpreted as referring to policy moves, where the former could be identified as breaching existing policy and the latter as modifying existing laws or implementing new ones. However, if responses to securitization are not considered as emerging within the realm of state-led public policy alone, then the actions of these NGOs may be understood as 'emergency' and 'extraordinary' measures to deal with trafficking (in light of the urgency of the needs of rescued victims of trafficking and the fact that these organizations are taking measures which would ordinarily be expected to originate from the state). Similarly, if the breaking of 'normal procedures and rules' is understood as measures in the absence of adequate state action in the face of insecurities faced by trafficking survivors and at-risk groups, Securitization Theory would be able to accommodate these actors better within its analysis. Ultimately, the resolution of these arguments may largely depend upon the clarification of one issue in Securitization Theory: who can 'do' security?

Conclusion

In Nepal, as in many South Asian states and other developing countries around the world, state agencies are often slow to respond to issues which do not directly threaten the safety and stability of the state or the regime in power. In many cases, a lack of political will, knowledge and misgovernance-related challenges such as corruption, weak state institutions and a politicized judiciary, lead to the concerns of the most vulnerable and weak sections of society being ignored or sidelined. Non-traditional security concerns which revolve around individuals and communities in the first instance, as opposed to the state, are therefore often addressed by NSAs operating at the grassroots level. In such cases, these actors may not only identify such concerns and raise them at suitable platforms in order to relay them to relevant state agencies and prompt adequate policy response at the national level, but also act to tackle the threat directly, and provide affected individuals and communities with the means required with which to prevent and deal with the threat in question.

In not accommodating this dynamics, Securitization Theory limits its analysis to the state level and focuses on those security acts which are carried out (or rejected) by state-led institutions. Its bias towards the state as the referent of security is easily identified, but its aversion to sub-state level dynamics involving actors such as the NGOs analysed here is embedded deeper within its conditions concerning who can securitize and how. While only the state has the power to introduce adequate legislation around trafficking and ensure its enforcement through its agencies, it is evidently not the only actor who can or does provide the necessary measures to help vulnerable and affected communities tackle the threat of human trafficking in Nepal. By allowing for actors other than the state to 'do' security, Securitization Theory would be able to reflect more accurately the dynamics of security in socio-political contexts where such actors are indeed often more active than state institutions in dealing with the security concerns of sub-state groups. As Hadiwinata has pointed out, 'a new concept of securitization is needed that may define emergency action beyond the public policy or government decision-making process' so that actors such as NGOs may be seen as 'legitimate security actors, especially in the context of non-traditional security issues'.[155]

The above analysis also emphasizes the importance of a contextualized approach to grasping how understandings of security emerge at various levels and result in preventative and protective measures led by a variety of actors. The powerful outcome of the NCTSN in March 2007, including the demands put forth to the Nepalese state by trafficking survivors who attended the conference, revealed that those who had been trafficked and survived the ordeal to return to their country and communities clearly perceived the phenomenon as a deep source of insecurity in many ways. The argument could be made that these projections of security perceptions in themselves are part of the processes through which the danger of human trafficking is being *constructed* as a security threat *and* successfully securitized insofar as the acceptance of relevant audiences (e.g. communities perceived to be at risk of being trafficked, trafficking survivors and their families, other NGOs and members of relevant policy communities) is concerned. As the next chapter demonstrates, the Copenhagen School approach to Securitization Theory is most accommodating of the role of NSAs as security practitioners when they are directly involved in formulating state-level responses to securitizing moves in relation to particular issues. In such a context, Securitization Theory's preference for the state as the ultimate security actor is met, yet the role NSAs may play when sitting within elite policy-making circles is also acknowledged.

Notes

1 It is important to point out here that just as the state at times may become a source of insecurity for its own people, such actors may – knowingly or unknowingly – also create conditions or behave in ways which compound rather than ease the insecurities of the referent groups they claim to be working to protect and safeguard. The aim of the chapter is not to provide an evaluation of the work of actors under scrutiny, but rather to demonstrate that in highlighting the insecurities of those who have experienced or are threatened by human trafficking, and in providing preventative and rehabilitative measures to those who may be in need, these NSAs are operating as security actors with respect to dealing with human trafficking.

2 For example, see B. Hadiwinata, 'Poverty and the Role of NGOs in Protecting Human Security in Indonesia', in M. Caballero-Anthony, R. Emmers and A. Acharya (eds), *Non-Traditional Security in Asia: Dilemmas in Securitization*, Aldershot: Ashgate, 2006, pp. 198–224.

3 'Human Trafficking: The Facts', *United Nations Global Initiative to Fight Human Trafficking (UN.GIFT)*. Online. HTTP: <http://www.unglobalcompact.org/docs/issues_doc/labour/Forced_labour/HUMAN_TRAFFICKING–THE_FACTS–final.pdf> (accessed 8 May 2011).

4 A. Brysk, 'Beyond Framing and Shaming: Human Trafficking, Human Security and Human Rights', *Journal of Human Security*, vol. 5, no. 3, 2009, pp .8–21.

5 Ibid.

6 'Human Trafficking and HIV: Exploring Vulnerabilities and Responses in South Asia', *UNDP Regional HIV and Development Programme for Asia Pacific*, UNDP Regional Centre in Colombo, 22 Aug. 2007. Online. HTTP: <http://www.hivpolicy.org/Library/HPP001346.pdf> (accessed 3 Mar. 2011).

7 For example, see 'Human Trafficking', *26th Report of Session 2005–2006*, UK Parliament Joint Committee on Human Rights, vol. 1, p. 10. Online. HTTP: <http://www.publications.parliament.uk/pa/jt200506/jtselect/jtrights/245/245.pdf> (accessed 24 Feb 2010); A. K. Jayasree, 'Searching for Justice for Body and Self in a Coercive Environment: Sex Work in Kerala, India', *Reproductive Health Matters*, vol. 12, no. 23, 2004, pp. 58–67; S. Y. Rana, R. Debabrata, G. P. Kumar, C. Castillejo and M. Mishra, 'From Challenges to Opportunities: Responses to Trafficking and HIV/AIDS in South Asia', *UNDP Regional HIV and Development Programme for South and North East Asia*, New Delhi, 2003 and M. Singh, 'Debate on Trafficking and Sex Slavery', *The Feminist Sexual Ethics Project*, Brandeis University, <http://www.brandeis.edu/projects/fse/index.html> (accessed 26 Feb. 2010).

8 For example, see F. Pickup, 'More Words but No Action? Forced Migration and Trafficking of Women', *Gender and Development*, vol. 6, no. 1, Mar.1998, pp. 44–51; L. Kelly, 'The Wrong Debate: Reflections on Why Force Is Not the Key Issue with Respect to Trafficking in Women for Sexual Exploitation', *Feminist Review*, vol. 73, no. 1, 2003, pp. 139–44; K. Barry, *The Prostitution of Sexuality*, New York: NYU Press,

1995; G. Pheterson, *A Vindication of the Rights of Whores*, Seattle, WA: Seal, 1989; F. Delacoste and P. Alexander, *Sex Work*, San Francisco: Cleis, 1998; R. Weitzer, *Sex for Sale*, New York: Routledge, 2000; W. Chapkis, 'Trafficking, Migration, and the Law: Protecting Innocents, Punishing Immigrants', *Gender and Society*, vol. 17, no. 6, Dec. 2003, pp. 923–37; C. Enloe, *Bananas, Beaches and Bases: Making Feminist Sense of International Politics*, Berkeley: University of California Press, 1989; T. D. Truong, *Sex, Money and Morality: Prostitution and Tourism in Southeast Asia*, London: Zed Books Ltd., 1990; M. Wijers and L. Lap-Chew, *Trafficking in Women Forced Labour and Slavery-like Practices in Marriage Domestic Labour and Prostitution*, Utrecht: Foundations Against Trafficking in Women (STV), 1997; P. Marshall, 'Globalisation, Migration and Trafficking: Some Thoughts from the South-East Asian Region', *Occasional Paper No. 1, Globalisation Workshop in Kuala Lumpur*, UN Inter-Agency Project on Trafficking in Women and Children in the Mekong Subregion, 8–10 May 2001 and N. Constable, 'Mail Order' Marriages, Berkeley: University of California Press, 2003.

9 For example, see 'Coalition Against Trafficking in Women' (CATW). Online. HTTP: <http://www.catwinternational.org/about/index.php> (accessed 12 June 2010); 'Foundation Against Trafficking in Women' (STV). Online. HTTP: <http://www.bayswan.org/FoundTraf.html> (accessed 12 June 2010); 'The Council of Europe Convention on Action against Trafficking in Human Beings', *Council of Europe*. Online. HTTP: <http://www.coe.int/t/dg2/trafficking/campaign/Docs/Convntn/default_en.asp> (accessed 26 Feb. 2010); 'Commonwealth Anti-Trafficking Legislation', *Department of Foreign Affairs and Trade*. Online. HTTP: <http://www.dfat.gov.au/illegal_immigration/laws.html> (accessed 1 Mar. 2010); P. Coonts and C. Griebel, 'International Approaches to Human Trafficking: The Call for a Gender-Sensitive Perspective in International Law', *Women's Health Journal*, April 2004, pp. 47–57. Online. HTTP: <http://www.reddesalud.org/english/datos/ftp/OpinionWHJ404.pdf> (accessed 3 Mar. 2010); E. E. Schuckman, 'Anti-Trafficking Policies in Asia and the Russian Far East: A Comparative Perspective', Heldref Publications, Winter 2006. Online. HTTP: <http://findarticles.com/p/articles/mi_qa3996/is_200601/ai_n16537201/pg_1> (accessed 26 Feb. 2010) and B. S. Zakhari, 'Legal Cases Prosecuted under the Victims of Trafficking and Violence Protection Act of 2000', in S. Stoecker, and L. Shelly, *Human Traffic and Transnational Crime: Eurasian and American Perspectives*, Lanham: Rowman and Littlefield Publishers, Inc., 2004, p. 131. For a detailed evaluation of anti-trafficking measures undertaken by countries around the world, see 'Trafficking in Persons (TIP) Report 2011', *US Department of State*. Online. HTTP: <http://www.state.gov/g/tip/rls/tiprpt/2011/index.htm> (accessed 10 July 2011).

10 'Revisiting the Human Trafficking Paradigm: The Bangladesh Experience', *Bangladesh Counter Trafficking Thematic Group*, IOM-CIDA Dhaka, 22 Apr. 2003. Online. HTTP: <http://www.childtrafficking.com/Docs/bangl_counter_traff_themati1.pdf> (accessed 12 May 2010).

11 'UN Protocol to Prevent, Suppress and Punish Trafficking in Persons Especially Women and Children, Supplementing the UN Convention against Transnational Organized Crime', *Office of the United Nations High Commissioner for Human Rights*, 2000. Online. HTTP: <http://www2.ohchr.org/english/law/protocoltraffic.htm> (accessed 2 Apr. 2010).

12 It should be pointed out here that some analysts consider it important to distinguish between prostitution and trafficking of women and children for the purpose of prostitution. According to Butcher, the key difference lies in agency, i.e. the trafficked individual is coerced or forced into prostitution while the non-trafficked individual may have chosen prostitution as means of income. For more see K. Butcher, 'Confusion between Prostitution and Sex Trafficking', *Lancet*, vol. 361, no. 9373, 2003, p. 1983.

13 B. Andrees and M. N. J. van der Linden, 'Designing Trafficking Research from a Labour Market Perspective: The ILO Experience', in F. Laczko and E. M. Gozdziak (eds), *Data and Research on Human Trafficking*, International Organization for Migration, 2005, pp. 57–58.

14 'UN Protocol to Prevent, Suppress and Punish Trafficking in Persons', 2000.
15 For a discussion of sex work, trafficking and migration, see N. Bandyopadhyay et. al., 'Streetwalkers Show the Way: Reframing the Debate on Trafficking from Sex Workers' Perspective', *Institute of Development Studies (IDS) Bulletin*, vol. 37, no.4, Sept. 2006, pp. 102–9; J. Doezema, 'Ouch! Western Feminists' Wounded Attachment to the Third World Prostitute', *Feminist Review*, vol. 67, Spring 2001, pp. 16–38; J. Doezema, 'Loose women or Lost Women? The Re-Emergence of the Myth of "White Slavery" in Contemporary Discourses of "Trafficking in Women"', *Gender Issues*, vol.18, no.1, 2000, pp. 23–50; D. Pranati, 'Population Movement from Nepal to West Bengal', *Indian Journal of Regional Science*, vol. 36, no. 1, 2001, pp. 88–102; and D. Huntingdon (ed.), 'Anti-Trafficking Programs in South Asia: Appropriate Activities, Indicators and Evaluation Methodologies – Summary Report of a Technical Consultative Meeting', *Horizons Project Population Council*, Kathmandu, 11–13 September 2001, p. 6. Online. HTTP: <http://www.popcouncil.org/pdfs/rr/anti_trafficking_asia.pdf> (accessed 12 Feb. 2010).
16 'Signatories to the CTOC Trafficking Protocol', *UN Office on Drugs and Crime (UNODC)*. Online. HTTP: <http://treaties.un.org/Pages/ViewDetails.aspx?src=TREATY&mtdsg_no=XVIII-12-a& chapter=18&lang=en> (accessed 4 July 2011).
17 'South Asia: Human Trafficking', *UNODC*, 2009. Online. HTTP: <http://www.unodc.org/southasia/en/topics/frontpage/2009/preventin-of-human-trafficking.html> (accessed 23 June 2011).
18 'Human Trafficking and HIV: Exploring Vulnerabilities and Responses in South Asia 2007', *UNDP Regional HIV and Development Programme for Asia Pacific*, UNDP Regional Centre Colombo, 2007, p. 10. Online. HTTP: <http://www.undp.org/hiv/docs/alldocs/human_traffick_hiv_undp2007.pdf> (accessed 7 Mar. 2010); 'Combating Trafficking of Women and Children in South Asia', *Regional Synthesis Paper for Bangladesh, India and Nepal*, Asian Development Bank, April 2003. Online. HTTP: <http://www.adb.org/gender/final_synthesis.pdf> (accessed 30 May 2011); and 'In Search of Dreams: Study on the Situation of the Trafficked Women and Children from Bangladesh and Nepal to India', *International Organisation for Migration (IOM)*, Dhaka: IOM, 2002. Online. HTTP: <http://publications.iom.int/bookstore/index.php?main_page=redirect&action=url&goto=publications.iom.int%2Fbookstore%2Ffree%2FIn_Search_of_Dreams.pdf > (accessed 20 Jan. 2011).
19 'South Asia: Human Trafficking', *UNODC*, 2009.
20 'Combating Trafficking of Women and Children in South Asia', Asian Development Bank, 2003.
21 'Human Trafficking and HIV', *UNDP*, p. 11.
22 Ibid.
23 'South Asia: Human Trafficking', *UNODC*, 2009.
24 'The Cost of Coercion: Global Report under the follow-up to the ILO Declaration on Fundamental Principles and Rights at Work', *ILO International Labour Conference*, 98th Session 2009, Report 1(B), p. 17. Online. HTTP: <http://www.ilo.org/wcmsp5/groups/public/--ed_norm/--declaration/documents/publication/wcms_106268.pdf> (accessed 22 June 2011).
25 Interviews with staff at USAID Nepal in Kathmandu and UNIFEM South Asia in New Delhi, Jul.–Aug. 2007. Also see 'Combating Trafficking of Women and Children in South Asia', Asian Development Bank, p. xi.
26 'Combatting Trafficking of Women and Children in South Asia: Guide for Integrating Trafficking Concerns into ADB Operations', *Asian Development Bank*, 2003, pp. 4–5. Online. HTTP: <http://www.adb.org/Documents/Guidelines/Combating_Trafficking/Guide_Integrating_Trafficking_Concerns.pdf> (accessed 28 June 2011).
27 'South Asia in Action: Preventing and Responding to Child Trafficking: Summary Report', *UNICEF Innocenti Research Centre*, Florence, August 2008, p. 6. Online. HTTP: <http://www.unicef.org/media/files/IRC_CT_Asia_Summary_FINAL4.pdf> (accessed

26 June 2011). Also see UN.GIFT, 'An Introduction to Human Trafficking: Vulnerability, Impact and Action', *UNODC Vienna 2008*, pp.71–75. Online. HTTP: <http://www. unodc.org/documents/human-trafficking/An_Introduction_to_Human_Trafficking–Background_Paper.pdf> (accessed 26 June 2011).

28 'Human Trafficking and HIV', *UNDP*, pp. 42–51.

29 Ibid.

30 TIP Report 2011, *US Department of State*, p. 247.

31 R. Wilkison, 'Human Trafficking Seen as a Security Threat in Ex-Communist Countries', *Voice of America News*, 9 Mar. 2005. Online. HTTP: <http://www.voanews. com/english/news/a-13-2005-03-09-voa45.html> (accessed 8 June 2010) and 'Counter-Trafficking', *International Organisation for Migration*. Online. HTTP: <http://www.iom. int/jahia/Jahia/activities/by-theme/regulating-migration/counter-trafficking> (accessed 10 June 2010).

32 For example, see R. Wilkison, 'Human Trafficking seen as a Security Threat'.

33 L. Shelley, *Human Trafficking: A Global Perspective*, Cambridge: Cambridge University Press, 2010, p. 87.

34 Trafficking in Persons Reports 2005 and 2008, ibid.

35 Y. Dandurand and V. Chin, 'Links Between Terrorism and Other Forms of Crime', *International Centre for Criminal Law Reform and Criminal Justice Policy*, Vancouver, December 2004, p. 7. Online. HTTP: <http://www.icclr.law.ubc.ca/Publications/Reports/LinksBetweenTerrorismLatest_updated.pdf> (accessed 23 June 2011).

36 For example, see F. E. Thoumi, *Political Economy and Illegal Drugs in Columbia*, Boulder, CO: Lynne Reinner, 1995; P. Bibes, 'Transnational Organized Crime and Terrorism: Colombia, a Case Study', *Journal of Contemporary Criminal Justice*, vol. 17, August 2001, pp. 243–58; J. Borger and M. Hodgson, 'US Drug Wars Aids Colombian Para-militaries', *Guardian*, 17 May 2001; A. Rabasa and P. Chalk, *Colombian Labyrinth: The Synergy of Drugs and Insurgency and its Implications for Regional Stability*, Santa Monica: RAND, 2001.

37 'An Introduction to Trafficking: Vulnerability, Impact and Action', *UNODC*, 2008, p. 9. Online. HTTP: <http://www.unodc.org/documents/human-trafficking/An_Introduction_to_Human_Trafficking–Background_Paper.pdf> (accessed 22 June 2011).

38 Huntingdon (ed.), 'Anti-Trafficking Programs in South Asia', p. 11. Also in interviews with staff at USAID Nepal, UNIFEM South Asia and NGOs in Kathmandu.

39 'Contemporary Forms of Slavery', *Fact Sheet No. 14*, UNOHCHR. Online. HTTP: 'Contemporary Forms of Slavery', *Fact Sheet No. 14*, <http://www.ohchr.org/Documents/Publications/FactSheet14en.pdf> (accessed 23 June 2011).

40 Ibid.

41 Shelley, *Human Trafficking*, pp. 60–61.

42 Ibid. Also see K. Archavanitkul, 'Combating the Trafficking in Children and their Exploitation in Prostitution and Other Intolerable Forms of Child Labouring in Mekong Basin Countries', *A subregional Report submitted to International Programme of the Elimination of Child Labour (IPEC)*, International Labour Organization (ILO), Bangkok, Thailand, June 1998, Chapter 7. Online. HTTP: <http://www.seameo.org/vl/combat/frame.htm> (25 June 2011).

43 Office of the Special Rapporteur on Trafficking in Women and Children (OSRT), 'Trafficking in Persons Especially in Women and Children in Nepal', *National Report 2008–2009*, National Human Rights Commission (NHRC) Nepal, p. 22. Online. HTTP: <http://www.nhrcnepal.org///publication/doc/reports/Trafficking-National Report%202008–9.pdf> (accessed 12 July 2011).

44 For an excellent record of accounts of experiences of being trafficked as narrated by victims themselves, see P. Bashford, 'A Sense of Direction: The Trafficking of Women and Children from Nepal 2006', *Asha Nepal*, March 2006. Online. HTTP: <http://www.childtrafficking.com/Docs/ashan250806.pdf> (accessed 10 Apr. 2010).

45 'Human Trafficking and HIV', *UNDP*, p. 5.

46 'Study: Sex Trafficking Spreading HIV in South Asia', *USA Today*, August 2007. Online. HTTP: <http://www.usatoday.com/news/health/2007-08-01-sex-trafficking-study_N.htm> (accessed 18 Apr. 2008). For more, see Silverman et. al., 'HIV Prevalence and Predictors of Infection in Sex-Trafficked Nepalese Girls and Women', *Journal of American Medical Association*, vol. 298, no. 5, August 2007, pp. 536–42.

47 Ibid.

48 'Article 27 of the Declaration of the Ninth SAARC Summit in Male', *SAARC Information Centre (SIC)*, 14 May 1997. Online. HTTP: <http://saarc-sic.org/_adm/editor/summits_9.php> (accessed 12 Mar. 2011).

49 The SAARC Trafficking Convention can be viewed at <http://www.saarc-sec.org/userfiles/conv-traffiking.pdf>, 12 June 2011.

50 Since the SAARC Trafficking Convention, other regional treaties such as the Council on Europe's Convention on Action Against Trafficking in Human Beings (2005) have followed, as pointed out in 'Review of the SAARC Convention and the Current Status of Implementation in Bangladesh', *International Organisation for Migration and Asian Development Bank*, 6448 REG, October 2009. Online. HTTP: <http://www.iom.org.bd/publications/Review%20of%20the%20SAARC%20Trafficking%20Convention%20Bangladesh.pdf> (accessed 21 June 2011).

51 'SAARC Trafficking Convention', Article 1.3, p.1, emphasis added.

52 Ibid., Article 1.5, p. 1, emphasis added.

53 'Review of the SAARC Convention', *IOM and ADB*, p. 15.

54 'Sub-Regional Initiatives Wide off the Mark', *Human Rights Features*, Special Edition for the 10th Annual Meeting of the Asia Pacific Forum of National Human Rights Institutions, Aug.–Sept. 2005, p. 11. Online. HTTP: <http://www.hrdc.net/sahrdc/hrfquarterly/apf10/PDF/SAHRDC_All.pdf> (accessed 4 July 2011).

55 'Review of the SAARC Convention', *IOM and ADB*, p. 24.

56 Ibid.

57 'Comments on the SAARC Convention on Preventing and Combating Trafficking Women and Children for Prostitution', *Forum for Women, Law and Development*, Kathmandu, 2002.

58 Interviews with NGOs and anti-trafficking experts in Kathmandu, New Delhi and Dhaka.

59 Ibid.

60 S. E. Thomas, 'Responses to Human Trafficking in Bangladesh, India, Nepal and Sri Lanka', *UNODC Regional Office for South Asia*, New Delhi: UNODC, 2011, p. 2.

61 Ibid.

62 Ibid.

63 Ibid., p. 4.

64 'Country Narratives: Nepal', in 'TIP Report 2011', *US Department of State*.

65 Ibid.

66 'Human Trafficking and HIV', *UNDP*, p. 30. The figure has been around for over a decade and a half, and may not accurately reflect overall figures today.

67 S. B. Prasai, 'Call for Global Action to Halt Nepalese Women and Girls Trafficking', *American Chronicle*, 10 Feb. 2008. Online. HTTP: <http://www.americanchronicle.com/articles/51873> (accessed 21 May 2011).

68 'Key Facts: Nepal', *Department for International Development*. Online. HTTP: <http://www.dfid.gov.uk/Where-we-work/Asia-South/Nepal/Key-facts/> (accessed 27 June 2011).

69 For more, see N. E. Levine, 'Caste, State and Ethnic Boundaries in Nepal', *The Journal of Asian Studies*, vol. 46, no. 1, Feb. 1987, pp. 71–88; S. Hangen, 'Race and the Politics of Identity in Nepal', *Ethnology*, vol. 44, no. 1, Winter 2005, pp. 49–64; N. Khadka, 'Democracy and Development in Nepal: Prospects and Challenges', *Pacific Affairs*, vol. 66, no. 1, Spring 1993, pp. 44–71; and L. Mahendra, *Towards a Democratic Nepal: Inclusive Political Institutions for a Multicultural Society*, New Delhi: Sage Publications, 2005.

70 S. Askvik, I. Jamil and T. N. Dhak, 'Citizens' Trust in Public and Political Institutions in Nepal', *International Political Science Review*, 17 Jan. 2011, p. 3.
71 G. B. Thapa and J. Sharma, 'From Insurgency to Democracy: The Challenges of Peace and Democracy-Building in Nepal', *International Political Science Review*, vol. 30, no. 2, Mar. 2009, p. 206.
72 Ibid.
73 J. Whelpton, *A History of Nepal*, Cambridge: Cambridge University Press, 2005, p. 86.
74 For more on the monarchy's politics in Nepal, see S. D. Muni (ed.), *Nepal: An Assertive Monarchy*, New Delhi: Chetana Publications, 1977; P. A. Raj, 'Monarchy in Nepal', in D. B. Gurung (ed.), *Nepal Tomorrow: Voices and Visions*, Kathmandu: Koselee Prakashan, 2003, pp. 113–23; J. D. Khand, 'The Contribution of Monarchy in Nepal', *Journal of Political Science*, vol. 7, nos. 1–2, 2003, pp. 25–44; T. Pokharel, 'Monarchy in Democratic Era: Need for Urgent Reform', in PlusMedium (ed.), *Forum Discussion: Threats to Nepali Democracy*, Kathmandu: Integrated Organization Systems (IOS) and DANIDA/HUGOU, 2003, pp. 69–77; B. Bhattarai, *Monarchy vs. Democracy: The Epic Fight in Nepal*, New Delhi: Samkaleen Teesari Duniya, 2005; and M. J. Hutt, 'Introduction: Monarchy, Democracy and Maoism in Nepal', in M. J. Hutt (ed.), *Himalayan People's War: Nepal's Maoist Rebellion*, London: Hurst & Company, 2004, pp. 1–20.
75 T. L. Brown, *The Challenge to Democracy in Nepal: A Political History*, London: Routledge, 1996, p. 153.
76 Thapa and Sharma, 'From Insurgency to Democracy', p. 208.
77 'Nepal's Decade of Conflict', *IRIN Humanitarian News and Analysis*, 10 Feb. 2006. Online. HTTP: <http://www.irinnews.org/InDepthMain.aspx?InDepthId=11&ReportId=33613> (accessed 17 Apr. 2010).
78 'Environmental Stress and Demographic Change: Underlying Conditions and Nepal's Instability', Report from event held at Woodrow Wilson Centre for International Scholars, 1 Nov. 2006. Online. HTTP: <http://www.wilsoncenter.org/index.cfm?fuseaction=events.event_summary&event_id=205735> (accessed 11 Apr. 2010).
79 'Nepal: State of Emergency Deepens Human Rights Crisis: Royal Takeover Prompts Fears for Safety of Critics', *Human Rights Watch*, 1 Feb. 2005. Online. HTTP: <http://www.hrw.org/english/docs/2005/02/01/nepal10100.htm> (accessed 12 Apr. 2010). Also see 'Nepal: State of Emergency May Go Too Far', *Amnesty International*, 30 Nov. 2001. Online. HTTP: <http://asiapacific.amnesty.org/library/Index/ENGASA310142001?open&of=ENG-2AS> (accessed 12 Apr. 2010).
80 Nepal's King Ends State of Emergency, Retains Power, *Daily Times*, 1 May 2005. Online. HTTP: <http://www.dailytimes.com.pk/default.asp?page=story_1-5-2005_pg4_2> (accessed 12 Jan. 2011).
81 R. Devraj, 'Maoists Put India on the Spot', *Asia Times Online*, 2 June 2005. Online. HTTP: <http://www.atimes.com/atimes/South_Asia/GF02Df01.html> (accessed 12 Jan. 2011).
82 See T. P. Pokharel and S. Sengupta, 'Nepal's Maoist Rebels Announce a Ceasefire', *New York Times*, 27 Apr. 2006. Online. HTTP: <http://www.nytimes.com/2006/04/27/world/asia/27nepal.html> (accessed 17 Apr. 2010).
83 See 'Peace Deal Ends Nepal's Civil War', *BBC News*, 21 Nov. 2006. Online. HTTP: <http://news.bbc.co.uk/2/hi/south_asia/6169746.stm> (accessed 17 Apr. 2010); S. Sengupta and T. P. Pokharel, 'Nepal Maoists Sign Peace Accord with Government', *International Herald Tribune*, 22 Nov. 2006. Online. HTTP: <http://www.iht.com/articles/2006/11/22/news/nepal.php> (accessed 17 Apr. 2010) and J. Page, 'Nepal Heads for Peace as Maoists Sign Deal', *The Times*, 21 Nov. 2006. Online. HTTP: <http://www.timesonline.co.uk/tol/news/world/asia/article644221.ece> (accessed 17 Apr. 2010).
84 'Nepal: Measuring the Economic Costs of the Conflict: The Effect of Declining Development Expenditures', Asian Development Bank, 27 June 2005. Online. HTTP: <http://www.reliefweb.int/rw/RWB.NSF/db900SID/RMOI-6DS49F?OpenDocument> (accessed 17 Apr. 2010).

85 Ibid. Also B. Pyakuryal and R. S. Sainju, *Nepal's Conflict: A Micro Impact Analysis on Economy*, Kathmandu: Pyakuryal & Sainju, 2007.
86 For example, see D. Boerema, 'As Deadline Draws Near, New Constitution in Nepal Still Far Away', Radio Netherlands Worldwide, 28 May 2011. Online. HTTP: <http://www.rnw.nl/english/article/deadline-draws-near-new-constitution-nepal-still-far-away> (accessed 28 June 2011); 'Party Disputes Affecting Peace, Statute: Nembag', *The Himalayan Times*, 21 July 2011. Online. HTTP: <http://www.thehimalayantimes.com/fullNews.php?headline=Party+disputes+affecting+peace%E2%80%209A+statute%3A+Nembang&NewsID=296381> (accessed 2 August 2011) and U. Parashar, 'Nepal Government May Fall', *The Hindustan Times*, 27 July 2011. Online. HTTP: <http://www.hindustantimes.com/Nepal-government-may-fall/H1-Article1-726208.aspx> (accessed 29 July 2011).
87 Bashford, 'A Sense of Direction', p. 25.
88 Ibid.
89 Interviews with journalists and social commentators in Nepal. For a more detailed understanding of the Badis and the Dalits in general in Nepal's socio-economic and political contexts, see T. Cox, 'The Badi: Prostitution as a Social Norm Among an Untouchable Caste of West Nepal', *Contributions to Nepalese Studies*, vol. 19, no. 1, 1992, pp. 51–71; P. Bishwakarma, 'Violence against Dalit Women in Nepal', *Nepalnews.com*, 21 May 2004. Online. HTTP: <http://www.countercurrents.org/gender-padma-lal210504.htm> (accessed 23 Apr. 2010); D. R. Dahal, 'Dalits in Governance', *The Telegraph Weekly*, 12 May 2004. Online. HTTP: <http://www.fesnepal.org/reports/2004/seminar_reports/paper_cets/paper_dahal.htm> (accessed 23 Apr. 2008); 'The Missing Piece of the Puzzle: Caste Discrimination and the Conflict in Nepal', *Centre for Human Rights and Global Justice*, NYU, 2005 and K. B. Bhattachan, K. Hemchuri, Y. Gurung and C. M. Biswakarma, 'Existing Practices of Caste-Based Untouchability in Nepal and Strategy for a Campaign for its Elimination', ActionAid Nepal, Kathmandu, 2003.
90 Bashford, 'A Sense of Direction', p. 25.
91 Ibid. Also in interviews with USAID Nepal, UNIFEM South Asia and anti-trafficking NGOs in Kathmandu.
92 'The Missing Piece of the Puzzle', Centre for Human Rights and Global Justice, p. 6. For a detailed understanding of the caste system in Nepal, see N. E. Levine, 'Caste, State and Ethnic Boundaries in Nepal', The Journal of Asian Studies, vol. 46, no. 1, Feb. 1987, pp. 71–88; J. N. Bhattacharyya, *Hindu Castes and Sects: An Exposition of the Origin of the Hindu Castes System and the Bearing of the Sects Towards Each Other and Towards Other Religious Systems*, New Delhi: Manohar, 1995; and E. Vansittart, *Tribes, Clans and Castes of Nepal*, Gurgaon: Vintage, 1992.
93 'Regional Study for the Harmonization of Anti-Trafficking Legal Framework in India, Bangladesh and Nepal with International Standards: Developing Rights Based Approaches for Anti-Trafficking Actions in South Asia', *Report published by Kathmandu School of Law (KSL) in cooperation with the TDH Consortium and SALS Forum*, May 2007, Kathmandu, Nepal, p. 37.
94 Ibid. For more on girl child labour in Nepal, see S. L. Singh, 'Work Burden of a Girl Child in Nepal: An Analysis by Poverty Levels', *Nepal Women Development SAARC Division*, United Nations Children's Fund, Nepal Office, Kathmandu, 1990.
95 For more, see S. Stash and E. Hannum, 'Who Goes to School? Educational Stratification by Gender, Caste, and Ethnicity in Nepal', *Comparative Education Review*, vol. 45, no. 3, Aug. 2001, pp. 354–78.
96 'Nepal Literacy', *International Labour Organisation (ILO)*. Online. HTTP: <http://www.ilo.org/public/english/region/asro/bangkok/skills-ap/skills/nepal_literacy.htm> (accessed 20 June 2011).
97 K. Sarup, 'Women Trafficking and Conflict', *Telegraph*, 14 Mar. 2005. Online. HTTP: <http://www.scoop.co.nz/stories/HL0503/S00100.htm> (accessed 9 May 2008).

98 M. Budhair, 'Human Trafficking in Nepal on Rise', 8 Sept. 2007. Online. HTTP: <http://www.madhuchandra.org/Women%20atroticities/Human%20trafficking%20from%20Nepal%20on%20rise.htm> (accessed 9 May 2008).

99 Interviews with anti-trafficking NGOs and other organizations in Nepal. Also see Sarup, 'Women Trafficking and Conflict'.

100 Interview with a senior SAARC official at the SAARC Secretariat in Kathmandu.

101 'Regional Study for the Harmonization of Anti-Trafficking Legal Framework', p. 105. Also as expressed in interviews with anti-trafficking NGOs and others organizations in Kathmandu.

102 S. K. Shunduna, 'Anti-Trafficking Challenges in Nepal', *Forced Migration Review*, vol. 25, May 2006, pp. 21–22. Online. HTTP: <http://www.fmreview.org/FMRpdfs/FMR25/FMR2510.pdf> (accessed 16 Apr. 2011). Also in interviews with anti-trafficking NGOs in Kathmandu.

103 Ibid.

104 Ibid.

105 'Regional Study for the Harmonization of Anti-Trafficking Legal Framework', p. 24. Also see 'More Nepalese Women Victims of Trafficking but Fewer Seeking Justice', *Feminist Daily Newswire*, 12 Feb. 2004. Online. HTTP: <http://www.feminist.org/news/newsbyte/uswirestory.asp?id=8240> (accessed 16 Apr. 2011).

106 Interviews with staff at Shakti Samuha. Also see, 'More Nepalese Women Victims of Trafficking but Fewer Seeking Justice', *Feminist Daily Newswire*.

107 Interviews with anti-trafficking NGOs and other organizations in Kathmandu.

108 'Regional Study for the Harmonization of Anti-Trafficking Legal Framework', p. 24.

109 'Prevention of Trafficking and the Care and Support of Trafficked Persons', *The Asia Council/Horizons Project Population Council*, February 2001, pp. 35–52. Online. HTTP: <http://www.popcouncil.org/pdfs/horizons/trafficking1.pdf> (accessed 21 June 2010).

110 Ibid.

111 Ibid.

112 'Trafficking in Persons Especially in Women and Children in Nepal', *National Report 2006–2007*, Office of the National Rapporteur on Trafficking in Women and Children (ONRT), National Human Rights Commission (NHRC), Nepal, p. 72. Online. HTTP: <http://www.nhrcnepal.org///publication/doc/reports/Nat_Rep2006–7.pdf> (accessed 19 Apr. 2009).

113 Interviews with anti-trafficking NGOs and UN agencies in Kathmandu and New Delhi.

114 Ibid. It is also important to point out here that much of the advocacy and awareness campaign work is carried out in the local Nepalese language.

115 Interviews with anti-trafficking NGOs, journalists, government officials, social commentators and members of law enforcement agencies in Kathmandu. Also as admitted by the ONRT in 'Trafficking in Persons', *National Report 2006–07*, p. 72.

116 For more, see Maiti Nepal. Online. HTTP: <http://www.maitinepal.org/> (accessed 30 June 2010); HimRights. Online. HTTP: <http://www.himrights.org/> (accessed 30 June 2010); FWLD. Online. HTTP: <http://www.fwld.org.np/> (accessed 30 June 2010); WOREC. Online. HTTP: <http://www.worecnepal.org> (accessed 30 June 2010) and ABC Nepal. Online. HTTP: <http://www.abcnepal.org.np/abc/index.php> (accessed 30 June 2010). These local actors are joined, supported and in many cases funded in their work by a growing number of INGOs such as the Asia Foundation, Save the Children Federation, TDH, and other international actors such as the International Labour Organisation (ILO), UNIFEM, and USAID.

117 Bashford, 'A Sense of Direction', p. 76. Also see R. Kaufman and M. Crawford, 'Sex Trafficking in Nepal: A Review of Intervention and Prevention Programs', *Violence Against Women*, vol. 17, no. 5, May 2011, pp. 651–65.

118 Bashford, 'A Sense of Direction', p. 76.

119 G. Ekberg and M. D. Manandhar, 'Final Report, Review of the Office of the National Rapporteur at the National Human Rights Commission Kathmandu, Nepal', *National Human Rights Commission*, 12 Aug. 2005, pp. 4–5. Online. HTTP: <http://www.nhrcnepal.org/publication/doc/reports/ONRT_REVIEW_REPORT. pdf> (accessed 19 Apr. 2011).
120 Ibid.
121 'Trafficking in Persons Especially in Women and Children in Nepal', *National Report 2006–2007*, Office of the National Rapporteur on Trafficking in Women and Children (ONRT), National Human Rights Commission (NHRC), Nepal, p. 70. Online. HTTP: <http://www.nhrcnepal.org///publication/doc/reports/Nat_Rep2006–7.pdf> (accessed 19 Apr. 2009).
122 Ibid., pp. 72–81.
123 Ibid., p. 72.
124 Interviews with anti-trafficking NGOs, journalists, government officials, social commentators and members of law enforcement agencies in Kathmandu.
125 See Shakti Samuha. Online. HTTP: <http://www.shaktisamuha.org.np/> (accessed 30 June 2008).
126 B. Gunnell, 'Nothing to Sell But Their Bodies', *New Statesman*, 1 Mar. 2004. Online. HTTP: <http://www.newstatesman.com/200403010023> (accessed 30 June 2010).
127 Interviews with staff at Shakti Samuha.
128 'Trafficking in Persons (TIP) Report 2007', US State Department, p. 39. Online. HTTP: <http://www.state.gov/documents/organization/82902.pdf> (accessed 1 May 2010).
129 Ibid. Also see 'Shakti Samuha: What We Do', *Free the Slaves*. Online. HTTP: <http://www.freetheslaves.net/Page.aspx?pid=294> (accessed 17 Apr. 2010).
130 'Links: A Newsletter on Gender for Oxfam GB Staff and Partners', Oxfam, Nov. 2005. Online. HTTP: <http://www.iiav.nl/ezines/email/Links/2005/November.pdf> (accessed 30 June 2010).
131 For more, see Asha Nepal. Online. HTTP: <http://www.asha-nepal.org/pages/home/index.php> (accessed 21 June 2010).
132 Ibid. Other organizations which assist Shakti Samuha financially and/or technically include WOREC, UNIFEM, Global Fund for Women (GFW), Action Aid Nepal, Free the Slaves and Save the Children Norway.
133 See '2011 Trafficking in Persons (TIP) Report Heros', US Department of State. Online. HTTP: <http://www.state.gov/g/tip/rls/tiprpt/2011/164227.htm> (accessed 27 June 2011).
134 Interviews with staff at Shakti Samuha.
135 See Maiti Nepal. Online. HTTP: <http://www.maitinepal.org/?page=prevention> (accessed 26 June 2011).
136 Ibid.
137 Ibid.
138 'About Anuradha Koirala', Mothers Home Nepal, May 2011. Online. HTTP: <http://www.mothershomenepal.org.au/about-anuradha-koirala/> (accessed 5 June 2011).
139 Interviews with staff at Shakti Samuha. Also see J. Sanghera, 'Trafficking of Women and Children in South Asia: Taking Stock and Moving Ahead', *Report sponsored by UNICEF Regional Office and Save the Children Alliance*, 21 Nov. 1999, p. 26.
140 Ibid.
141 'Trafficking in Persons', *National Report 2006–2007*, p. 72.
142 Interviews with anti-trafficking NGOs, INGOs and journalists in Kathmandu. Also see 'Impoverished Nepalese Girls Tricked into Prostitution', *IRIN Asia News*, 9 May 2007. Online. HTTP: <http://www.irinnews.org/Report.aspx?ReportId=72037> (accessed 20 Apr. 2009).
143 'Second National Conference of Trafficking Survivors of Nepal, September 2008', Concept Note and Request for Support, Shakti Samuha, April 2008.

144 Interviews with government officials, journalists and anti-trafficking NGOs in Kathmandu.
145 Y. Fujikura, 'Repatriation of Nepali Girls 1996: Social Workers' Experience', *Himalayan Research Bulletin*, vol. 21, no. 1, 2001, p. 39. Online. HTTP: <http://digitalcommons. macalester.edu/cgi/viewcontent.cgi?article=1674&context=himalaya> (accessed 10 July 2011).
146 J. G. Silverman, M. R. Decker, J. Gupta, A. Maheshwari, B. M. Willis and A. Raj, 'HIV Prevalence and Predictors of Infection in Sex-Trafficked Nepalese Girls and Women', *Journal of the American Medical Association (JAMA)*, vol. 298, no. 5, 1 Aug. 2007, pp. 536–42.
147 B. Buzan, O. Wæver and J. de Wilde, *Security: A New Framework for Analysis*, CO: Lynne Rienner, 1998, p. 37.
148 Interviews with government officials, journalists, anti-trafficking NGOs, USAID Nepal in Kathmandu and UNIFEM South Asia in New Delhi.
149 'Trafficking in Persons', *National Report 2006–2007*, p. 72.
150 For example, see 'UN Refugee Agency Launches HIV/AIDS Prevention Project in Nepal', *People's Daily Online*, 16 Oct. 2007. Online. HTTP: <http://english.people. com.cn/90001/90782/6284364.html> (accessed 12 April 2008).
151 'USAID Nepal Budget Summary 2003–4', USAID. Online. HTTP: <http://www.usaid. gov/policy/budget/cbj2004/asia_near_east/Nepal.pdf> (accessed 12 Apr. 2010).
152 See Friends of Maiti Nepal. Online. HTTP: <http://www.friendsofmaitinepal.org/ index.htm> (accessed 23 June 2010).
153 'Social security' here refers more to the notion of *societal* security as referred to by Buzan and Wæver, rather than social security on the lines of the US Federal Old-Age, Survivors, and Disability Insurance (OASDI) programme.
154 Kaufman and Crawford, 'Sex Trafficking in Nepal', p. 5.
155 B. Hadiwinata, 'Poverty and the Role of NGOs in Protecting Human Security in Indonesia', in Caballero-Anthony, Emmers and Acharya (eds), *Non-Traditional Security in Asia*, p. 221.

5 Shaping India's national action plan on climate change

The Energy and Resources Institute (TERI) and the Centre for Science and Environment (CSE)

The phenomenon of climate change as a scientific reality is now widely accepted around the world.[1] The adverse impacts of climate change are seen as posing significant challenges to the survival, safety and well-being of communities as well as states in most parts of the world. Calls for coordinated action at the international level in order to mitigate and adapt to the impacts of climate change have become increasingly louder over the decades. Consequently, the realm of international environmental politics is teeming with a diverse variety of actors. These include states, international organizations such as the World Meteorological Organization (WMO) and the United Nations Environment Programme (UNEP), local and global media organizations, lobbying networks like the Climate Action Network (CAN) (including environmental groups like Greenpeace International, World Wide Fund for Nature (WWF) and Environmental Defence Fund (EDF)), and epistemic communities such as the Working Groups (WGs) of the UN Intergovernmental Panel on Climate Change (IPCC). These actors and their agencies may be driven by different sets of interests, which may or may not overlap, and each may wield varying degrees of social and political influence in shaping actions through public policy or other means in the area of climate change at the local, national and international levels.

In India too, the debate on climate change and how it should be tackled has involved a range of voices – state actors such as senior officials and relevant state agencies, as well as non-state actors (NSAs) such as epistemic communities, think-tanks, civil society groups and the media. Many of these actors are often part of wider policy networks or communities focused on climate change and related issues.[2] This chapter analyses the role played by key scientific policy communities (SPCs) in India in shaping the discourse on climate change at the national level, and in influencing the country's National Action Plan on Climate Change (NAPCC) launched in 2008. It begins by exploring the nature of SPCs as epistemic communities, and the perceived security implications of climate change for states and sub-state groups in South Asia. The chapter then focuses on the key dynamics and implications of climate change in India. It investigates the development of the discourse on climate change in the country, and how it has increasingly been linked with the survival, safety and well-being of those most vulnerable to the adverse impacts of the phenomenon. Using Securitization Theory, it examines securitizing moves by Indian state representatives constructing climate change as a threat to the people of India, and the articulations and efforts of two SPCs in particular – The Energy and Resources Institute (TERI) and the Centre for Science and Environment (CSE). The analysis demonstrates that Securitization Theory as formulated by the Copenhagen School is most effective in identifying NSAs as securitizing agents and security practitioners when they are situated directly within relevant policy-making circles and have direct access to authorities of the state.

Scientific policy communities

SPCs fall into the category of epistemic communities, that is, 'knowledge-based groups of experts and specialists who share common beliefs about cause and effect relationships in the world and some political values concerning the ends to which policies should be addressed'.[3] SPCs have 'become increasingly important to environmental governance through policy advocacy and through contribution to knowledge about the causes and consequences of environmental change'.[4] According to Elliot, scientists who work as part of governments, intergovernmental organizations and scientific non-government organizations (NGOs) have heavily influenced environmental discussions at the international level, and 'the dissemination of information and knowledge about environmental problems. In doing so, they have become part of the political process, contributing to and becoming involved in decision-making and standard-setting.'[5]

Haas makes a similar argument when pointing out that 'the behaviour [of states] in the area of environment differs dramatically from traditional forms of international behaviour', where policy formulation has benefited from 'new patterns of reasoning ... which reflected a more sophisticated understanding of the complex array of causal interconnections between human environmental and economic activities'.[6] This is largely thanks to the work of 'actors and processes that are commonly neglected by the more orthodox system approaches [such as neorealism], and a more eclectic, mid-level approach involving epistemic communities is required to theoretically explain the process by which such changes have come about'.[7] Adler and Haas insist that,

> In international coordination games concerning issues of a technical nature, cooperative outcomes may depend ... on the extent to which nation-states, after taking everything into consideration ... apply their power on behalf of a practice that epistemic communities may have helped create and perpetuate ... if we know the winning epistemic community, we can deduce the likely policy alternatives available for political selection.[8]

The work of the IPCC and its WGs, for example, provides a significant case for analysis where a scientific community has had great influence in the formulation of international agreements on climate change.[9] In this scenario, the IPCC has been largely regarded as the 'winning' epistemic community. The four assessment reports produced by the IPCC in 1990, 1995, 2001 and 2007 have been widely accepted as authoritative accounts of the state of climate science and have played a central role in 'setting benchmarks for international action' on climate change over the last two decades or so.[10] Unfortunately, since late 2009 the credibility of the organization has suffered a setback following a string of controversies over some inaccuracies in its 2007 assessment report, and allegations of political bias.[11] The events led to an independent review of the processes and procedures of the IPCC by the InterAcademy Council (IAC), a multinational organization of science academies. The IAC in its August 2010 report recommended a number of measures and actions for the IPCC to strengthen its processes and procedures, many of which have now been adopted by the latter.[12] It remains, however, that 'the findings of the [IPCC] generally concur with those of major scientific associations ... such as the U.S. National Academy of Sciences' and that 'within the community of experts on climate science, few believe that IPCC reports overestimate the state of the problem'.[13] Moreover, the recent setback in the IPCC's reputation does little to change the fact that it has been, and arguably remains, the most influential body in national and international policy debates on climate change, and has played a pivotal role in raising concerns over the issue.

In the specific case of India, it may be argued that epistemic communities in the form of SPCs such as TERI and CSE have significantly influenced policy-making on the issue of climate change at the national level. Both have strong and long-running reputations in India and beyond as organizations producing high-quality research and analysis on environmental and sustainable development issues, including climate change.[14] They are actively engaged in a range of projects dealing with climate change in India, including conducting research and carrying out capacity-building activities for other actors including the Indian state.[15] Moreover, there is evidence that their work is held in high esteem within policy-making circles in India, and this is explored in further detail in this case study. Both organizations have worked for Indian state agencies as advisers on different environmental issues, and their respective directors are non-official members of the Prime Minister's Council on Climate Change (PMCCC), the body responsible for drafting India's NAPCC in June 2008.[16]

Climate change as a security issue

Climate change is generally understood as the warming of the earth's surface and atmosphere as a result of an increase in the concentration of greenhouse gases (GHGs) in the atmosphere. Today, there is widespread agreement among states and other groups that 'increasing levels of man-made greenhouse gases are leading to global climate change', with consequences such as climbing temperatures and rising sea levels.[17] The academic literature on climate change as a key scientific development and a significant issue of political consideration has grown considerably since the late 1980s. The initial stream of writing and research on the issue mainly concentrated on grappling with the nature and scale of the dangers posed by the phenomenon.[18] By the early 1990s, however, it began to focus increasingly on the political nature of the issue, as the international climate change regime began to evolve rapidly.[19] In 1988, the WMO and UNEP jointly established the IPCC to assess all aspects of climate change.[20] The IPCC's mandate is to assess published data and provide credible conclusions on climate change. As mentioned earlier, its assessment reports over the years have played a key role in the establishment of the international climate change regime.[21]

As the political debate around climate change intensified, the focus of the literature diverged. Some analysts questioned the formulation of short-term policy to deal with climate change based on existing evidence on the phenomenon.[22] Another key area of discussion was how to mitigate the causes of climate change with the maximum effectiveness and efficiency, while others questioned the economic cost of such policy action and whether it was necessary at all.[23] As international engagement in this realm intensified following the adoption of the United Nations Framework Convention on Climate Change (UNFCCC) at the Earth Summit in Rio de Janeiro in 1992, it also became a key focus of analysts interested in studying the development of the international climate change regime.[24]

The literature citing climate change as a threat to human, national and international security has also been growing steadily.[25] It is argued that climate change is a key threat not only to 'human development and environmental conservation but also … a major threat to human security at national and livelihood levels'.[26] In the lobbying sphere, NGOs such as Greenpeace International, WWF and Oxfam have been actively drawing attention to climate change as a risk with catastrophic consequences for the most vulnerable groups on earth.[27] Climate change has also come to be understood as a 'national' security threat in countries around the world.[28] In recent years, state actors have increasingly expressed the need to act together to curb climate change. In 2003, for example, the Pentagon produced a report around a 'plausible' climate change scenario which would challenge 'United States national security in ways that should be considered immediately'.[29] In April 2007, British Foreign Secretary Margaret Becket insisted that there were few greater threats to global security than climate change.[30] At the 2006 UN Climate Change Conference in Nairobi, former UN Secretary General Kofi Annan warned that climate change is an 'all-encompassing threat' which endangers the world's food supply, health, peace and security among other things.[31] The German Advisory Council on Global Change (WBGU) has argued that climate change 'amplifies mechanisms which lead to insecurity and violence'.[32] In December 2009, ahead of the much-hyped fifteenth UN Climate Change Conference, Denmark's Minister for Climate and Energy Connie Hedegaard, also the summit chairperson, insisted that 'As such, climate policy is also *security* policy.'[33] At the same time, leaders of Commonwealth countries urged for a global response to a problem which they saw as 'central to the survival of peoples and one which posed an "existential" threat particularly to small island states, low-lying coastal states and least developed countries'.[34] Climate change has also become the subject of discussions around food and water security, and some argue that it is driving many of the present ongoing conflicts in the world and could potentially be the source of similar conflicts in the future.[35] According to

UN Secretary General Ban Ki-Moon, climate change 'affects ... poverty, water scarcity, disease, regional and political instability, global health ... the future of humanity, and ... the future of the planet Earth'.[36] He has argued that increasing competition between states and communities for scarce resources 'is increasing, exacerbating old security dilemmas and creating new ones', and trends driven by climate change such as environmental refugees, increasing desertification and rising sea levels 'are all threats to human security as well as to international peace and security'.[37]

Climate change in South Asia: Key impacts

South Asia is considered to be highly vulnerable to the effects of climate change.[38] One of the greatest impacts of climate change in the region is predicted to be the decline in water resources.[39] According to the IPCC, two of the major rivers in the Indo-Gangetic Plains (IGP), the Brahmaputra and the Indus, will see a reduction in their annual run-offs by 14 per cent and 27 per cent respectively,[40] resulting in 'tremendous downstream consequences'.[41] Initially the rise in temperature is expected to lead to accelerated 'glacial melt' in the Himalayan range, leading to glacial lakes overflowing and causing glacial lake outburst floods (GLOFs). For a country like Bangladesh, which sees flooding every year in its key river basin area during the monsoon season, climate change means a potential increase in the magnitude and extent of flooding.[42] In the Maldives, where people are almost entirely dependent on groundwater and rainfall for their freshwater supply, climate change threatens saltwater intrusion into freshwater sources.[43] Sri Lanka, another island-state, is projected to lose most of its freshwater from heavy rainfall as run-off to the sea.[44]

Climate change is also seen as a threat to agricultural yields and livelihoods in South Asia. According to the World Bank, around 70 per cent of the region's population lives in rural areas, and accounts for 75 per cent of South Asians living in poverty.[45] Agriculture is the main form of livelihood for the majority of these people, employing 60 per cent of the work force.[46] The estimated and measured impacts of climate change on agricultural yields and on those who depend on agriculture for their livelihoods are therefore substantial. The IPCC suggests that in South Asia yields of cereal crops could decrease by up to 30 per cent, even when taking into account the beneficial effects of a CO_2-enriched atmosphere on plant growth.[47] While wheat and rice crop yields in the region are predicted to suffer directly from temperature increases, indirect impacts 'due to water availability and changing soil moisture status and pest and disease incidence' are also key concerns.[48] Given the extent to which South Asian economies rely on agriculture and the seasonal monsoons in this context, any variation in the duration and pattern of rainfall stands to have a bearing on the performance of local and national economies.

In January 2011, the WMO stated that South Asian countries faced rising temperatures and extreme weather patterns as the world recorded the warmest year in 2010,[49] chiming with the IPCC's projections that the occurrence of extreme weather events would increase in the region as a result of rising temperatures.[50] At present, it is estimated that around 65 per cent of South Asia's disasters are climate-related.[51] The region's poor socio-economic indicators and weak infra-structure further exacerbate the vulnerability of its people to the impact of natural disasters.[52] Coastal cities in South Asia are at the frontline of such climatic changes. Apart from the threat of flooding, saltwater intrusion into freshwater sources, and death and destruction from increasingly intense and frequent cyclones, hurricanes and rainstorms, they also face accelerated coastal erosion as a result of rising sea levels. According to the IPCC, sea levels are set to rise at least by round 40 centimetres (cm) by the end of the twenty-first century, and it is projected that this will increase the number of people flooded in coastal popula-tions per year from 13 million to 94 million.[53] 'Almost 60 per cent of this increase will occur in South Asia (along coasts from Pakistan, through India, Sri Lanka and Bangladesh to Burma) ... '[54] The rise in sea levels will impact most on island countries such as Sri Lanka and the Maldives, while low-lying coastal cities such as Karachi, Dhaka and Mumbai will also be amongst the most vulnerable.[55] As high sea levels provide a higher base for storm surges to build on, coastal cities face a greater risk of being devastated by floods during rainstorms.[56] Over the years, there has been an increasing movement of people from coastal regions to other cities, sometimes across national borders, creating the phenomenon of climate refugees. In India, for example, there are rising concerns that as coastal regions in Bangladesh face higher sea levels, the number of climate refugees crossing over to India will increase significantly, putting additional strain on local infrastructure and causing socio-political instability.[57]

Key dynamics of climate change in India

It is argued that climate change in India may put 'additional stresses on ecological and socioeconomic systems that already face tremendous pressures from rapid urbanization, industrialization and economic development'.[58] Some human security experts argue that as freshwater resources get stressed further, this could create new or exacerbate existing political conflicts between Indian states sharing common water sources.[59] Others have raised alarm over the potential devastation which would result from the impact of increasingly intense natural disasters and rising sea levels in coastal urban metropolitan cities such as Mumbai and Chennai.[60]

India's official position on climate change at the national and international level has been conflicting. In the past, India's Prime Minister Manmohan Singh has cited climate change as 'a real threat' challenging the future of the country.[61] At the Gleneagles G8 Summit in 2005, the Indian Ministry of External Affairs (MEA) presented a country paper on 'Dealing with the Threat of Climate Change' which stated that the phenomenon posed an 'especially serious threat to a country like India, which is dependent on weather for its agricultural output'.[62] However, since then Indian state representatives have rejected calls by countries such as the US, UK and others to label climate change as a threat specifically to 'international peace and security', to be considered under the ambit of the UN Security Council (UNSC).[63] Nirupam Sen, India's former Permanent Representative to the UN, has for example argued that climate change does not fit the bill of a 'security threat' as defined in Article 39 and Article 41 of the UN charter, 'both of which call for "action with respect to threats to the peace, breaches of the peace, and acts of aggression."'[64] India, together with others like China and Brazil, insists that 'The appropriate forum for discussing issues relating to climate change [is] the United Nations Framework Convention on Climate Change.'[65] Therefore, although India describes climate change as a 'global threat' in its main domestic policy document on the issue, the NAPCC 2008, it has vehemently resisted the framing of climate change as a threat to 'international peace and security', i.e. a security threat with military-political consequences at the international level, and opposes its consideration within the forum of the UNSC. According to some analysts, this is because India does not wish to give the UNSC the mandate to intervene domestically when it comes to enforcing international obligations in the area of climate change. Ahead of the Copenhagen climate change summit, in 2009, the MEA issued a pamphlet clarifying India's position on climate change, emphasizing that India viewed its NAPCC as distinct from any international agreement on climate change which 'reflects a careful balance of interests of parties to the agreement and not merely a collation of nationally determined intentions to act'.[66] While this case study notes this distinction between the Indian state's position on climate change within a security context at home and abroad, it focuses specifically on the state-level discourse, where the state appears to have accepted securitizing moves made by its own representatives as well as NSAs around climate change as a threat to communities in India.

In their assessments, analysts broadly identify three main areas of impact as posing serious threats to India and the wider region of South Asia – 'agriculture, sea level rise leading to submergence of coastal areas as well as increased frequency of extreme events'.[67] It is estimated that the agricultural sector in India employs around 60 per cent of the country's workforce and accounts for around 17 per cent of the country's Gross Domestic Product (GDP).[68] Almost 70 per cent of the country's population lives in rural areas, the majority of whom depend on rain-fed agriculture (i.e. farming which is entirely reliant on rainfall for irrigation) and forests for their livelihoods.[69] Increasing temperatures would have a severe impact on the annual monsoon rainfall,[70] resulting in 'severe droughts and intense flooding in parts of India' with 'a 20 per cent rise in all summer monsoon rainfall'.[71] They could also upset the monsoon pattern in India and other South Asian countries.[72] With millions of farmers relying on the timing and predictability of the monsoon season to plant and grow crops, changes in the weather pattern and amount of rainfall could lead to disastrous consequences for food availability in India and the wider region, and livelihoods dependent on farming.[73]

A quarter of India's population lives along its coastline, which stretches for over 7,500 kilometres along nine states and four union territories.[74] The IPCC predicts that in India, coastal levels will to rise by 2.4 millimetres (mm) per year, leading to an increase of 38 cm by the middle of the twenty-first century.[75] Such a rise in sea levels would 'inundate low-lying areas, drown coastal marshes and wetlands, erode beaches, exacerbate flooding and increase the salinity of rivers, bays and groundwater'.[76] Mumbai, India's financial hub, is the capital of the state of Maharashtra and located on the west coast of India. It is India's largest city, and also the second most populated city in the world, with an estimated population of over 13.5 million.[77] The devastating flooding of the city in 2005 demonstrated how the city's geographical location and character and its inadequate infrastructure make it extremely vulnerable to heavy rainfall and rising sea levels.[78]

India is reportedly the world leader when it comes to natural disasters.[79] According to research at the Earth Institute at Columbia University, 'almost the entire country is significantly impacted by at least one hazard and mortality impacts are particularly concentrated in the north and north-eastern regions'.[80] It is proposed that the impact of climate change is aggravating these existing problems across India.[81] Densely populated regions such as coastal areas face increased risk of exposure to cyclones and storm surges, while changes in precipitation patterns increase the risk of droughts, floods and famines. These events not only disrupt normal life dramatically but also cause a trail of disastrous consequences, such as falls in food production levels and outbursts of incidences of sickness: 'mainly water-borne illness such as cholera, diarrhoea and dysentery are reported due to poor sanitation, poor sewerage systems and access to potable drinking water facilities during floods'.[82] They lead to 'a breakdown of livelihoods' which depend on farming, and also adversely affect other sources of livelihood, such as dairy activities and manual labour.[83]

Securitizing climate change in India

The discourse on climate change in India emerged in the early 1990s, coalescing around international negotiations on the issue. In 1992, the first Earth Summit was organized by the UN Conference on Environment and Development (UNCED), in Rio de Janeiro.[84] Among other things, the summit resulted in the production of the UNFCCC, which 'sets an overall framework for intergovernmental efforts to tackle the challenge posed by climate change'.[85] The Convention has been ratified by 192 countries, and undertakes the task 'to stabilize greenhouse gas concentrations in the atmosphere'.[86] The Kyoto agreement, the implementing protocol for Annex I of the Convention, was adopted in 1997 and set 'binding targets for 37 industrialized countries and the European community for reducing greenhouse gas (GHG) emissions'.[87]

As preparations for the Rio Earth summit took place, the internal debate on climate change in India gathered momentum. The essence of this debate revolved around India's own development goals and the costs of cutting GHG emissions. As with other developing countries, India's political elite reflected a perspective which saw the richer, industrialized countries as primarily responsible for causing climate change through 'unsustainable consumption patterns'.[88] In 1993, India ratified the UNFCCC, which stipulated that developing countries would not have binding GHG mitigation commitments under the convention, given their small contribution to the greenhouse problem and low financial and technical capacities.[89] Between 23 October and 1 November 2002, New Delhi hosted the Eighth Conference of the Parties (COP 8) to the UNFCCC, providing further impetus for environmental groups in the country to take the opportunity to generate debate around the impact of climate change on India, finding economically viable ways to cut and share GHG emissions on a fair basis, and moving towards an economy not dependent on fossil fuels for its energy needs.[90] A key example of this is the 'Climate Justice Summit' held on 26–8 October that year, organized by the India Climate Justice Forum, a coalition of Indian and international NGOs, 'to provide a platform for people and communities most affected by climate change who have been left out of the UN negotiations'. The summit included 'workshops and discussions to articulate the issues and define just solutions around climate change from a human rights, social justice and labour perspective'.[91]

At the 2007 G8 Summit in Berlin, where climate change was high on the agenda,[92] Prime Minister Singh argued the need to take into consideration the cost of development for any action plan on the environment.[93] He made this argument in the context of developmental progress being crucial in order to lift millions out of poverty in developing countries.[94] Back home in India, the climate change debate further intensified around concerns about India's poor being hit the hardest by the impacts of the phenomenon.[95] The debate reached a new peak on 30 June 2008 when India released its 'National Action Plan on Climate Change', or NAPCC. This document outlines an action plan of key measures the country needs to take to simultaneously promote its development objectives 'while yielding co-benefits for addressing climate change effectively'.[96] The NAPCC came ahead of the G8 summit in 2008 in Japan, where the Indian Prime Minister again reiterated that climate change was one of the key challenges facing the world and 'could be overcome only through global, collaborative and cooperative efforts'.[97] At the same time, he rejected US President George Bush's suggestion that 'countries like India and China should accept the same emission reduction goals as developed nations'.[98]

State securitizing actors

As the above discussion demonstrates, over the last two decades or so the issue of climate change in India has gradually gained prominence at the national level. In high-profile articulations of state actors, it has been constructed as a 'security' threat to the people of India, 'a major threat' which 'may alter the distribution and quality of India's natural resources and adversely affect the livelihoods of people'.[99] The language used by state actors in speeches, official documents and publications in relation to climate change and its impacts on the people of India and the rest of the world has steadily increased in urgency. For example, in his speech at the High Level Segment of the COP 8 in New Delhi on 30 October

2002, India's then serving Prime Minister Atal Bihari Vajpayee described climate change as 'one of the most serious environmental concerns of our times'; 'a global phenomenon with diverse local impacts'.[100] By 2005, the language of 'threat' and 'risk' was being used directly in relation to climate change and its impacts. While it is true that since the G8 summit at Gleneagles in 2005, India has actually opposed the framing of climate change as a threat to 'international peace and security', preferring instead to discuss responses to climate change at the international level within a sustainable development context, it has nonetheless continued to use the rhetoric of 'security' in the domestic realm, as demonstrated below.

On June 6 2006, the PMCCC was launched with the Prime Minister as Chair and the Ministers of Agriculture, Finance, Science and Technology, Energy and the Deputy Chairman of the Planning Commission as official members.[101] Non-official members included individual experts with strong backgrounds in research and analysis in the area of climate change. These individuals, while not recruited to represent organizations they hold affiliations to, are associated with some of the most high-profile and well-respected scientific research and policy communities in India.[102] The mandate of the council was to coordinate national action plans for the assessment and mitigation of, and adaptation to the impacts of climate change in India. Almost a year after the formation of the PMCCC, and before leaving for the G8 summit in Berlin in 2007, Prime Minister Singh addressed the country on World Environment Day and warned that, 'The threat of climate change is real and unless we alter our lifestyles and pursue a sustainable model of development, our future will be at peril.'[103] Thus, he constructed climate change as a threat to the people of India, using a 'point of no return' argument, and as one which required 'extraordinary' measures in order to be mitigated. In 2008, the PMCCC presented India's NAPCC following a two-year drafting process. The document is India's key policy statement on climate change, and states that: 'India is faced with the challenge of sustaining its rapid economic growth while dealing with the global threat of climate change.'[104] It needs 'a national strategy to ... adapt to climate change and ... to further enhance the ecological sustainability of India's development path.'[105]

According to the Copenhagen School, when analysing a speech act two sets of conditions must be taken into consideration: The first set relates to internal conditions, i.e. 'the grammar of security' and the construction of 'a plot that includes existential threat, point of no return, and a possible way out'.[106] It is clear from the above discussion that Indian state representatives have been constructing such a plot around the threat of climate change using all of these elements. The second set is the external conditions, which include (1) 'the social capital of the enunciator', i.e. the securitizing actor 'who must be in a position of authority', and (2) the threat in question should ideally be something 'generally held to be threatening', such as 'tanks, hostile sentiments, or polluted waters'.[107] The first external condition is met with ease in these efforts to securitize climate change in India. As demonstrated above, in the recent past two different Prime Ministers have expressed urgency around the need to deal with the threat of climate change on various occasions, while one has explicitly called it a 'threat' to the 'security' of the country. In addition, this language has been embedded in official documents such as the country paper to the G8 summit in Gleneagles and the NAPCC. Thus, as far as the Copenhagen School is concerned, the Indian Prime Minister and other state agencies such as the MEA have the essential character-istics required to fit the role of securitizing actors. As for the requirement that the phenomenon in question be generally viewed as threatening, it can be argued that climate change has over the past few decades come to be viewed as a highly threatening phenomenon globally, with substantial scientific evidence to support this perception.[108]

The Copenhagen School also stipulates that the securitizing move alone does not actually constitute a successful securitization on its own. In order for this to happen, the securitizing move must be accepted by the target audience and the securitizing actor must, in making the move, break free of 'normal procedures and rules'. At the same time, the deployment of emergency measures demanded by the securitizing actor, however, is not a necessary condition for a successful securitization.[109] In his June 2007 statement, the Indian Prime Minister projected climate change as a threat to the people of India, arguing that unless 'we', i.e. not only the Indian people but also the Indian state (given that Singh is its prime representative), change their ways and specifically adopt policies to pursue a sustainable development model, the future of these referent groups is at risk of going beyond a point of no return. Thus, it may be logical to assume that the audience of this securitizing move appears to be the Indian people (as this was a public statement) as well as state officials such as the Members of Parliament (MPs) who would subsequently discuss the draft NAPCC. Using the Copenhagen School approach to Securitization Theory, the above analysis makes a good case for its argument that state actors are the 'best fit' as securitizing actors and security practitioners. Not only do state representatives such as the Prime Minister arguably have the necessary social capital and authority which the Copenhagen School demands from a securitizing actor, they also have the ability to break what might be defined as 'normal procedures and rules', i.e. regular laws and policies, and facilitate the introduction and implementation of new ones.

As far as audience acceptance signalling a successful securitization is concerned, the Copenhagen School would argue that in a parliamentary democracy such as in India, the Prime Minister would be restricted by the country's Parliament in terms of how far he could act without its consent, and so would require by way of audience acceptance the support of a majority of MPs to make any draft bill into a law – as it did in case of the NAPCC. While in principle this is a sound argu-ment, as the case study on misgovernance in Bangladesh highlighted, corruption is a huge problem in South Asian states and deeply entrenched within many of their key institutions. In recent years in India, even the parliamentary process has come under scrutiny. A key example here is an incident during the first term of the Congress Party-led United Progressive Alliance (UPA) coalition government, surviving a 'no-confidence motion' in Parliament. The motion was called for by the

Opposition in July 2008.[110] The situation arose after one of the UPA's coalition partners, the Communist Party of India-Marxist (CPI-M) withdrew its support to the government following the Prime Minister's insistence on pushing through a controversial civilian nuclear cooperation deal with the US despite heavy opposition from CPI-M and other domestic factions. The move reduced the strength of the UPA government to a minority in the Lok Sabha, the lower house of Parliament.[111] What followed was a desperate attempt by the UPA to cobble together the majority of MPs required to survive the vote, from various parties in the opposition using methods allegedly including 'bribery ... political arm-twisting, media manipulation and offers of the loaves and fishes of office in return for opposition MPs voting against their own parties' whips'.[112] Ahead of the confidence vote, three opposition MPs came forward on the floor of the Lok Sabha waving 'wads of money' they claimed they had been given as part of bribes by the government's coalition partner, the Samajwadi Party, in exchange for abstaining from the vote.[113] It was only after the intervention of the Supreme Court, following a petition by a group of retired bureaucrats in April 2011, that the police investigation into the matter gathered pace, resulting in two arrests in July and six indictments under the Prevention of Corruption Act in August.[114] The incident serves as a stark reminder that in countries where corruption and embezzlement of public funds have become common phenomena, it is harder to make a case for the sanctity of democratic principles and values, and even the parliamentary process, at all times. It also further strengthens the argument for the need for Securitization Theory to look beyond the practices of state actors and state-led institutional processes, to also consider the practices of NSAs and the processes in which they are involved, which may not necessarily conform to traditional state-led, institutionalized practices in the context of security.

CSE and TERI

CSE and TERI have been two leading voices in the debate on climate change and other environmental issues in India. Both are members of the Climate Action Network South Asia (CANSA) established in 1991 by South Asian NGOs and scientists concerned and engaged with 'the emerging challenge and threat of climate change'.[115] CSE was established in 1980 by Anil Aggarwal as 'one of India's first environmental NGOs to analyse and study the relationship between environment and development and create public consciousness about the need for sustainable development'.[116] It describes itself as a 'public interest research and advocacy organization', which 'researches into, lobbies for and communicates the urgency of development that is both sustainable and equitable'. Other than communication for awareness, research and advocacy, it is also involved in pollution monitoring, and in educating and training professionals, public administrators, private sector executives, NGO workers and students in environmental issues.[117] Since it was set up, CSE has been churning out high-quality and internationally recognized research and analysis on environmental issues in India. This includes its Citizens' Reports on 'The State of India's Environment', which have focused on a range of issues such as environmental degradation, the management of the environment by rural communities, causes and consequences of floods in the floodplains of the Ganges and Brahmaputra rivers, the need to preserve and implement India's traditional knowledge in rainwater harvesting technology management to combat problems such as drought and land degradation, and more.[118]

Based in Delhi, CSE claims to follow a strategy of 'knowledge-based activism', using its research and publications to support its lobbying campaigns. It aims to promote solutions to environmental threats facing India such as 'ecological poverty' and extensive land degradation on the one hand, and rapidly growing toxic degradation of uncontrolled industrialization and economic growth on the other.[119] It is funded by a number of different international organizations such as the Swedish International Development Agency, Rockefeller Foundation, Ford Foundation, UNDP and UNICEF, as well as a number of national trusts such as the Sir Ratan Tata Trust, Sir Dorabjee Tata Trust and the Rajiv Gandhi Mission for Watershed Management. On occasions, it has also undertaken projects for the Indian Ministry of Environment and Forests (MEF). It also supports itself through sales of CSE publications and audio visual films.[120] CSE's work has been recognized both at home and abroad through various awards; both its founder Anil Aggarwal and its director Sunita Narain have been awarded the Padma Shree in 1986 and 2005 respectively.[121] CSE was also given the prestigious Stockholm Water Prize in 2005.

Over the years, CSE representatives have campaigned strongly on the issue of climate change – both in relation to domestic policy as well as on India's handling of negotiations on the issue at the international level – from a sustainable development perspective.[122] In December 2007, a CSE press briefing described the people of South Asia as 'climate victims'.[123] It claimed that changes in rainfall patterns will affect 'water security' in large parts of India. Elsewhere, CSE activists have argued that this will also pose 'a serious threat to agriculture, and therefore to the country's economy and food security'.[124] CSE claims that climate change does not only pose a threat to food and economic security, but as a consequence of the impacts of climate change, 'our survival is also affected'.[125] In terms of its influence on climate change policy in India, there are two significant points to consider. In 1990, CSE challenged a key report by the World Resources Institute (WRI) which contained the total emissions of greenhouse gases by all countries as calculated by the WRI.[126] The report was viewed as designed to push developing countries towards sharing the responsibility for global warming, and CSE in turn published a booklet entitled 'Global Warming in an Unequal World', which contained its own analysis of the data and what it considered to be an equitable way (in per capita emissions) to address the problem.[127] The document not only laid the foundations for CSE's campaign work around climate change, but was also presented to the MEA and the MEF. Subsequently, the Indian state adopted the CSE analysis as India's official position for an equitable solution to climate change. Furthermore, it chose CSE analysts to be a part of the official Indian delegation to the 1992 Rio Earth Summit.[128]

Second, CSE director Sunita Narain has been serving as a non-official member of the PMCCC. Narain is a well-known and highly respected figure in the field of environment and sustainable development,[129] and a leading voice on the issue of climate change in India. She has been explicit in expressing urgency around the need to tackle the threat of climate change, warning that 'the whisper is becoming a shout. Climate change signs are here. We are ... running out of time.'[130] Other than contributing to the deliberations over the drafting of the NAPCC within the PMCCC, she also gave private consultations to the Prime Minister's office on the matter of climate change.[131] As the council proceeds with formulating more detailed plans for each of the eight missions mentioned in the action plan, Narain's participation in its activities continues. These examples are key indicators of how CSE and its work have fed into the climate change policy-making process in India. In both cases, it is clear that the Indian state accepts CSE as a trusted and respected SPC, and holds its research and analysis in high esteem. CSE also regularly presents the government with briefings papers on aspects of climate change.[132]

TERI is another key SPC in India operating in the realm of environment, climate change and sustainable development issues. It was established as a research organization in 1974 with the aim of dealing with the 'immense and acute problems that mankind is likely to be faced with in the years ahead' as a result of the misuse and depletion of resources, and pollution as a result of misuse.[133] With over 700 employees today, TERI has grown into a large organization which has diversified into a range of issue-areas. The organization has its headquarters in New Delhi, and launched its own university, the TERI University, in 1998. It has a presence not only in different parts of the country, but also in North America, Europe, Japan, Malaysia and the Gulf. TERI launched and hosts the annual Delhi Sustainable Development Summit (DSDS), 'a major event focusing on sustainable development, the pursuit of the Millennium Development Goals (MDGs) and assessment of worldwide progress in these critical areas'. It has also established the World Sustainable Development Forum (WSDF), 'guided by the patronage of a group of select world leaders'.[134]

TERI funds itself mainly through project-based activities undertaken for multilateral and bilateral agencies (including UN organizations, the World Bank, etc.), state departments and ministries, foundations (e.g. the Ford Foundation, Rockefeller Foundation, etc.) and the corporate sector.[135] Thus, its income is generated through its own research-based activities for various clients for non-profit purposes. It has been engaged in research on climate change since 1989 and has since then carried out several projects on climate change, focusing on 'awareness generation and capacity building for different stakeholders' such as 'governments, industries and civil society organizations'.[136] TERI has focused on areas such as impacts and vulnerability assessment, adaptation strategies, exploring GHG mitigation options and issues therein, climate change policies and climate-modelling activities.[137] Today, it is considered one of the leading research organizations in India, and is led by Dr Rajendra Pachauri, Chairman of the IPCC since April 2002.

Through their research, analysis and outreach activities, TERI analysts and associates have consistently been raising the threat posed by climate change to food and energy security in India.[138] Pachauri himself has been at the forefront of voicing these concerns in the Indian media as well as at various national and international seminars, conferences and workshops in India and abroad. He has argued that environmental refugees as a consequence of climate change 'could disrupt peace and security' across borders and have serious implications for social stability in India and other countries.[139] He insists that 'the scale and nature of human-induced climate change requires the immediate inclusion of the impacts of climate change in our preparedness to protect human life and property'.[140] In the years after of the formation of the PMCCC and its efforts around drafting the NAPCC, Pachauri argued that 'India ... is particularly vulnerable [to climate change and] needs to formulate and implement a forward looking policy on climate change ... '[141]

TERI's research and expertise is highly regarded within Indian policy-making circles. Under Pachauri's leadership, TERI has been invited to advise state agencies on climate change-related policies at the national and sub-state level in India. In February 2008, for example, the Chief Minister of West Bengal, Buddhadeb Bhattacharjee,[142] revealed he was seeking advice from Pachauri on climate change-related problems that the state was facing, particularly the threat to the Sundarbans.[143] Bhattacharjee and Pachauri held a detailed meeting to discuss these problems in West Bengal in August 2008, where Pachauri submitted a proposal to the former to set up a climate-related research centre in the state. The government of West Bengal is already operating a scheme to give a 'green rating' to environment-friendly buildings (residential and corporate) in the state – an initiative proposed and launched by TERI in collaboration with the Union Ministry of New and Renewable Energy and Green Power Corporation (the corporate entity of the West Bengal Renewable Energy Development Agency).[144] At the national level also, TERI's influence on policy-making in the realm of climate change is evident. Pachauri, like Narain, is a non-official member of the PMCCC, along with three other experts affiliated to TERI as 'Distinguished Fellows' – Dr Nitin Desai, Dr Prodipto Ghosh and Ambassador Chandrashekhar Dasgupta.[145] Moreover, at the request of the MEF, TERI drafted the technical document containing the 'quantitative analysis and assessment of options by which the [NAPCC] could be considered in light of various activities and initiatives, which could be included in it'.[146] This meant that 'a large number of TERI staff ... beyond the membership of the [PMCCC] provided valuable inputs in the formulation of the National Action Plan'.[147] The individuals sitting on the council were also involved in 'giving feedback to the various drafts of the NAPCC and in the final acceptance of the plan'.[148]

Bearing in mind the internal and external conditions laid out by the Copenhagen School in the context of analysing securitizing moves, the work and articulations of CSE and TERI representatives fits the requirements rather well. Both sets of actors have been using the 'grammar of security' to construct a plot which revolves around a threat, a point of no return and a possible way out. As demonstrated above, under Narain's leadership, CSE has argued that climate change threatens food, water and economic security in the country, endangering the very survival of Indians, whom she describes as 'climate victims'. Similarly, Pachauri has on several occasions claimed publicly that climate change is one of the most serious challenges facing India, and argued that unless people change their ways, and the state adopts forward-looking policies to deal with its impacts, the lives of ordinary Indians are at peril.[149]

In terms of the external conditions stipulated by the Copenhagen School, the first one is met with ease: climate change, as demonstrated earlier, is an issue which has come to be generally perceived as threatening. It is harder to determine the extent to which the second external condition, stipulating that the securitizing actor must have social capital and authority, is met by CSE and TERI. This is because of the lack of clarity around what type of 'authority' is referred to here by the Copenhagen School. If 'authority' relates to knowledge and expertise on the issue-area or sector from which the threat is seen to emerge, the case for both CSE and TERI as securitizing actors becomes strong. Within India, these are arguably two of the most influential and active SPCs working in the realm of climate change, other environmental issues and sustainable development. Both are led by individuals who have established their credibility in the field at the national and international levels. As mentioned earlier, CSE's Narain has been bestowed with prestigious honours at home and abroad. In August 2007 in a special issue marking the sixtieth anniversary of India's independence, *Time* magazine listed Narain as one of India's most influential individuals.[150] Pachauri, for his part, has been awarded the Padma Bhushan in India,[151] and the US Environmental Protection Agency (EPA) has honoured him for his 'outstanding efforts and impeccable leadership in spreading the awareness about the importance of environmental issues to protect the Earth's climate'.[152] His association with the IPCC as chair since 2002 has also been crucial in further entrenching his influence in the field, and under his chairmanship the IPCC was awarded the Nobel Peace Prize in 2007.[153] Securitization Theory specifies that a securitizing actor must have the necessary social capital and authority to raise an issue as a 'security' threat in relation to a particular referent group, and be able to influence the target audience to accept his or her argument. In light of the above, it may be argued that both Narain and Pachauri possess the required social capital and expert authority in the field of their work, given the robust credentials of their respective organizations as well as their personal achievements. The fact that both are members of the PMCCC is indicative of the influence they may hold over any public policy which emerges on the issue. Pachauri's positions at TERI and IPCC further strengthen his influence and credibility. Similarly, Narain has in the past worked closely with state agencies in India such as the MEF on issues such as the management of tiger reserves in the country,[154] and continues to be a member of the Environment Pollution (Prevention and Control) Authority for the National

Capital Region, where her role is to help monitor and implement strategies for reducing pollution in Delhi and in other cities across the country.

If, however, 'authority' in this context refers to 'political' authority – and the Copenhagen School is ambiguous here – it becomes uncertain whether CSE and TERI would meet this criterion. Given the emphasis on public policy outcomes within securitization studies, the lack of clarity around how a successful securitization takes place, and insufficient distinction between the securitizing actor and the securitizing agent or security practitioner, it becomes harder to determine to what extent Securitization Theory would be able to factor in the roles played by CSE and TERI in the securitization of climate change in India. While these actors may have the social capital and expert authority to make securitizing moves towards this effort, they do not have the direct power to determine whether or not their recommendations (by way of consultations to governments or through their participation in policy drafting committees) are ultimately accepted and incorporated into the policies adopted and implemented by the state. It may be argued here that such a lack of power on the part of these SPCs is irrelevant as it is not the adoption of 'emergency' measures (by way of public policy) which determines the success of a securitizing move, but the acceptance of the relevant move by the target audience. Since the Indian state has in recent years accepted climate change as a 'security' issue at the national level, most significantly in its NAPCC, securitizing moves made by actors such as CSE and TERI could be seen as successful as they have been accepted by one of their target audiences – the Indian state.

Conclusion

The notion of climate change as a non-traditional security issue, threatening the survival, livelihoods and welfare of communities and the stability of states around the world, has now gained widespread recognition. This is reflected in, among other things, the sense of urgency surrounding recent UN climate change conferences, and the rhetoric adopted by those involved in direct negotiations as well as those lobbying and commenting from the sidelines.

In South Asia, the problem of climate change has particular resonance. States in the region, particularly Sri Lanka, the Maldives, Bangladesh and India – have over the last two decades acknowledged climate change and its impacts as having grave consequences for their people, particularly in the shape of changing rainfall patterns and the consequences for agricultural sectors, the risk posed by rising sea levels to coastal cities, and the devastation which would follow the increase in the intensity and incidence of natural disasters such as cyclones, droughts, floods, heatwaves and rainstorms. A vast network of NSAs has also been actively raising awareness around the issue and pressuring the states in the region to limit human action contributing to climate change, while keeping in mind its goals for sustainable development.

Using Securitization Theory to study the dynamics of climate change as a security challenge in India, it becomes evident that securitizing actors in this context include state actors as well as NSAs such as TERI and CSE. The latter have evidently been at the forefront of generating debate on climate change and its impacts in India, particularly with respect to its coastal cities, rural communities, the agricultural sector and the wider economy. Indian state representatives, despite being opposed to labelling climate change as a matter of 'international peace and security', have also moved to construct the challenge in security terms at the national level, as demonstrated in the lead-up to and with the launch of the NAPCC in 2008.

The focus on TERI and CSE and the impact their research, analysis and related activities have had on the state's outlook on climate change in security-related terms also draws attention to the weaknesses in Securitization Theory when it comes to determining a successful securitization. These SPCs have articulated the adverse impacts of climate change as a security threat to people in India, using the 'grammar of security', on several occasions and called upon the state to take the necessary steps to deal with the challenges. There are two things to consider here. First, in doing so they may not be breaking any 'normal procedures and rules' as required by the Copenhagen School in order for the move to qualify as a case of successful securitization. Second, the Copenhagen School simultaneously requires audience acceptance of the securitizing move in order for a successful securitization to take place. When observing the role of TERI and CSE in securitizing climate change in India, it may be argued that by the first requirement, their attempts to securitize climate change may not be considered successful, while judging by the second requirement, they would appear to have been successful owing to the Indian state's adoption of such an approach in its official policy on climate change.

Securitization Theory remains focused on security practices as they unfold within state-led institutional processes. Although the adoption of 'emergency measures', generally understood as changes or developments in public policy in order to address the issue at the heart of securitizing moves, is not considered necessary for a successful securitization, Securitization Theory is nonetheless interested in public policy as the main instrument by which state actors are engaged in addressing security issues. Therefore, in the absence of clarity around what exactly it takes for a securitizing move to be successful, the fact that representatives of TERI and CSE were involved in drafting the country's NAPCC and offered consultations to state officials on climate change-related matters, is rather helpful. This is because these actors were involved in working with state officials to directly shape state policy on climate change, and therefore may be viewed as having direct influence in shaping the state's approach towards climate change.

Thus, there are two conclusions to be drawn from the preceding analysis. First, securitizing actors raising climate change as a security threat have included state actors in India, who have been forthcoming in using the 'grammar of security' and constructing 'a plot that includes existential threat, point of no return and a possible way out'.[155] These actors, including former and current Prime Ministers, arguably have the highest level of political authority an individual could possess in a state-system, and a high degree of social capital. Thus, not only do the words of these actors have the necessary ability to influence state agencies and public opinion, but they also have the authority or ability to take decisions on behalf of the state. Since state actors have been among those at the forefront of efforts to securitize climate change in India, Securitization Theory is quick to identify this dynamic and point to the role of the state as the securitizing actor and security practitioner in this context. Second, the NSAs in this case study are relatively large, well-funded organizations. Their leaders have credible reputations, bolstered by the quality of research each organization produces and the nature of projects it undertakes. The fact that these actors are substantially integrated into the policy-making process at the state-level as far as climate change is concerned, is perhaps most significant. If it is considered that the success of a securitizing move depends on audience acceptance, i.e. to 'just gain enough resonance for a platform to be made from which it is possible to legitimize emergency measures',[156] it may be argued that these SPCs have helped create the platform which state actors have then been able to use to launch India's NAPCC.

Notes

1　A. Dupont and G. Pearman, 'Heating up the Planet', *Lowy Institute Paper 12*, Lowy Institute for International Policy, 2006, p. 3.
2　While a policy network is 'a group of individuals and organizations that share similar belief systems, codes of conduct and established patterns of behaviour', a policy or epistemic community is 'a more tightly-knit group of elite experts who have access to certain information and knowledge, which excludes those who do not have such access'. For more, see R. Sutton, 'The Policy Process: An Overview', *Working Paper*, Overseas Development Institute, August 1999, p. 12. Online. HTTP: <http://www.odi.org.uk/resources/odi-publications/working-papers/118-policy-process.pdf> (accessed 1 Nov. 2008).
3　P. Haas, *Saving the Mediterranean: The Politics of International Environmental Cooperation*, New York: Columbia University Press, 1990, p. xviii. For more on epistemic communities, see Haas, 'Epistemic Communities and International Policy Coordination', *International Organization*, vol. 46, no. 1, Winter 1992, pp. 1–35; E. Adler, 'The Emergence of Cooperation: National Epistemic Communities and the International Evolution of the Idea of Nuclear Arms Control', *International Organization*, vol. 46, no. 1, Winter 1992, pp. 101–45; E. Adler and P. Haas, 'Conclusion: Epistemic Communities, World Order, and the Creation of a Reflective Research Program', *International Organization*, vol. 46, no. 1, Winter 1992, pp. 367–90; J. K. Sebenius, 'Challenging Conventional Explanations of International Cooperation: Negotiation Analysis and the Case of Epistemic Communities', *International Organization*, vol. 46, no. 1, Winter 1992, pp. 323–65; E. A. Kolodziej, 'Epistemic Communities Searching for Regional Cooperation', *Mershon International Studies Review*, vol. 41, no. 1, May 1997, pp. 93–98; and C. W. Thomas, 'Public Management as Interagency Cooperation: Testing Epistemic Community Theory at the Domestic Level', *Journal of Public Administration Research and Theory*, vol. 7, no. 2, Apr. 1997, pp. 221–46.
4　L. Elliot, *The Global Politics of the Environment* (2nd edn), New York: Palgrave Macmillan, 2004, p. 114.
5　Ibid., p. 115.
6　Haas, *Saving the Mediterranean*, p. xxii.
7　Ibid.
8　Adler and Haas, 'Conclusion', p. 372.

9 Haas, *Saving the Mediterranean*.
10 'The Global Climate Change Regime', *Council on Foreign Relations*, 29 Nov. 2010. Online. HTTP: <http://www.cfr.org/climate-change/global-climate-change-regime/p21831> (accessed 20 June 2011).
11 For more, see F. Pearce, 'Claims Himalayan Glaciers Could Melt By 2035 Were False, Says UN Scientist', *Guardian*, 20 Jan. 2010. Online. HTTP: <http://www.guardian.co.uk/environment/2010/jan/20/himalayan-glaciers-melt-claims-false-ipcc> (accessed 4 Jan. 2011); 'Controversy Behind Climate Science's "Hockey Stick" Graph', *Guardian*, 2 Feb. 2010. Online. HTTP: <http://www.guardian.co.uk/environment/2010/feb/02/hockey-stick-graph-climate-change?INTCMP=ILCNETTXT3487> (accessed 7 Jan. 2011); D. Carrington, 'In Defence of the IPCC: Critics Ignore the Real Scandal', *Guardian*, 28 July 2011. Online. HTTP: <http://www.guardian.co.uk/environment/damian-carrington-blog/2011/jul/28/ipcc-climate-change-science-pachauri> (accessed 3 Aug. 2011); P. Stanford, 'Can Prof Rajendra Pachauri Really Survive Glaciergate?', 26 July 2011. Online. HTTP: <http://www.telegraph.co.uk/earth/environment/climatechange/8660714/Can-Prof-Rajendra-Pachauri-really-survive-Glaciergate.html> (accessed 4 Aug. 2011).
12 For more see 'InterAcademy Council Report Recommends Fundamental Reform of IPCC Management Structure', *Press release from InterAcademy Council*, Review of the IPCC, 30 Aug. 2010. Online. HTTP: <http://reviewipcc.interacademycouncil.net/ReportNewsRelease.html> (accessed 30 July 2011).
13 'The Global Climate Change Regime', *Council on Foreign Relations*.
14 Interviews with environmental activists, scientists and journalists in New Delhi.
15 Ibid.
16 It must be clarified here that while each organization funds the majority of its work through project-based activities for a variety of clients, both are non-governmental actors, i.e. they do not depend on funding from the Indian state for their basic survival.
17 For example, see 'Understanding and Responding to Climate Change', *Highlights of the National Academies Reports*, 2008. Online. HTTP: <http://americasclimatechoices.org/climate_change_2008_final.pdf> (accessed 3 Mar. 2011); 'Key Findings', *United States Global Change Research Group*. Online. HTTP: <http://www.globalchange.gov/publications/reports/scientific-assessments/us-impacts/key-findings> (accessed 3 Mar. 2011); 'Climate Change', *The Royal Society*. Online. HTTP: <http://royalsociety.org/landing.asp?id=1278> (accessed 1 Aug. 2010). For more, see M. A. Benarde, *Global Warming ... Global Warming*, New York: Wiley, 1992; R. Bate and J. Morris, *Global Warming: Apocalypse or Hot Air?*, London: Institute of Economic Affairs, 1994; N. Arnell, *Global Warming, River Flows and Water Resources*, Chichester, England: Wiley, 1996; J. J. Berger, *Beating the Heat: Why and How We Must Combat Global Warming*, Berkeley, CA: Berkeley Hills Books, 2000; R. Bailey (ed.), *Earth Report 2000: Revisiting the True State of the Planet*, New York: McGraw-Hill, 2000; C. Perrings, 'The Economics of Abrupt Climate Change', Philosophical Transactions of the Royal Society of London. Series A, Mathematical and Physical Sciences, vol. 361, 15 Sept. 2003, pp. 2043–59; H. Brauch et al. (eds), Security and Environment in the Mediterranean: Conceptualising Security Conflicts, Berlin: Springer, 2003; L. Hinzman et al., 'Evidence and Implications of Recent Climate Change in Northern Alaska and Other Arctic Regions', Climatic Change, vol. 72, Oct. 2005, pp. 251–98; and 'Special Report: Climate Change', *New Scientist*. Online. HTTP: <http://environment.newscientist.com/channel/earth/climate-change> (accessed 28 Aug. 2010).
18 For example, see S. Boyle and J. Ardill, *The Greenhouse Effect: A Practical Guide to the World's Changing Climate*, London: New English Library, 1989; S. H. Schneider, *Global Warming: Are We Entering the Greenhouse Century?* San Francisco: Sierra Club Books, 1989; and J. Legett, *Global Warming: The Greenpeace Report*, Oxford: Oxford University Press, 1990.
19 P. Newell, *Climate for Change: Non-State Actors and the Global Politics of the Greenhouse*, Cambridge: Cambridge University Press, 2000, p. 30. Also see, see M. J. Chadwick,

I. M. Mintzer and J. A. Leonard (eds), *Negotiating Climate Change: The Inside Story of the Rio Convention*, Cambridge, New York: Cambridge University Press, 1994; T. O'Riordan and J. Jager, *Politics of Climate Change: A European Perspective*, London: Routledge, 1996; and W. D. Nordhaus, *Economics and Policy Issues in Climate Change*, Washington DC: RFF Press, 1998.

20 'The IPCC: Who Are They and Why Do Their Climate Reports Matter?', *Union of Concerned Scientists*. Online. HTTP: <http://www.un.org/Pubs/chronicle/2007/webArticles/101907_nobel_prize_ipcc.html> (accessed 28 Aug. 2010).

21 'IPCC Eighteenth Plenary Session, London, September 24–29 2001', *Institute for International Sustainable Development*, 2001. Online. HTTP: <http://www.iisd.ca/climate/ipcc18/> (accessed 2 Aug. 2010) and 'What is the IPCC?', Max Planck Institute for Meteorology. Online. HTTP: <http://www.mpimet.mpg.de/en/news/press/faq-frequently-asked-questions/what-is-the-ipcc.html> (accessed 2 Aug. 2010). For IPCC's assessment reports as well as other publications, see 'IPCC Reports', *Intergovernmental Panel on Climate Change (IPCC)*. Online. HTTP: <http://www.ipcc.ch/publications_and_data/publications_and_data.shtml> (accessed 2 Aug. 2010).

22 For example, see C. B. Gray and D. B. Rivkin, 'A "No Regrets" Environmental Policy', *Foreign Policy*, vol. 83, Summer 1991, pp. 47–65 and J. Leggert, 'Energy and the New Politics of the Environment', *Energy Policy*, vol. 19, March 1991, pp. 161–70.

23 Newell, *Climate for Change*, p. 30. Also see Z. Kaczmarek, *Water Resources Management in the Face of Climatic/Hydrologic Uncertainties*, Springer, 1996; H. F. Diaz and B. J. Morehouse, *Climate and Water: Transboundary Challenges in the Americas*, Boston: Kluwer Academic Publishers, 2003; and D. Molden, *Water for Food, Water for Life: A Comprehensive Assessment of Water Management in Agriculture*, London: Earthscan, 2007.

24 For example, see F. Yamin and J. Depledge, *The International Climate Change Regime: A Guide to Rules, Institutions and Procedures*, Cambridge: Cambridge University Press, 2004; T. G. Moore, *In Sickness or in Health: The Kyoto Protocol Versus Global Warming*, Stanford: Hoover Institute Press, 2000 and D. G. Victor, *The Collapse of The Kyoto Protocol and the Struggle to Slow Global Warming*, Princeton, NJ: Princeton University Press, 2001.

25 For example, see A. Grossman and C. Owren, 'Gender, Climate Change and Human Security: Lessons from Bangladesh, Ghana and Senegal', *Prepared by The Women's Environment and Development Organization (WEDO) with ABANTU for Development in Ghana*, ActionAid Bangladesh and ENDA in Senegal, May 2008. Online. HTTP: <http://www.wedo.org/files/HSN%20Study%20Final%20May%2020,%202008.pdf> (accessed 2 Aug. 2010); 'Climate Change and Security', *Royal United Services Institute for Defence and Security Studies (RUSI)*. Online. HTTP: <http://www.rusi.org/climate/> (accessed 2 Aug. 2010); C. Abbott, 'Climate Change: The Real Threat to Security', *China Dialogue*, 23 June 2006. Online. HTTP: <http://www.chinadialogue.net/article/show/single/en/132-Climate-Change-the-real-threat-to-security> (accessed 2 Aug. 2010); 'Human Security, Climate Change, and Environmentally Induced Migration', *United Nations University, Institute for Environment and Human Security*, 28 June 2008. Online. HTTP: <http://www.each-for.eu/documents/ELIAMEP.pdf> (accessed 2 Aug. 2010) and 'Military Panel: Climate Change Threatens U.S. National Security', *Environment News Service*, 16 Apr. 2007. Online. HTTP: <http://www.ens-newswire.com/ens/apr2007/2007-04-16-05.asp> (accessed 2 Aug. 2010).

26 Grossman and Owren, 'Gender, Climate Change and Human Security', p. 5.

27 For more, see 'Climate Impacts and Adaptations', *World Wildlife Fund (WWF)*. Online. HTTP: <http://www.worldwildlife.org/climate/impactsandadaptation.html> (accessed 10 Aug. 2010); 'Adapting to Climate Change: What's Needed in Poor Countries, and Who Should Pay', *Oxfam Briefing Paper*, 29 May 2007. Online. HTTP: <http://www.oxfam.org/files/adapting%20to%20climate%20change.pdf> (accessed 10 Aug. 2010) and 'Impacts', *Greenpeace International*. Online. HTTP: <http://www.greenpeace.org/international/campaigns/climate-change/impacts> (accessed 10 Aug. 2010).

28 For example, see 'Climate Change and Security', *RUSI*. Online. HTTP: <http://www.rusi.org/climate/> (accessed 10 Aug. 2010); 'Does Global Warming Comprise National Security?', *Time*, 17 Apr. 2008. Online. HTTP: http://www.time.com/time/specials/2007/article/0,28804,1730759_1731383_1731632,00.html> (accessed 10 Aug. 2008); J. Wihbey, 'Covering Climate Change as a National Security Issue', *Yale Forum on Climate Change and the Media*, 17 July 2008. Online. HTTP: <http://www.yaleclimatemediaforum.org/features/0708_security.htm> (accessed 10 Aug. 2008) and CAN Corporation, 'National Security and the Threat of Climate Change', April 2007, p. 3. Online. HTTP: <http://securityandclimate.cna.org/report/National%20Security%20and%20the%20Threat%20of%20Climate%20Change.pdf> (accessed 14 Aug. 2010). This report received widespread media attention. For example, see 'Military Panel', *Environment News Service* and 'Climate Change: A Threat to Global Security', *Green Energy News*, 15 Apr. 2007. Online. HTTP: <http://www.green-energy-news.com/arch/nrgs2007/20070050.html> (accessed 21 Aug. 2008). Also see 'The Age of Consequences: The Foreign Policy and National Security Implications of Global Climate Change', *Center for Strategic and International Studies*, November 2007, p. 10. Online. HTTP: <http://csis.org/publication/age-consequences> (accessed 14 Aug. 2008).

29 P. Schwartz and D. Randall, 'An Abrupt Climate Change Scenario and Its Implications for United States National Security', *Greenpeace*, October 2003. Online. HTTP: <http://www.greenpeace.org/raw/content/international/press/reports/an-abrupt-climate-change-scena.pdf> (accessed 31 May 2009).

30 A. Clark, 'Climate Change Threatens Security: UK Tells UN', *Guardian*, 18 Apr. 2007. Online. HTTP: <http://www.guardian.co.uk/environment/2007/apr/18/greenpolitics.climatechange> (accessed 13 Aug. 2010).

31 K. Annan, 'Global Warming an All-Encompassing Threat', *Environment News Service*, 15 Nov. 2006. Online. HTTP: <http://www.ens-newswire.com/ens/nov2006/2006-11-15-insann.asp> (accessed 14. Aug. 2010).

32 R. Schubert et al., *Climate Change as a Security Risk*, London: Earthscan, 2008.

33 C. Hedegaard, 'Copenhagen Climate Summit: Tough Times Not an Excuse to Avoid Hard Decisions', *Daily Telegraph*, 7 Dec. 2009. Online. HTTP: <http://www.telegraph.co.uk/earth/copenhagen-climate-change-confe/6712272/Copenhagen-climate-summit-tough-times-not-an-excuse-to-avoid-hard-decisions.html> (accessed 12 July 2011).

34 'Port of Spain Climate Change Consensus: The Commonwealth Climate Change Declaration 2009', *Commonwealth Secretariat*, 28 Nov. 2009. Online. HTTP: <http://www.thecommonwealth.org/files/216780/FileName/PortofSpainClimateChange-Consensus-TheCommonwealthClimateChangeDeclaration.PDF> (accessed 12 July 2011).

35 For example, see J. T. Mathews, 'Redefining Security', *Foreign Affairs*, vol. 68, no. 2, Spring 1989, pp. 162–77; B. Rodal, 'The Environment and Changing Concepts of Security', *Canadian Security Intelligence Service Commentary*, no. 47, Aug. 1994. Online. HTTP: <http://www.csis-scrs.gc.ca/pblctns/cmmntr/cm47-eng.asp> (accessed 14 Aug. 2010); M. A. Levy, 'Is the Environment a National Security Issue?', *International Security*, vol. 20, no. 2, Autumn 1995, pp. 35–62; T. Homer-Dixon, 'On the Threshold: Environmental Changes as Causes of Acute Conflict', *International Security*, vol. 16, no. 2, Autumn 1991, pp. 76–116; N. Myers, 'Environmental Refugees in a Globally Warmed World', *BioScience*, vol. 43, Dec. 1993, pp. 752–61 and B. R. Döös, 'Environmental Degradation, Global Food Production, and Risk for Large-Scale Migrations', *Ambio*, vol. 23, Mar. 1994, pp. 124–30.

36 B. Walsh, 'Q& a: The UN's Ban Ki-Moon on Climate Change', *Time*, 11 Dec. 2009. Online. HTTP: <http://www.time.com/time/specials/packages/article/0,28804,1929071_1929070_1947173,00.html> (accessed 12 July 2011).

37 M. Besheer, 'UN: Climate Change Could Cause Instability for Some Nations', *Voice of America*, 20 July 2011. Online. HTTP: <http://www.voanews.com/english/news/environment/UN-Climate-Change-Could-Cause-Instability-for-Some-Nations-125915354.html> (accessed 27 July 2011).

38 U. Kelkar and S. Bhadwal, 'South Asia Regional Study on Climate Change, Impacts and Adaptations: Implications for Human Development', *Paper prepared by TERI and Human Development Report Office 2007/08*, p. 4. Online. HTTP: <http://hdr.undp.org/en/reports/global/hdr2007–8/> (accessed 1 Aug. 2008).

39 'Climate Change 2001: Working Group II: Impacts, Adaptation and Vulnerability', *Intergovernmental Panel on Climate Change (IPCC)*, 2001. Online. HTTP: <http://www.grida.no/publications/other/ipcc_tar/?src=/climate/IPCC_tar/wg2/439.htm> (accessed 29 Apr. 2009).

40 Ibid.

41 Kelkar and Bhadwal, 'South Asia Regional Study on Climate Change', p. 15.

42 Ibid., p. 16.

43 'National Adaptation Programme of Action', *Ministry of Environment, Energy and Water, Republic of Maldives 2007*, p. 32. Online. HTTP: <http://env.rol.net.mv/docs/Reports/National%20Adaptation%20Programme%20of%20Action%20-%20Maldives/NAPA_Maldives_optimised.pdf> (accessed 29 Apr. 2011).

44 Kelkar and Bhadwal, 'South Asia Regional Study on Climate Change', p. 17. For more on impacts of climate change on Sri Lanka, see F. Samath, 'Sri Lanka: Climate Change Worse Than Civil War – UN Expert', *IPS News*, 24 Apr. 2007. Online. HTTP: <http://ipsnews.net/news.asp?idnews=37463> (accessed 29 Apr. 2009) and 'Sri Lanka Climate Change May Ravage Agriculture, Coast Areas', *Lanka Business Online*, 18 Dec. 2007. Online. HTTP: <http://www.lankabusinessonline.com/fullstory.php?newsID=1301661969&no_view=1&SEARCH_TERM=1> (accessed 20 Apr. 2011).

45 'Climate Change and South Asia: Rural Lives and Livelihoods of Millions at Risk', *World Bank*, 30 Nov. 2007. Online. HTTP: <http://web.worldbank.org/WBSITE/EXTERNAL/COUNTRIES/SOUTHASIAEXT/0,contentMDK:21571064~pagePK:146736~piPK:146830~theSitePK:223547,00.html> (12 Aug. 2010).

46 Ibid.

47 IPCC, 'Impacts, Adaptation and Vulnerability', *The Working Group II contribution to the IPCC Fourth Assessment Report 'Climate Change 2007'*, p. 475. Online. HTTP: <http://www.ipcc-wg2.org/index.html> (accessed 12 Aug. 2010).

48 Kelkar and Bhadwal, 'South Asia Regional Study on Climate Change', p. 7.

49 '2010 Warmest Year on Record', *The Australian*, 14 Jan. 2011. Online. HTTP: <http://www.theaustralian.com.au/news/world/warmest-year-on-record/story-e6frg6so-1225987372032> (accessed 13 Mar. 2011).

50 'India, S Asian Nations Face Extreme Weather', *Deccan Herald*, 23 Jan. 2011. Online. HTTP: <http://www.deccanherald.com/content/131598/india-s-asian-nations-face.html> (accessed 12 July 2011). Also see IPCC, 'Impacts, Adaptation and Vulnerability', p. 479; 'Extreme Weather: A Global Problem', *International Herald Tribune*, 7 Aug. 2007. Online. HTTP: <http://www.iht.com/articles/2007/08/07/news/weather.php> (accessed 13 Aug. 2010); L. MacInnis, 'Early 2007 Saw Record-Breaking Extreme Weather: UN', *Stopglobalwarming.org*, 8 Aug. 2007. Online. HTTP: <http://www.stopglobalwarming.org/sgw_read.asp?id=122858882007> (accessed 13 Aug. 2010); 'The Impact of Climate Change on Least Developed Countries and Small Island Developing States', *United Nations Office of the High Representative for the Least Developed Countries, Landlocked Developing Countries and Small Island Developing States*, New York, June 2007, p. 8. Online. HTTP: <http://www.iied.org/CC/documents/ClimateChange-ReportFinal.pdf> (accessed 13 Aug. 2010); and 'Climate Change and Small Island States, The Alliance of Small Island States (AOSIS)', *Ministerial Conference on Environment and Development in Asia and the Pacific 2000*, Kitakyushu, Japan, Aug. 31 – Sept. 5 2000. Online. HTTP: <http://www.unescap.org/mced2000/pacific/background/AOSIS.htm> (accessed 13 Aug. 2010).

51 'Human Failure Exacerbates Scale of Natural Disasters: Oxfam', *InfoChange News and Features*, April 2008. Online. HTTP: <http://infochangeindia.org/200804237081/

Disasters/Related-Reports/Human-failure-exacerbates-scale-of-natural-disasters-Oxfam.html> (accessed 13 Aug. 2010).

52 'Enhanced Disaster Preparedness in South Asia: Through Community-Based and Regional Approaches', *Annual Programme Statement (APS), USAID/DCHA/OFDA*, ReliefWeb, 24 Apr. 2002. Online. HTTP: <http://www.reliefweb.int/rw/RWB. NSF/db900SID/OCHA-64CEVD?OpenDocument> (accessed 13 Aug. 2010). Also see R. S. Negi, 'Disaster Lessons Call for Greater Preparedness', *OneWorld South Asia*, 19 July 2008. Online. HTTP: <http://southasia.oneworld.net/todaysheadlines/disaster-lessons-call-for-greater-preparedness> (accessed 13 Aug. 2010) and BCAS at 'Research Areas', *Climate Change Network South Asia*, 13 Aug. 2008. Online. HTTP: <http://www.can-sa.net/cansa/research_areas.htm> (accessed 13 Aug. 2010).

53 IPCC, 'Impacts, Adaptation and Vulnerability', p. 484.

54 Ibid.

55 Kelkar and Bhadwal, 'South Asia Regional Study on Climate Change', p. 13.

56 Ibid.

57 Interviews with environmental activists and journalists in New Delhi. Also see L. Friedman, 'How Will Climate Change Impact National Security?', *Scientific American*, 23 Mar. 2009. Online. HTTP: <http://www.scientificamerican.com/article.cfm?id=climage-refugees-national-security> (accessed 31 May 2011) and 'Climate Change Refugees Seek a New International Deal', *ClimateChangeCorp*, 27 Dec. 2008. Online. HTTP: <http://www.climatechangecorp.com/content.asp?ContentID=5871> (accessed 31 May 2011).

58 'Climate Change Scenarios for India', Keysheet 2, *India–UK collaboration on impacts of climate change in India*. Online. HTTP: <http://www.defra.gov.uk/environment/climatechange/internat/devcountry/pdf/india-climate-2-climate.pdf> (accessed 15 Aug. 2010).

59 For example, see K. L. Babu et al., 'Possible Enhanced Conflict Situations on Account of Climate Change on Account of Water Sharing: A Case Study of Three States of India', *Human Security and Climate Change – An International Workshop*, 21–23 June 2005. Online. HTTP: <http://www.gechs.org/downloads/holmen/Babu_etal.pdf> (accessed 15 Aug. 2010).

60 For example, see R. Sanchez-Rodriguez et al., 'Introduction to the "Global Environmental Change, Natural Disasters, Vulnerability and their Implications for Human Security in Coastal Urban Areas" Issue', *IHDP Update*, Issue 2, October 2007. Online. HTTP: <http://www.ihdp.uni-bonn.de/Pdf_files/Updates/IHDPUpdate2_2007.pdf> (accessed 15 Aug. 2010).

61 'Climate Change Threat Real, Change Lifestyle: PM', *The Times of India*, 5 June 2007. Online. HTTP: <http://www.hindustantimes.com/storypage/storypage.aspx?id=7aba6298-7bce-4c6a-8b6d-2f78fad93cc2&ParentID=90fc013b-af57-40d2-b066-a5ac1995828d&MatchID1=4468&TeamID1=2&TeamID2=4&MatchType1=1&SeriesID1=11> (accessed 15 Aug. 2010).

62 'Dealing with the Threat of Climate Change – India Country Paper', *MEA India*. Online. HTTP: <http://www.meaindia.nic.in/speech/2005/07/07ss02.pdf> (accessed 15 Aug. 2010).

63 Interviews with climate change experts in New Delhi.

64 T. Deen, 'Climate Change: Legitimacy of Security Council Meeting Challenged', *IPS News*, 7 Apr. 2007. Online. HTTP: <http://ipsnews.net/news.asp?idnews=37382> (accessed 4 May 2011).

65 'Security Council Holds First-Ever Debate on Impact of Climate Change on Peace, Security, Hearing Over 50 Speakers', *UNSC Department of Public Information*, 17 Apr. 2007. Online. HTTP: <http://www.un.org/News/Press/docs/2007/sc9000.doc.htm> (accessed 4 May 2011).

66 'The Road to Copenhagen: India's Position on Climate Change Issues', *Ministry of External Affairs*, Government of India, 27 Feb. 2009, p. 10. Online. HTTP: <http://www.indiaenvironmentportal.org.in/files/climate_0.pdf> (accessed 4 May 2011).

67 J. K. Parikh and K. Parikh, 'Climate Change – India's Perceptions, Positions, Policies and Possibilities', *Indira Gandhi Institute for Development Research and Organization for Economic Co-operation and Development (OECD) 2002*, p. 6. Online. HTTP: <http://www.oecd.org/dataoecd/22/16/1934784.pdf> (accessed 15 Aug. 2010).

68 'India at a Glance', *World Bank Development Data*, 25 Jan. 2011. Online. HTTP: <http://devdata.worldbank.org/AAG/ind_aag.pdf> (accessed 12 July 2011).
   'Empowering Farmers Through Real Time Weather and Price Information: Reuters Market Light', *WBCSD-SNV Alliance*. Online. HTTP: <http://www.inclusivebusiness.org/2008/06/reuters-market.html> (accessed 16 Aug. 2010). Also see 'India's Role in World Agriculture', *MAP*, no. 03/07, Dec. 2007. Online. HTTP: <http://ec.europa.eu/agriculture/publi/map/03_07_sum.pdf> (accessed 16 Aug. 2010) and 'India: Priorities for Agriculture and Rural Development', *World Bank*. Online. HTTP: <http://web.worldbank.org/WBSITE/EXTERNAL/COUNTRIES/SOUTHASIA EXT/EXTSAREGTOPAGRI/0,contentMDK:20273764~menuPK:548214~page PK:34004173~piPK:34003707~theSitePK:452766,00.html> (accessed 15 Aug. 2010).

69 C. R. Hazra, 'Crop Diversification in India', in M. K. Papademetriou and F. J. Dent (eds.), *Crop Diversification in the Asia-Pacific Region*, FAO Regional Office for Asia and the Pacific, Bangkok 2001. Online: <http://www.fao.org/docrep/003/x6906e/x6906e06.htm> (accessed 15 Aug. 2010). For more see S. Sengupta, 'Climate Change Threatens Food Production in India, UN Experts Warn', *International Herald Tribune*, 8 Aug. 2007. Online. HTTP: <http://www.iht.com/articles/2007/08/08/news/india.php> (accessed 15 Aug. 2010).

70 See 'How Will Climate Change Affect India's Monsoon Season?', *Science Daily*, 12 Mar. 2007. Online. HTTP: <http://www.sciencedaily.com/releases/2007/03/070308121808.htm> (accessed 14 Aug. 2010).

71 Ibid.

72 'Climate Change 2001: Impacts, Adaptation and Vulnerability', *IPCC*, p. 543. Online. HTTP: <http://www.ipcc.ch/ipccreports/tar/wg2/pdf/wg2TARchap11.pdf> (accessed 19 Aug. 2010).

73 For example, see R. Ramesh, 'Monsoon Floods Displace 19 Million', *Guardian*, 3 Aug. 2007. Online. HTTP: <http://www.guardian.co.uk/world/2007/aug/03/india.randeepramesh> (accessed 15 Aug. 2010).

74 M. S. R. Khan, 'Securing India's Coastline', *Institute for Peace and Conflict Studies (IPCS)*, 7 Feb. 2008. Online. HTTP: <http://www.ipcs.org/whatsNewArticle11.jsp?action= showView&kValue=2503&status=article&mod=b> (accessed 19 Aug. 2010). Union Territories are administered by the Indian President through an administrator whom he appoints.

75 IPCC in R. Kumar, P. Jawale and S. Tandon, 'Economic Impact of Climate Change on Mumbai, India', *Regional Health Forum*, vol. 12, no. 1, 2008, p. 38. Online. HTTP: <http://searo.who.int/LinkFiles/Regional_Health_Forum_Volume_12_No_1_Econo mic_impact_of.pdf> (accessed 19 Aug. 2010).

76 Ibid. Also see T. V. Padma, 'Development Versus Climate Change in India', *SciDev Net*, 31 Aug. 2006. Online. HTTP: <http://www.scidev.net/en/features/development-versus-climate-change-in-india.html> (accessed 19 Aug. 2010).

77 'India: Largest Cities and Towns and Statistics of their Population', *World Gazetteer*. Online. HTTP: <http://www.world-gazetteer.com/wg.php?x=&men=gcis&lng=en& dat=80&geo=-104&srt=pnan&col=aohdq&msz=1500&pt=c&va=&srt=pnan> (accessed 20 Aug. 2010).

78 For more, see 'Millions Suffer in Indian Monsoon', *BBC News*, 1 Aug. 2005. Online. HTTP: <http://news.bbc.co.uk/2/hi/south_asia/4733897.stm> (accessed 20 Aug. 2010); 'Tackling the Tides and Tremors: South Asia Disaster Report 2005', *Report by Duryog Nivaran*, South Asia Network for Disaster Risk Reduction, 2006, p. 94. Online. HTTP: <http://duryognivaran.org/sadr/pdfs/chapter5.pdf> (accessed 20 Aug. 2010) and 'India Counts the Costs of Floods', *BBC News*, 2 Aug. 2005. Online.

HTTP: <http://news.bbc.co.uk/2/hi/south_asia/4737187.stm > (accessed 20 Aug. 2010).

79 S. S. A. Aiyer, 'India, World Leader in Natural Disasters', *The Times of India*, 14 May 2006. Online. HTTP: <http://timesofindia.indiatimes.com/articleshow/1528671. cms> (accessed 21 Aug. 2010); and A. Gupta, 'Information Technology and Disaster Management in India'. Online. HTTP: <http://www.gisdevelopment.net/aars/acrs/ 2000/ts8/hami0001.asp> (accessed 21 Aug. 2010).

80 'India Natural Disaster Profile', *LDEO*, The Earth Institute at Columbia University. Online. HTTP: <http://www.ldeo.columbia.edu/chrr/research/profiles/pdfs/india_- profile.pdf> (accessed 21 Aug. 2010).

81 'Climate Change Impacts and India', *UNDP*. Online. HTTP: <http://www.undp.org. in/index.php?option=com_content&task=view&id=297&Itemid=466> (accessed 21 Aug. 2010).

82 Kelkar and Bhadwal, 'South Asia Regional Study on Climate Change', p. 18.

83 Ibid.

84 For more on the 1992 Rio Earth Summit, see 'UNCED 1999 Earth Summit', *United Nations*. Online. HTTP: <http://www.un.org/geninfo/bp/enviro.html> (accessed 22 Aug. 2010); E. A. Parson, P. M. Haas and M. A. Levy, 'A Summary of the Major Documents Signed at the Earth Summit and the Global Forum', *Center for International Earth Science Information Network*. Online. HTTP: <http://www.ciesin.org/docs/003–312. html> (accessed 22 Aug. 2010); J. G. Speth, 'A Post-Rio Compact', Foreign Policy, vol. 88, Autumn 1992, pp. 145–61 and J. Davidson, 'The Earth Summit', Development in Practice, vol. 2, no. 3, Oct. 1992, pp. 201–3.

85 'The United National Framework Convention on Climate Change', *UNFCCC*. Online. HTTP: <http://unfccc.int/essential_background/convention/items/2627.php> (accessed 23 Aug. 2010).

86 W. J. McKibbin, 'Climate Change Policy for India', Lowy Institute for International Policy, 30 Apr. 2004, p. 1. Online. HTTP: <http://www.lowyinstitute.org/Publication. asp?pid=128> (accessed 23 Aug. 2010).

87 'Kyoto Protocol', *UNFCCC*. Online. HTTP: <http://unfccc.int/kyoto_protocol/ items/2830.php> (accessed 23 Aug. 2010). As of April 2008, 172 countries had signed and ratified the protocol. The US remains amongst those countries that have yet to ratify it.

88 Parikh and Parikh, 'Climate Change', p. 25.

89 'India and UNFCCC', *Government of India*. Online. HTTP: <http://envfor.nic.in/cc/ india_unfccc.htm> (accessed 23 Aug. 2010).

90 For example, see A. G. Bhaya, 'Children's Charter on Climate Change', *The Times of India*, 25 Oct. 2002. Online. HTTP: <http://timesofindia.indiatimes.com/article- show/26195613.cms> (accessed 26 Aug. 2010); S. Narain, 'All Said and Done: Too Important for just Governments', *Equity Watch*, CSE Newsletter, 23 Oct. 2002. Online. HTTP: <http://www.cseindia.org/campaign/ew/ew_cop-8/government.htm> (accessed 26 Aug. 2010); 'NGO Events During COP 8', *Government of India*. Online. HTTP: <http://envfor.nic.in/cc/cop8/ngo.htm> (accessed 26 Aug. 2010) and A. Bischoff, 'Climate Justice at COP 8', *Greenspiration*. Online. HTTP: <http://www. greenspiration.org/environ/articles/ClimateJustice.htm> (accessed 26 Aug. 2010).

91 N. Khastagir, 'A Human Face to a Human Problem: Climate Justice Summit', *India Resource Centre*, 1 Nov. 2002. Online. HTTP: <http://www.indiaresource.org/issues/ energycc/2003/humanfacehumanproblem.html> (accessed 26 Aug. 2010).

92 P. Sekhsaria, 'G8, Clean Up Your Act', *The Times of India*, 8 July 2005. Online. HTTP: <http://timesofindia.indiatimes.com/articleshow/1164468.cms> (accessed 26 Aug. 2010).

93 'Eco-Sense at G8', *Indian Express*, 9 July 2005. Online. HTTP: <http://www.indianex press.com/archive_full_story.php?content_id=74087 > (accessed 26 Aug. 2010).

94 Ibid.

95 'Climate Change Will Affect India's Farming, Water Supply, Health', *MedIndia*, 31 Oct. 2007. Online. HTTP: <http://www.medindia.net/news/Climate-Change-Will-Hit-Indias-Farming-Water-Supply-Health-28712-1.htm> (accessed 26 Aug. 2010); 'Climate Change: Why India Must Act', *The Indian Economy Blog*, 12 June 2007. Online. HTTP: <http://indianeconomy.org/2007/06/12/climate-change-why-india-must-act/> (accessed 26 Aug. 2010); A. B. Sharma, 'Icrisat Cautions Indian Against the Impacts of Climate Change', *Financial Express*, 24 Sept. 2007. Online. HTTP: <http://www.financialexpress.com/news/Icrisat-cautions-India-against-impact-of-climate-change/220432/> (accessed 26 Aug. 2010) and C. E. Karunakaran, 'Climate Change – Should India Change?', *The Hindu*, 3 Dec. 2007. Online. HTTP: <http://www.hinduonnet.com/2007/12/03/stories/2007120354921100.htm> (accessed 26 Aug. 2010).
96 'National Action Plan on Climate Change (NAPCC)', *Government of India*, p. 2. Online. HTTP: <http://www.pmindia.nic.in/Pg01–52.pdf> (accessed 21 Aug. 2010).
97 'PM for Equitable and Fair Global Climate Change Framework', *Indiatimes.com*, 30 June 2008. Online. HTTP: <http://articles.economictimes.indiatimes.com/2008-06-30/news/27696064_1_climate-change-national-action-plan-capita-ghg-emissions> (accessed 28 June 2010).
98 Ibid.
99 NAPCC, *Government of India*, p. 1.
100 'Speech of Prime Minister Shri Atal Bihari Vajpayee at the High Level Segment of the Eighth Session of Conference of the Parties to the UN Framework Convention on Climate Change New Delhi, 30th October, 2002', *Government of India*. Online. HTTP: <http://unfccc.int/cop8/latest/ind_pm3010.pdf> (accessed 27 Aug. 2010).
101 'Council on Climate Change Constituted', *The Hindu*, 6 June 2007. Online. HTTP: <http://www.hinduonnet.com/2007/06/06/stories/2007060605991300.htm> (accessed 2 Sept. 2010).
102 For a full list of the members of the PMCCC, see 'PM's Council on Climate Change', *Prime Minister of India*, 6 June 2008. Online. HTTP: <http://pmindia.nic.in/climate-body.htm> (accessed 3 Sept. 2011)
103 In 'Climate Change Threat Real, Change Lifestyle: PM', *Hindustan Times*, 5 June 2007. Online. HTTP: <http://www.hindustantimes.com/storypage/storypage.aspx?sectionName=&id=7aba6298–7bce-4c6a-8b6d-2f78fad93ce2&&Headline=%27Climate+change+threat+real%2c+change+lifestyle%27&strParent=strParentID> (accessed 27 Aug. 2010).
104 NAPCC, *Government of India*, p. 1.
105 Ibid.
106 B. Buzan, O. Wæver and J. de Wilde, *Security: A New Framework for Analysis*, Boulder, CO: Lynne Rienner, 1998, pp. 32–33.
107 Ibid., p. 33.
108 The UN Secretary General, for example, has said that how the world addresses the threat of climate change 'will define us, our era and ultimately our global legacy'. See 'Secretary-General Challenges World Community to Tackle Climate Change', *Press release of 61st UN General Assembly Informal Thematic Debate*, 31 July 2007. Online. HTTP: <http://www.un.org/News/Press/docs/2007/ga10607.doc.htm> (accessed 1 Sept. 2010).
109 Buzan et al., *Security*, p. 25.
110 'Opposition Mounts Attack on PM in LS on Cash-for-Votes Scam', *The India Daily*, 23 Mar. 2011. Online. HTTP: <http://www.theindiadaily.com/opposition-mounts-attack-on-pm-in-ls-on-cash-for-votes-scam/> (accessed 5 April 2011).
111 P. Bidwai, 'Politics-India: Costly Vote of Confidence', *IPS News*, 24 July 2008. Online. HTTP: <http://ipsnews.net/news.asp?idnews=43293> (accessed 23 Aug. 2010).
112 Ibid. For more, see 'Indian Govt Hit by Bribery Claims Ahead of Confidence Vote', *AFP*, 21 July 2008. Online. HTTP: <http://afp.google.com/article/ALeqM5j2dA4PDAQFxLne-xWZZoi4TJCFOw> (accessed 23 Aug. 2008); R. Bedi, 'Indian Government's

Victory Marred by Bribery Accusations', *The Telegraph*, 23 July 2008. Online. HTTP: <http://www.telegraph.co.uk/news/worldnews/asia/india/2446203/Indian-govern ments-victory-marred-by-bribery-accusations.html> (accessed 23 Aug. 2010); and S. Sengupta, 'India Confidence Vote Opens Way for US Nuclear Agreement', *International Herald Tribune*, 22 July 2008. Online. HTTP: <http://www.iht.com/articles/2008/ 07/22/asia/india.php> (accessed 12 Aug. 2010).

113 'Cash for Votes? Oppn MPs Show Wads of Currency Notes in LS', *The Indian Express*, 22 July 2008. Online. HTTP: <http://www.expressindia.com/latest-news/- Cash-for-votes-Oppn-MPs-show-wads-of-currency-notes-in-LS/338932/> (accessed 2 Sept. 2010). The matter is now the subject of an ongoing investigation by the Delhi police.

114 T. Biswas, 'Cash-for-Votes Scam: Amar Singh, Sudheendra Kulkarni chargesheeted', NDTV, 24 August 2011. Online. HTTP: <http://www.ndtv.com/article/india/cash- for-votes-scam-amar-singh-sudheendra-kulkarni-chargesheeted-128665&cp> (accessed 25 August 2011).

115 See CANSA Website. Online. HTTP: <http://www.cansouthasia.net/> (accessed 12 July 2011).

116 'About CSE: Anil Agarwal', *CSE India*. Online. HTTP: <http://www.cseindia.org/ node/216> (accessed 12 July 2011).

117 Ibid.

118 Ibid. For more on CSE and the impact of its research and analysis, see 'Fighting for a Better, Cleaner World', *India Together*, 27 Apr. 2005. Online. HTTP: <http://www. indiatogether.org/2005/apr/env-csenarain.htm> (accessed 29 July 2011).

119 Ibid.

120 R. Menon, 'Fighting for a Better, Cleaner World', *India Together*, 17 Apr. 2005. Online. HTTP: <http://www.indiatogether.org/2005/apr/env-csenarain.htm> (accessed 29 Aug. 2010).

121 The Padma Shri is awarded by the Indian state to citizens recognizing their dis- tinguished contribution in various spheres of activity. It is the fourth-highest civilian award in India.

122 For example, see letter to Indian Prime Minister Atal Bihari Vajpayee from CSE Director Anil Aggarwal and Deputy Director Sunita Narain, 19 Oct. 1998. Online. HTTP: <http://www.cseindia.org/html/eyou/climate/pm_letter.htm> (accessed 23 Aug. 2010); 'Two Decades of Breathless Development', *CSE Press Release*, 1 Nov. 1998. Online. HTTP: <http://www.cseindia.org/AboutUs/press_releases/au4_ 110198.htm> (31 Aug. 2008); 'How to make PUC More Effective', *CSE Press Release*, 4 Oct. 2002. Online. HTTP: <http://www.cseindia.org/campaign/apc/press_ 20021004.htm> (accessed 31 Aug. 2010); 'Unclean Business: The Sad Truth About CDM', *CSE Press Release*, 8 Nov. 2005. Online. HTTP: <http://www.cseindia.org/ AboutUs/press_releases/20051108.htm> (accessed 31 Aug. 2010) and 'CSE Warns Delhi: Time to Breathe Easy Over, Air Pollution Reaching Critical Levels Again in City', *CSE Press Release*, 6 Nov. 2007. Online. HTTP: <http://www.cseindia.org/ AboutUs/press_releases/press_20071106.htm> (accessed 31 Aug. 2010).

123 'Climate Change: The Road to Bali and Beyond', *CSE India*, 5 Dec. 2007. Online. HTTP: <http://www.cseindia.org/AboutUs/press_releases/press_20071205.htm> (accessed 29 Aug. 2010).

124 'Impacts of Climate Change: West and Central India', *CSE India*. Online. HTTP: <http://www.cseindia.org/programme/geg/pdf/western.pdf> (accessed 29 Aug. 2010).

125 'Report of Regional Consultation of WSSD (Western Region)', *CSE India*, 12–13 July 2002, p. 9. Online. HTTP: <http://www.cseindia.org/programme/geg/pdf/geg.pdf> (accessed 29 Aug. 2010).

126 See World Resources Institute, *World Resources 1990–91: A Guide to the Global Environment*, Oxford: Oxford University Press, 1990.

127 As pointed out by a senior expert at CSE. For the CSE report, see A. Agarwal and S. Narain, *Global Warming in an Unequal World: A Case of Environmental Colonialism*, New Delhi: CSE, 1991.

128 Ibid.

129 For a good summary of Narain's achievements and impact, see 'Sunita Narain-India', *World People's Blog*. Online. HTTP: <http://word.world-citizenship.org/wp-archive/699> (accessed 1 Sept. 2010).

130 S. Narain, 'Sublimating Climate Change', *Down To Earth*, 31 Dec. 2003. Online. HTTP: <http://www.downtoearth.org.in/content/sublimating-climate-change> (accessed 1 Sept. 2010).

131 Interview with a senior official at CSE.

132 For example, see A. Agarwal, 'Climate Change: A Challenge to India's Economy', Briefing Paper for Members of Parliament, *CSE*. Online. HTTP: <http://www.cseindia.org/html/eyou/climate/pdf/cse_briefing.pdf> (accessed 29 Aug. 2010).

133 'About TERI', *The Energy and Resources Institute (TERI)*. Online. HTTP: <http://www.teriin.org/index.php?option=com_content&task=view&id=17> (accessed 2 Sept. 2010).

134 Ibid.

135 For more on funding, see 'How is TERI Funded?', *The Energy and Resources Institute (TERI)*. Online. HTTP: <http://www.teriin.org/cocacola1_faq.php#2> (accessed 7 Oct. 2010).

136 'Earth Science and Climate Change', *The Energy and Resources Institute (TERI)*. Online. HTTP:<http://www.teriin.org/index.php?option=com_division&task=view_div&id=26> (accessed 31 Aug. 2010).

137 Ibid.

138 For example, S. Mitra et al., 'Climate Change and Vulnerability in Indian Agriculture: A Major Hurdle Towards Food Security', in R.B. Singh (ed.), *Natural Hazards and Disaster Management: Vulnerability and Mitigation*, New Delhi: Rawat, 2006, pp. 273–88; K. O'Brien et al., 'Vulnerability of Indian Agriculture to Climate Change and Economic Changes 2003', *Mainstreaming Biodiversity and Climate Change: Proceedings of the Asia Regional Workshop*, Dehra Dun, India: TERI, 6–11 Apr. 2003, pp. 41–47; and R. Pachauri and P. Mehrotra, 'Alternative Energy Sources', *2020 Focus 7 (Appropriate Technology for Sustainable Food), Brief 8 of 9*, August 2001.

139 R. Pachauri, 'Act Now on Climate Change, No Need to Wait: Top UN Scientist', *The Times of India*, 23 Oct. 2007. Online. HTTP: < http://economictimes.indiatimes.com/environment/act-now-on-climate-no-need-to-wait-top-un-scientist/articleshow/9300276.cms> (accessed 29 Aug. 2010).

140 R. Pachauri, 'Scary Future: More Hot Days, Floods Likely', *The Times of India*, 23 Oct. 2005. Online. HTTP: <http://www.teriin.org/upfiles/pub/articles/art15.pdf> (accessed 29 Aug. 2010).

141 R. Pachauri, 'Can Global Warming Be Controlled? Enough Resources Available for Mitigation', *The Times of India*, 5 Dec. 2005. Online. HTTP: <http://www.teriin.org/upfiles/pub/articles/art27.pdf> (accessed 29 Aug. 2010).

142 In India, a Chief Minister is the elected head of government at the level of states, and has most of the executive powers at this level.

143 See 'Durgawati Project: Centre to Fund 90% Cost', *Express India*, 11 Feb. 2008. Online. HTTP: <http://www.expressindia.com/latest-news/Durgadwani-project-Centre-to-fund-90-cost/271578/> (accessed 7 Oct. 2010).

144 'TERI Working on Sunderbans Project', *The Hindu*, 8 Aug. 2008. Online. HTTP: <http://www.hindu.com/2008/08/08/stories/2008080856120900.htm> (accessed 29 Aug. 2010).

145 'PM's Council on Climate Change', *Prime Minister of India*.

146 'Annual Report 2007/08', *The Energy and Resources Institute (TERI)*, p. 4. Online. HTTP: <http://www.teriin.org/about/Annual08.pdf> (accessed 4 May 2011).

147 Ibid.

148 Ibid.
149 See V. Sharma, 'Global Warming: Let's Take It Seriously', *The Tribune*, 13 May 2007. Online. HTTP: <http://www.tribuneindia.com/2007/20070513/edit.htm#5> (accessed 2 Sept. 2010).
150 See 'India's Most Influential', *Time*, 13 Aug. 2008. Online. HTTP: <http://www.time.com/time/specials/2007/0,28757,1652689,00.html> (accessed 29 Aug. 2010).
151 The Padma Bhushan is India's third-highest civilian award, one rank higher than the Padma Shri. See 'Biography: R. K. Pachauri', *US Climate Change Science Program*. Online. HTTP: <http://www.climatescience.gov/Library/bios/pachauri.htm> (accessed 31 Aug. 2010).
152 'Dr. R. K. Pachauri Conferred with Climate Protection Award by EPA', *The Financial Express*, 29 May 2008. Online. HTTP: <http://www.financialexpress.com/news/dr-r-k-pachauri-conferred-with-climate-protection-award-by-epa/316177/> (accessed 31 May 2011).
153 'Pachauri's IPCC, Al Gore Share Nobel Peace Prize', *Express India*, 12 Oct. 2007. Online. HTTP: <http://www.expressindia.com/latest-news/Pachauris-IPCC-Al-Gore-share-Nobel-Peace-Prize/227572/> (accessed 31 May 2011).
154 'Joining the Dots: The Report of the Tiger Task Force', *CSE India*, 19 Apr. 2005. Online. HTTP: <www.cseindia.org/userfiles/ttf_report.pdf> (accessed 31 Aug. 2010).
155 Buzan et al., *Security*, p. 33.
156 Ibid., p. 25.

6 Conclusion

NSAs, Securitization Theory and security practices in South Asia

South Asia remains one of the most volatile regions in the world. The history of violent conflict in the region, its enduring inter-state hostilities and the potential threat of nuclear conflict have all served to entrench the notion that security in South Asia remains mainly about military-political challenges. The relevance, therefore, of realist assumptions when analysing security in South Asia is regularly emphasized by regional analysts. For a long time, this has served to hinder the emergence of a more nuanced and broadened understanding of security in a region where 'internal insecurity is of much greater consequence ... than external insecurity'.[1] Despite the emergence of new ways of conceptualizing security in recent decades, the prevailing story of security in South Asia continues to be one told mainly through the perspectives of state elites, and remains largely disconnected from those security perspectives which resonate with a majority of South Asians, regardless of nationality.

For millions of South Asians, life is riddled with insecurities emerging from a wide range of issues, which do not necessarily reflect the security concerns of the state. Some of these insecurities are linked to the question of how to stay alive (i.e. the challenge of existential survival); others are more about how to be able to live a life which is not 'sub-human'.[2] They emerge from challenges ranging from poverty, hunger and lack of access to basic healthcare and education, to political violence and oppression, corruption, and socio-economic inequality resulting from 'many layers of social exclusion: religious, linguistic, gender, access to land/occupation, zaats/kinships/caste-like structures among others',[3] particularly in countries like India, Pakistan, Nepal, Bangladesh and Sri Lanka. The sheer scale of deprivation in South Asia helps put the significance of these insecurities for sub-state communities in the region into perspective. Despite impressive economic growth over the last two decades, South Asia continues to have the largest number of the poorest people in the world – more than 600 million.[4] In India alone, there are almost as many poor as in the twenty-six poorest countries in Africa.[5] The region also accounts for more than half of the world's undernourished children, one reflection of the fact that 'the burden of this human deprivation falls heavily on children and women' in South Asia.[6] High levels of deprivation have served to '[accentuate] the hierarchies of caste and gender and ethnic and religious inequities' in the region, and 'have led to the perpetuation of a vicious cycle of conflict and made South Asia the battleground for some of the world's long-standing religious, ethnic and caste conflicts'.[7] Unfortunately, rather than viewing these challenges from the perspectives of those who are most affected by them, states in the region have largely chosen to view them in terms of how they affect 'national' security. Subsequently, major policies to address some of these challenges have tended to be oriented towards protecting the interests of the state and those who rule, as opposed to those who are ruled.

In such a scenario, a security analysis which remains limited to examining the security policies of states and the articulations of those who are in particular positions of authority is inadequate. The analysis of security – if 'security' is to be understood as more than the safety of the state from military-political threats – needs to be informed by the concerns of state as well as sub-state groups. It also needs to be informed by the practices of actors other than states, especially when states are still mired in the process of democratization and may lack capacity, or are challenged by problems of misgovernance. It is in this context that this book has tried to highlight the role of non-state actors (NSAs) in South Asia. Private actors in the region, such as non-governmental organizations (NGOs), media organizations, civil society groups and epistemic communities, have been at the forefront of highlighting the insecurities of sub-state groups linked to different non-military issue areas. Their activities include working with vulnerable and affected groups to increase awareness and capacity to prevent and mitigate these insecurities; advocacy and lobbying state representatives to place the insecurities of sub-state groups at the centre of policy-making on these issues, and also devising and implementing measures to directly address the causes of insecurities at the sub-state level through their own efforts, often outside the state-led public policy realm.

The three case studies in this book demonstrate these different dynamics, and at the same time raise questions around how they may be analysed in a theoretically sophisticated and analytically coherent manner. The concept of Human Security and the Welsh School's critical approach to security are useful in gaining insights into the insecurities which may exist among sub-state groups in South Asia. Using a Critical Security Studies (CSS) approach, it becomes possible to analyse the prevailing, state-centric understanding of security in South Asia with respect to how it emerged, whose interests it serves, and how it may possibly be changed to reflect the concerns of the most deprived, marginalized and excluded groups in the region. At the practical level, Human security, broadly defined, emphasizes a range of components to security at the sub-state level. In doing so, it helps identify insecurities emerging from 'real world' issues such as lack of availability of or access to adequate healthcare, education and food; social and economic injustice and inequalities; environmental degradation, natural disasters and political violence, among others. When it comes to the *practice* of security, Securitization Theory provides a unique theoretical framework to identify how an issue is constructed as a 'security' threat by a specific type of actor, and possibly to what effect. The theory's approach, however, to identify who 'does' security (i.e. its preference for state actors) and how (i.e. its focus on state-led public policy as the only legitimate 'security' response), and its relative apathy towards the wider cultural and political contexts within which these dynamics occur, remains problematic. Recent developments towards fleshing out a sociological or pragmatic variant of Securitization Theory have helped emphasize the importance of factors such as cultural and political contexts within which securitization processes may occur; the multiplicity of audiences in determining what is or is not considered a 'security' threat; and the evolving nature of security policies.[8] As the case studies in the book show, however, key aspects of the theory continue to hinder its ability to produce a comprehensive and inclusive analysis, especially when applied to studying security practices in socio-political contexts such as in South Asia. These are briefly summarized below.

Who 'does' security?

Securitization Theory, as proposed by the Copenhagen School and also when underpinned by a sociological approach, continues to focus on the state level in looking for security responses. The state continues to be the preferred security actor, and the lack of clarity around the role of the securitizing actor and the securitizing agent or security practitioner, facilitates this preference to an extent. For example, the Copenhagen School argues that when a securitizing *actor* manages to 'break free of procedures and rules he and she would otherwise be bound by, we are witnessing a case of securitization'.[9] This creates ambiguity around whether it is the actor making the securitizing move who must have social capital and authority not only in relation to the issue (i.e. being an expert authority on the matter) at the heart of the securitizing move, but also be able to legitimately carry out the breaking of 'normal procedures and rules' (and therefore act as the securitizing agent). The concept of the breaking of 'normal procedures and rules' itself remains vague, although within the securitization studies literature it appears to have been widely interpreted as generally referring to those rules and procedures which relate to policy-making at the state-level. The concepts of 'extra-ordinary' and 'emergency' measures have similarly been left inadequately explained but have again generally been understood as urgent or even unprecedented measures in the context of policy-making (e.g. the suspension of regular parliamentary procedures ahead of action by state representatives or ahead of passing a bill into law). Consequently, analyses of security practices using Securitization Theory exclude those practices which may be led by NSAs, such as those discussed in this book, at the sub-state level. In particular, such an analysis overlooks the role of those NSAs which may not be involved in delivering services in conjunction with or on behalf of state institutions as part of a formal arrangement, such as the anti-trafficking NGOs in Nepal analysed in Chapter 4. By examining those security practices which unfold at the sub-state level and fall outside the domain of state-led public policies, Securitization Theory can move towards providing a more inclusive analysis of security dynamics in parts of the world such as South Asia. In order for this to occur, the requirement of breaking 'normal procedures and rules' needs to be reconsidered in a way which allows for a broader range of ways to 'securitize'; simultaneously, the distinction between the securitizing agent and the securitizing actor needs to be clarified. This is important because *how* an issue may be securitized relates to *who* is considered a valid securitizing actor. For example, individuals fighting for the rights of communities being forced to evict their homes to make room for developmental projects (such as dams and highways), without being adequately compensated and rehabilitated by the state, or for the rights of agricultural communities being forced to sell their lands to private corporations at nominal rates in the absence of clear land acquisition rights, may not have social capital and authority as conceived by the Copenhagen School. They may also not have the power or legitimacy to break 'normal procedures and rules' in the context of policy-making. Nonetheless, it may be argued that they are legitimately expressing the security concerns of those who are most endangered by the phenomenon, and risk losing their livelihoods and way of life as a consequence.

The role of the audience

Although conflicting with other parts of its theorizing, the Copenhagen School puts the audience at the centre of the success of a securitizing move without sufficiently elaborating on who the audience may be and what specific role(s) it may play at different stages of securitization. There have now, however, been solid efforts to develop the concept of the audience further by delineating the different types of audiences involved in different stages of the policy-making process.[10] While this is valuable in creating a more nuanced understanding of how security responses emerge at the state level in the form of public policy, it does not, however, address a key problem which arises particularly when considering security practices in developing socio-political contexts. If the final audience of a securitizing move (with the power and authority to reject or accept, and possibly implement, measures required to deal with the relevant issue in the form of public policy) consists of state representatives and state-led institutions, what does it mean for security practices in states where misgovernance is a significant problem? Furthermore, in instances where the state rejects, or even accepts but does not implement, suggested measures to deal with the relevant issue, the idea that the issue has been securitized is problematic. Such an approach not only places more emphasis on rhetoric than on action-led responses, but also discounts the possibility that other actors may emerge to respond on the ground in the absence of adequate responses from the state. The question therefore arises: what defines a successful securitization?

What defines a successful securitization?

There continues to be disagreement within the securitization studies literature over what may constitute a successful securitization. The Copenhagen School itself has provided conflicting statements on this matter. On the one hand, it has insisted that the implementation of 'extraordinary' or 'emergency' measures is not required for a successful securitization; all that is required is that the intended audience accepts the securitizing move and thereby allows for the creation of a platform 'from which is it possible to legitimize' such measures. On the other hand, it also proposes that the securitizing actor needs to break free of 'normal procedures and rules' in making a securitizing move. More recently, it has been argued that a definitive change in policy, or at least one which is proposed and accepted by the audience (if not implemented), is the mark of a successful securitization.[11] It may, however, be more useful to identify outcomes in which the insecurities of affected and vulnerable sub-state groups gain cognizance (1) within these groups themselves as factors significantly undermining their physical existence, livelihoods or way of life,[12] and (2) also among other, different audiences such as those groups with expert knowledge on the issues driving these insecurities, and their perceived as well as measurable impact (where relevant) on group members. Thus, a successful securitization would not necessarily have to lead to *public policy* responses – thereby weakening the emphasis placed so far within securitization studies on the role of state actors (as the final audience of securitizing moves around a particular issue), and opening up the scope to analyse other kinds of responses. In this context, the breaking of 'normal procedures and rules' becomes less significant, and it becomes possible to analyse the role of NSAs as securitizing agents or security practitioners, providing vulnerable and affected groups with measures to prevent and mitigate insecurities emerging from a range of issue areas.

NSAs, Securitization Theory and South Asia

The work of the Copenhagen School evolved in response to the European security problematique, particularly in the post-Cold War years.[13] This period saw 'the emergence of a large number of new bilateral and multilateral security institutions. ... [organized around] systems of rule through which state and non-state actors can organize their common and competing interests in individual, national, regional and global security'.[14] The practice of security through these institutions relies on a particular security regime, i.e. a set of 'principles, rules, and norms that permit [actors] ... to be restrained in their behaviour in the belief that others will reciprocate'.[15] Consequently, the Copenhagen School's theorizing has 'an explicitly European flavour',[16] and may explain why, barring a few exceptions, most theoretically driven discussions within securitization studies have emerged from this part of the world.[17]

When applied in regions like South Asia where development is ongoing, most states have poor governance records, and many have traditionally adopted an authoritarian approach to ruling their populations, the assumptions underpinning Securitization Theory are not very reliable. Historically, key state institutions and their representatives in countries like Sri Lanka, Pakistan, Bangladesh, Bhutan and Nepal have not always been restrained by, or conformed to, the kind of security regimes described above. Even in India, where democratic norms and principles are relatively more entrenched, aspects of misgovernance such as corruption and lack of sufficient accountability are widespread. Thus, in the absence of (adequate) state responses, it becomes even more important to consider whether the security needs of sub-state groups are being addressed by other, private actors. Responses by such actors may or may not be adequate; they may even have the effect of further increasing the insecurities of those they are aimed at protecting. It remains, however, that these actions are 'security' responses and therefore require further scholarly attention in order to be better understood and accounted for within a broadened security analysis. This has particular relevance for the study of non-traditional security issues, as the emergence of NSAs as security actors seems to have occurred mainly (though not exclusively) in non-military issue areas, or those where the state has lacked political interest and will, or capacity, to engage in an effective manner.

Despite the hostilities, rivalries and disputes which dominate state and regional security perceptions in South Asia, the existence of non-traditional challenges to the security of sub-state groups across the region also presents new opportunities for regional cooperation. Issues such as human trafficking, climate change, environmental degradation, water scarcity, food insecurity and forced population movements affect the majority, if not all, of South Asia's states. Such problems cannot be adequately addressed in the absence of cooperation across borders. In many of these issue areas, the work of NSAs has built solid foundations for effective cooperative mechanisms to emerge horizontally at the sub-state level and cutting across borders, as well as vertically at the state and regional levels. In the area of anti-trafficking, for example, a growing number of NGOs in the region have developed partnerships across borders which allow them to be more effective in their anti-trafficking efforts. These include detecting traffickers and identifying victims at border locations; rescuing them from brothels across state borders; and boarding them in safe houses and rehabilitation centres before and after repatriation to home countries respectively. In the area of renewable energy and sustainable development, the Energy and Resources Institute (TERI) in India is just one NSA which has forged networks such as those formed under the auspices of the Asia Energy Institute (AEI), which includes member institutes from the region and beyond, and aims to promote and facilitate greater information exchange between members, as well as joint research and training activities. The Centre for Science and Environment (CSE), another scientific policy community (CSE) analysed in this book, is also actively engaged in dialogues with similar NSAs in the region on environmental issues of common concern, with the aim of influencing policy at the national and regional levels.[18] The region has such active networks of NSAs operating in many other non-traditional issue areas. These networks, and the work being done by different NSAs within them, potentially provide states in South Asia with solid foundations upon which cooperative approaches to security may be further developed at the inter-state and regional levels.

Notes

1 P. R. Chari, 'Preface', in P. R. Chari (ed.), *Perspectives on National Security in South Asia*, New Delhi: Manohar, 1999, p. 7.

2 Ken Booth makes this very important distinction between security and survival, arguing that 'survival is not synonymous with security, it is the necessary condition'. For more, see K. Booth, *Theory of World Security*, Cambridge: Cambridge University Press, 2007, p. 107.

3 A. Kumar, 'A Review of Human Development Trends in South Asia: 1990–2009', *Human Development Research Paper 2010/44*, UNDP, Nov. 2010, p. 28. Online. HTTP: <http://hdr.undp.org/en/reports/global/hdr2010/papers/HDRP_2010_44.pdf> (accessed 6 July 2011).

4 Ibid., p. 1.

5 Ibid.

6 M. Haq, 'Human Development Challenge in South Asia', Introductory Speech at the launch of the report on *Human Development in South Asia 1997*, 9 Apr. 1997, Islamabad, p. 2. Online. HTTP: <http://www.mhhdc.org/Dr%20haq%20reports/Human% 20Development%20Challenge%20in%20South%20Asia.pdf> (accessed 6 July 2011).

7 Kumar, 'A Review of Human Development Trends', pp. 1–2.

8 For example, see contributions in T. Balzacq (ed.), *Securitization Theory: How Security Problems Emerge and Dissolve*, Abingdon: Routledge, 2011.

9 B. Buzan, O. Wæver and J. de Wilde, *Security: A New Framework for Analysis*, Boulder, CO: Lynne Rienner, 1998, p. 204.

10 For example, see S. Leonard and K. Kaunert, 'Reconceptualising the Audience', in T. Balzacq (ed.), *Securitization Theory: How Security Problems Emerge and Dissolve*, Abingdon: Routledge, 2011, pp. 58–61.

11 For example, see M. Salter, 'When Securitization Fails', in Balzacq (ed.), *Securitization Theory*, p. 126.

12 In order to analyse whether such cognizance exists and to what extent, ethnographic approaches such as participant analysis and semi-structured interviews would prove to be useful methodologies. For more, see T. Balzacq, 'Enquiries into Methods: A New Framework for Securitization Analysis', in Balzacq (ed.), *Securitization Theory*, pp. 31–53.

13 See J. Huysmans, 'Revisiting Copenhagen: Or, On the Creative Development of a Security Studies Agenda in Europe', *European Journal of International Relations*, vol. 4, no. 4 (Dec. 1998), pp. 479–505.

14 E. Krahmann, 'The Emergence of Security Governance in Post-Cold War Europe', *ESRC 'One Europe or Several?' Programme Working Paper 36/01*, Sept. 2001.

15 R. Jervis, 'Security Regimes', *International Organization*, vol. 36, no. 2, Spring 1982, p. 357.

16 Huysmans, 'Revisiting Copenhagen', p. 480.

17 These exceptions include, for example, contributions in M. Caballero-Anthony, R. Emmers and A. Acharya (eds), *Non-Traditional Security in Asia*, Aldershot, Hants: Ashgate, 2006.

18 For example, in August 2011 CSE co-organized a one-day workshop in Dhaka with the Bangladesh Institute of Planners on lake conservation. The workshop was attended by researchers, activists, planners, advocates and regulators from both Bangladesh and India. A key objective of the meeting was to create a network of people involved in the conservation of lakes in both countries, and the initiative was aimed at influencing the policy debate on lakes in the wider region. For more, see 'Towards Lake Conservation', *CSE*, 7 Aug. 2011. Online. HTTP: <http://www.cseindia.org/content/towards-lake-conservation> (accessed 21 Aug. 2011).

Bibliography

'2010 Warmest Year on Record', *The Australian*, 14 Jan. 2011. Online. HTTP: <http://www.theaustralian.com.au/news/world/warmest-year-on-record/story-e6frg6so-122598 7372032> (accessed 13 Mar. 2011).

'2011 Regional Operations Profile – South Asia', *UNHCR*. Online. HTTP: <http://www.unhcr.org/pages/49e45b156.html> (accessed 15 Apr. 15 2011).

'2011 Trafficking in Persons (TIP) Report Heroes', US Department of State. Online. HTTP: <http://www.state.gov/g/tip/rls/tiprpt/2011/164227.htm> (accessed 27 June 2011).

'A Matter of Magnitude: The Impact of the Economic Crisis on Women and Children in South Asia', *UNICEF*, June 2009. Online. HTTP: <http://www.unicef.org/rosa/Latest_Matter_of_magnitude.pdf> (accessed 12 Mar. 2011).

Abbott, C., 'Climate Change: The Real Threat to Security', *China Dialogue*, 23 June 2006. Online. HTTP: <http://www.chinadialogue.net/article/show/single/en/132-Climate-Change-the-real-threat-to-security> (accessed 2 Aug. 2010).

'About Anuradha Koirala', *Mothers Home Nepal*, May 2011. Online. HTTP: <http://www.mothershomenepal.org.au/about-anuradha-koirala/> (accessed 5 June 2011).

'About CSE: Anil Agarwal', *CSE India*. Online. HTTP: <http://www.cseindia.org/node/216> (accessed 12 July 2011).

'About TERI', *The Energy and Resources Institute (TERI)*. Online. HTTP: <http://www.teriin.org/index.php?option=com_content&task=view&id=17> (accessed 2 Sept. 2010).

Acharya, A., 'Securitization in Asia', in M. Caballero-Anthony, R. Emmers and A. Acharya (eds), *Non-Traditional Security in Asia: Dilemmas in Securitization*, Aldershot, Hants: Ashgate, 2006, pp. 247–250.

'Adapting to Climate Change: What's Needed in Poor Countries, and Who Should Pay', *Oxfam Briefing Paper*, 29 May 2007. Online. HTTP: <http://www.oxfam.org/files/adapting%20to%20climate%20change.pdf> (accessed 10 Aug. 2010).

Adhikari, D., 'Nepal Risks Political Chaos over Constitutional Task', *Agence France-Presse*, 20 June 2011. Online. HTTP: <http://au.news.yahoo.com/world/a/-/world/9679744/nepal-risks-political-chaos-over-constitution-task/> (accessed 26 June 2011).

Adorno, T. and Horkheimer, M., *Dialectic of Enlightenment*, trans. by J. Cumming, London: Verso, 1979.

'Address to the IISS by HE Mr Sabiluddin Ahmed, High Commissioner for Bangladesh to the UK', *International Institute for Strategic Studies*, 30 June 2006. Online. HTTP: <http://www.iiss.org/recent-key-addresses/sabiluddin-ahmed-address/> (accessed 15 Mar. 2011).

Adler, E., 'The Emergence of Cooperation: National Epistemic Communities and the International Evolution of the Idea of Nuclear Arms Control', *International Organization*, vol. 46, no. 1, Winter 1992, pp. 101–45.

Adler, E. and Haas, P., 'Conclusion: Epistemic Communities, World Order, and the Creation of a Reflective Research Program', *International Organization*, vol. 46, no. 1, Winter 1992, pp. 367–90.

Agarwal, A., 'Climate Change: A Challenge to India's Economy', *Briefing Paper for Members of Parliament*, CSE India. Online. HTTP: <http://www.cseindia.org/html/eyou/climate/pdf/cse_briefing.pdf> (accessed 29 Aug. 2010).

Aggarwal, K. S., *Dynamics of Identity and Intergroup Relation in North East India*, Shimla: Indian Institute of Advanced Studies, 1999.

Ahmad, Q. K., 'People's Freedoms and Development in Bangladesh', *New Age*, 8 Jan. 2005.

Ahmar, M., *Chronology of Conflict and Cooperation in South Asia 1947–2001*, Karachi: Karachi University Press, 2001.

Ahmed, A. U., et al., 'Considering Adaptation to Climate Change: Towards a Sustainable Development of Bangladesh', *Report Prepared for South Asia Region, World Bank, Washington DC*, Oct. 1999. Online. HTTP: <http://www.mungo.nl/CC_Bangla.htm> (accessed 12 Mar. 2008).

Ahmed, E., 'The Military and Democracy in Bangladesh', in R. J. May and V. Selochan (eds), *The Military and Democracy in Asia and the Pacific*, Canberra: ANU E-Press, 2004.

Ahmed, I., *State, Nation and Ethnicity in Contemporary South Asia*, London: Pinter, 1996.

——, 'Bangladesh: Amid Hope and Despair', *South Asia Journal*, vol. 13, July–Sept. 2006. Online. HTTP: <http://www.southasianmedia.net/magazine/journal/13_amid-hope.htm> (accessed 15 Mar. 2008).

Ahmed, M., *Democracy and the Challenge of Development: A Study of Politics and Military Interventions in Bangladesh*, Dhaka: University Press Ltd., 1995.

Aiyer, S. S. A., 'India, World Leader in Natural Disasters', *The Times of India*, 14 May 2006. Online. HTTP: <http://timesofindia.indiatimes.com/articleshow/1528671.cms> (accessed 21 Aug. 2010).

Akbar, M. J., 'India-Pakistan: Take the Good News Cautiously', *International Herald Tribune*, 30 Oct. 2002. Online. HTTP: <http://www.nytimes.com/2002/10/30/opinion/30iht-edakbar_ed3_.html> (accessed 12 July 2011).

Alamgir, J., 'We Need Local Leaders Not National Personalities', *The Daily Star*, 15 Feb. 2007. Online. HTTP: <http://www.thedailystar.net/2007/02/15/d70215020324.htm> (accessed 24 Oct. 2009).

Alker, H., 'Emancipation in the Critical Security Studies Project', in Booth (ed.), *Critical Security Studies and World Politics*, London: Lynne Rienner, 2005.

Allred, K. J., 'Analysis: Combating Human Trafficking', *NATO Review*, Summer 2006. Online. HTTP: <http://www.nato.int/docu/review/2006/issue2/english/Analysis.html> (accessed 10 Mar. 2009).

'Amendment to Strip ACC of Freedom: TIB', *BDnews24.com*, 29 Jan. 2011. Online. HTTP: <http://www.bdnews24.com/details.php?id=185894&cid=2> (accessed 19 Feb. 2011).

'An Introduction to Trafficking: Vulnerability, Impact and Action', *UNODC*, 2008, p. 9. Online. HTTP: <http://www.unodc.org/documents/human-trafficking/An_Introduction_to_Human_Trafficking-Background_Paper.pdf> (accessed 22 June 2011).

'Analysis: A Tale of Two Women', *BBC News*, 2 Oct. 2001. Online. HTTP: <http://news.bbc.co.uk/2/hi/south_asia/1575704.stm> (accessed 12 Oct. 2007).

Anderson, C. P., 'Causes and Consequences of the Maoist Rebellion in Nepal: 1996–2006', *International Affairs Journal at UC Davis*, vol. 3, no. 2, Winter 2007.

Andrees, B. and van der Linden, M. N. J., 'Designing Trafficking Research from a Labour Market Perspective: The ILO Experience', in F. Laczko and E. M. Gozdziak (eds), *Data and Research on Human Trafficking*, pp. 57–58.

Annan, K., 'Global Warming an All-Encompassing Threat', *Environment News Service*, 15 Nov. 2006. Online. HTTP: <http://www.ens-newswire.com/ens/nov2006/2006-11-15-insann.asp> (accessed 14. Aug. 2010).

'Annual Report 2007/08', *The Energy and Resources Institute (TERI)*, p. 4. Online. HTTP: <http://www.teriin.org/about/Annual08.pdf> (accessed 4 May 2011).

Archavanitkul, K., 'Combating the Trafficking in Children and their Exploitation in Prostitution and Other Intolerable Forms of Child Labouring in Mekong Basin Countries', *A subregional report submitted to International Programme of the Elimination of Child Labour (IPEC)*, International Labour Organization (ILO), Bangkok, Thailand, June 1998, Chapter 7. Online. HTTP: <http://www.seameo.org/vl/combat/frame.htm> (25 June 2011).

'Army to "Stop Election Violence"', *BBC News*, 4 Jan. 2007. Online. HTTP: <http://news.bbc.co.uk/2/hi/south_asia/6230965.stm > (accessed 4 Oct. 2009).

Arnell, N., *Global Warming, River Flows and Water Resources*, Chichester, England: Wiley, 1996.

Article 27 of the Declaration of the Ninth SAARC Summit, *SAARC*, Male, Maldives, 12–14 May 1997. Online. HTTP: http://www.saarc-sec.org/userfiles/Summit%20Declarations/09%20-%20Maldives%20-%209th%20Summit%201997.pdf (accessed 14 May 2010).

Arts, B., Noortmann, M. and Reinialda, B. (eds), *Non-State Actors in International Relations*, Aldershot: Ashgate, 2001.

Asadullah Khan, M., 'Poor Governance Fuels Corruption', *The Daily Star* 17 May 2008. Online. HTTP: <http://www.thedailystar.net/story.php?nid=36841> (accessed 23 May 2010).

Askvik, S., Jamil, I. and Dhak, T. N., 'Citizens' Trust in Public and Political Institutions in Nepal', *International Political Science Review*, 17 Jan. 2011, pp. 1–21.

'Assam Assessment 2011', *South Asian Terrorism Portal*. Online. HTTP: <http://www.satp.org/satporgtp/countries/india/states/assam/index.html> (accessed 12 Jan. 2011).

'Assam Playing Host to Anti-Insurgency Plays', *The Indian News*, 15 Mar. 2009. Online. HTTP: <http://www.thaindian.com/newsportal/india-news/assam-playing-host-to-anti-insurgency-plays_100166637.html> (accessed 26 May 2010).

'Authoritarianism and Political Party Reform in Pakistan', *International Crisis Group*, Asia Report no. 102, 28 Sept. 2005. Online. HTTP: <http://www.crisisgroup.org/en/regions/asia/south-asia/pakistan/102-authoritarianism-and-political-party-reform-in-pakistan.aspx> (accessed 27 Oct. 2009).

Ayoob, M., 'Defining Security: A Subaltern Realist Perspective', in K. Krause and M. Williams (eds), *Critical Security Studies: Concepts and Cases*, London: UCL Press, 1997, pp. 121–148.

Aziz-al Hasan, S. and Chakma, B., 'Problems of National Integration in Bangladesh', *Asian Survey*, vol. 29, no. 10 Oct. 1989, pp. 959–70.

Babu, K. L., et al., 'Possible Enhanced Conflict Situations on Account of Climate Change on Account of Water Sharing: A Case Study of Three States of India', *Human Security and Climate Change – An International Workshop*, 21–23 June 2005. Online. HTTP: <http://www.gechs.org/downloads/holmen/Babu_etal.pdf> (accessed 15 Aug. 2010).

Bachrach, P. and Baratz, M. S., 'Two Faces of Power', *The American Political Science Review*, vol. 56, no. 4, Dec. 1962, pp. 947–52.

'Bad Governance Breeds Militancy, Says Expert', *The Tribune*, 22 Oct. 2007.

Bahree, M., 'The Forever War: Inside India's Maoist Conflict', *World Policy Journal*, vol. 27, no. 2, Summer 2010, pp. 83–9.

Bailey, R. (ed.), *Earth Report 2000: Revisiting the True State of the Planet*, New York: McGraw-Hill, 2000.

Balachandran, V., 'Insurgency, Terrorism and Transnational Crime in South Asia', *Transnational Trends: Middle Eastern and Asian Views*, June 2008, pp. 117–19. Online. HTTP:

<http://kms1.isn.ethz.ch/serviceengine/Files/ISN/95193/ichaptersection_singledocument/
c8178933-7827-4b08-ad45-27e6b6284a83/en/6.pdf> (accessed 11 Mar. 2009).

Baldor, L. C., 'Terror Attacks Spike in Pakistan, Afghanistan', *MSNBC*, 28 Apr. 2010.
Online. HTTP: <http://www.msnbc.msn.com/id/36820196/ns/world_news-south_and_
central_asia/> (accessed 12 Mar. 2011).

Balzacq, T., 'The Three Faces of Securitization: Political Agency, Audience and Context',
European Journal of International Relations, vol. 11, no. 2, June 2005, pp. 171–201.

——(ed.), *Securitization Theory: How Security Problems Emerge and Dissolve*, London: Routledge,
2011.

——, 'Enquiries into Methods: A New Framework For Securitization Analysis', in Balzacq (ed.),
Securitization Theory: How Security Problems Emerge and Dissolve, London: Routledge, 2011,
pp. 31–53.

Bandyopadhyay, N., et al., 'Streetwalkers Show the Way: Reframing the Debate on Trafficking from Sex Workers' Perspective', *Institute of Development Studies (IDS) Bulletin*, vol. 37,
no. 4, Sept. 2006, pp. 102–9.

Banerjee, K. and Saha, P., 'The NREGA, the Maoists and the Developmental Woes of the
Indian State', *Economic and Political Weekly*, vol. 45, no. 28, 10 July 2010, pp. 42–47.

Banerji, P., Chaudhury, S. B. R. and Das, S.K. (eds), *Internal Displacement in South Asia*,
London: Sage Publications, 2005.

'Bangladesh: EU Commission Suspends Election Observation Mission', *European Commission*,
11 Jan. 2007. Online. HTTP: <http://www.europa-eu-un.org/articles/en/article_
6669_en.htm> (accessed 10 Oct. 2009).

'Bangladesh Election Winner Urges Loser to Concede', *International Herald Tribune*, 31 Dec.
2008. Online. HTTP: <http://www.iht.com/articles/ap/2008/12/31/asia/AS-Bangladesh-
Election.php> (accessed 12 Jan. 2009).

'Bangladesh Emergency Laws Lifted', *Al Jazeera*, 17 Dec. 2008. Online. HTTP: <http://
english.aljazeera.net/news/asia/2008/12/2008121620156401684.html> (accessed 12
Jan. 2009).

'Bangladesh: Flood Waters Recede, But Challenges Remain', *IRIN Humanitarian News and
Analysis*, 27 Aug. 2007. Online. HTTP: <http://www.irinnews.org/report.aspx?ReportId=
73966> (accessed 23 Oct. 2007).

'Bangladesh Has a Population of 164.4 Million: UN', *Sify News*, 21 Oct. 2010. Online.
HTTP: <http://www.sify.com/news/bangladesh-has-a-population-of-164-4-million-un-
news-international-kkvpawhdead.html> (accessed 20 Apr. 2011).

'Bangladesh Leader Vows Crackdown', *BBC News*, 22 Jan. 2007. Online. HTTP: <http://
news.bbc.co.uk/2/hi/south_asia/6285685.stm> (accessed 10 Oct. 2009).

'Bangladesh Parliament', *National Web Portal of Bangladesh*. Online. HTTP: <http://www.
bangladesh.gov.bd/index.php?option=com_content&task=view&id=116&Itemid=190>
(accessed 10 Mar. 2010).

'Bangladesh Results Seen As Fair, Though Loser Disputes Results', *International Herald Tribune*, 30 Dec. 2008. Online. HTTP: <http://www.iht.com/articles/2008/12/30/asia/
bangla.php> (accessed 12 Jan. 2009).

'Bangladesh State of Emergency Lifted', *The Age*, 18 Dec. 2008. Online. HTTP: <http://
www.theage.com.au/world/bangladeshs-state-of-emergency-lifted-20081217-70q9.html>
(accessed 12 Jan. 2009).

'Bangladesh Today', *International Crisis Group Report*, 23 Oct. 2006, p. 3. Online. HTTP:
<http://www.crisisgroup.org/home/index.cfm?id=4462> (accessed 27 May 2009).

'Bangladesh Tops Most Corrupt List', *BBC News*, 18 Oct. 2005. Online. HTTP: <http://
news.bbc.co.uk/2/hi/south_asia/4353334.stm> (accessed 11 Nov. 2009).

'Bangladesh "Will Lift Emergency"', *BBC News*, 10 Dec. 2008. Online. HTTP: <http://news.bbc.co.uk/2/hi/south_asia/7776085.stm> (accessed 12 Jan. 2009).

Barnett, M. and Duvall, R. (eds), *Power in Global Governance*, Cambridge: Cambridge University Press, 2005.

Barry, K., *The Prostitution of Sexuality*, New York: NYU Press, 1995.

Bashford, P., 'A Sense of Direction: The Trafficking of Women and Children from Nepal 2006', *Asha Nepal*, March 2006. Online. HTTP: <http://www.childtrafficking.com/Docs/ashan250806.pdf> (accessed 10 Apr. 2010).

Basrur, R. M., *South Asia's Cold War*, London: Routledge, 2008.

Bate, R. and Morris, J., *Global Warming: Apocalypse or Hot Air?*, London: Institute of Economic Affairs, 1994.

Bates, R., *States and Markets in Tropical Africa: The Political Basis of Agricultural Policy*, Berkeley: University of California Press, 1981.

Bayes, A., 'Beyond the Border Basics', *The Daily Star*, 28 Sept. 2004.

Bedi, R., 'Indian Government's Victory Marred by Bribery Accusations', *The Telegraph*, 23 July 2008. Online. HTTP: <http://www.telegraph.co.uk/news/worldnews/asia/india/2446203/Indian-governments-victory-marred-by-bribery-accusations.html> (accessed 23 Aug. 2010).

——, 'India Reserves Right to Attack Pakistan in Response to Mumbai Attack', *Jane's Defence News*, 5 Dec. 2008. Online. HTTP: <http://www.janes.com/news/defence/triservice/jdw/jdw081205_1_n.shtml> (accessed 11 Mar. 2009).

Benarde, M. A., *Global Warming … Global Warming*, New York: Wiley, 1992.

Berger, J. J., *Beating the Heat: Why and How We Must Combat Global Warming*, Berkeley, CA: Berkeley Hills Books, 2000.

Besheer, M., 'UN: Climate Change Could Cause Instability for Some Nations', *Voice of America*, 20 July 2011. Online. HTTP: <http://www.voanews.com/english/news/environment/UN-Climate-Change-Could-Cause-Instability-for-Some-Nations-125915354.html> (accessed 27 July 2011).

Bhattachan, K. B., Hemchuri, K. Gurung, Y. and Biswakarma, C. M., Existing Practices of Caste-Based Untouchability in Nepal and Strategy for a Campaign for its Elimination, Kathmandu: ActionAid Nepal, 2003.

Bhattacharjee, J.B. (ed.), *Roots of Insurgency in Northeast India*, New Delhi: Eastern Book Corporation, 2007.

Bhattacharjee, S. and Dhamala, R. R., *Human Rights and Insurgency: The North-East India*, New Delhi: Shipra Publications, 2002.

Bhattacharya, P. and Hazra, S. (eds), *Environment and Human Security*, New Delhi: Lancer's Books, 2003.

Bhattacharyya, J. N., *Hindu Castes and Sects: An Exposition of the Origin of the Hindu Castes System and the Bearing of the Sects Towards Each Other and Towards Other Religious Systems*, New Delhi: Manohar, 1995.

Bhattarai, B., *Monarchy vs. Democracy: The Epic Fight in Nepal*, New Delhi: Samkaleen Teesari Duniya, 2005.

Bhaumik, S., 'Mob Attacks India Grain Warehouse', *BBC News*, 18 Sept. 2007. Online. HTTP: <http://news.bbc.co.uk/2/hi/south_asia/7000535.stm> (accessed 6 Dec. 2007).

Bhaya, A. G., 'Children's Charter on Climate Change', *The Times of India*, 25 Oct. 2002. Online. HTTP: <http://timesofindia.indiatimes.com/articleshow/26195613.cms> (accessed 26 Aug. 2010).

Bhowmick, R., 'Preventing Trafficking of Women', *The New Nation*, 28 July 2006. Online. HTTP: <http://www.wunrn.com/news/2006/07_31_06/080106_trafficking_south.htm> (accessed 19 May 2009).

'Bhutanese Refugees in Nepal: Point of No Return', *The Economist*, 15 Jan. 2009. Online. HTTP: <http://www.economist.com/world/asia/displaystory.cfm?story_id=12941086> (accessed 10 Mar. 2009).

Bibes, P., 'Transnational Organized Crime and Terrorism: Colombia, a Case Study', *Journal of Contemporary Criminal Justice*, vol. 17, August 2001, pp. 243–58.

Bidwai, P., 'Politics-India: Costly Vote of Confidence', *IPS News*, 24 July 2008. Online. HTTP: <http://ipsnews.net/news.asp?idnews=43293> (accessed 23 Aug. 2010).

Bigo, D., 'Security and Immigration: Toward a Critique of the Governmentality of Unease', *Alternatives: Global, Local, Political*, vol. 27, no. 1, Jan. 2002, pp. 64–92.

'Biography: R.K. Pachauri', *US Climate Change Science Program*. Online. HTTP: <http://www.climatescience.gov/Library/bios/pachauri.htm> (accessed 31 Aug. 2010).

Bischoff, A., 'Climate Justice at COP 8', *Greenspiration*. Online. HTTP: <http://www.greenspiration.org/environ/articles/ClimateJustice.htm> (accessed 26 Aug. 2010).

Bishwakarma, P., 'Violence against Dalit Women in Nepal', *Nepalnews.com*, 21 May 2004. Online. HTTP: <http://www.countercurrents.org/gender-padmalal210504.htm> (accessed 23 Apr. 2010).

T. Biswas, 'Cash-for-Votes Scam: Amar Singh, Sudheendra Kulkarni chargesheeted', *NDTV*, 24 August 2011. Online. HTTP: <http://www.ndtv.com/article/india/cash-for-votes-scam-amar-singh-sudheendra-kulkarni-chargesheeted-128665&cp> (accessed 25 August 2011).

'Blame and Retribution', *The Economist*, 4 Dec. 2009. Online. HTTP: <http://www.economist.com/world/asia/displaystory.cfm?story_id=12724858> (accessed 11 Mar. 2010).

'Blasts Hit Bangladesh Party Rally', *BBC News*, 22 Aug. 2004. Online. HTTP: <http://news.bbc.co.uk/2/hi/south_asia/3586384.stm> (accessed 20 May 2010).

Boerema, D., 'As Deadline Draws Near, New Constitution in Nepal Still Far Away', *Radio Netherlands Worldwide*, 28 May 2011. Online. HTTP: <http://www.rnw.nl/english/article/deadline-draws-near-new-constitution-nepal-still-far-away> (accessed 28 June 2011).

Booth, K., 'Security and Emancipation', *Review of International Studies*, vol.17, no. 4, Oct. 1991, pp. 313–26.

——, 'Human Wrongs and International Relations', *International Affairs*, vol. 71, no. 1, Jan. 1995, p. 103–26.

——(ed.), *Critical Security Studies and World Politics*, Boulder, CO: Lynne Rienner, 2004.

——, *Theory of World Security*, Cambridge: Cambridge University Press, 2007.

Booth, K. and Dunne, T. (eds), *Worlds in Collision: Terror and the Future of Global Order*, Houndmills and New York: Palgrave Macmillan, 2002.

Borger, J. and Hodgson, M., 'US Drug Wars Aids Colombian Paramilitaries', *Guardian*, 17 May 2001.

Bose, S., *States, Nations and Sovereignty: Sri Lanka, India and the Tamil Eelam Movement*, New Delhi: Sage Publications, 1994.

——, 'Kashmir: Sources of Conflict, Dimensions of Peace', *Economic and Political Weekly*, vol. 34, no. 13, 27 Mar.–2 Apr., 1999, pp. 762–68.

——, 'Kashmir: Sources of Conflict, Dimensions of Peace', *Survival*, vol. 41, no. 3, Autumn 1999, pp. 149–71.

Bosold, D., 'Development of the Human Security Field: A Critical Examination', in D. Chandler and N. Hynek (eds), *Critical Perspectives on Human Security*, Abingdon: Routledge, 2011.

Boyden, J., Hart, J., de Berry, J. and Feeney, T., 'Children Affected by Armed Conflict in South Asia: A Review of Trends and Issues Identified Through Secondary Research', *RSC Working Paper Series 7*, International Development Centre, 2002, Oxford University.

Boyle, S. and Ardill, J., *The Greenhouse Effect: A Practical Guide to the World's Changing Climate*, London: New English Library, 1989.

Brauch, H., et al. (eds), *Security and Environment in the Mediterranean: Conceptualising Security Conflicts*, Berlin: Springer, 2003.

Broendel, K. and Goodwin, G., 'State Dept. Releases Human Trafficking Report', *All Africa*, 17 June 2004. Online. HTTP: <http://allafrica.com/stories/200406170721.html> (accessed 10 Mar. 2009).

Brown, T. L., *The Challenge to Democracy in Nepal: A Political History*, London: Routledge, 1996.

Bruderlein, C., 'The Role of Non-State Actors in Building Human Security: The Case of Armed Groups in Intra-State Wars', *Centre for Humanitarian Dialogue*, Geneva, 2000. Online. HTTP: <http://www.hdcentre.org/files/the%20role%20of%20non-state%20actors.pdf> (accessed 2 June 2011).

Bryant, N., 'Maldives: Paradise Soon to be Lost', *BBC News*, 28 July 2004. Online. HTTP: <http://news.bbc.co.uk/1/hi/world/south_asia/3930765.stm> (accessed 27 Apr. 2008).

Brysk, A., 'Beyond Framing and Shaming: Human Trafficking, Human Security and Human Rights', *Journal of Human Security*, vol. 5, no. 3, 2009, pp. 8–21.

Burall, S. and Neligan, C., 'The Accountability of International Organizations', *GPPi Research Paper Series No. 2*, Global Public Policy Institute, 2005. Online. HTTP: <http://www.gppi.net/fileadmin/gppi/IO_Acct_Burall_05012005.pdf> (accessed 12 Jan. 2011).

Burgess, J. P. and Owen, T. (eds), 'Special Section: What Is Human Security?', *Security Dialogue*, vol. 35, no. 3, Sept. 2004, pp. 345–87.

Butcher, K., 'Confusion between Prostitution and Sex Trafficking', *Lancet*, vol. 361, no. 9373, 2003, p. 1983.

Buzan, B., 'Rethinking security after the Cold War', *Cooperation and Conflict*, vol. 32, no. 1, Mar. 1997, pp. 5–28.

——*People, states and fear: The national security problem in international relations*, Chapel Hill: University of North Carolina Press, 1983.

Buzan, B. and L. Hansen, *The evolution of international security studies*, Cambridge: Cambridge University Press, 2009.

Buzan, B. and Waever, O., 'Macrosecuritization and security constellations: reconsidering scale in securitization theory', *Review of international studies*, vol. 35, no. 2, pp. 253–276.

Buzan, B., Wæver, O., and Kelstrup, M. et al., *Identity, Migration and the New Security Agenda in Europe*, London: Pinter, 1993.

Buzan, B., Wæver, O. and de Wilde, J., *Security: A New Framework for Analysis*, Boulder, CO: Lynne Rienner, 1998.

Buzan, B. and Wæver, O., *Regions and Powers: The Structure of International Security*, Cambridge: Cambridge University Press, 2003.

Cahnman, W. J., 'Ideal Type Theory: Max Weber's Concept and Some of Its Derivations', *Sociological Quarterly*, vol. 6, no. 3, Summer 1965, pp. 268–80.

CAN Corporation, 'National Security and the Threat of Climate Change', Apr. 2007, p. 3. Online. HTTP: <http://securityandclimate.cna.org/report/National%20Security%20and%20the%20Threat%20of%20Climate%20Change.pdf> (accessed 14 Aug. 2010).

CANSA Website. Online. HTTP: <http://www.cansouthasia.net/> (accessed 12 July 2011).

Carrington, D., 'In Defence of the IPCC: Critics Ignore the Real Scandal', *Guardian*, 28 July 2011. Online. HTTP: <http://www.guardian.co.uk/environment/damian-carrington-blog/2011/jul/28/ipcc-climate-change-science-pachauri> (accessed 3 Aug. 2011).

'Cash for Votes? Oppn MPs Show Wads of Currency Notes in LS', *The Indian Express*, 22 July 2008. Online. HTTP: <http://www.expressindia.com/latest-news/Cash-for-votes-Oppn-MPs-show-wads-of-currency-notes-in-LS/338932/> (accessed 2 Sept. 2010).

Cha, V.D., 'Globalization and the Study of International Security', *Journal of Peace Research*, vol. 37, no. 3, May 2000, pp. 391–403.

Chadwick, M. J., Mintzer, I. M. and Leonard, J. A. (eds), *Negotiating Climate Change: The Inside Story of the Rio Convention*, Cambridge and New York: Cambridge University Press, 1994.

Chalk, P., 'Pakistan's Role in the Kashmir Insurgency', Jane's Intelligence Review, 1 Sept. 2001. Online. HTTP: <http://www.rand.org/commentary/090101JIR.html> (accessed 12 Oct. 2010).

Chanda, R., 'Internal Politics in Bangladesh: An Insight', *IPCS*, 4 Oct. 1999. Online. HTTP: <http://www.ipcs.org/article/bangladesh/internal-politics-in-bangladesh-an-insight-269.html> (accessed 23 Oct. 2009).

Chandler, D. and Hynek, N., 'Emancipation and Power in Human Security', in D. Chandler and N. Hynek (eds), *Critical Perspectives on Human Security*, Abingdon: Routledge, 2011, pp. 1–10.

Chapkis, W., 'Trafficking, Migration, and the Law: Protecting Innocents, Punishing Immigrants', *Gender and Society*, vol. 17, no. 6, Dec. 2003, pp. 923–37.

Chari, P. R., 'India's Nuclear Doctrine: Confused Ambitions', *The Non-Proliferation Review*, Fall–Winter 2000, pp. 123-35.

——(ed.), *Perspectives on National Security in South Asia*, New Delhi: Manohar, 1999.

——(ed.), *Alternative Approaches to Security: National Integration, Governance, Non-Military Challenges*, Dhaka: The University Press Limited, 2000.

——(ed.), *Security and Governance in South Asia*, Colombo: Manohar, 2001.

——, 'Security and Governance in South Asia: Their Linkages', in P.R. Chari (ed.), *Security and Governance in South Asia*, Manohar: New Delhi, 2001.

Chari, P. R. and Gupta, S. (eds), *Human Security in South Asia: Energy, Gender, Migration and Globalisation*, New Delhi: Social Science Press, 2003.

Chari, P. R., Joseph, M. and Chandran, S. (eds), *Missing Boundaries: Refugees, Migrants, Stateless and Internally Displaced People in South Asia*, New Delhi: Manohar, 2003.

Chopra, P. N., *India at The Crossroads*, New Delhi: Sterling Publishers Pvt. Ltd., 2004.

Chowdhury, M. R., 'Bangladesh State Emergency an Opportunity', *Washington Post*, 7 May 2007. Online. HTTP: <http://newsweek.washingtonpost.com/postglobal/needtoknow/2007/05/bangladeshs_political_emergenc.html> (accessed 6 Dec. 2009).

Clark, A., 'Climate Change Threatens Security: UK Tells UN', *Guardian*, 18 Apr. 2007. Online. HTTP: <http://www.guardian.co.uk/environment/2007/apr/18/greenpolitics.climatechange> (accessed 13 Aug. 2010).

'Climate Change', *The Energy and Resources Institute (TERI)*. Online. HTTP: <http://www.teriin.org/index.php?option=com_division&task=view_div&id=26> (accessed 31 Aug. 2010).

'Climate Change', *The Royal Society*. Online. HTTP: <http://royalsociety.org/landing.asp?id=1278> (accessed 1 Aug. 2010).

'Climate Change 2001: Impacts, Adaptation and Vulnerability', *IPCC*, p. 543. Online. HTTP: <http://www.ipcc.ch/ipccreports/tar/wg2/pdf/wg2TARchap11.pdf> (accessed 19 Aug. 2010).

'Climate Change 2001: Working Group II: Impacts, Adaptation and Vulnerability', *Intergovernmental Panel on Climate Change (IPCC)*, 2001. Online. HTTP: <http://www.grida.no/publications/other/ipcc_tar/?src=/climate/IPCC_tar/wg2/439.htm> (accessed 29 Apr. 2009).

'Climate Change 2007: The Physical Science Basis', *Contribution of Working Group I to the Fourth Assessment Report of the Intergovernmental Panel on Climate Change*, IPCC, 2007. Online. <HTTP: <http://www.ipcc.ch/publications_and_data/publications_ipcc_fourth_assessment_ report_wg1_report_the_physical_science_basis.htm> (accessed 20 July 2011).

'Climate Change and Security', *Royal United Services Institute for Defence and Security Studies (RUSI)*. Online. HTTP: <http://www.rusi.org/climate/> (accessed 2 Aug. 2010).

'Climate Change and Security', *RUSI*. Online. HTTP: <http://www.rusi.org/climate/> (accessed 10 Aug. 2010).

'Climate Change and Small Island States, The Alliance of Small Island States (AOSIS)', *Ministerial Conference on Environment and Development in Asia and the Pacific 2000*, Kitakyushu, Japan, 31 Aug. –5 Sept. 2000. Online. HTTP: <http://www.unescap.org/mced2000/pacific/background/AOSIS.htm> (accessed 13 Aug. 2010).

'Climate Change and South Asia: Rural Lives and Livelihoods of Millions at Risk', *World Bank*, 30 Nov. 2007. Online. HTTP: <http://web.worldbank.org/WBSITE/EXTERNAL/COUNTRIES/SOUTHASIAEXT/0,contentMDK:21571064~pagePK:146736~piPK:146830~theSitePK:223547,00.htm> (12 Aug. 2010).

'Climate Change Debate Hots Up', *The Times of India*, 13 Apr. 2010. Online. HTTP: <http://articles.timesofindia.indiatimes.com/2010-04-13/delhi/28137197_1_highest-temperature-degree-climate-change> (accessed 12 Jan. 2011).

'Climate Change Impacts and India', *UNDP*. Online. HTTP: <http://www.undp.org.in/index.php?option=com_content&task=view&id=297&Itemid=466> (accessed 21 Aug. 2010).

'Climate Change Refugees Seek a New International Deal', *ClimateChangeCorp*, 27 Dec. 2008. Online. HTTP: <http://www.climatechangecorp.com/content.asp?ContentID=5871> (accessed 31 May 2011).

'Climate Change Scenarios for India', *Keysheet 2*, India–UK collaboration on impacts of climate change in India. Online. HTTP: <http://www.defra.gov.uk/environment/climatechange/internat/devcountry/pdf/india-climate-2-climate.pdf> (accessed 15 Aug. 2010).

'Climate Change Threat Real, Change Lifestyle: PM', *Hindustan Times*, 5 June 2007. Online. HTTP: <http://www.hindustantimes.com/storypage/storypage.aspx?sectionName=&id=7aba6298-7bce-4c6a-8b6d-2f78fad93ce2&&Headline=%27Climate+change+threat+real%2c+change+lifestyle%27&strParent=strParentID> (accessed 27 Aug. 2010).

'Climate Change Will Affect India's Farming, Water Supply, Health', *MedIndia*, 31 Oct. 2007. Online. HTTP: <http://www.medindia.net/news/Climate-Change-Will-Hit-Indias-Farming-Water-Supply-Health-28712-1.htm> (accessed 26 Aug. 2010)

'Climate Change: A Threat to Global Security', *Green Energy News*, 15 Apr. 2007. Online. HTTP: <http://www.green-energy-news.com/arch/nrgs2007/20070050.html> (accessed 21 Aug. 2008).

'Climate Change: The Road to Bali and Beyond', *CSE India*, 5 Dec. 2007. Online. HTTP: <http://www.cseindia.org/AboutUs/press_releases/press_20071205.htm> (accessed 29 Aug. 2010).

'Climate Change: Why India Must Act', *The Indian Economy Blog*, 12 June 2007. Online. HTTP: <http://indianeconomy.org/2007/06/12/climate-change-why-india-must-act/> (accessed 26 Aug. 2010)

'Climate Impacts and Adaptations', *World Wildlife Fund (WWF)*. Online. HTTP: <http://www.worldwildlife.org/climate/impactsandadaptation.html> (accessed 10 Aug. 2010).

Clemens, Jr., W. C., *Dynamics of International Relations (2nd ed.)*, Boulder: Rowman and Littlefield Publishers Inc., 2004.

'Coalition Against Trafficking in Women' (CATW). Online. HTTP: <http://www.catwinternational.org/about/index.php> (accessed 12 June 2010).

Cohen, R., 'Threat Perception in International Crisis', *Political Science Quarterly*, vol. 93, no. 1, Spring 1978, pp. 93–107.

Cohen, S., 'Nuclear Weapons and Nuclear War in South Asia', in R. Thakur and O. Wiggen (eds), *South Asia in the World: Problem Solving Perspectives on Security, Sustainable Development and Good Governance*, Hong Kong: United Nations University Press, 2004, pp. 39–57.

'Combating Trafficking of Women and Children in South Asia', *Asian Development Bank*, Manila: ABD, 2003.

'Combating Trafficking of Women and Children in South Asia', *Regional Synthesis Paper for Bangladesh, India and Nepal*, Asian Development Bank, Apr. 2003. Online. HTTP: <http://www.adb.org/gender/final_synthesis.pdf> (accessed 30 May 2011).

'Combatting Trafficking of Women and Children in South Asia: Guide for Integrating Trafficking Concerns into ADB Operations', *Asian Development Bank*, 2003. Online. HTTP: <http://www.adb.org/Documents/Guidelines/Combating_Trafficking/Guide_Integrating_Trafficking_Concerns.pdf> (accessed 28 June 2011).

'Comments on the SAARC Convention on Preventing and Combating Trafficking Women and Children for Prostitution', *Forum for Women, Law and Development*, Kathmandu: FWLD, 2002.

'Commonwealth Anti-Trafficking Legislation', *Department of Foreign Affairs and Trade*. Online. HTTP: <http://www.dfat.gov.au/illegal_immigration/laws.html> (accessed 1 Mar. 2010)

Conner, W., *Ethnonationalism: The Quest for Understanding*, Princeton: Princeton University Press, 1994.

Constable, N., 'Mail Order' Marriages, Berkeley: University of California Press, 2003.

'Contemporary Forms of Slavery', *Fact Sheet No. 14*, UNOHCHR. Online. HTTP: <http://www.ohchr.org/Documents/Publications/FactSheet14en.pdf> (accessed 23 June 2011).

'Controversy Behind Climate Science's "Hockey Stick" Graph', *Guardian*, 2 Feb. 2010. Online. HTTP: <http://www.guardian.co.uk/environment/2010/feb/02/hockey-stick-graph-climate-change?INTCMP=ILCNETTXT3487> (accessed 7 Jan. 2011).

Coonts, P. and Griebel, C., 'International Approaches to Human Trafficking: The Call for a Gender-Sensitive Perspective in International Law', *Women's Health Journal*, April 2004, pp. 47–57. Online. HTTP: <http://www.reddesalud.org/english/datos/ftp/OpinionWHJ404.pdf> (accessed 3 Mar. 2010).

'Corruption in the Public Sector: Its Manifestations, Causes and Suggested Remedies', *Report by Transparency International Bangladesh*. Online. HTTP: <http://www.ti-bangladesh.org/index.php?page_id=338> (accessed 11 Nov. 2009).

'Council on Climate Change Constituted', *The Hindu*, 6 June 2007. Online. HTTP: <http://www.hinduonnet.com/2007/06/06/stories/2007060605991300.htm> (accessed 2 Sept. 2010).

'Counter-Trafficking', *International Organisation for Migration*. Online. HTTP: <http://www.iom.int/jahia/Jahia/activities/by-theme/regulating-migration/counter-trafficking> (accessed 10 June 2010).

'Country Narratives: Nepal', in 'Trafficking in Persons (TIP) Report 2011', *US Department of State*. Online. HTTP: <http://www.state.gov/g/tip/rls/tiprpt/2011/index.htm> (accessed 10 July 2011).

Cox, R., 'Social Forces, States and World Orders: Beyond International Relations Theory', *Millennium: Journal of International Studies*, vol. 10, no. 2, 1981, pp. 126–55.

Cox, T., 'The Badi: Prostitution as a Social Norm Among an Untouchable Caste of West Nepal', *Contributions to Nepalese Studies*, vol. 19, no. 1, 1992, pp. 51–71.

'Cricket World Cup: India PM Invites Pakistan Leaders', *BBC News*, 25 Mar. 2011. Online. HTTP: <http://www.bbc.co.uk/news/world-south-asia-12864679> (accessed 4 Apr. 2011).

'CSE Warns Delhi: Time to Breathe Easy Over, Air Pollution Reaching Critical Levels Again in City', *CSE Press Release*, 6 Nov. 2007. Online. HTTP: <http://www.cseindia.org/AboutUs/press_releases/press_20071106.htm> (accessed 31 Aug. 2010).

Dahal, D. R., 'Dalits in Governance', *The Telegraph Weekly*, 12 May 2004. Online. HTTP: <http://www.fesnepal.org/reports/2004/seminar_reports/paper_cets/paper_dahal.htm> (accessed 23 Apr. 2008).

Dahl, R. A., 'The Concept of Power', *Behavioural Science*, vol. 2, no. 3, 1957, pp. 201–15.

——, 'A Critique of the Ruling-Elite Model', *American Political Science Review*, vol. 52, no. 2, June 1958, pp. 463–69.

Dandurand, Y. and Chin, V., 'Links Between Terrorism and Other Forms of Crime', *International Centre for Criminal Law Reform and Criminal Justice Policy*, Vancouver, December 2004, p. 7. Online. HTTP: <http://www.icclr.law.ubc.ca/Publications/Reports/Links BetweenTerrorismLatest_updated.pdf> (accessed 23 June 2011).

Datta, R., 'Hum honge kamiyab … [We shall overcome …]: Non-governmental organizations, the state and human security in India', in R. Thakur and O. Wiggen (eds), *South Asia in the World: Problem Solving Perspectives on Security, Sustainable Development, and Good Governance*, Tokyo: United Nations University Press, 2004, pp. 335–54.

Datta, S., 'Bangladesh's Political Evolution: Growing Uncertainties', *Strategic Analysis*, vol. 27, no. 2, Apr.–Jun. 2003. Online. HTTP: <http://www.idsa.in/publications/strategic-analysis/2003/april/Sreeradha%20Datta.pdf> (accessed 12 Mar. 2010).

Davidson, J., 'The Earth Summit', Development in Practice, vol. 2, no. 3, Oct. 1992, pp. 201–3.

de Silva, K., 'Terrorism and Political Agitation in Post-Colonial South Asia: Jammu-Kashmir and Sri Lanka', in R. Thakur and O. Wiggen (eds), *South Asia in the World: Problem Solving Perspectives on Security, Sustainable Development and Good Governance*, Hong Kong: United Nations University Press, 2004, pp. 84–103.

de Silva, N., *An Introduction to Tamil Racism in Sri Lanka*, Colombo: Chintana Prashadaya, 1997.

de Sotto, H., *The Other Path: The Invisible Revolution in the Third World*, New York: Harper and Row, 1989.

'Dealing with the Threat of Climate Change – India Country Paper', *MEA India*. Online. HTTP: <http://www.meaindia.nic.in/speech/2005/07/07ss02.pdf> (accessed 15 Aug. 2010).

Deen, T., 'Climate Change: Legitimacy of Security Council Meeting Challenged', *IPS News*, 7 Apr. 2007. Online. HTTP: <http://ipsnews.net/news.asp?idnews=37382> (accessed 4 May 2011).

Delacoste, F. and Alexander, P., *Sex Work*, San Francisco: Cleis, 1998.

'Democracy and State Security', *New Age*, 28 Jan. 2007.

Den Boer, M. and de Wilde, J. (eds), *The Viability of Human Security*, Amsterdam: Amsterdam University Press, 2008.

Denyer, S., 'Ghani Says Afghanistan Must Take Its "Second Chance"', *Reuters India*, 3 Mar. 2009. Online. HTTP: <http://in.reuters.com/article/southAsiaNews/idINIndia-38310 720090303> (accessed 7 Apr. 2009).

R. Deshpande, 'Centre won't bypass House rules for Lokpal', *The Times of India*, 22 Aug. 2011. Online. HTTP: <http://articles.timesofindia.indiatimes.com/2011-08-22/india/29914533_1_anna-hazare-agitation-lokpal-anti-corruption-ombudsman> (accessed 26 Aug. 2011).

Devraj, R., 'Maoists Put India on the Spot', *Asia Times Online*, 2 June 2005. Online. HTTP: <http://www.atimes.com/atimes/South_Asia/GF02Df01.html> (accessed 12 Jan. 2011).

Diaz, H. F. and Morehouse, B. J., *Climate and Water: Transboundary Challenges in the Americas*, Boston: Kluwer Academic Publishers, 2003.

'Does Global Warming Comprise National Security?', *Time*, 17 Apr. 2008. Online. HTTP: http://www.time.com/time/specials/2007/article/0,28804,1730759_1731383_1731632,00.html> (accessed 10 Aug. 2008).

Doezema, J., 'Loose Women or Lost Women? The Re-emergence of the Myth of "White Slavery" in Contemporary Discourses of "Trafficking in Women"', *Gender Issues*, vol. 18, no. 1, 2000, pp. 23–50.

——, 'Ouch! Western Feminists' Wounded Attachment to the Third World Prostitute', *Feminist Review*, vol. 67, Spring 2001, pp. 16–38.

Döös, B. R., 'Environmental Degradation, Global Food Production, and Risk for Large-Scale Migrations', *Ambio*, vol. 23, Mar. 1994, pp. 124–30.

Douglas, N., *Institutions, Institutional Change and Economic Performance*, Cambridge: Cambridge University Press, 1990.

'Dr. R. K. Pachauri Conferred with Climate Protection Award by EPA', *The Financial Express*, 29 May 2008. Online. HTTP: <http://www.financialexpress.com/news/dr-r-k-pachauri-conferred-with-climate-protection-award-by-epa/316177/> (accessed 31 May 2011).

Dubey, R. K., *Indo-Sri Lankan Relations with Special Reference to the Tamil Problem*, New Delhi: Deep & Deep Publications, 1989.

Duenas, C., 'Water Champion: Hamidur Khan on Flood Management – Coping with the Worst of Floods', *Asian Development Bank*, August 2004. Online. HTTP: <http://www.adb.org/Water/Champions/khan.asp#footnote> (accessed 6 Oct. 2009).

Dupont, A. and Pearman, G., 'Heating up the Planet', *Lowy Institute Paper 12*, Lowy Institute for International Policy, 2006.

'Durgawati Project: Centre to Fund 90% Cost', *Express India*, 11 Feb. 2008. Online. HTTP: <http://www.expressindia.com/latest-news/Durgadwani-project-Centre-to-fund-90-cost/271578/> (accessed 7 Oct. 2010).

ECDPM, 'The Cotonou Agreement: A User's Guide for Non-State Actors', *African, Caribbean and Pacific (ACP) Secretariat*, Brussels: ACP Secretariat, Nov. 2003. Online. HTTP: <http://www.acpsec.org/en/nsa/nsa_users_guide_en_rev1.pdf> (accessed 22 June 2011).

'Eco-Sense at G8', *Indian Express*, 9 July 2005. Online. HTTP: <http://www.indianexpress.com/archive_full_story.php?content_id=74087> (accessed 26 Aug. 2010).

Ekberg, G. and Manandhar, M. D., 'Final Report, Review of the Office of the National Rapporteur at the National Human Rights Commission Kathmandu, Nepal', *National Human Rights Commission*, 12 Aug. 2005. Online. HTTP: <http://www.nhrcnepal.org/publication/doc/reports/ONRT_REVIEW_REPORT.pdf> (accessed 19 Apr. 2011).

Elliot, L., *The Global Politics of the Environment* (2nd edn), New York: Palgrave Macmillan, 2004.

'Emergency Declared; Iajuddin Quits As Chief Adviser', *The Daily Star*, 12 Jan. 2007. Online. HTTP: <http://thedailystar.net/2007/01/12/d7011201011.htm> (accessed 10 Oct. 2009).

'Emerging Non-Traditional Security Challenges in Asia', *Centre for Strategic and International Studies*, Washington D.C., 6 Mar. 2007.

Emirates Center for Strategic Studies (ECSS), *The Balance of Power in South Asia*, Abu Dhabi: I. B. Tauris, 2003.

'Empowering Farmers Through Real Time weather and Price Information: Reuters Market Light', *WBCSD-SNV Alliance*. Online. HTTP: <http://www.inclusivebusiness.org/2008/06/reuters-market.html> (accessed 16 Aug. 2010).

'Enhanced Disaster Preparedness in South Asia: Through Community-Based and Regional Approaches', *Annual Programme Statement (APS), USAID/DCHA/OFDA*, ReliefWeb, 24 Apr. 2002. Online. HTTP: <http://www.reliefweb.int/rw/RWB.NSF/db900SID/OCHA-64CEVD?OpenDocument> (accessed 13 Aug. 2010).

Enloe, C., *Bananas, Beaches and Bases: Making Feminist Sense of International Politics*, Berkley: University of California Press, 1989.

'Environmental Stress and Demographic Change: Underlying Conditions and Nepal's Instability', Report from event held at Woodrow Wilson Centre for International Scholars, 1 Nov. 2006. Online. HTTP: <http://www.wilsoncenter.org/index.cfm?fuseaction=events.event_summary&event_id=205735> (accessed 11 Apr. 2010).

Erikkson, J., 'Observers or Advocates? On The Political Role of Analysts', *Cooperation and Conflict*, vol. 34, no. 3, Sept. 1999, pp. 311–30.

Fierke, K., *Critical Approaches to International Security*, London: Polity Press, 2007.

'Fighting for a Better, Cleaner World', *India Together*, 27 Apr. 2005. Online. HTTP: <http://www.indiatogether.org/2005/apr/env-csenarain.htm> (accessed 29 July 2011).

Foong Khong, Y. and MacFarlane, S. N., *Human Security and the UN: A Critical History*, Bloomington, IN: Indiana University Press, 2006.

Foster, P. and Zaman, R., 'Riots Halt Bangladesh Elections', *The Telegraph*, 12 Jan. 2007. Online. HTTP: <http://www.telegraph.co.uk/news/main.jhtml?xml=/news/2007/01/12/wbangla12.xml> (accessed 4 Oct. 2009).

'Foundation Against Trafficking in Women' (STV). Online. HTTP: <http://www.bayswan.org/FoundTraf.html> (accessed 12 June 2010).

'Freedom in the World – Bangladesh', *Freedom House*, 16 Apr. 2007. Online. HTTP: <http://www.unhcr.org/cgi-bin/texis/vtx/refworld/rwmain?docid=473c55ad48> (accessed 10 Dec. 2009).

'Freedom in the World – Bangladesh', *Freedom House*, 2010. Online. HTTP: <http://www.freedomhouse.org/template.cfm?page=22&year=2010&country=7778> (accessed 12 Jan. 2011).

Friedman, L., 'How Will Climate Change Impact National Security?', *Scientific American*, 23 Mar. 2009. Online. HTTP: <http://www.scientificamerican.com/article.cfm?id=climage-refugees-national-security> (accessed 31 May 2011).

Fujikura, Y., 'Repatriation of Nepali Girls 1996: Social Workers' Experience', *Himalayan Research Bulletin*, vol. 21, no. 1, 2001, pp. 36–40. Online. HTTP: <http://digitalcommons.macalester.edu/cgi/viewcontent.cgi?article=1674&context=himalaya> (accessed 10 July 2011).

Ganguly, R., *Kin State Intervention in Ethnic Conflicts: Lessons from South Asia*, New Delhi: Sage Publications, 1998.

——, 'India, Pakistan and the Kashmir Insurgency: Causes, Dynamics and Prospects for Resolution', *Asian Studies Review*, vol. 25, no. 3, Sept. 2001, pp. 309–34.

Ganguly, S., 'Explaining the Kashmir Insurgency: Political Mobilization and Institutional Decay', International Security, vol. 21, no. 2, Autumn, 1996, pp. 76–107.

——, *The Crisis in Kashmir*, Washington, D.C.: Woodrow Wilson Center Press, 1997.

——, 'Explaining the Kashmir Conundrum: Prospects and Limitations', *Asia Policy*, no. 3, Jan. 2007, pp. 196–98.

——, *Conflict Unending: India Pakistan Tensions Since 1947*, New York: Columbia University Press, 2001.

——, 'India's Territorial Disputes with Pakistan and China: Understanding Security Relations', in P. Sahadevan (ed.), *Conflict and Cooperation in South Asia*, New Delhi: Lancer's Books, 2001.

——, 'Six Decades of Independence', *Journal of Democracy*, vol. 18, no. 2, 2007, pp. 30–40.

Ganguly, S. and Biringer K. L. in Dittmer, L. (ed.), *South Asia's Nuclear Dilemma: India, Pakistan and China*, New York: M. E. Sharpe Inc., 2005.

Ganguly, S. and Paul Kapur, S., 'The Sorcerer's Apprentice: Islamist Militancy in South Asia', *The Washington Quarterly*, vol. 33, no. 1, Jan. 2010, pp. 47–59.

Gaudin, J. P., 'Modern Governance, Yesterday and Today: Some Clarifications to be Gained from French Policies', *International Social Science Journal*, vol. 50, no. 155, Mar. 1998, pp. 47–56.

Ghate, P., 'Kashmir: The Dirty War', Economic and Political Weekly, vol. 37, no. 4, 26Jan.–1 Feb. 2002, pp. 313–22.

Ghosh, B., 'How to Defeat Insurgencies: Sri Lanka's Bad Example', *Time*, 10 May 2009. Online. HTTP: <http://www.time.com/time/world/article/0,8599,1899762,00.html> (accessed 26 May 2009).

Ghosh, P.S., *Migrants and Refugees in South Asia: Political and Security Dimensions*, Shillong: ICSSR-NERC, 2001.

'Glynn Berry Programme 2007–8', *Foreign Affairs and International Trade Canada*. Online. HTTP: <http://www.international.gc.ca/glynberry/program-gb-programme/0708. aspx> (accessed 7 February 2011).

Gohain, H., 'Ethnic Unrest in the North-East', *Economic and Political Weekly*, vol. 32, no. 8, 22–28 Feb., 1997, pp. 389–91.

Gopal, A., 'Afghanistan: Taliban Fill Power Void in Kabul?', *IPS News*, 20 Aug. 2008. Online. HTTP: <http://ipsnews.net/news.asp?idnews=43614> (accessed 7 Apr. 2009).

Gopinath, M., 'Trenches, Boundaries, Spaces: The Dialectics of Governance and Security in India', in P. R. Chari (ed.), *Security and Governance in South Asia*, Colombo: Manohar, 2001.

Gossman, P., 'Afghanistan in the Balance', *Middle East Report*, no. 221, Winter 2001, pp. 8–15.

'Governance Matters 2007: Worldwide Governance Indicators 1996–2006', *The Worldwide Governance Indicators (WBI) Project*. Online. HTTP: <http://info.worldbank.org/govern-ance/wgi2007/> (accessed 1 Oct. 2009).

'Governance Programmes and Activities for Development Partners in Bangladesh', *Local Consultative Groups in Bangladesh (LCG Bangladesh)*, 2007. Online. HTTP: <http://www. lcgbangladesh.org/inventory/13_inventory.pdf> (accessed 12 June 2011).

'Graft level Stays Same', *The Daily* Star, 27 Oct. 2010. Online. HTTP: <http://www.the-dailystar.net/newDesign/news-details.php?nid=160096> (accessed 12 Jan. 2011).

Gramsci, A., *Prison Notebooks*, New York: International Publishers, 1971.

'Grand Alliance Boycotts Jan 22 Election', *The Daily Star*, 4 Jan. 2007. Online. HTTP: <http://www.thedailystar.net/2007/01/04/d7010401011.htm> (accessed 4 Oct. 2009).

Gray, C. B. and Rivkin, D. B., 'A "No Regrets" Environmental Policy', *Foreign Policy*, vol. 83, Summer 1991, pp. 47–65.

'Grenades Kill 18 at Rally in Bangladesh', *CNN*, 21 Aug. 2004. Online. HTTP: <http:// edition.cnn.com/2004/WORLD/asiapcf/08/21/bangladesh.blasts/index.html> (acces-sed 20 May 2010).

Grossman, A. and Owren, C., 'Gender, Climate Change and Human Security: Lessons from Bangladesh, Ghana and Senegal', *Prepared by The Women's Environment and Development Organization (WEDO) with ABANTU for Development in Ghana*, ActionAid Bangladesh and ENDA in Senegal, May 2008. Online. HTTP: <http://www.wedo.org/files/HSN% 20Study%20Final%20May%2020,%202008.pdf> (accessed 2 Aug. 2010).

Gunaratna, R., *Indian Intervention in Sri Lanka: The Role of India's Intelligence Agencies*, Colombo: South Asian Network on Conflict Research, 1994.

Gunnell, B., 'Nothing to Sell But Their Bodies', *New Statesman*, 1 Mar. 2004. Online. HTTP: <http://www.newstatesman.com/200403010023> (accessed 30 June 2010).

Gupta, A., 'Information Technology and Disaster Management in India'. Online. HTTP: <http://www.gisdevelopment.net/aars/acrs/2000/ts8/hami0001.asp> (accessed 21 Aug. 2010).

Gurung, S. M., 'Good Governance, Participation, Gender and Disadvantaged Groups', *Dialogue on National Strategies for Sustainable Development in Nepal*, 23 Dec. 2000.

Jay, M., *The Dialectical Imagination: The History of the Frankfurt School and the Institute of Social Research: 1923–1950*, Berkeley: University of California Press, 1973.

Haas, P., 'Epistemic Communities and International Policy Coordination', *International Organization*, vol. 46, no. 1, Winter 1992, pp. 1–35.

——, *Saving the Mediterranean: The Politics of International Environmental Cooperation*, New York: Columbia University Press, 1990.

Habermas, J., *The Theory of Communicative Action, Volume 1: Reason and the Rationalization of Society*, trans. S. Verlg, Boston: Beacon Press, 1981.

——, *Between Facts and Norms: Contributions to a Discourse Theory of Law and Democracy*, trans. W. Rehg, Cambridge: Polity Press: 1996.

Hadar, L. T., 'Pakistan in America's War against Terrorism Strategic Ally or Unreliable Client?', *Policy Analysis*, no. 436, CATO Institute, 8 May 2002. Online. HTTP: <http://www.cato.org/pubs/pas/pa436.pdf> (accessed 27 Feb. 2009).

Hadiwinata, B. S., 'Poverty and the Role of NGOs in Protecting Human Security in Indonesia', in M. Caballero-Anthony, R. Emmers and A. Acharya (eds), *Non-Traditional Security in Asia: Dilemmas in Securitization*, Aldershot: Ashgate, 2006.

——, 'Securitizing Poverty: The Role of NGOs in the Protection of Human Security in Indonesia', paper presented at *IDSS, Nanyang University-Ford Foundation workshop on 'The Dynamics of Securitization in Asia'*, Singapore, 3–5 Sept. 2004, p. 4. Online. HTTP: <http://www.rsis-ntsasia.org/resources/publications/research-papers/poverty/Bob%20Hadiwinata.pdf> (accessed 16 February 2011).

Hagerty, D. T., 'India's Regional Security Doctrine', *Asian Survey*, vol. 31, no. 4, Apr. 1991, pp. 351–63.

Halder, D., 'Anna domini', Mid-Day, 28 Aug. 2011. Online. HTTP: <http://www.mid-day.com/news/2011/aug/280811-News-Mumbai-Indian-Parliament-Anna-Hazare.htm> (accessed 29 Aug. 2011).

Hangen, S., 'Race and the Politics of Identity in Nepal', *Ethnology*, vol. 44, no. 1, Winter 2005, pp. 49–64.

Hansen, L., 'The Little Mermaid's Silent Security Dilemma and the Absence of Gender in the Copenhagen school', *Millennium*, vol. 29, no. 2, 2000, pp. 285–306.

——and H. Nissenbaum, 'Digital Disaster, Cyber Security and the Copenhagen School', *International Studies Quarterly*, vol. 53, no. 4, 2009, pp. 1155–75.

Haq, M., 'Human Development Challenge in South Asia', Introductory speech at the launch of the report on *Human Development in South Asia 1997*, 9 Apr. 1997, Islamabad. Online. HTTP: <http://www.mhhdc.org/Dr%20haq%20reports/Human%20Development%20Challenge%20in%20South%20Asia.pdf> (accessed 6 July 2011).

——'Human Development Report in South Asia 1999 – The Crisis of Governance', Mahbub ul Haq Human Development Centre, 1999. Online. HTTP: <http://www.mhhdc.org/reports/HDRSA%201999.pdf> (accessed 12 Oct. 2009).

——, *Human Development in South Asia 1999: The Crisis of Governance*, Karachi: Oxford University Press, 2000.

Harshe, R., 'Understanding Conflicts in South Asia', in S. George (ed.), *Intra and Inter-State Conflicts in South Asia*, New Delhi: South Asian Publishers Pvt. Ltd., 2001.

Hashmi, T., 'An Open Letter', *New Age*, 18 Sept. 2007.——, 'Power Politics in Bangladesh', *Countercurrents.org*, 16 Nov. 2006. Online. HTTP: <http://www.countercurrents.org/bangla-hashmi160107.htm> (accessed 12 Mar. 2008).

'Hasina Urges People to Resist Jan 22 Elections', *New Age*, 5 Jan. 2007. Online. HTTP: <http://www.bangladesh-web.com/view.php?hidRecord=144963> (accessed 10 Oct. 2009).

Haviland, C., 'Despair of Nepal's Unwanted Exiles', *BBC News*, 30 Aug. 2005. Online. HTTP: <http://news.bbc.co.uk/1/hi/world/south_asia/4194616.stm> (accessed 10 Mar. 2010).

Hay, C., *Political Analysis*, New York: Palgrave, 2002.

Haynes, J., 'Transnational Religious Actors and International Politics', *Third World Quarterly*, vol. 22, no. 2, Apr. 2001, pp. 143–58.

Hedegaard, C., 'Copenhagen Climate Summit: Tough Times Not an Excuse to Avoid Hard Decisions', *Daily Telegraph*, 7 Dec. 2009. Online. HTTP: <http://www.telegraph.co.uk/earth/copenhagen-climate-change-confe/6712272/Copenhagen-climate-summit-tough-times-not-an-excuse-to-avoid-hard-decisions.html> (accessed 12 July 2011).

Heffernen, J. W., 'Being Recognised as Citizens: A Human Security Dilemma in South and Southeast Asia', Nov. 2002. Online. HTTP: <http://www.humansecuritychs.org/activities/research/citizenship_asia.pdf> (accessed 12 Mar. 2011).

Hegel, G.W.F., *The Philosophy of Right*, Oxford: Oxford University Press, 1967.

——,*Phenomenology of Spirit*, Oxford: Oxford University Press, 1977.

Hekman, S. J., 'Weber's Ideal Type: A Contemporary Reassessment', *Polity*, vol. 16, no. 1, Autumn, 1983, pp. 119–37

Held, D. and McGrew, A. (eds), *Governing Globalization: Power, Authority and Global Governance*, Cambridge: Polity Press, 2002.

Hellman-Rajanayagam, D., *The Tamil Tigers' Armed Struggle for Identity*, Stuttgart: Franz Steiner Verlag, 1994.

Hennayake, S. K., 'The Peace Accord and the Tamils in Sri Lanka', *Asian Survey*, vol. 29, no. 4, Apr. 1989, pp. 401–15.

Herson, L. J. R., 'In the Footsteps of Community Power', *American Political Science Review*, vol. 51, Dec. 1961, pp. 817–31.

Higgott, R. A., Underhill, G. and Bieler, A. (eds), *Non-State Actors and Authority in the Global System*, London: Routledge, 2000.

Hinzman, L., et al., 'Evidence and Implications of Recent Climate Change in Northern Alaska and Other Arctic Regions', *Climatic Change*, vol. 72, Oct. 2005, pp. 251–98.

Homer-Dixon, T., 'On the Threshold: Environmental Changes as Causes of Acute Conflict', *International Security*, vol. 16, no. 2, Autumn 1991, pp. 76–116.

Horkheimer, M., 'Traditional and Critical Theory', trans. M.J. O'Connell et al., in *Critical Theory: Selected Essays*, New York: Seabury Press, 1972.

Hossain, K., 'Struggling for Democracy 1986–2006', *Forum*, 21 Jan. 2007. Online. HTTP: <http://www.thedailystar.net/forum/2006/november/struggling.htm> (accessed 12 Mar. 2010).

'How is TERI Funded?', *The Energy and Resources Institute (TERI)*. Online. HTTP: <http://www.teriin.org/cocacola1_faq.php#2 > (accessed 7 Oct. 2010).

'How to make PUC More Effective', *CSE Press Release*, 4 Oct. 2002. Online. HTTP: <http://www.cseindia.org/campaign/apc/press_20021004.htm> (accessed 31 Aug. 2010)

'How Will Climate Change Affect India's Monsoon Season?', *Science Daily*, 12 Mar. 2007. Online. HTTP: <http://www.sciencedaily.com/releases/2007/03/070308121808.htm> (accessed 14 Aug. 2010).

Huggler, J., 'Bangladesh Gripped By Rioting As Political Rivalry Threatens Election', *The Independent*, 8 Jan. 2007. Online. HTTP: <http://news.independent.co.uk/world/asia/article2134843.ece> (accessed 4 Oct. 2007).

'Human Development Report 1997', *United Nations Development Report*. Online. HTTP: <http://hdr.undp.org/reports/global/1997/en/> (accessed 11 Mar. 2009).

'Human Failure Exacerbates Scale of Natural Disasters: Oxfam', *InfoChange News and Features*, Apr. 2008. Online. HTTP: <http://infochangeindia.org/200804237081/Disasters/Related-Reports/Human-failure-exacerbates-scale-of-natural-disasters-Oxfam.html> (accessed 13 Aug. 2010).

'Human Rights Report 2010', *Odhikar Report on Bangladesh*, 1 Jan. 2011. Online. HTTP: <http://www.odhikar.org/documents/2010/English_Reports/Annual_Human_Rights_Report_2010_Odhikar.pdf> (accessed 12 Apr. 2011).

'Human Security, Climate Change, and Environmentally Induced Migration', *United Nations University, Institute for Environment and Human Security*, 28 June 2008. Online. HTTP: <http://www.each-for.eu/documents/ELIAMEP.pdf> (accessed 2 Aug. 2010).

'Human Security in Bangladesh: Recent Trends and Responses', *Centre for Policy Dialogue*, no. 77, November 2003. Online. HTTP: <http://www.cpd.org.bd/pub_attach/DR-77.pdf> (accessed 14 Jan. 2011).

'Human Security Now', *Report of the Commission on Human Security*, 2003. Online. HTTP: <http://reliefweb.int/sites/reliefweb.int/files/resources/91BAEEDBA50C6907C1256D19006A9353-chs-security-may03.pdf > (accessed 18 May 2009).

'Human Trafficking', *26th Report of Session 2005–2006*, UK Parliament Joint Committee on Human Rights, vol. 1. Online. HTTP: <http://www.publications.parliament.uk/pa/jt200506/jtselect/jtrights/245/245.pdf> (accessed 24 Feb 2010).

'Human Trafficking and HIV: Exploring Vulnerabilities and Responses in South Asia', *UNDP Regional HIV and Development Programme for Asia Pacific*, UNDP Regional Centre in Colombo, 22 Aug. 2007. Online. HTTP: <http://www.hivpolicy.org/Library/HPP001346.pdf> (accessed 3 Mar. 2011).

'Human Trafficking and HIV: Exploring Vulnerabilities and Responses in South Asia 2007', *UNDP Regional HIV and Development Programme for Asia Pacific*, UNDP Regional Centre Colombo, 2007. Online. HTTP: <http://www.undp.org/hiv/docs/alldocs/human_traffick_hiv_undp2007.pdf> (accessed 7 Mar. 2010).

'Human Trafficking: The Facts', *United Nations Global Initiative to Fight Human Trafficking (UN. GIFT)*. Online. HTTP: <http://www.unglobalcompact.org/docs/issues_doc/labour/Forced_labour/HUMAN_TRAFFICKING–THE_FACTS-final.pdf> (accessed 8 May 2011).

Huntingdon, D. (ed.), 'Anti-Trafficking Programs in South Asia: Appropriate Activities, Indicators and Evaluation Methodologies – Summary Report of a Technical Consultative Meeting', *Horizons Project Population Council*, Kathmandu, 11–13 September 2001. Online. HTTP: <http://www.popcouncil.org/pdfs/rr/anti_trafficking_asia.pdf> (accessed 12 Feb. 2010).

Hussain, M., 'Governance and Electoral Processes in India's North-East', *Economic and Political Weekly*, vol. 38, no. 10, 8-14 Mar. 2003, pp. 981–90.

Hussain, Z., *Frontline Pakistan: The Path to Catastrophe and the Killing of Benazir Bhutto*, London: I. B. Tauris, 2008.

——, 'Pakistan Sends 20,000 Troops to Indian Frontier', *The Times*, 17 Dec. 2008. Online. HTTP: <http://www.timesonline.co.uk/tol/news/world/asia/article5400650.ece> (accessed 12 Feb. 2010).

Hutt, M. J., 'Introduction: Monarchy, Democracy and Maoism in Nepal', in M. J. Hutt (ed.), *Himalayan People's War: Nepal's Maoist Rebellion*, London: Hurst & Company, 2004, pp. 1–20.

Huysmans, J., 'Revisiting Copenhagen: Or, On the Creative Development of a Security Studies Agenda in Europe', *European Journal of International Relations*, vol. 4, no. 4, Dec. 1998, pp. 479–505.

'Impacts', *Greenpeace International*. Online. HTTP: <http://www.greenpeace.org/international/campaigns/climate-change/impacts> (accessed 10 Aug. 2010).

'Impacts of Climate Change: West and Central India', *CSE India*. Online. HTTP: <http://www.cseindia.org/programme/geg/pdf/western.pdf> (accessed 29 Aug. 2010).

'Impoverished Nepalese Girls Tricked into Prostitution', *IRIN Asia News*, 9 May 2007. Online. HTTP: <http://www.irinnews.org/Report.aspx?ReportId=72037> (accessed 20 Apr. 2009).

'In Search of Dreams: Study on the Situation of the Trafficked Women and Children from Bangladesh and Nepal to India', *International Organisation for Migration (IOM)*, Dhaka, 2002. Online. HTTP: <http://publications.iom.int/bookstore/index.php?main_age= redirect&action=url&goto=publications.iom.int%2Fbookstore%2Ffree%2FIn_Search_ of_Dreams.pdf> (accessed 20 Jan. 2011).

'India and UNFCCC', *Government of India*. Online. HTTP: <http://envfor.nic.in/cc/india_ unfccc.htm> (accessed 23 Aug. 2010).

'India at a Glance', *World Bank Development Data*, 25 Jan. 2011. Online. HTTP: <http://devdata.worldbank.org/AAG/ind_aag.pdf> (accessed 12 July 2011).

'India Counts the Costs of Floods', *BBC News*, 2 Aug. 2005. Online. HTTP: <http://news.bbc.co.uk/2/hi/south_asia/4737187.stm> (accessed 20 Aug. 2010).

'India: Desperately Seeking Doctors in Orissa's Red Zone', *Radio Netherlands Worldwide*, 23 June 2011. Online. HTTP: <http://www.rnw.nl/english/article/india-desperately-seeking-doctors-orissas-red-zone> (accessed 28 June 2011).

'India: Largest Cities and Towns and Statistics of their Population', *World Gazetteer*. Online. HTTP: <http://www.world-gazetteer.com/wg.php?x=&men=gcis&lng=en&dat=80&geo= -104&srt=pnan&col=aohdq&msz=1500&pt=c&va=&srt=pnan> (accessed 20 Aug. 2010).

'India's Maoist Challenge', *IISS Strategic Comments*, vol. 16, no. 24, Sep. 2010.

'India's Most Influential', *Time*, 13 Aug. 2008. Online. HTTP: <http://www.time.com/time/specials/2007/0,28757,1652689,00.html> (accessed 29 Aug. 2010).

'India Natural Disaster Profile', *LDEO*, The Earth Institute at Columbia University. Online. HTTP: <http://www.ldeo.columbia.edu/chrr/research/profiles/pdfs/india_profile.pdf> (accessed 21 Aug. 2010).

'India: Priorities for Agriculture and Rural Development', *World Bank*. Online. HTTP: <http://web.worldbank.org/WBSITE/EXTERNAL/COUNTRIES/SOUTHASIAEX T/EXTSAREGTOPAGRI/0,contentMDK:20273764~menuPK:548214~pagePK:3400 4173~piPK:34003707~theSitePK:452766,00.html> (accessed 15 Aug. 2010).

'India, S Asian Nations Face Extreme Weather', *Deccan Herald*, 23 Jan. 2011. Online. HTTP: <http://www.deccanherald.com/content/131598/india-s-asian-nations-face.html> (accessed 12 July 2011).

'India's Corruption Scandals', BBC News, 19 August 2011. Online. HTTP: <http://www.bbc.co.uk/news/world-south-asia-12769214> (accessed 24 Aug. 2011).

'India's Role in World Agriculture', *MAP*, no., Dec. 2007. Online. HTTP: <http://ec.europa.eu/agriculture/publi/map/03_07_sum.pdf> (accessed 16 Aug. 2010)

'India Talks Tough with Pakistan over Mumbai Terror Attack', *Rediff India Abroad*, 28 Nov. 2008. Online. HTTP: <http://www.rediff.com/news/2008/nov/28mumterror-india-talks-tough-with-pakistan.htm> (accessed 12 Feb. 2009).

'India–Pakistan Composite Dialogue On Hold', *The Hindu*, 5 Dec. 2008. Online. HTTP: <http://www.hindu.com/thehindu/holnus/000200812051421.htm>, 12 Feb. 2009.

'India Pakistan Leaders Meet at South Asia Summit', *USA Today*, 4 Jan. 2004. Online. HTTP: <http://www.usatoday.com/news/world/2004-01-04-summit_x.htm> (accessed 10 Mar. 2010).

Indian External Affairs Minister Pranab Mukherjee's statement in Parliament on the Mumbai terror attacks, 13 Feb. 2009. Online. HTTP: <http://www.satp.org/satporgtp/countries/india/document/papers/09fab13.htm> (accessed Mar. 11 2009).

'Indian Govt Hit by Bribery Claims Ahead of Confidence Vote', *AFP*, 21 July 2008. Online. HTTP: <http://afp.google.com/article/ALeqM5j2dA4PDAQFxLne-xWZZoi4TJCFOw> (accessed 23 Aug. 2008)

'InterAcademy Council Report Recommends Fundamental Reform of IPCC Management Structure', *Press release from InterAcademy Council*, Review of the IPCC, 30 Aug. 2010. Online. HTTP: <http://reviewipcc.interacademycouncil.net/ReportNewsRelease.html> (accessed 30 July 2011).

'IOM Resettles Over 10,000 Bhutanese Refugees from Nepal', *United Nations Radio*, 17 Feb. 2009. Online. HTTP: <http://www.unmultimedia.org/radio/english/detail/69588.html> (accessed 19 Mar. 2010).

'Insecurity of the Marginalised', in 'Democracy: Object of Desire', Special Report in *Himal South Asian*, vol. 20, no. 1, Jan. 2007.

'International Human Development Indicators: Bangladesh', *UNDP Human Development Report*. Online. HTTP: <http://hdrstats.undp.org/en/countries/profiles/BGD.html> (accessed 21 Jan. 2010).

IPCC, 'Extreme Weather: A Global Problem', *International Herald Tribune*, 7 Aug. 2007. Online. HTTP: <http://www.iht.com/articles/2007/08/07/news/weather.php> (accessed 13 Aug. 2010).

——, 'Impacts, Adaptation and Vulnerability', *The Working Group II contribution to the IPCC Fourth Assessment Report 'Climate Change 2007'*. Online. HTTP: <http://www.ipcc-wg2.org/index.html> (accessed 12 Aug. 2010).

'IPCC Eighteenth Plenary Session, London, September 24–29 2001', *Institute for International Sustainable Development*, 2001. Online. HTTP: <http://www.iisd.ca/climate/ipcc18/> (accessed 2 Aug. 2010).

'IPCC Reports', *Intergovernmental Panel on Climate Change (IPCC)*. Online. HTTP: <http://www.ipcc.ch/publications_and_data/publications_and_data.shtml> (accessed 2 Aug. 2010).

Islam, N., 'Military Role May Bear on Dhaka's Peacekeeping UN, EU Suspend Election Observation missions', *New Age*, 12 Jan. 2007.

Jalal, A., *Democracy and Authoritarianism in South Asia: A Comparative and Historical Perspective*, Cambridge: Cambridge University Press, 1995.

Jayasree, A. K., 'Searching for Justice for Body and Self in a Coercive Environment: Sex Work in Kerala, India', *Reproductive Health Matters*, vol. 12, no. 23, 2004, pp. 58–67.

Jayatilleka, D., *The Indian Intervention in Sri Lanka, 1987–1990: The North-East Provincial Council and Devolution of Power*, Kandy: International Centre for Ethnic Studies, 1991.

——, *Sri Lanka: The Travails of a Democracy, Unfinished War, Protracted Crisis*, Colombo: ICES, 1995.

Jervis, R., 'Security Regimes', *International Organization*, vol. 36, no. 2, Spring 1982, pp. 357–78.

'Joining the Dots: The Report of the Tiger Task Force', *CSE India*, 19 Apr. 2005. Online. HTTP: <www.cseindia.org/userfiles/ttf_report.pdf> (accessed 31 Aug. 2010).

Johnston, H. and Khan, S. (eds), *Trafficking in Persons in South Asia*, Alberta: Shastri Indo-Canadian Institute, 1998.

Jones, S. G., 'Pakistan's Dangerous Game', *Survival*, vol. 49, no. 1, Spring 2007, pp. 15–32.

——, 'The Rise of Afghanistan's Insurgency', *International Security*, vol. 32, no. 4, Spring 2008, pp. 7–40.

Joseph, M., 'Security Threat Assessment of Naxalites in India', *IPCS*, 15 Aug. 2001. Online. HTTP: < http://www.ipcs.org/article/naxalite-violence/security-threat-assessment-of-naxalites-in-india-541.html> (accessed 23 Oct. 2009).

Kabir, E., 'Why Small Arms Jeopardise Human Security', *The Daily Star*, 23 Sept. 2004. Online. HTTP: <http://www.thedailystar.net/2004/09/23/d40923020527.htm> (accessed 10 Dec. 2009).

Kaczmarek, Z., Strzepek, K. M., Somlyódy, L. and Priazhinskaya, V. (eds.), *Water Resources Management in the Face of Climatic/Hydrologic Uncertainties*, Dordrecht: Kluwer; Laxenburg, Austria: International Institute for Applied Systems Analysis, 1996.

Kaldor, M., *Human Security: Reflections on Globalization and Interventions*, Cambridge: Polity Press, 2007.

Kanitkar, S., *Refugee Problems in South Asia*, New Delhi: Rajat Publications, 2000.

Karunakaran, C. E., 'Climate Change – Should India Change?', *The Hindu*, 3 Dec. 2007. Online. HTTP: <http://www.hinduonnet.com/2007/12/03/stories/2007120354921100.htm> (accessed 26 Aug. 2010).

Kashani, S., 'SAARC: 25 years of existence but little to show', The Hindustan Times, 28 Apr. 2010. Online. HTTP: <http://www.hindustantimes.com/SAARC-25-years-of-existence-but-little-to-show/Article1-536770.aspx> (accessed 23 Feb. 2011);

Kashyap, S.C., *Institutions of Governance in South Asia*, New Delhi: Konark Publishers, 2000.

Kaufman, R. and Crawford, M., 'Sex Trafficking in Nepal: A Review of Intervention and Prevention Programs', *Violence Against Women*, vol. 17, no. 5, May 2011, pp. 651–65.

Kaufman, S. J., 'Approaches to Global Politics in the Twenty-First Century: A Review Essay', *International Studies Review*, vol. 1, no. 2, Summer 1999, pp. 201–18.

Kazancigil, A., 'Governance and Science: Market-Like Modes of Managing Society and Producing Knowledge', *International Social Science Journal*, vol. 50, no. 155, Mar. 1998, pp. 69–79.

Keefer, P. and Knack, S., 'Why Don't Poor Countries Catch Up? A Cross-Country Test for an Institutional Explanation', *Economic Enquiry*, vol. 35, no. 3, 1997, pp. 590–602.

Keefer, S. L., 'Human Trafficking and the Impact on National Security for the United States', *USAWC Strategy Research Project*, 15 Mar. 2006. Online. HTTP: <http://stinet.dtic.mil/cgi-bin/GetTRDoc?AD=ADA448573&Location=U2&doc=GetTRDoc.pdf> (accessed 10 Mar. 2009).

Keith, K., 'The Key to a Powerful Agenda, If Properly Defined', in J. P. Burgess and T. Owen (eds), 'Special Section: What Is Human Security?', *Security Dialogue*, vol. 35, no. 3, Sept. 2004, pp. 345–87.

Kelkar, U. and Bhadwal, S., 'South Asia Regional Study on Climate Change, Impacts and Adaptations: Implications for Human Development', *Paper prepared by TERI and Human Development Report Office 2007/08*, p. 4. Online. HTTP: <http://hdr.undp.org/en/reports/global/hdr2007-8/> (accessed 1 Aug. 2008).

Kelly, L., 'The Wrong Debate: Reflections on Why Force Is Not the Key Issue with Respect to Trafficking in Women for Sexual Exploitation', *Feminist Review*, vol. 73, no. 1, 2003, pp. 139–44.

Kent, A., 'Reconfiguring Security: Buddhism and Moral Legitimacy in Cambodia', *Security Dialogue*, vol. 37, no. 3, Sept. 2006, pp. 343–61.

Keohane, R. O. (ed.), *Neorealism and Its Critics*, New York: Columbia University Press, 1986.

Keohane, R. O., and Nye, J., *Power and Interdependence*, Glenview: Scott Foresman, 1977, 2nd edn. 1989.

'Key Facts: Nepal', *Department for International Development.* Online. HTTP: <http://www. dfid.gov.uk/Where-we-work/Asia-South/Nepal/Key-facts/> (accessed 27 June 2011).

'Key Findings', *United States Global Change Research Group.* Online. HTTP: <http://www. globalchange.gov/publications/reports/scientific-assessments/us-impacts/key-findings> (accessed 3 Mar. 2011).

Khadka, N., 'Democracy and Development in Nepal: Prospects and Challenges', *Pacific Affairs,* vol. 66, no. 1, Spring 1993, pp. 44–71.

Khan, M. and Rahman, M., 'Partnership Approach to Disaster Management in Bangladesh: a Critical Policy Assessment', *Natural Hazards,* vol. 41, no. 2, May 2007, pp. 359–78.

Khan, M. S. R., 'Securing India's Coastline', *Institute for Peace and Conflict Studies (IPCS),* 7 Feb. 2008. Online. HTTP: <http://www.ipcs.org/whatsNewArticle11.jsp?action=show View&kValue=2503&status=article&mod=b> (accessed 19 Aug. 2010).

Khan, Y., *The Great Partition: The Making of India and Pakistan,* New Haven: Yale University Press, 2008.

Khand, J. D., 'The Contribution of Monarchy in Nepal', *Journal of Political Science,* vol. 7, nos. 1–2, 2003, pp. 25–44.

Khastagir, N., 'A Human Face to a Human Problem: Climate Justice Summit', *India Resource Centre,* 1 Nov. 2002. Online. HTTP: <http://www.indiaresource.org/issues/energycc/ 2003/humanfacehumanproblem.html> (accessed 26 Aug. 2010).

Khatri, S. K. (ed.), *Regional Security in South Asia,* Kathmandu: Centre for Nepal and Asian Studies, Tribhuvan University, 1987.

Knill, C. and Lehmkuhl, C., 'Private Actors and the State: Internationalization and Changing Patterns of Governance', *Governance,* vol. 15, no. 1, Jan. 2002, pp. 41–63.

Knudsen, O., 'Post-Copenhagen Security Studies', *Security Dialogue,* vol. 32, no. 3, Sept. 2001, pp. 355–68.

Kodikara, S. U., 'The Separatist Eelam Movement in Sri Lanka: An Overview', *India Quarterly,* vol. 37, Apr.–June 1981, pp. 194–212.

Kolodziej, E. A., 'Epistemic Communities Searching for Regional Cooperation', *Mershon International Studies Review,* vol. 41, no. 1, May 1997, pp. 93–98.

Korey, W., *NGOs and the Universal Declaration of Human Rights,* New York: Palgrave, 1998.

Krahmann, E., 'The Emergence of Security Governance in Post-Cold War Europe', ESRC 'One Europe or Several?' Programme, Working Paper, Sep. 2001.

Krause, K. and Williams, M., 'Broadening the Agenda of Security Studies: Politics and Methods', *Mershon International Studies Review,* vol. 40, no. 2, Oct. 1996, pp. 229–54.

——(eds), *Critical Security Studies: Concepts and Cases,* Minneapolis: University of Minneapolis Press, 1997.

Kronstadt, K. A., 'International Terrorism in South Asia', *CRS Report for Congress No. RS21658,* Washington, DC, 3 Nov. 2003. Online. HTTP: <http://www.fas.org/irp/crs/ RS21658.pdf> (accessed 10 Mar. 2009).

Kumar, A., 'A Review of Human Development Trends in South Asia: 1990–2009', Human Development Research Paper 2010/ 44, UNDP, November 2010. Online. HTTP:> (accessed 6 July 2011).

'Kyoto Protocol', *UNFCCC.* Online. HTTP: <http://unfccc.int/kyoto_protocol/items/ 2830.php> (accessed 23 Aug. 2010).

R. Kumar, P. Jawale and S. Tandon, 'Economic Impact of Climate Change on Mumbai, India', *Regional Health Forum,* vol. 12, no. 1, 2008, pp. 38–42. Online. HTTP: <http:// searo.who.int/LinkFiles/Regional_Health_Forum_Volume_12_No_1_Economic_impact_ of.pdf > (accessed 19 Aug. 2010).

Lamb, A., *Kashmir: A Disputed Legacy 1846–1990,* Hertingfordbury: Roxford Books, 1991.

Lamberton, D., *Managing the Global: Globalization, Employment and Quality of Life*, London: I. B. Tauris in association with the Toda Institute for Global Peace and Policy Research, 2002.

Landell-Mills, P. and Seregeldin, I., 'Governance and the External Factors', *Proceedings of the 1991 World Bank Annual Conference on Economic Development*, Washington DC: World Bank, 1991.

Legett, J., *Global Warming: The Greenpeace Report*, Oxford: Oxford University Press, 1990.

Leggert, J., 'Energy and the New Politics of the Environment', *Energy Policy*, vol. 19, March 1991, pp. 161–70.

Leonard, S. and Kaunert, C., 'Reconceptualising the Relationship Between the Audience and the Securitizing Actor', in T. Balzacq (ed.), *Securitization Theory: How Security Problems Emerge and Dissolve*, London: Routledge, 2011, pp. 57–76.

'Letter to Indian Prime Minister Atal Bihari Vajpayee from CSE Director Anil Aggarwal and Deputy Director Sunita Narain', 19 Oct. 1998. Online. HTTP: <http://www.cseindia.org/html/eyou/climate/pm_letter.htm> (accessed 23 Aug. 2010).

Levine, N. E., 'Caste, State and Ethnic Boundaries in Nepal', The Journal of Asian Studies, vol. 46, no. 1, Feb. 1987, pp. 71–88.

Levy, M. A., 'Is the Environment a National Security Issue?', *International Security*, vol. 20, no. 2, Autumn 1995, pp. 35–62.

Lindsey, T. and Dick, H., *Corruption in Asia: Rethinking the Governance Paradigm*, Annadale: Freedom Press, 2002.

'Links: A Newsletter on Gender for Oxfam GB Staff and Partners', Oxfam, Nov. 2005. Online. HTTP: <http://www.iiav.nl/ezines/email/Links/2005/November.pdf> (accessed 30 June 2010).

Liton, S. and Hasan, R., 'BNP Pledges to Work with Govt for Nation's Progress', *The Daily Star*, 2 Jan. 2009. Online. HTTP: <http://www.thedailystar.net/newDesign/news-details.php?nid=71529> (accessed 19 Jan. 2009).

Lukes, S., *Power: A Radical View* (2nd edn), New York: Palgrave Macmillan, 2005.

MacInnis, L., 'Early 2007 Saw Record-Breaking Extreme Weather: UN', *Stopglobalwarming.org*, 8 Aug. 2007. Online. HTTP: <http://www.stopglobalwarming.org/sgw_read.asp?id=122858882007> (accessed 13 Aug. 2010).

Maclean, S. J., Black, D. R. and Shaw, T. M. (eds), *A Decade of Human Security: Global Governance and New Multilateralisms*, Ashgate: Aldershot, 2006.

Madhab, J., 'North East: Crisis of Identity, Security and Underdevelopment', *Economic and Political Weekly*, vol. 34, no. 6, Feb. 6–12, 1999, pp. 320–22.

Mahendra, L., *Towards a Democratic Nepal: Inclusive Political Institutions for a Multicultural Society*, New Delhi: Sage Publications, 2005.

Malik, I. H., 'Pakistan: Misgovernance to Meltdown', *Open Democracy*, 19 Nov. 2007. Online. HTTP:<http://www.opendemocracy.net/article/conflicts/india_pakistan/pakistan_melt down> (accessed 12 Apr. 2011).

Mamun, M., 'The Challenge of Governance in South Asia: Good Governance in Bangladesh', *Occasional Paper 2000*, Peace Studies Group, University of Calcutta.

Maniruzzaman, T., 'Bangladesh Politics: Secular and Islamic Trends', in R. Ahmed (ed.), *Religion, Nationalism and Politics in Bangladesh*, New Delhi: South Asian Publishers, 1990.

——., *Politics and Security of Bangladesh*, Dhaka: University Press Ltd., 1994.

Manivannan, R., *Shadows of a Long War: Indian Intervention in Sri Lanka*, New Delhi: Kumar & Manivannan, 1988.

Marshall, P., 'Globalisation, Migration and Trafficking: Some Thoughts from the South-East Asian Region', *Occasional Paper No. 1, Globalisation Workshop in Kuala Lumpur*, UN Inter-Agency Project on Trafficking in Women and Children in the Mekong Subregion, 8–10 May 2001.

Marwah, O., 'India's Military Intervention in East Pakistan, 1971–72', *Modern Asian Studies*, vol. 13, no. 4, 1979, pp. 549–80.

Marwah, V., 'Rise in Violence and Governance in South Asia', in V. A. P. Panandiker (ed.), *Problems of Governance in South Asia*, Dhaka: University Press Limited, 2000.

Marx, K., *Capital Vol. 1*, London: Penguin Books, 1990.

Masud Ali, A. K. M., 'Treading along a Treacherous Trail: Research on Trafficking in Persons in South Asia', *International Migration*, vol. 42, no. 1–2, Jan. 2005, pp. 141–64.

Matinuddin, K., *The Nuclearization of South Asia*, Oxford: Oxford University Press, 2002.

Mathews, J. T., 'Redefining Security', *Foreign Affairs*, vol. 68, no. 2, Spring 1989, pp. 162–77.

Mattoo, A., 'Summer of Discontent', *Harvard International Review*, vol. 32, no. 4, Winter 2011, pp. 54–58.

Mauro, P., 'Corruption and Growth', *Quarterly Journal of Economics*, vol. 110, 1995, pp. 681–712.

May, R.J. and Ray, B. (eds), *Corruption, Governance and Democracy in South Asia: Bangladesh, India and Pakistan*, Kolkata: Towards Freedom, 2006.

McCombs, M., *The Agenda-Setting Role of the Mass Media in the Shaping of Public Opinion*, Oxford: Polity Press, 2004.

McCormack, T., *Critical Security Theory and Contemporary Power Relations: Emancipation, Critique and the International Order*, London: Routledge, 2009.

McIntosh, D., 'The Objective Bases of Max Weber's Ideal Types', *History and Theory*, vol. 16, no. 3, Oct. 1977, pp. 265–79.

McKibbin, W. J., 'Climate Change Policy for India', Lowy Institute for International Policy, 30 Apr. 2004. Online. HTTP: <http://www.lowyinstitute.org/Publication.asp?pid=128> (accessed 23 Aug. 2010).

McNair, B., *An Introduction to Political Communication*, Abingdon: Routledge, 2003.

McSweeney, B., 'Identity and Security: Buzan and the Copenhagen school', *Review of International Studies*, vol. 22, no. 1, 1996, pp. 81–89.

Mehrotra, O. N., 'Ethnic Strife in Sri Lanka', *Strategic Analysis*, vol. 21, Jan. 1988, pp. 346–61.

Mehta, M., 'India's Turbulent Northeast', *The South Asia Monitor*, Number 35, 5 July 2001. Online. HTTP: <http://www.ciaonet.org/pbei/csis/sam/sam35/index.html> (accessed 11 Mar. 2009).

Menon, R. K., 'A Case for Proportional Representation', *The Daily Star*, 31 Jan. 2004. Online. HTTP: <http://www.thedailystar.net/suppliments/anni2004/demo_04.html> (accessed 6 Dec. 2009).

——, 'Fighting for a Better, Cleaner World', *India Together*, 17 Apr. 2005. Online. HTTP: <http://www.indiatogether.org/2005/apr/env-csenarain.htm> (accessed 29 Aug. 2010).

Merelman, R., 'On the Neo-Elitist Critique of Community Power', *American Political Science Review*, vol. 62, no. 2, 1968, pp. 451–60.

'Military Panel: Climate Change Threatens U.S. National Security', *Environment News Service*, 16 Apr. 2007. Online. HTTP: <http://www.ens-newswire.com/ens/apr2007/2007-04-16-05.asp> (accessed 2 Aug. 2010).

Millar, L., 'Bin Laden operation strains US-Pakistan ties', *ABC News*, 27 May 2011. Online. HTTP: <http://www.abc.net.au/news/2011-05-10/bin-laden-operation-strains-us-pakistan-ties/2713696> (accessed 16 Jun. 2011).

'Millions Suffer in Indian Monsoon', *BBC News*, 1 Aug. 2005. Online. HTTP: <http://news.bbc.co.uk/2/hi/south_asia/4733897.stm> (accessed 20 Aug. 2010).

'Minister Vows to Root Out Corruption in PDS', *The Hindu Online*, 28 May 2006. Online. HTTP: <http://www.hinduonnet.com/thehindu/2006/05/28/stories/2006052812270100.htm> (accessed 6 Dec. 2009).

Mitra, S., et al., 'Climate Change and Vulnerability in Indian Agriculture: A Major Hurdle Towards Food Security', in R.B. Singh (ed.), *Natural Hazards and Disaster Management: Vulnerability and Mitigation*, New Delhi: Rawat, 2006.

Mohsin, A., 'Governance and Security: The Experience of Bangladesh', in Chari, P. R. (ed.), *Security and Governance in South Asia*, Colombo: Manohar, 2001.

Molden, D., *Water for Food, Water for Life: A Comprehensive Assessment of Water Management in Agriculture*, London: Earthscan, 2007.

Moore, T. G., *In Sickness or in Health: The Kyoto Protocol Versus Global Warming*, Stanford: Hoover Institute Press, 2000.

'More Democracy, Not Less', 29 Sept. 2006. Online. HTTP: <http://www.thedailystar.net/2006/09/29/d60929020319.htm> (accessed 19 May 2010).

'More Nepalese Women Victims of Trafficking but Fewer Seeking Justice', *Feminist Daily Newswire*, 12 Feb. 2004. Online. HTTP: <http://www.feminist.org/news/newsbyte/uswirestory.asp?id=8240> (accessed 16 Apr. 2011).

Muni, S. D. (ed.), *Nepal: An Assertive Monarchy*, New Delhi: Chetana Publications, 1977.

——, *Pangs of Proximity: India and Sri Lanka's Ethnic Crisis*, New Delhi: Sage Publications, 1993.

Myers, N., 'Environmental Refugees in a Globally Warmed World', *BioScience*, vol. 43, Dec. 1993, pp. 752–61.

Nadarajah, S. and Sriskandarajah, D., 'Liberation Struggle or Terrorism? The Politics of Naming the LTTE', *Third World Quarterly*, vol. 26, no. 1, 2005, pp. 87–100.

Najam, A., 'The Environmental Challenge to Human Security in South Asia', in R. Thakur and O. Wiggen (eds), *South Asia in the World: Problem Solving Perspectives on Security, Sustainable Development and Good Governance*, Hong Kong: United Nations University Press, 2004, pp. 225–47.

Narain, S., 'All Said and Done: Too Important for just Governments', *Equity Watch*, CSE Newsletter, 23 Oct. 2002. Online. HTTP: <http://www.cseindia.org/campaign/ew/ew_cop-8/government.htm> (accessed 26 Aug. 2010).

——, 'Sublimating Climate Change', *Down To Earth*, 31 Dec. 2003. Online. HTTP: <http://www.downtoearth.org.in/content/sublimating-climate-change> (accessed 1 Sept. 2010).

National Action Plan on Climate Change (NAPCC), *Government of India*, p. 2. Online. HTTP:<http://www.pmindia.nic.in/Pg01–52.pdf > (accessed 21 Aug. 2010).

National Adaptation Programme of Action, *Ministry of Environment, Energy and Water*, Republic of Maldives 2007. Online. HTTP: <http://env.rol.net.mv/docs/Reports/National%20Adaptation%20Programme%20of%20Action%20-%20Maldives/NAPA_Maldives_optimised.pdf > (accessed 29 Apr. 2011).

'National Security Internal & External Dimensions for India', *India International Centre ARSIPSO Seminar Summary*, 4 Dec. 2007.

Nefzger, B., 'The Ideal-Type: Some Conceptions and Misconceptions', *Sociological Quarterly*, vol. 6, no. 2, Spring, 1965, pp. 166–74.

Negi, R. S., 'Disaster Lessons Call for Greater Preparedness', *OneWorld South Asia*, 19 July 2008. Online. HTTP: <http://southasia.oneworld.net/todaysheadlines/disaster-lessons-call-for-greater-preparedness> (accessed 13 Aug. 2010).

'Nepal Literacy', *International Labour Organisation (ILO)*. Online. HTTP: <http://www.ilo.org/public/english/region/asro/bangkok/skills-ap/skills/nepal_literacy.htm> (accessed 20 June 2011).

'Nepal: Measuring the Economic Costs of the Conflict – The Effect of Declining Development Expenditures', *Asian Development Bank*, 27 June 2005. Online. HTTP: <http://www.reliefweb.int/rw/RWB.NSF/db900SID/RMOI-6DS49F?OpenDocument> (accessed 17 Apr. 2010).

'Nepal: State of Emergency Deepens Human Rights Crisis: Royal Takeover Prompts Fears for Safety of Critics', *Human Rights Watch*, 1 Feb. 2005. Online. HTTP: <http://www. hrw.org/english/docs/2005/02/01/nepal10100.htm> (accessed 12 Apr. 2010).

'Nepal: State of Emergency May Go Too Far', *Amnesty International*, 30 Nov. 2001. Online. HTTP: <http://asiapacific.amnesty.org/library/Index/ENGASA310142001?open& of=ENG-2AS> (accessed 12 Apr. 2010).

'Nepal's Decade of Conflict', *IRIN Humanitarian News and Analysis*, 10 Feb. 2006. Online. HTTP: <http://www.irinnews.org/InDepthMain.aspx?InDepthId=11&ReportId=33613> (accessed 17 Apr. 2010).ORDER

'Nepal's King Ends State of Emergency, Retains Power', *Daily Times*, 1 May 2005. Online. HTTP: <http://www.dailytimes.com.pk/default.asp?page=story_1-5-2005_pg4_2> (acce ssed 12 Jan. 2011).

'Nepal's Peace Agreement: Making it Work', *International Crisis*, Group Asia Report No.126, 15 December 2006. Online. HTTP: <http://www.crisisgroup.org/~/media/Files/asia/ south-asia/nepal/126_nepals_peace_agreement–making_it_work.ashx> (accessed 20 Jul. 2010).

'New Dimensions of Human Security', *UNDP Human Development Report 1994*, Oxford University Press, 1994, p.22. Online. HTTP: <http://hdr.undp.org/en/reports/global/ hdr1994/chapters/> (accessed 30 Jan. 2011).

'New India–Pakistan Bus on Trial', *BBC News*, 11 Dec. 2005. Online. HTTP: <http:// news.bbc.co.uk/2/hi/south_asia/4518096.stm> (accessed 4 July 2011)

Newell, P., *Climate for Change: Non-State Actors and the Global Politics of the Greenhouse*, Cambridge: Cambridge University Press, 2000.

Newman, E., 'Critical Human Security Studies', *Review of International Studies*, vol. 36, no.1, Jan. 2010, p. 77–94.

Newman, E. and Richmond, O. P. (eds), *The United Nations and Human Security*, Basingstoke: Palgrave Macmillan, 2001.

'NGO Events During COP 8', *Government of India*. Online. HTTP: <http://envfor.nic.in/ cc/cop8/ngo.htm> (accessed 26 Aug. 2010).

Nietzsche, F., *The Birth of Tragedy and the Geneology of Morals*, trans. F. Golffing, London: Doubleday, Random House Inc., 1956.

'Non-Traditional and Human Security in South Asia', *Institute of Regional Studies: National Commission for Human Development*, Islamabad, 2006.

Nordhaus, W. D., *Economics and Policy Issues in Climate Change*, Washington DC: RFF Press, 1998.

O'Brien, K., et al., 'Vulnerability of Indian agriculture to Climate Change and Economic Changes 2003', *Mainstreaming Biodiversity and Climate Change: Proceedings of the Asia Regional Workshop*, Dehra Dun, India, 6–11 Apr. 2003.

Office of the Special Rapporteur on Trafficking in Women and Children (OSRT), 'Trafficking in Persons Especially in Women and Children in Nepal', *National Report 2008– 2009*, National Human Rights Commission (NHRC) Nepal. Online. HTTP: <http:// www.nhrcnepal.org//publication/doc/reports/Trafficking-NationalReport%202008–9. pdf> (accessed 12 July 2011).

O'Neill, B. E., *Insurgency & Terrorism: Inside Modern Revolutionary Warfare*, Washington, DC: Brassey's, 1990.

'Opposition Mounts Attack on PM in LS on Cash-for-Votes Scam', *The India Daily*, 23 Mar. 2011. Online. HTTP: <http://www.theindiadaily.com/opposition-mounts-attack-on-pm-in-ls-on-cash-for-votes-scam/> (accessed 5 Apr. 2011).

O'Riordan, T. and Jager, J., *Politics of Climate Change: A European Perspective*, London: Routledge, 1996.

Osman, F. A., 'Bangladesh Politics: Confrontation, Monopoly and Crisis in Governance', *Asian Journal of Political Science*, vol. 18, no. 3, 2010, pp. 310–33.

'Our Global Neighbourhood', *Report of The Commission on Global Governance*, Oxford University Press: Oxford, 1995.

Owen, T., 'Human Security – Conflict, Critique and Consensus: Colloquium Remarks and a Proposal for a Threshold-Based Definition', *Security Dialogue*, vol. 35, no. 3, 2004, pp. 373 – 87.

Pachauri, R., 'Scary Future: More Hot Days, Floods Likely', *The Times of India*, 23 Oct. 2005. Online. HTTP: <http://www.teriin.org/upfiles/pub/articles/art15.pdf> (accessed 29 Aug. 2010).

——, 'Can Global Warming Be Controlled? Enough Resources Available for Mitigation', *The Times of India*, 5 Dec. 2005. Online. HTTP: <http://www.teriin.org/upfiles/pub/articles/art27.pdf> (accessed 29 Aug. 2010).

——, 'Act Now on Climate Change, No Need to Wait: Top UN Scientist', *The Times of India*, 23 Oct. 2007. Online. HTTP: <http://economictimes.indiatimes.com/environment/act-now-on-climate-no-need-to-wait-top-un-scientist/articleshow/9300276.cms> (accessed 29 Aug. 2010).

Pachauri, R., and Mehrotra, P., 'Alternative Energy Sources', *2020 Focus 7 (Appropriate Technology for Sustainable Food), Brief 8 of 9*, August 2001.

'Pachauri's IPCC, Al Gore Share Nobel Peace Prize', *Express India*, 12 Oct. 2007. Online. HTTP: <http://www.expressindia.com/latest-news/Pachauris-IPCC-Al-Gore-share-Nobel-Peace-Prize/227572/> (accessed 31 May 2011).

Padma, T. V., 'Development Versus Climate Change in India', *SciDev Net*, 31 Aug. 2006. Online. HTTP: <http://www.scidev.net/en/features/development-versus-climate-change-in-india.html> (accessed 19 Aug. 2010).

Page, J., 'Nepal Heads for Peace as Maoists Sign Deal', *The Times*, 21 Nov. 2006. Online. HTTP: <http://www.timesonline.co.uk/tol/news/world/asia/article644221.ece> (accessed 17 Apr. 2010).

'Pakistan Government Does Deal with Taliban on Sharia law', *CNN*, 18 Feb. 2009. Online. HTTP: <http://www.cnn.com/2009/WORLD/asiapcf/02/16/pakistan.taliban.sharia.law/index.html> (accessed 7 Apr. 2009).

Panandiker, V. A. P., 'Introduction', in V. A. P. Panandiker (ed.), *Problems of Governance in South Asia*, Dhaka: University Press Limited, 2000.

Parashar, U., 'Nepal Government May Fall', *The Hindustan Times*, 27 July 2011. Online. HTTP: <http://www.hindustantimes.com/Nepal-government-may-fall/H1-Article1–72 6208.aspx> (accessed 29 July 2011).

Parikh, J. K. and Parikh, K., 'Climate Change – India's Perceptions, Positions, Policies and Possibilities', *Indira Gandhi Institute for Development Research and Organization for Economic Co-operation and Development (OECD) 2002*, p. 6. Online. HTTP: <http://www.oecd.org/dataoecd/22/16/1934784.pdf> (accessed 15 Aug. 2010).

Paris, R., 'Human Security: Paradigm Shift or Hot Air?', *International Security*, vol. 26, no. 2, 2001, pp. 87-102.

Parmar, I., *Think Tanks and Power in Foreign Policy: A Comparative Study of the Role and Influence of the Council on Foreign Relations and the Royal Institute of International Affairs, 1939–1945*, New York: Palgrave Macmillan, 2004.

Parson, E. A., Haas, P. M. and Levy, M. A., 'A Summary of the Major Documents Signed at the Earth Summit and The Global Forum', *Center for International Earth Science Information Network*. Online. HTTP: <http://www.ciesin.org/docs/003-312.html> (accessed 22 Aug. 2010).

'Party Disputes Affecting Peace, Statute: Nembag', *The Himalayan Times*, 21 July 2011. Online. HTTP: <http://www.thehimalayantimes.com/fullNews.php?headline=Party+disputes+

affecting+peace%E2%80%9A+statute%3A+Nembang&NewsID=296381> (accessed 2 August 2011).

Patil, V. T. and Jha, N. K., *Peace and Cooperative Security in South Asia*, Delhi: P R Books, 1999.

Patil, V.T. and Trivedi, P.R., *Migration, Refugees and Security in the 21st Century*, New Delhi: Authorspress, 2000.

Pattanaik, S. S., 'Making Sense of Regional Cooperation: SAARC at 20', *Strategic Analysis*, vol. 30, no. 1, Jan.–Mar. 2006, pp. 139–60.

——, 'SAARC at 25: Time to reflect', IDSA Comment, 7 May 2010. Online. HTTP: <http://www.idsa.in/idsacomments/SAARCat25TimetoReflect_sspattanaik_070510> (accessed 23 Feb. 2011).

'Patterns of Global Terrorism 2000', Report by the *Office of the Coordinator for Counterterrorism*, US Department of State. Online. HTTP: <http://www.state.gov/s/ct/rls/crt/2000/2432.htm> (accessed 11 Mar. 2010).

'Peace Deal Ends Nepal's Civil War', *BBC News*, 21 Nov. 2006. Online. HTTP: <http://news.bbc.co.uk/2/hi/south_asia/6169746.stm> (accessed 17 Apr. 2010).

Pearce, F., 'Claims Himalayan Glaciers Could Melt By 2035 Were False, Says UN Scientist', *Guardian*, 20 Jan. 2010. Online. HTTP: <http://www.guardian.co.uk/environment/2010/jan/20/himalayan-glaciers-melt-claims-false-ipcc> (accessed 4 Jan. 2011).

Pepper, G. B., 'A Re-Examination of the Ideal Type Concept', *The American Catholic Sociological Review*, vol. 24, no. 3, Autumn, 1963, pp. 185–201.

Perlez, J. and Masood, S., 'Pakistanis Deny Any Role in Attacks', *The New York Times*, 29 Nov. 2008. Online. HTTP: <http://www.nytimes.com/2008/11/30/world/asia/30pstan.html> (accessed 12 Feb. 2010).

Perrings, C., 'The Economics of Abrupt Climate Change', Philosophical transactions of the Royal Society of London. Series A, Mathematical and Physical Sciences, vol. 361, 15 Sept. 2003, pp. 2043–59.

Phadnis, U., *Ethnicity and Nation Building in South Asia*, New Delhi: Sage Publications, 1990.

Pheterson, G., *A Vindication of the Rights of Whores*, Seattle, WA: Seal, 1989.

Pickup, F., 'More Words but No Action? Forced Migration and Trafficking of Women', *Gender and Development*, vol. 6, no. 1, Mar.1998, pp. 44–51.

'PM for Equitable and Fair Global Climate Change Framework', *India Times*, 30 June 2008. Online. HTTP: <http://articles.economictimes.indiatimes.com/2008-06-30/news/27696064_1_climate-change-national-action-plan-capita-ghg-emissions> (accessed 28 June 2010).

'PM's Council on Climate Change', *Prime Minister of India*, 6 June 2008. Online. HTTP: <http://pmindia.nic.in/climatebody.htm> (accessed 3 Sept. 2011)

Pokharel, T., 'Monarchy in Democratic Era: Need for Urgent Reform', in PlusMedium (ed.), *Forum Discussion: Threats to Nepali Democracy*, Kathmandu: Integrated Organization Systems (IOS) and DANIDA/HUGOU, 2003, pp. 69–77.

Pokharel, T. P. and Sengupta, S., 'Nepal's Maoist Rebels Announce a Ceasefire', *New York Times*, 27 Apr. 2006. Online. HTTP: <http://www.nytimes.com/2006/04/27/world/asia/27nepal.html> (accessed 17 Apr. 2010).

——, 'Nepal Maoists Sign Peace Accord with Government', *International Herald Tribune*, 22 Nov. 2006. Online. HTTP: <http://www.iht.com/articles/2006/11/22/news/nepal.php> (accessed 17 Apr. 2010)

'Policy Bulletin: Nontraditional Security Threats in South East Asia', *The Stanley Foundation*, Warrenton, Virginia, 16–18 Oct. 2003.

'Political Unrest and Democracy in Bangladesh', *Asian Survey*, vol. 37, no. 3, Mar. 1997, pp. 254–68.

'Politics of Hate: An Ancient Vendetta Continues To Eat Away At Public Life', *The Economist*, 10 Nov. 2010. Online. HTTP: <http://www.economist.com/node/17525830> (accessed 20 Apr. 2011).

Polsby, N. W., *Community Power and Political Theory* (2nd edn), New Haven: Yale University Press, 1980.

'Port of Spain Climate Change Consensus: The Commonwealth Climate Change Declaration 2009', *Commonwealth Secretariat*, 28 Nov. 2009. Online. HTTP: <http://www.thecommonwealth.org/files/216780/FileName/PortofSpainClimateChangeConsensus-The CommonwealthClimateChangeDeclaration.PDF> (accessed 12 July 2011).

'Potential Impact of Sea-Level Rise on Bangladesh', *UNEP*. Online. HTTP: <http://www.grida.no/publications/vg/climate/page/3086.aspx> (accessed 12 Mar. 2010).

Pranati, D., 'Population Movement from Nepal to West Bengal', *Indian Journal of Regional Science*, vol. 36, no. 1, 2001, pp. 88–102.

Prasai, S. B., 'Call for Global Action to Halt Nepalese Women and Girls Trafficking', *American Chronicle*, 10 Feb. 2008. Online. HTTP: <http://www.americanchronicle.com/articles/51873> (accessed 21 May 2011).

'Present "EC" Must Go: Khaleda', *The Daily Star*, 1 May 2011. Online. HTTP: <http://www.thedailystar.net/newDesign/latest_news.php?nid=29590> (accessed 2 May 2011).

'Prevention of Trafficking and the Care and Support of Trafficked Persons', *The Asia Council/Horizons Project Population Council*, February 2001. Online. HTTP: <http://www.popcouncil.org/pdfs/horizons/trafficking1.pdf> (accessed 21 June 2010).

'Profile: India's Maoist Rebels', *BBC News*, 4 Mar. 2011. Online. HTTP: <http://www.bbc.co.uk/news/world-south-asia-12640645> (accessed 14 June 2011).

'Protecting Refugees and the Role of UNHCR', *UNHCR*, Report 2007–8. Online. HTTP: <http://www.unhcr.org/basics/BASICS/4034b6a34.pdf> (accessed 12 Mar. 2009).

Puri, B., *Kashmir: Insurgency and After*, New Delhi: Orient Longman Private Limited, 2008.

Pyakuryal, B. and Sainju, R. S., *Nepal's Conflict: A Micro Impact Analysis on Economy*, Kathmandu: Pyakuryal & Sainju, 2007.

'Q and A: Kashmir Dispute', *BBC News*, 6 Nov. 2008. Online. HTTP: <http://news.bbc.co.uk/1/hi/world/south_asia/2739993.stm> (accessed 31 Oct., 2010).

Quraishi, A., 'Chance of India, Pakistan Thaw', *CNN News*, 22 July 2004. Online. HTTP: <http://edition.cnn.com/2004/WORLD/asiapcf/07/21/saarc.meeting/index.html> (accessed 10 Mar. 2009).

Qadeer, M. A., 'Will the Falling Dominoes Reach Pakistan?', *Open Democracy*, 30 Mar. 2011. Online. HTTP: <http://www.opendemocracy.net/mohammad-aqadeer/will-falling-dominoes-reach-pakistan> (accessed 4 Apr. 2011).

Quader, G. M., 'The Ultimate Target', *The Daily Star* 22 Oct. 2007. Online. HTTP: <http://www.the dailystar.net/story.php?nid=8282> (accessed 23 May 2010).

Rabasa, A. and Chalk, P., *Colombian Labyrinth: The Synergy of Drugs and Insurgency and its Implications for Regional Stability*, Santa Monica: RAND, 2001.

Radhakrishnan, R., 'More Tamil Refugees Expected to Return: UNHCR', *The Hindu*, 10 Jan. 2011. Online. HTTP: <http://www.thehindu.com/news/international/article 1076016.ece> (accessed 4 Apr. 2011).

Rahman, M., Hossain, S. and Ahmed, F., *Endemic Corruption in Bangladesh: A Handful of Corrupt Hurt Millions*, Dhaka: News Network, 2003.

Rahman, N., 'A Civil War of the Soul', *Forum*, vol. 2, no. 1, Jan. 2007. Online. HTTP: <http://www.thedailystar.net/forum/2007/january/civil.htm> (accessed 23 Oct. 2007).

Rahman, W., 'Is Bangladesh Heading Towards Disaster?', *BBC News*, 8 Jan. 2007. Online. HTTP: <http://news.bbc.co.uk/2/hi/south_asia/6241263.stm> (accessed 4 Oct. 2009).

Rais, R. B., 'Post-Cold War Security Studies in Pakistan: Continuity and Change' in D. Banerjee (ed.), *Security Studies in South Asia: Change and Challenges*, New Delhi: Vedam Books, 2000.

Raj, P. A., 'Monarchy in Nepal' in D. B. Gurung (ed.), *Nepal Tomorrow: Voices and Visions*, Kathmandu: Koselee Prakashan, 2003.

Rama Rao, M., 'India–Pakistan Begin a New Round of Talks on Nuke CBMs', *Asian Tribune*, 5 Aug. 2005. Online. HTTP: <http://www.asiantribune.com/news/2005/08/05/india-pakistan-begin-new-round-talks-nuke-cbms> (accessed 4 July 2011).

Ramesh, R., 'Monsoon Floods Displace 19 Million', *Guardian*, 3 Aug. 2007. Online. HTTP: <http://www.guardian.co.uk/world/2007/aug/03/india.randeepramesh> (accessed 15 Aug. 2010).

Ramesh, R. and Burke, J., 'At War Level: India Raises Security Status Amid Grief', *Guardian*, 1 Dec. 2008. Online. HTTP: <http://www.guardian.co.uk/world/2008/dec/01/mumbai-terror-attacks-india-pakistan3> (accessed 12 Feb. 2009).

Ramesh, R. and Dodd, V., 'Mumbai Terror Attacks: India Fury at Pakistan as Bloody Siege is Crushed', *Guardian*, 30 Nov. 2008. Online. HTTP: <http://www.guardian.co.uk/world/2008/nov/30/mumbai-terror-attacks-india3> (accessed 12 Feb. 2011).

Rana, S. Y., Debabrata, R., Kumar, G. P., Castillejo, C. and Mishra, M., 'From Challenges to Opportunities – Responses to Trafficking and HIV/AIDS in South Asia', *UNDP Regional HIV and Development Programme for South and North East Asia*, New Delhi, 2003.

Rao, J. L. N., 'Jihad and Cross-Border Terrorism in South Asia', in A. S. Raju (ed.), *Terrorism in South Asia: Views from India*, New Delhi: India Research Press, 2004.

Rashiduzzaman, M., 'Political Unrest and Democracy in Bangladesh', *Asian Survey*, vol. 37, no. 3, Mar. 1997, pp. 254–68.

'Red Storm Rising: India's Intractable Maoist Insurgency', *Jane's Information Group*, 20 May 2008. Online. HTTP: <http://www.janes.com/news/security/countryrisk/jir/jir080520_1_n.shtml> (accessed 7 Apr. 2009).

'Reform of the Caretaker Government', *Keynote paper given by Shah A.M.S. Kibria at a seminar organized by Bangladesh Foundation for Development Research (BFDR)*, 31 Jan. 2005. Online. HTTP: <http://www.kibria.org/publications/caretaker_govt.pdf> (accessed 12 Mar. 2008).

'Refugee Watch Special Issue', *Mahaniban Calcutta Research Group*, nos. 24 – 6, Oct. 2005. Online. HTTP: <www.mcrg.ac.in/rw%20files/RW24.doc> (accessed 12 Apr. 2011).

'Regional Study for the Harmonization of Anti-Trafficking Legal Framework in India, Bangladesh and Nepal with International Standards: Developing Rights Based Approaches for Anti-Trafficking Actions in South Asia', *Report published by Kathmandu School of Law (KSL) in cooperation with the TDH Consortium and SALS Forum*, May 2007, Kathmandu, Nepal.

Rehman, H. Z. (ed.), 'Unbundling Governance: Bangladesh Governance Report 2007', *Power and Participation Research Centre (PPRC)*, Dhaka, 2007.

Reiss, H. (ed.), *Kant's Political Writings*, Cambridge: Cambridge University Press, 1989.

'Report of Regional Consultation of WSSD (Western Region)', *CSE India*, 12–13 July 2002, p. 9. Online. HTTP: <http://www.cseindia.org/programme/geg/pdf/geg.pdf> (accessed 29 Aug. 2010).

'Research Areas', *Climate Change Network South Asia*, 13 Aug. 2008. Online. HTTP: <http://www.can-sa.net/cansa/research_areas.htm> (accessed 13 Aug. 2010).

'Review of the SAARC Convention and the Current Status of Implementation in Bangladesh', *International Organisation for Migration and Asian Development Bank*, 6448 REG, October 2009. Online. HTTP: <http://www.iom.org.bd/publications/Review%20of%20the%

20SAA RC%20Trafficking%20Convention%20Bangladesh.pdf> (accessed 21 June 2011).

'Revisiting the Human Trafficking Paradigm: The Bangladesh Experience', *Bangladesh Counter Trafficking Thematic Group*, IOM-CIDA Dhaka, 22 Apr. 2003. Online. HTTP: <http://www.childtrafficking.com/Docs/bangl_counter_traff_themati1.pdf> (accessed 12 May 2010).

Rhodes, R., 'The New Governance: Governing Without Governance', *Political Studies*, Vol. 44, No. 4, 1996, pp. 652–67.

Riaz, A., 'Bangladesh in 2004: The Politics of Vengeance and the Erosion of Democracy', *Asian Survey*, vol. 45, no. 1, Jan.–Feb. 2005, pp. 112–18.

——'The politics of Islamization in Bangladesh', in A. Riaz (ed.), *Religion and Politics in South Asia*, Abingdon: Routledge, 2010, pp. 45–70.

Richmond, O., 'Post-Colonial Hybridity and the Return of Human Security', in D. Chandler and N. Hynek (eds), *Critical Perspectives on Human Security*, Abingdon: Routledge, 2011.

Richter, J. and Wagner, C. (eds), *Regional Security, Ethnicity and Governance: The Challenges for South Asia*, New Delhi: Manohar, 1998.

Roberts, D., *Global Governance and Biopolitics: Regulating Human Security*, Zed: London, 2009.

——, 'Human Security, Biopoverty and the Possibility for Emancipation', in D. Chandler and N. Hynek (eds), *Critical Perspectives on Human Security*, Abingdon: Routledge, 2011.

——, 'Human Security or Human Insecurity? Moving the Debate Forward', *Security Dialogue*, vol. 37, no. 249, 2006, pp. 249 – 61.

Rodal, B., 'The Environment and Changing Concepts of Security', *Canadian Security Intelligence Service Commentary*, no. 47, Aug. 1994. Online. HTTP: <http://www.csis-scrs.gc.ca/pblctns/cmmntr/cm47-eng.asp> (accessed 14 Aug. 2010).

Roe, P., 'Actor, Audience(s) and Emergency Measures: Securitization and the UK's Decision to Invade Iraq', *Security Dialogue*, vol. 39, no. 6, 2008, pp. 615–35.

Rogers, P., *A War on Terror: Afghanistan and After*, London: Pluto Press, 2004.

——, 'Climate Change: Threat and Promise', *Open Democracy*, 2 Nov. 2006. Online. HTTP: <http://www.opendemocracy.net/conflict/climatechange_4055.jsp> (accessed 27 Apr. 2008).

Rubin, B. R., 'Saving Afghanistan', *Foreign Affairs*, vol. 86, no. 1, Jan.–Feb. 2007, pp. 57–78.

Ruiz, H. A. and Berg, M., 'Unending Limbo: Warehousing Bhutanese Refugees in Nepal', *U.S. Committee for Refugees and Immigrants*, Report 98–105, Washington DC, 2004. Online. HTTP: <www.cnsp.ca/pdf%20files/bhutanese_refugees_in_nepal.pdf> (accessed 23 Nov. 2010).

Russett, B. and Starr, H., *Choices in World Politics: Sovereignty and Interdependence*, New York: Freeman, 1989.

——, 'When Securitization Fails', in T. Balzacq (ed.), *Securitization Theory: How Security Problems Emerge and Dissolve*, London: Routledge, 2011.

'SAARC Charter', *South Asian Association for Regional Cooperation (SAARC)*. Online. HTTP: <http://www.saarc-sec.org/SAARC-Charter/5/> (accessed 10 Mar. 2009).

L. Saez, *The South Asian Association for Regional Cooperation (SAARC): An Emerging Collaboration Architecture*, London: Routledge, 2011.

Sahadevan, P., 'Ethnic Conflict and Militarism in South Asia', *Kroc Institute Occasional Paper*, vol. 16, Joan B. Kroc Institute for International Peace Studies, University of Notre Dame, June 1999. Online. HTTP: <http://www.ciaonet.org/wps/sap01/> (accessed 5 Dec. 2009).

——(ed.), *Conflict and Cooperation in South Asia*, New Delhi: Lancer's Books, 2001.

Salter, M., 'Securitization and Desecuritization: Dramaturgical Analysis and the Canadian Aviation Transport Security Authority', *Journal of International Relations and Development*, vol. 11, no. 4, 2008, pp. 321–49.

——, "When Securitization Fails", in T. Balzacq (ed.), *Securitization Theory: How Security Problems Emerge and Dissolve*, London: Routledge, 2011, pp. 116–31.

Samad, S., 'Awami League and Its Allies Said They Will Boycott Forthcoming Parliamentary Elections', *Durdesh Weekly*, 3 Jan. 2007.

——, 'State of Minorities in Bangladesh: From Secular to Islamic Hegemony', *Country Paper presented at 'Regional Consultation on Minority Rights in South Asia' organised by South Asian Forum for Human Rights (SAFHR)*, Kathmandu, Nepal, 20–22 Aug. 1998. Online. HTTP: <http://www.sacw.net/DC/CommunalismCollection/ArticlesArchive/ssamad_Bangaldesh.html> (accessed 23 Sept. 2009).

Samath, F., 'Sri Lanka: Climate Change Worse Than Civil War – UN Expert', *IPS News*, 24 Apr. 2007. Online. HTTP: <http://ipsnews.net/news.asp?idnews=37463> (accessed 29 Apr. 2009).

Sanchez-Rodriguez, R., et al., 'Introduction to the "Global Environmental Change, Natural Disasters, Vulnerability and their Implications for Human Security in Coastal Urban Areas" Issue', *IHDP Update*, Issue 2, October 2007. Online. HTTP: <http://www.ihdp.uni-bonn.de/Pdf_files/Updates/IHDPUpdate2_2007.pdf> (accessed 15 Aug. 2010).

Sanghera, J., 'Trafficking of Women and Children in South Asia: Taking Stock and Moving Ahead', *Report sponsored by UNICEF Regional Office and Save the Children Alliance*, 21 Nov. 1999.

Sappenfield, M. and Yusuf, H., 'Public Anger Strains Indian–Pakistani Cooperation', *The Christian Science Monitor*, 5 Dec. 2008. Online. HTTP: <http://www.csmonitor.com/2008/1205/p06s02-wosc.html> (accessed 11 Mar. 2009).

Sarup, K., 'Women Trafficking and Conflict', *Telegraph*, 14 Mar. 2005. Online. HTTP: <http://www.scoop.co.nz/stories/HL0503/S00100.htm> (accessed 9 May 2008).

Saxena, P., 'Creating Legal Space for Refugees in India: the Milestones Crossed and the Roadmap for the Future', *International Journal of Refugee Law*, vol. 19, 2007, pp. 246–72.

Schneider, S. H., *Global Warming: Are We Entering the Greenhouse Century?* San Francisco: Sierra Club Books, 1989.

Schubert, R., et al., *Climate Change as a Security Risk*, London: Earthscan, 2008.

Sebenius, J. K., 'Challenging Conventional Explanations of International Cooperation: Negotiation Analysis and the Case of Epistemic Communities', *International Organization*, vol. 46, no. 1, Winter 1992, pp. 323–65.

'Second National Conference of Trafficking Survivors of Nepal, September 2008', *Concept Note and Request for Support*, Shakti Samuha, Apr. 2008.

'Secretary-General Challenges World Community to Tackle Climate Change', *Press release of 61st UN General Assembly Informal Thematic Debate*, 31 July 2007. Online. HTTP: <http://www.un.org/News/Press/docs/2007/ga10607.doc.htm> (accessed 1 Sept. 2010).

'Security Council Holds First-Ever Debate on Impact of Climate Change on Peace, Security, Hearing Over 50 Speakers', *UNSC Department of Public Information*, 17 Apr. 2007. Online. HTTP: <http://www.un.org/News/Press/docs/2007/sc9000.doc.htm> (accessed 4 May 2011).

Sekhsaria, P., 'G8, Clean Up Your Act', *The Times of India*, 8 July 2005. Online. HTTP: <http://timesofindia.indiatimes.com/articleshow/1164468.cms> (accessed 26 Aug. 2010).

Sen, S. R., 'Bangladesh: Retrospect and Prospect', *Economic and Political Weekly*, vol. 26, no. 13, Mar. 30, 1991, pp. 826–39.

Sengupta, S., 'Climate Change Threatens Food Production in India, UN Experts Warn', *International Herald Tribune*, 8 Aug. 2007. Online. HTTP: <http://www.iht.com/articles/2007/08/08/news/india.php> (accessed 15 Aug. 2010).

——, 'India Confidence Vote Opens Way for US Nuclear Agreement', *International Herald Tribune*, 22 July 2008. Online. HTTP: <http://www.iht.com/articles/2008/07/22/asia/india.php> (accessed 12 Aug. 2010).

Schofield, V., *Kashmir in the Crossfire*, London: I. B. Tauris, 1996.

Schwartz, P. and Randall, D., 'An Abrupt Climate Change Scenario and Its Implications for United States National Security', *Greenpeace*, October 2003. Online. HTTP: <http://www.greenpeace.org/raw/content/international/press/reports/an-abrupt-climate-change-scena.pdf> (accessed 31 May 2009).

Schuckman, E. E., 'Anti-Trafficking Policies in Asia and the Russian Far East: A Comparative Perspective', *Demokratizatsiya*, vol. 14, no. 1, 2006, pp. 85-102. Online. HTTP: <http://findarticles.com/p/articles/mi_qa3996/is_200601/ai_n16537201/pg_1> (accessed 26 Feb. 2010).

'Shakti Samuha: What We Do', *Free the Slaves*. Online. HTTP: <http://www.freetheslaves.net/Page.aspx?pid=294> (accessed 17 Apr. 2010).

Shani, G., 'Securitizing "Bare Life": Critical Perspectives on Human Security Discourse', in D. Chandler and N. Hynek (eds), *Critical Perspectives on Human Security*, Abingdon: Routledge, 2011.

Sharma, A. B., 'Icrisat Cautions Indian Against the Impacts of Climate Change', *Financial Express*, 24 Sept. 2007. Online. HTTP: <http://www.financialexpress.com/news/Icrisat-cautions-India-against-impact-of-climate-change/220432/> (accessed 26 Aug. 2010).

Sharma, V., 'Global Warming: Let's Take It Seriously', *The Tribune*, 13 May 2007. Online. HTTP: <http://www.tribuneindia.com/2007/20070513/edit.htm#5> (accessed 2 Sept. 2010).

Shaw, T.M., 'The Commonwealth(s): Inter- and Non-State: At the Start of the Twenty-First Century: Contributions to Global Development and Governance', Third World Quarterly, vol. 24, no.4, Aug. 2003, pp. 729–44.

Shawkat Ali, A. M. M., 'What are the signposts of a Failed State?', *The Daily Star*, 11 May 2004. Online. HTTP: <http://www.thedailystar.net/2004/05/11/d40511020330.htm> (accessed 10 Dec. 2009).

Shehzad, M., 'The South Asian Paradox', *Frontline*, vol. 20, no. 3, Feb. 2003. Online. HTTP: <http://www.hinduonnet.com/fline/fl2003/stories/20030214010508000.htm> (accessed 6 Dec. 2007).

Shelley, L., *Human Trafficking: A Global Perspective*, Cambridge: Cambridge University Press, 2010.

Shunduna, S. K., 'Anti-Trafficking Challenges in Nepal', *Forced Migration Review*, vol. 25, May 2006, pp. 21–22. Online. HTTP: <http://www.fmreview.org/FMRpdfs/FMR25/FMR2510.pdf> (accessed 16 Apr. 2011).

Siddiky, C. I. A., 'Coercive Stability Needs to be Transformed into Consensual Stability', *New Age*, 9 July 2007.

Singh, G., 'Punjab Since 1984: Disorder, Order and Legitimacy', Asian Survey, vol. 36, no. 4, Apr. 1996, pp. 410–21.

'Signatories to the CTOC Trafficking Protocol', *UN Office on Drugs and Crime (UNODC)*. Online. HTTP: <http://treaties.un.org/Pages/ViewDetails.aspx?src=TREATY&mtdsg_no=XVIII-12-a& chapter=18&lang=en> (accessed 4 July 2011).

Silverman, J. G., Decker, M. R., Gupta, J., Maheshwari, A., Willis, B. M. and Raj, A., 'HIV Prevalence and Predictors of Infection in Sex-Trafficked Nepalese Girls and Women', *Journal of the American Medical Association (JAMA)*, vol. 298, no. 5, 1 Aug. 2007, pp. 536–42.

Singh, M., 'Debate on Trafficking and Sex Slavery', *The Feminist Sexual Ethics Project*, Brandeis University, <http://www.brandeis.edu/projects/fse/index.html> (accessed 26 Feb. 2010).

Singh, S. L., 'Work Burden of a Girl Child in Nepal: An Analysis by Poverty Levels', *Nepal Women Development SAARC Division*, United Nations Children's Fund, Nepal Office, Kathmandu, 1990.

'South Asia in Action: Preventing and Responding to Child Trafficking: Summary Report', *UNICEF Innocenti Research Centre*, Florence, August 2008. Online. HTTP: <http://www.unicef.org/media/files/IRC_CT_Asia_Summary_FINAL4.pdf> (accessed 26 June 2011).

Skidmore, D., 'Review: Security: A New Framework for Analysis by Barry Buzan et al.', *The American Political Science Review*, vol. 93, no. 4, Dec. 1999, p. 1010–11.

Smith, A. D., *The Ethnic Origin of Nations*, Oxford: Blackwell, 1986.

Smouts, M.C., 'The Proper Use of Governance in International Relations', *International Social Science Journal*, vol. 50, no. 155, Mar. 1998, pp. 81–89.

Sobhan, R., 'South Asia's Weak Development: The Role Of Governance', *Centre for Policy Dialogue Dhaka*, November 1999. Online. HTTP: <http://www.cias.org/publications/briefing/1999/weakdev.pdf.pdf> (accessed 23 Oct. 2009).

——, 'Problems of Governance in South Asia: An Overview' in V. A. P. Panandikar (ed.), *Problems of Governance in South Asia*, Dhaka: University Press Limited, 2000.

——, 'Aid, Governance and Policy Ownership in Bangladesh', *Centre for Policy Dialogue*, Dhaka, January 2003. Online. HTTP: <http://www.cpd-bangladesh.org/publications/rs/rs1.PDF> (accessed 7 Apr. 2009).

Sobhan, Z., 'Human Security in Bangladesh', *The Daily Star* 17 Oct. 2004. Online. HTTP: <http://www.thedailystar.net/2004/10/17/d41017020320.htm> (accessed 23 May 2010).

——, 'Freedom from Fear', *The Daily Star*, 4 May 2007. Online. HTTP: <http://www.thedailystar.net/2007/05/04/d70504020330.htm> (accessed 5 Dec. 2009).

'South Asia: Human Trafficking', *UNODC*. Online. HTTP: <http://www.unodc.org/southasia/en/topics/frontpage/2009/preventin-of-human-trafficking.html> (accessed 23 June 2011).

'Special Report: Climate Change', *New Scientist*. Online. HTTP: <http://environment.newscientist.com/channel/earth/climate-change> (accessed 28 Aug. 2010).

'Speech of Prime Minister Shri Atal Bihari Vajpayee at the High Level Segment of the Eighth Session of Conference of the Parties to the UN Framework Convention on Climate Change New Delhi, 30th October, 2002', *Government of India*. Online. HTTP: <http://unfccc.int/cop8/latest/ind_pm3010.pdf> (accessed 27 Aug. 2010).

Speth, J. G., 'A Post-Rio Compact', *Foreign Policy*, vol. 88, Autumn 1992, pp. 145–61.

'Sri Lanka Climate Change May Ravage Agriculture, Coast Areas', *Lanka Business Online*, 18 Dec. 2007. Online. HTTP: <http://www.lankabusinessonline.com/fullstory.php?newsID=1301661969&no_view=1&SEARCH_TERM=1> (accessed 20 Apr. 2011).

'Sri Lanka Probe Urged as Video Airs in US', *Agence France-Presse*, 15 July 2011. Online. HTTP: http://news.yahoo.com/sri-lanka-probe-urged-video-airs-us-213152566.html (accessed 29 July 2011).

Stanford, P., 'Can Prof Rajendra Pachauri Really Survive Glaciergate?', 26 July 2011. Online. HTTP: <http://www.telegraph.co.uk/earth/environment/climatechange/8660714/Can-Prof-Rajendra-Pachauri-really-survive-Glaciergate.html> (accessed 4 Aug. 2011).

Stash, S. and Hannum, E., 'Who Goes to School? Educational Stratification by Gender, Caste, and Ethnicity in Nepal', *Comparative Education Review*, vol. 45, no. 3, Aug. 2001, pp. 354–78.

'Study: Sex Trafficking Spreading HIV in South Asia', *USA Today*, August 2007. Online. HTTP: <http://www.usatoday.com/news/health/2007-08-01-sex-trafficking-study_N.htm> (accessed 18 Apr. 2008).

'Sub-Regional Initiatives Wide off the Mark', *Human Rights Features*, Special Edition for the 10th Annual Meeting of the Asia Pacific Forum of National Human Rights Institutions, Aug.–Sept. 2005, p. 11. Online. HTTP: <http://www.hrdc.net/sahrdc/hrfquarterly/apf10/PDF/SAHRDC_All.pdf> (accessed 4 July 2011).

Suhrke, A., 'Human Security and the Interests of States', *Security Dialogue*, vol. 30, no. 3, Sept. 1999, pp. 268–69.

Sullivan, M. P., 'Transnationalism, Power Politics, and the Realities of the Present System', in M. Williams (ed.), *International Relations in the Twentieth Century*, London: MacMillan, 1989.

'Sunita Narain-India', *World People's Blog*. Online. HTTP: <http://word.world-citizenship.org/wp-archive/699> (accessed 1 Sept. 2010).

Sutton, R., 'The Policy Process: An Overview', Working Paper, Overseas Development Institute, August 1999. Online. HTTP: <http://www.odi.org.uk/resources/odi-publications/working-papers/118-policy-process.pdf> (accessed 1 Nov. 2008).

'State of Democracy in South Asia: A Report', *Prepared by the Centre for the Study of Developing Societies (CSDS) New Delhi in collaboration with International IDEA and the Department of Sociology, Oxford University*, 4 Dec. 2006.

Stoker, G., 'Governance as Theory: Five Propositions', *International Social Science Journal*, vol. 50, no. 155, Mar. 1998, pp. 17–28.

Strange, S., *The Retreat of the State: The Diffusion of Power in the World Economy*, Cambridge: Cambridge University Press, 1996.

Stritzel, H., 'Towards a Theory of Securitization: Copenhagen and Beyond', *European Journal of International Relations*, vol. 13, no. 3, Sept. 2007, pp. 357–83.

'Strong Democratic Institutions a Must to Face External Threats', *The Daily Star*, 30 Mar. 30 2005. Online. HTTP: <http://www.thedailystar.net/2005/03/30/d50330060269.htm> (accessed 10 Dec. 2009).

'Tackling the Tides and Tremors: South Asia Disaster Report 2005', *Report by Duryog Nivaran*, South Asia Network for Disaster Risk Reduction, 2006, p. 94. Online. HTTP: <http://duryognivaran.org/sadr/pdfs/chapter5.pdf> (accessed 20 Aug. 2010).

Tadjbakhsh, S. and Chenoy, A. M., *Human Security: Concepts and Implications*, London: Routledge, 2007.

Tarzi, A., 'South Asia: Pakistan–Afghanistan Conflicts Continue', *Radio Free Europe/Radio Liberty*, 29 Sept. 2006. Online. HTTP: <http://www.rferl.org/featuresarticle/2006/09/260c90a0–1f41–44ab6-a580–21bcc8a914f5.html> (accessed 12 Nov. 2010).

Tavares, R., 'Resolving the Kashmir Conflict: Pakistan, India, Kashmiris and Religious Militants', *Asian Journal of Political Science*, vol. 16, no. 3, 2003, pp. 276–302.

Taureck, R., 'Positive and Negative Securitization – Bringing Together Securitization Theory and Normative Critical Security Studies', paper prepared for the *COST Doctoral Training School, 'Critical Approaches to Security in Europe, ACTION A24: The Evolving Social Construction of Threats'*, Centre Européen, Institut d'Etudes Politiques de Paris, France, June 2005.

Taylor, P., *Non-State Actors in International Politics: From Transregional to Sub-State Organizations*, Boulder, CO: Westview Press, 1984.

Tellis, A. J., 'Pakistan and the War on Terror: Conflicted Goals, Compromised Performance', Carnegie Endowment Report, Jan. 2008. Online. HTTP: <http://www.carnegieendowment.org/files/tellis_pakistan_final.pdf> (accessed 27 Feb. 2009).

'TERI Working on Sunderbans Project', *The Hindu*, 8 Aug. 2008. Online. HTTP: <http://www.hindu.com/2008/08/08/stories/2008080856120900.htm> (accessed 29 Aug. 2010).

Thakur, R., 'Minorities, Women and Elections in Bangladesh – Part-II', *Asian Tribune*, 17 Oct. 2007. Online. HTTP: <http://www.asiantribune.com/index.php?q=node/7845> (accessed 6 Dec. 2009).

Thakur, R. and Newman, E., *Broadening Asia's Security Discourse and Agenda*, Tokyo: United Nations University Press, 2004.

Thapa, G. B. and Sharma, J., 'From Insurgency to Democracy: The Challenges of Peace and Democracy-Building in Nepal', *International Political Science Review*, vol. 30, no. 2, Mar. 2009, pp. 205–19.

'The Age of Consequences: The Foreign Policy and National Security Implications of Global Climate Change', *Center for Strategic and International Studies*, November 2007, p. 10. Online. HTTP: <http://csis.org/publication/age-consequences> (accessed 14 Aug. 2008).

The Conflict, Security & Development Group Bulletin, The Conflict, Security & Development Group, Oct. 1999.

'The Cost of Coercion: Global Report under the follow-up to the ILO Declaration on Fundamental Principles and Rights at Work', *ILO International Labour Conference*, 98th Session 2009, Report 1(B). Online. HTTP: <http://www.ilo.org/wcmsp5/groups/public/–ed_norm/–declaration/documents/publication/wcms_106268.pdf> (accessed 22 June 2011).

'The Council of Europe Convention on Action against Trafficking in Human Beings', *Council of Europe*. Online. HTTP: <http://www.coe.int/t/dg2/trafficking/campaign/Docs/Convntn/default_en.asp> (accessed 26 Feb. 2010)

'The Global Climate Change Regime', *Council on Foreign Relations*, 29 Nov. 2010. Online. HTTP: <http://www.cfr.org/climate-change/global-climate-change-regime/p21831> (accessed 20 June 2011).

'The Impact of Climate Change on Least Developed Countries and Small Island Developing States', *United Nations Office of the High Representative for the Least Developed Countries, Landlocked Developing Countries and Small Island Developing States*, New York, June 2007. Online. HTTP: <http://www.iied.org/CC/documents/ClimateChangeReportFinal.pdf> (accessed 13 Aug. 2010).

'The Insurgency in Afghanistan's Heartland', *International Crisis Group*, Asia Report no. 207, 27 June 2011. Online. HTTP: <http://www.crisisgroup.org/en/regions/asia/south-asia/afghanistan/207-the-insurgency-in-afghanistans-heartland.aspx> (accessed 2 July 2011).

'The IPCC: Who Are They and Why Do Their Climate Reports Matter?', *Union of Concerned Scientists*. Online. HTTP: <http://www.un.org/Pubs/chronicle/2007/webArticles/101907_nobel_prize_ipcc.html> (accessed 28 Aug. 2010).

'The Missing Piece of the Puzzle: Caste Discrimination and the Conflict in Nepal', *Centre for Human Rights and Global Justice*, NYU, 2005.

'The Road to Copenhagen: India's Position on Climate Change Issues', *Ministry of External Affairs*, Government of India, 27 Feb. 2009, p. 10. Online. HTTP: <http://www.indiaenvironmentportal.org.in/files/climate_0.pdf> (accessed 4 May 2011).

'The Story of a Nepali Girl Sold into Sexual Slavery', *Kanchenjunga Social Network*, 17 Apr. 2009. Online. HTTP: <http://www.ksnonline.org/profiles/blogs/survivor-the-story-of-a-nepali> (accessed 12 July 2011).

'The United National Framework Convention on Climate Change', *UNFCCC*. Online. HTTP: <http://unfccc.int/essential_background/convention/items/2627.php> (accessed 23 Aug. 2010).

Thomas, C., *Global Governance, Development and Human Security*, London: Pluto, 2000.

Thomas, C. W., 'Public Management as Interagency Cooperation: Testing Epistemic Community Theory at the Domestic Level', *Journal of Public Administration Research and Theory*, vol. 7, no. 2, Apr. 1997, pp. 221–46.

Thomas, R.G.C. (ed.), *Perspectives on Kashmir: the Roots of Conflict in South Asia*, Boulder, CO: Westview Press, 1992.

——, 'South Asian Security in the 1990s', Adelphi Paper 278, International Institute for Strategic Studies, July 1993.

Thomas, S. E., 'Responses to Human Trafficking in Bangladesh, India, Nepal and Sri Lanka', *UNODC Regional Office for South Asia*, New Delhi, 2011.

Thoumi, F. E., *Political Economy and Illegal Drugs in Columbia*, Boulder, CO: Lynne Reinner, 1995.

'TISS Report on the Narmada Dam: Sardar Sarovar Project', Tata Institute of Social Sciences, 20 Aug. 20 2008. Online. HTTP: <http://aidindia.org/main/content/view/764/376/> (accessed 4 Apr. 2011).

Tiwari, C. K., *Security in South Asia: Internal and External Dimensions*, London: University Press of America, 1989.

'Towards Lake Conservation', *CSE*, 7 August 2011. Online. HTTP: <http://www.cseindia.org/content/towards-lake-conservation> (accessed August 21 2011).

'Trafficking in Persons (TIP) Report 2007', *US State Department*, p. 39. Online. HTTP: <http://www.state.gov/documents/organization/82902.pdf> (accessed 1 May 2010).

'Trafficking in Persons (TIP) Report 2011', *US Department of State*. Online. HTTP: <http://www.state.gov/g/tip/rls/tiprpt/2011/index.htm> (accessed 10 July 2011).

'Trafficking in Persons Especially in Women and Children in Nepal', *National Report 2006–2007*, Office of the National Rapporteur on Trafficking in Women and Children (ONRT), National Human Rights Commission (NHRC), Nepal. Online. HTTP: <http://www.nhrcnepal.org///publication/doc/reports/Nat_Rep2006–7.pdf> (accessed 19 Apr. 2009).

'Transparency International Corruption Perceptions Index 2005', *Transparency International*, 2005. Online. HTTP: <http://www.transparency.org/news_room/in_focus/2005/cpi_2005#cpi> (accessed 30 Nov. 2010).

'Transparency International Corruption Perceptions Index 2010', *Transparency International*, 2010. Online. HTTP: <http://www.transparency.org/policy_research/surveys_indices/cpi/2010/results> (accessed 30 Nov. 2010).

Trombetta, M.J., 'Rethinking the Securitization of the Environment', in T. Balzacq (ed.), *Securitization Theory: How Security Problems Emerge and Dissolve*, London: Routledge, 2011, pp. 135–49.

True, J. and Mintrom, M., 'Transnational Networks and Policy Diffusion: The Case of Gender Mainstreaming', *International Studies Quarterly*, vol. 45, no. 1, March 2001, pp. 27–57.

Truong, T. D., *Sex, Money and Morality: Prostitution and Tourism in Southeast Asia*, London: Zed Books Ltd., 1990.

'Two Decades of Breathless Development', *CSE Press Release*, 1 Nov. 1998. Online. HTTP: <http://www.cseindia.org/AboutUs/press_releases/au4_110198.htm> (31 Aug. 2008)

Turner, M., Cooper, N. and Pugh, M., 'Institutionalised and Co-opted: Why Human Security Has Lost Its Way', in D. Chandler and N. Hynek (eds), *Critical Perspectives on Human Security*, Abingdon: Routledge, 2011.

UN.GIFT, 'An Introduction to Human Trafficking: Vulnerability, Impact and Action', *UNODC Vienna 2008*, pp.71–75. Online. HTTP: <http://www.unodc.org/documents/human-trafficking/An_Introduction_to_Human_TraffickingBackground_Paper.pdf> (accessed 26 June 2011).

'UN Protocol to Prevent, Suppress and Punish Trafficking in Persons Especially Women and Children, supplementing the United Nations Convention against Transnational Organised Crime', *United Nations*, 2000. Online. HTTP: <http://www.uncjin.org/Documents/Conventions/dcatoc/final_documents_2/convention_%20traff_eng.pdf> (accessed 12 Mar. 2009).

'UN Refugee Agency Launches HIV/AIDS Prevention Project in Nepal', *People's Daily Online*, 16 Oct. 2007. Online. HTTP: <http://english.people.com.cn/90001/90782/6284364.html> (accessed 12 Apr. 2008).

'UNCED 1999 Earth Summit', *United Nations*. Online. HTTP: <http://www.un.org/geninfo/bp/enviro.html> (accessed 22 Aug. 2010).

'Unclean Business: The Sad Truth About CDM', *CSE Press Release*, 8 Nov. 2005. Online. HTTP: <http://www.cseindia.org/AboutUs/press_releases/20051108.htm> (accessed 31 Aug. 2010)

'Understanding and Responding to Climate Change', *Highlights of the National Academies Reports*, 2008. Online. HTTP: <http://americasclimatechoices.org/climate_change_2008_final.pdf> (accessed 3 Mar. 2011).

UNHCR. Online. HTTP: <www.unhcr.org> (accessed 12 Mar. 2010).

United Nation Development Programme (UNDP), 'The Real Wealth of Nations: Pathways to Human Development', *Human Development Report 2010*, p. 98. Online. HTTP: <http://hdr.undp.org/en/media/HDR_2010_EN_Complete_reprint.pdf> (accessed 12 June 2011).

'US Report: Insurgency on the Rise in Afghanistan', Press TV, 3 Feb. 2010. Online. HTTP: <http://www.presstv.ir/detail.aspx?id=84484&sectionid=351020403> (accessed 12 Mar. 2009).

'USAID Nepal Budget Summary 2003–4', USAID. Online. HTTP: <http://www.usaid.gov/policy/budget/cbj2004/asia_near_east/Nepal.pdf> (accessed 12 Apr. 2010).

Vansittart, E., *Tribes, Clans and Castes of Nepal*, Gurgaon: Vintage, 1992.

Vaughn, J., 'The Unlikely Securitizer: Humanitarian Organizations and the Securitization of Indistinctiveness', *Security Dialogue*, vol. 40, no. 3, June 2009, pp. 263–85.

Victor, D. G., *The Collapse of The Kyoto Protocol and the Struggle to Slow Global Warming*, Princeton, NJ: Princeton University Press, 2001.

Vuori, J., 'Illocutionary Logic and Strands of Securitization: Applying the Theory of Securitization to the Study of Non-Democratic Political Orders', *European Journal of International Relations*, vol. 14, no. 1, 2008, pp. 65–99.

Wæver, O., 'Securitization and Desecuritization', in R. Lipschutz (ed.), *On Security*, New York: Columbia University Press, 1995.

Walsh, B., 'Q& a: The UN's Ban Ki-Moon on Climate Change', *Time*, 11 Dec. 2009. Online. HTTP: <http://www.time.com/time/specials/packages/article/0,28804,1929071_1929070_1947173,00.html> (accessed 12 July 2011).

'Weak Governance, Judiciary Root Cause of Human Insecurity', *The Daily Star*, 26 Jan. 2007. Online. HTTP: <http://www.thedailystar.net/2007/01/26/d70126060171.htm> (accessed 12 Nov. 2009).

Weber, M., *The Methodology of the Social Sciences*, New York: Free Press, 1949.

Weitzer, R., *Sex for Sale*, New York: Routledge, 2000.

'What is the IPCC?', *Max Planck Institute for Meteorology*. Online. HTTP: <http://www.mpimet.mpg.de/en/news/press/faq-frequently-asked-questions/what-is-the-ipcc.html> (accessed 2 Aug. 2010).

Whelpton, J., *A History of Nepal*, Cambridge: Cambridge University Press, 2005.

'Where is the Emergency Leading Us?', *The Bangladesh Today*, 12 Jan. 2008.

Wiebe, H., 'Flood Action Plan in Bangladesh', *Contributing Paper, Northwest Hydraulic Consultants, Canada*. Online. HTTP: <http://www.slideshare.net/willwilliams7/bangladesh-flood-action-plan> (accessed 23. Oct. 2007).

Wihbey, J., 'Covering Climate Change as a National Security Issue', *Yale Forum on Climate Change and the Media*, 17 July 2008. Online. HTTP: <http://www.yaleclimatemedia-forum.org/features/0708_security.htm> (accessed 10 Aug. 2008).

Wijers, M., and Lap-Chew, L., *Trafficking in Women Forced Labour and Slavery-like Practices in Marriage Domestic Labour and Prostitution*, Utrecht: Foundations Against Trafficking in Women (STV), 1997.

Wilkinson, C, 'The Copenhagen School on Tour in Kyrgyzstan: Is Securitization Theory Usable Outside Europe?', *Security Dialogue*, vol. 38, no. 1, March 2007, pp. 5–25.

——, 'The Limits of the Spoken Word: From Meta-narratives to Experiences of Security', in T. Balzacq (ed.), *Securitization Theory: How Security Problems Emerge and Dissolve*, London: Routledge, 2011, pp. 94–115.

Wilkison, R., 'Human Trafficking Seen as a Security Threat in Ex-Communist Countries', *Voice of America News*, 9 Mar. 2005. Online. HTTP: <http://www.voanews.com/english/news/a-13-2005-03-09-voa45.html> (accessed 8 June 2010).

Willetts, P. (ed.), *The Conscience of the World: The Influence of Non-governmental Organisations in the UN System*, London: Hurst & Co., 1996.

Williams, M., 'Words, Images, Enemies: Securitization and International Politics', *International Studies Quarterly*, vol. 47, no. 4, Dec. 2003, pp. 511–31.

——, 'The Continuing Evaluation of Securitization Theory', in T. Balzacq (ed.), *Securitization Theory: How Security Problems Emerge and Dissolve*, London: Routledge, 2011.

Wonacott, P., 'Sri Lanka Declares Rebel Chief Dead, Ending War', *The Wall Street Journal*, 18 May 2010. Online. HTTP: <http://online.wsj.com/article/SB124263479362029841.html> (accessed 26 May 2009).

'World Reaction to Osama Bin Laden's Death', NPR, 2 May 2011. Online. HTTP: <http://www.npr.org/2011/05/02/135919728/world-reaction-to-osama-bin-ladens-death> (accessed 16 Jun. 2011).

World Resources Institute, *World Resources 1990–91: A Guide to the Global Environment*, Oxford: Oxford University Press, 1990.

Wyn Jones, R., *Security, Strategy, and Critical Theory*, Boulder, CO: Lynne Rienner, 1999.

——, 'Message in a Bottle? Theory and Praxis in Critical Security Studies', *Contemporary Security Policy*, vol. 16, no.3, Sept. 1995, pp. 299–319.

Yamin, F. and Depledge, J., *The International Climate Change Regime: A Guide to Rules, Institutions and Procedures*, Cambridge: Cambridge University Press, 2004.

Zakhari, B. S., 'Legal Cases Prosecuted under the Victims of Trafficking and Violence Protection Act of 2000', in S. Stoecker and L. Shelley (eds), *Human Traffic and Transnational Crime: Eurasian and American Perspectives*, Lanham: Rowman and Littlefield Publishers, Inc., 2004.

Index

Printed in Great Britain
by Amazon.co.uk, Ltd.,
Marston Gate.